THE MYTH OF SOUTHERN EXCEPTIONALISM

THE MYTH OF SOUTHERN EXCEPTIONALISM

Edited by
Matthew D. Lassiter and
Joseph Crespino

OXFORD
UNIVERSITY PRESS

2010

OXFORD
UNIVERSITY PRESS

Oxford University Press, Inc., publishes works that further
Oxford University's objective of excellence
in research, scholarship, and education.

Oxford   New York
Auckland   Cape Town   Dar es Salaam   Hong Kong   Karachi
Kuala Lumpur   Madrid   Melbourne   Mexico City   Nairobi
New Delhi   Shanghai   Taipei   Toronto

With offices in
Argentina   Austria   Brazil   Chile   Czech Republic   France   Greece
Guatemala   Hungary   Italy   Japan   Poland   Portugal   Singapore
South Korea   Switzerland   Thailand   Turkey   Ukraine   Vietnam

Published by Oxford University Press, Inc.
198 Madison Avenue, New York, New York 10016

www.oup.com

Library of Congress Cataloging-in-Publication Data

The myth of southern exceptionalism / edited by
Matthew D. Lassiter and Joseph Crespino.
p.   cm.
Includes bibliographical references and index.
ISBN 978-0-19-538474-1; 978-0-19-538475-8 (pbk.)
1. Southern States—Historiography.   2. Regionalism—Southern States—
Historiography.   3. African Americans—Segregation—Historiography.
4. United States—Race relations—Historiography.   5. Southern States—
Social conditions.   6. Group identity—Southern States.
I. Lassiter, Matthew D., 1970–
II. Crespino, Joseph.
F208.2.M98 2009
975'.043—dc22   2009010766

9 8 7 6 5 4 3 2 1

Printed in the United States of America
on acid-free paper

PREFACE

"The white South's uncontrollable urge to self-obituarize actually became a steady source of supplementary income for a select squadron of the usual academic and journalistic suspects who convened with amazing frequency to deliver shamelessly recycled speeches at countless symposia dedicated to kissing southern distinctiveness good-bye one more time."

James C. Cobb, *Away Down South*

We begin with a confession. In March 2006, we convened a conference at Emory University, the goals of which could be construed to resemble those of the long line of southern symposia described above. We called the conference "The End of Southern History? Integrating the Modern South and the Nation." We even invited Jim Cobb to speak. He indulged us with a gracious, incisive, knee-slapping commentary on a panel. It was one of many rich and provocative intellectual exchanges that took place that weekend, as we debated whether to keep the question mark in the conference title, take it out, or perhaps replace it with an exclamation point.

We organized the Emory conference in order to produce this anthology, and we deliberately recruited half of the contributors from outside the ranks of "southern history" as traditionally defined. Readers can decide for themselves whether or not we offer something new or have simply continued the recycling process, but it says something about the staying power of the myths of southern exceptionalism that scholars can't stop having this debate. We should be clear that "kissing southern distinctiveness good-bye" was never really our goal. The concern that motivated our conference and that informs this volume is not whether the South has come to an end, so much as what it means to recognize that it is time for a distinctive southern history and historiography to end.

We take it for granted that there is, and will continue to be, some entity called "the South," and that people will continue to love it or hate it, defend it or deride it—or, in that great Faulknerian tradition, do all at the same time. And we trust that readers will recognize that we are not arguing that "there are no regional differences anymore" because "the South is the same as every place else," to reference some of the critiques that we have heard in the process of compiling this book. Our concern is how the idea of "the South"—defined as a unified region that is not just different in some matters of degree but *exceptional* from the rest of America and in historical opposition to dominant national trends—has shaped and continues to shape the kinds of narratives that we tell about the region and the nation. This book explores regional history and reconsiders southern exceptionalism as a way to address broader questions about American history, the equally problematic category of "the North," and the related myths of American exceptionalism.

We are deeply indebted to each of the scholars who participated in the conference at Emory. In addition to Professor Cobb and the contributors to this volume, they include Jane Dailey, Jacquelyn Dowd Hall, Doug Flamming, Charles Payne, Bryant Simon, Susan Ashmore, Merle Black, Michelle Brattain, Cliff Kuhn, Andrew Lewis, Allen Tullos, and Earl Lewis. We thank, in particular, President Jimmy Carter and John Egerton for their keynote addresses.

We are grateful to Emory University for granting us the resources to assemble such a distinguished group of scholars, specifically the Emory Conference Center Subvention Fund, Hightower Lecture Fund, Emory Academic Exchange, and the Departments of History, African American Studies, and Political Science. Becky Herring, Rosalyn Page, and Allison Adams provided indispensable help with conference logistics. We also thank Emory College and Dean Christine Levenduski for supplying funds for the illustrations used in the book.

The anonymous peer reviewers provided many valuable suggestions and wisely counseled us to clarify that this volume represents a contribution to the consolidation of a paradigm shift that has been under way for some years now (in the academy much more than in popular discourse), as the doctrine of southern exceptionalism has been exerting less and less influence on the best scholarship about the South and about other parts of the United States. Kevin Kruse has been instrumental in the development of this book from the beginning, and he generously arranged for us to present draft versions of our chapters to the Modern America Workshop at Princeton University. Susan Ferber, our editor at Oxford University Press, supported this project with energy and enthusiasm from its earliest stages, and she supplied great advice and welcome feedback throughout the process.

Editing this anthology took much more time than we initially anticipated when the idea for a combined conference and book project began to take shape in the hallways and bars of a conference meeting almost four years ago. For their patience and for so much else, we especially thank Tracy Davis, Caroline Herring, and Carrie and Sam Crespino.

CONTENTS

CONTRIBUTORS

JOSEPH CRESPINO is Associate Professor of History at Emory University. He is the author of *In Search of Another Country: Mississippi and the Conservative Counterrevolution* (2007). He is currently working on a political biography of Strom Thurmond.

KARI FREDERICKSON is Associate Professor of History at the University of Alabama. She is the author of *The Dixiecrat Revolt and the End of the Solid South, 1932–1968* (2001). Her chapter is drawn from a new book project, *The Cold War in Dixie: Transforming the Modern South, 1945–1980*.

ALLISON GRAHAM is Professor of Communication at the University of Memphis. She is the author of *Framing the South: Hollywood, Television, and Race during the Civil Rights Struggle* (2001). She also has worked on two PBS documentaries about the civil rights era, as associate producer of *Hoxie: The First Stand* (2003), and co-producer of *At the River I Stand* (1993).

GRACE ELIZABETH HALE is Associate Professor of History at the University of Virginia. She is the author of *Making Whiteness: The Culture of Segregation in the South, 1890–1940* (1998). Her chapter is drawn from a forthcoming book, *The Romance of the Outsider: How Middle-Class Whites Fell in Love with Rebellion in Postwar America* (Oxford University Press, 2010).

KEVIN M. KRUSE is Associate Professor of History at Princeton University. He is the author of *White Flight: Atlanta and the Making of Modern Conservatism* (2005), co-editor of *The New Suburban History* (2006), and co-editor of *The Spaces of the Modern City: Imaginaries, Politics, and Everyday Life* (2008). His chapter is drawn from a book in progress, *One Nation Under God: Cold War Christianity and the Origins of the Religious Right*.

MATTHEW D. LASSITER is Associate Professor of History at the University of Michigan. He is the author of *The Silent Majority: Suburban Politics in the Sunbelt South* (2006) and co-editor of *The Moderates' Dilemma: Massive Resistance to School Desegregation in Virginia* (1998). His chapter is drawn in part from a book in progress, *The Suburban Crisis: The Pursuit and Defense of the American Dream*.

NANCY MACLEAN is Professor of History and African American Studies at Northwestern University. She is the author of *Freedom Is Not Enough: The Opening of the American Workplace* (2006); *The American Women's Movement, 1945–2000: A Brief History with Documents* (2008); *Debating the American Conservative Movement, 1945 to the Present*, with Donald T. Critchlow (2009); and *Behind the Mask of Chivalry: The Making of the Second Ku Klux Klan* (Oxford University Press, 1994).

MARY E. ODEM is Associate Professor of History and Women's Studies at Emory University. She is the author of *Delinquent Daughters: Protecting and Policing Adolescent Female Sexuality in the United States, 1885–1920* (1995) and co-editor of *Latino Immigration and the Transformation of the U.S. South* (2009).

DOUGLAS SMITH is Visiting Assistant Professor of History at Occidental College and a John Randolph and Dora Haynes Foundation Fellow at the Huntington Library. He is the author of *Managing White Supremacy: Race, Politics, and Citizenship in Jim Crow Virginia* (2002). His chapter is drawn from a book project on *Reynolds v. Sims, Baker v. Carr*, and the "reapportionment revolution" of the 1960s.

JAMES T. SPARROW is Assistant Professor of History at the University of Chicago. His chapter is drawn from a forthcoming book, *Americanism and Entitlement: The Social Politics of Big Government in an Age of Total War, 1937–50*.

JEANNE THEOHARIS is Endowed Chair in Women's Studies and Associate Professor of Political Science at Brooklyn College of the City University of New York. She is co-author of *Not Working: Latina Immigrants, Low-Wage Jobs, and the Failure of Welfare Reform* (2006), co-editor of *Groundwork: Local Black*

Freedom Movements in America (2005), and co-editor of *Freedom North: Black Freedom Struggles Outside the South, 1940–1980* (2003).

HEATHER ANN THOMPSON is Associate Professor in the Department of African American Studies and the Department of History at Temple University. She is the author of *Whose Detroit: Politics, Labor and Race in a Modern American City* (2001). Her chapter is drawn from a forthcoming book on the Attica prison uprising of 1971 and its legacy.

ANDREW WIESE is Professor of History at San Diego State University. He is the author of *Places of Their Own: African American Suburbanization in the Twentieth Century* (2004) and co-editor of *The Suburb Reader* (2006).

THE MYTH OF SOUTHERN EXCEPTIONALISM

INTRODUCTION: THE END
OF SOUTHERN HISTORY

Matthew D. Lassiter and Joseph Crespino

LITTLE ROCK, ARKANSAS, SEPTEMBER 1957. Three years after the *Brown* decision, nine black students carefully selected by the Little Rock school board were prepared to desegregate Central High School. Governor Orval Faubus, however, upended months of community preparations and defied the federal court order by mobilizing the Arkansas National Guard to prevent "the forcible integration of Negroes and whites." On September 4, about one hundred white onlookers and a throng of journalists watched the National Guardsmen turn the black students away. *Time* magazine blamed Faubus for manufacturing a racial crisis and observed that the vast majority of white residents of Little Rock were ready to comply with the constitutional requirement to desegregate their public schools. The governor removed the National Guard after a three-week legal standoff, which allowed a mob of four hundred segregationists to surround Central High when the "Little Rock Nine" tried to enter for the second time. The mayor of Little Rock requested federal assistance to prevent violence, and President Dwight Eisenhower sent U.S. Army troops to restore order and avert a constitutional crisis. With bayonets fixed, members of the 101st Airborne escorted the black students to school, and an international audience observed the first military occupation of a southern city since Reconstruction (figure I.1). These indelible images soon became seared into the dramatic storyline of the civil rights era: massive resistance to school integration, unruly white segregationists confronting peaceful black activists, the exposed violence at the heart of the Jim Crow system, a global humiliation in the Cold War struggle, the latest stage in the South's timeless defiance of national norms.[1]

FIGURE I.1. White students at Central High School in Little Rock watch as federal troops escort six members of the "Little Rock Nine" to classes, October 16, 1957. Six weeks earlier, Governor Orval Faubus mobilized the Arkansas National Guard to prevent school desegregation in Little Rock. This forced President Dwight Eisenhower to intervene in order to uphold the authority of the *Brown* decision. © Bettmann/ CORBIS.

LEVITTOWN, PENNSYLVANIA, AUGUST 1957. Two weeks before national and international attention focused on the Little Rock Nine, the first African-American family moved into the model postwar suburb of Levittown, a middle-class community of 60,000 located on the outskirts of Philadelphia. The NAACP previously had challenged the segregationist policy of the Levitt Corporation, because the racially exclusionary mortgage programs of the U.S. government insured all of the homes in the all-white development, but the federal courts refused to apply the *Brown* principle to the allegedly private issue of housing discrimination. "If we sell one house to a Negro family," builder William Levitt explained, "then 90 to 95 percent of our white customers will not buy into the community." When William and Daisy Myers and their young children arrived at their Levittown home, four hundred residents formed a mob that threw rocks through their picture window, harassed them with loud music and car horns, unfurled a Confederate battle flag, and burned a cross in the yard of a neighbor deemed too friendly to the newcomers (figure I.2). The governor of Pennsylvania dispatched state troopers to protect the Myers family, leading to a week of violent confrontations between law enforcement and the Levittown segregationists. Homeowners in the grassroots resistance movement blamed outside agitators in the NAACP for the troubles and warned of a mass Negro invasion of their suburban enclave. Before descending on Little Rock, the national media briefly registered the Levittown storyline: a "peaceful community suddenly turned upside down by racial tension," an unseemly eruption of racial prejudice in "a Northern community in a state which legally has no color bars."[2]

Why do Americans remember Little Rock but not Levittown? Popular narratives about the "American Dilemma" of racial inequality reinforce a selective historical consciousness about the civil rights era, which is typically portrayed as an epic showdown between the retrograde South and a progressive nation. Many students still learn about the civil rights movement's "classic period," from the *Brown* decision of 1954 through the Voting Rights Act of 1965, through the filter of *Eyes on the Prize* dramas set only in Little Rock, Greensboro, Albany, Birmingham, Selma, and rural

FIGURE I.2. August 20, 1957: Roughly two weeks before the Little Rock school desegregation crisis, neighbors gather outside the home of Mr. and Mrs. William Myers, Jr., the first African-American family to move into the all-white community of Levittown, Pennsylvania. The Myers family received police protection during several weeks of threats and harassment from white homeowners in the Philadelphia suburb, which typified federally subsidized patterns of housing segregation in postwar America. © Bettmann/CORBIS.

Mississippi.[3] Published in 2007, on the fiftieth anniversary of the concurrent riots in Levittown and Little Rock, a Pulitzer Prize-winning account of "how America awakened to its race problem" celebrated the national media coverage of the "shocking indignities and injustices of racial segregation in the South" while barely even acknowledging parallel civil rights conflicts in the North and West.[4] In recent years, academic historians have dismantled the "myth of the liberal consensus" and excavated a "hidden era" of civil rights activism and white resistance in cities and suburbs across the nation from the 1940s through the 1960s.[5] Yet the burgeoning literature on the "long civil rights movement" has failed to alter popular understanding and journalistic tropes about the "Second Reconstruction," a region-specific framework that keeps the spotlight focused on the most troubled parts of the Deep South. In the traditional narrative (and the second installment of the *Eyes on the Prize* documentary series), when attention finally shifts northward and westward in the mid-1960s, urban race riots and the Black Power movement emerge without historical context as the catalysts for white backlash and the seemingly sudden "southernization of American politics."[6]

These interpretations have contributed to a distorted account of political realignment that attributes the rise of modern conservatism primarily to white southern backlash against the civil rights movement. The decline of New Deal liberalism and the ascendance of the New Right "can be summed up in just five words," according to influential *New York Times* columnist Paul Krugman: "Southern whites started voting Republican. . . . End of story."[7] The GOP dominates the South, in the conventional wisdom summarized by political scientist Thomas Schaller, because of the "southern strategy invented by Barry Goldwater, accelerated by Richard Nixon, and perfected by Ronald Reagan." Schaller's *Whistling Past Dixie* concludes that "southerners hold distinctly conservative values and have long prided themselves for their obstinancy, for resisting the social transformations unfolding elsewhere across America. . . . The South is different . . . because it's still full of southerners."[8]

These formulations ignore more than six decades of dynamic growth in the metropolitan Sunbelt, the longstanding political divisions between the Deep South and the much more populous states of the Outer South (where a majority of white voters supported Eisenhower in the 1950s), and the inconvenient fact that about one-third of the present-day southern electorate consists of migrants born outside the region. The "southern strategy" thesis is popular and ubiquitous precisely because it reduces a complex phenomenon of national political transformation to another familiar story of southern white backlash. Yet Richard Nixon and Ronald Reagan did not need to learn their political strategies from southern demagogues such as George Wallace. They honed their conservative platforms in the segregated suburbs of postwar California, and each secured forty-nine states in his presidential reelection campaign.[9] The current binary of red state–blue state polarization represents the latest version of this simplistic dichotomy between southern backlash and American progress, an intractable region alternately deviating from and dominating an otherwise liberal nation.[10]

We argue in this volume that the notion of the exceptional South has served as a myth, one that has persistently distorted our understanding of American history. Although scholars and journalists have repeatedly chronicled the decline of regional distinctiveness for more than a century now, the basic features of southern exceptionalism still structure the popular mythology of American exceptionalism—a story of white racial innocence (occasionally compromised by the "southernization" of northern race relations), of a benevolent superpower (that temporarily tasted the "southern experience" of defeat after Vietnam), of an essentially liberal national project (if only the red states would stop preventing the blue states from resurrecting the Great Society).[11] In challenging southern exceptionalism, our agenda is not to absolve the South but to implicate the nation. We write during an era dominated by color-blind myths of American innocence from the burdens of the past, when our political culture turns Martin Luther King Jr. into a sanitized national hero, while the Supreme Court requires public school districts across the nation to abandon racial integration plans by drawing a direct analogy between affirmative-action remedies and Jim Crow segregation.[12] Today the "blue states" of the Northeast and Midwest have the nation's highest rates of school and housing segregation, but our suburban students from Michigan and Atlanta and New England and Virginia know much more about the civil rights movement in Mississippi and Alabama than they do about what happened in their own states and hometowns.[13] Discarding the framework of southern exceptionalism is a necessary step in overcoming the mythology of American exceptionalism, transforming the American Dilemma into a truly national ordeal, and traversing regional boundaries to rewrite the American past on its own terms and in full historical perspective.

The most insightful observers of southern history have always insisted that the region is inseparable from the nation, that the South is not the antithesis of a progressive America but, rather, has operated as a mirror that reveals its fundamental values and practices. In *The Southern Mystique*, published in 1964 as national attention focused on Mississippi's racial violence, Howard Zinn argued that the American Dilemma "has never been the tension between an American dream and Southern reality, but between the American dream and national reality."[14] In a similar fashion, C. Vann Woodward's *Strange Career of Jim Crow* (1955) located the origins of legal segregation in the antebellum North and highlighted the nation's complicity in the establishment and maintenance of the South's racial order. While civil rights reform and economic modernization have "already leveled many of the old monuments of regional distinctiveness," Woodward observed in 1958, "national myths have been waxing in power and appeal,...national legends of opulence and success and innocence."[15] In 1960, at the height of massive resistance to the civil rights movement, a

new generation of southern historians marked the centennial of the outbreak of the Civil War with an anthology titled *The Southerner as American*.
The contributors attacked notions of southern exceptionalism and national
innocence, and they warned white southerners against a second "revolt
against the larger society of which they have always been a part, against
social values which they have always shared."[16] More recently, James C.
Cobb has counseled historians not to define "southern peculiarities solely
in relation to 'the North.' In this usage, the North actually represented
not simply another region...but an 'emotional idea' of the remainder of
a triumphantly superior America,...that mythical non-South [that] had
become virtually synonymous with the idea of America itself."[17]

   The modern field of southern history came of age during the reign of
the "liberal consensus," when the myths of American exceptionalism were
at their most powerful, and when the conflation of "the North" with a triumphant narrative of American history was most pronounced. During the
early years of the Cold War, leading figures in southern history felt, with as
much anxiety as optimism, that traditional patterns of regional distinctiveness were giving way to the homogenizing forces of nationalization and
the bellicose ideology of the American Way. In this context, C. Vann Woodward outlined an intellectual project of southern exceptionalism as a strategic maneuver to critique the excesses of American empire, the underside of
American capitalism, and the myth of American innocence from responsibility for the past. In a series of essays published during the 1950s, and then
compiled in *The Burden of Southern History* (1960), Woodward argued that
nothing in the South remained "immune from the disintegrating effect of
nationalism and the pressure for conformity" except for the unique history
of the region itself, the "collective experience of the Southern people." He
therefore proposed that the South's "un-American" historical identity—pervasive poverty instead of economic abundance, military defeat instead of
confidence in inevitable victory, a "tortured conscience" instead of "moral
complacency"—could serve as the critical vantage point to deflate the "illusions and myths of American nationalism."[18] Citing Woodward as inspiration, David M. Potter then advised scholars to "confine Southern history
to phenomena which have some kind of regional distinctiveness" and to
exclude all "manifestations within the region of national phenomena."[19]
In short, liberal historians in the postwar decades called for a distinctive
southern history based not on a set of empirical differences between region
and nation but, rather, on the presumed divergence of a collective southern
identity from national *myths* and American *ideals*.

   In retrospect, it seems clear that the strategy of policing the boundaries
of southern exceptionalism has done far more to sustain than to dismantle
the myths of American exceptionalism. In this sense, the problem of southern distinctiveness should be of concern not only to regional specialists but
also to the many scholars of the "non-South" who have tended to ignore
this debate altogether.[20] "The South...has been an American problem,"

Larry Griffin and Don Doyle observe, "because it became the repository for problems that were really 'American' all along and that were only thought to be peculiar to the region and antithetical to mainstream American values."[21] For much too long, to take one prominent example, the sway of the "liberal consensus" and the dominance of southern history in explorations of the American Dilemma worked to obscure the transregional origins and national (indeed transnational) scope of "Jim Crow" racial systems. Recent scholars working outside of southern history have documented the early segregation laws targeting Chinese immigrants in San Francisco in the 1880s, the extensive history of statutory discrimination against Mexican Americans in the Southwest, the exportation of racial apartheid as part of the American twentieth-century imperialist project, the many northern and western states that permitted or required black-white segregation in public schools in the century before *Brown*, and the federal and municipal policies that segregated metropolitan housing markets across the country.[22] New studies of the civil rights era also have critiqued the Little Rock/Levittown binary of de jure/de facto segregation, which rested on an untenable regional dichotomy that naturalized the racial system in "the North" by describing postwar metropolitan development, not on its own terms as an emerging national (not simply northern) racial system, but as the amorphous opposite of the state-mandated Jim Crow system of the South.[23]

The tendency to isolate distinctive regional characteristics from a normative American narrative has set southern history in false opposition to an idealized national standard and has encouraged oversimplifications and overgeneralizations about all parts of the country. At the same time, the constant need to mine the South for its symbolic possibilities has often come at the expense of exploring the deeper currents of American history and the particular conditions of local places. Scholars, journalists, and politicians frequently have compartmentalized outbreaks of racial backlash in the "non-South" by drawing on a reliable reservoir of southern metaphors: opposition to housing integration makes Cicero, Illinois, the "the Selma of the North"; resistance to school desegregation means Boston is "the Little Rock of the North"; ending affirmative action makes California the "Mississippi of the 1990s"; the racially motivated murder of a black man in Queens is something "expect[ed] . . . to happen in the Deep South."[24] Civil rights activists often employed a related strategy of denouncing racial discrimination in the North and West through direct analogies to the specter of southernization: "No Mississippi Here!" implored the unsuccessful open-housing movement in California in 1964 (figure I.3).[25] This framework attributes episodes of racism and racial violence inside the South to the social and political structures of the region, while portraying similar events elsewhere as anomalous incidents that really should have happened down in Mississippi or Alabama.[26] When regional compartmentalization fails, the "southernization of America" metaphor works to erase the longer trends of white backlash and political conservatism in a

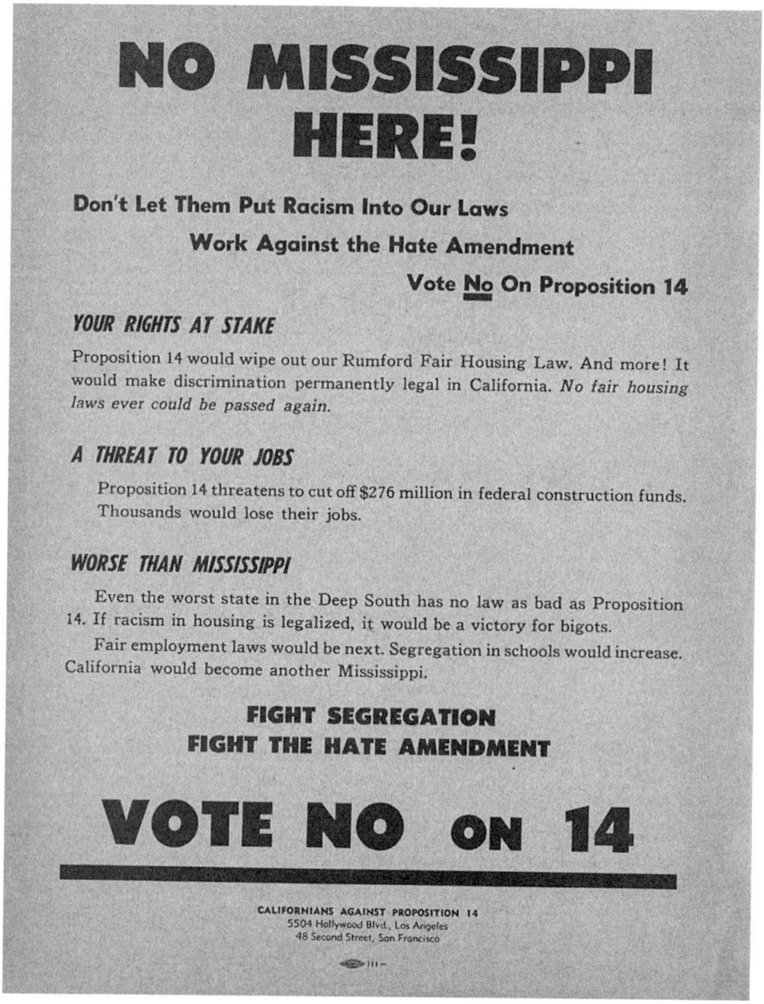

NO MISSISSIPPI HERE!

Don't Let Them Put Racism Into Our Laws

Work Against the Hate Amendment

Vote No On Proposition 14

YOUR RIGHTS AT STAKE

Proposition 14 would wipe out our Rumford Fair Housing Law. And more! It would make discrimination permanently legal in California. *No fair housing laws ever could be passed again.*

A THREAT TO YOUR JOBS

Proposition 14 threatens to cut off $276 million in federal construction funds. Thousands would lose their jobs.

WORSE THAN MISSISSIPPI

Even the worst state in the Deep South has no law as bad as Proposition 14. If racism in housing is legalized, it would be a victory for bigots.

Fair employment laws would be next. Segregation in schools would increase. California would become another Mississippi.

FIGHT SEGREGATION
FIGHT THE HATE AMENDMENT

VOTE NO ON 14

CALIFORNIANS AGAINST PROPOSITION 14
5504 Hollywood Blvd., Los Angeles
48 Second Street, San Francisco

FIGURE I.3. "No Mississippi Here!" In 1964, the fair-housing movement in California charged that passage of Proposition 14, a ballot referendum to restore the right to discriminate based on race and religion in the sale and rental of property, would mean that "California would become another Mississippi." The liberal coalition Californians Against Proposition 14 deployed the metaphor of southernization in the attempt to preserve the 1963 Rumford Fair Housing Act, but white homeowners in California did not need to import their segregationist politics from the Jim Crow South. During the two decades following World War II, public policies and private discrimination combined to prohibit racial minorities from living in about 98 percent of new suburban developments in the state of California. In 1964, 65 percent of the state's voters, and three-fourths of white residents of the suburbs, supported Proposition 14 and amended the state constitution to guarantee the private right to discriminate. Courtesy of the Max Mont Collection, Urban Archives Center, Oviatt Library, California State University, Northridge.

different but equally problematic way. "The Southern Strategy therefore had a Northern flank of fundamental importance," according to the tortured logic of a book about suburban opposition to housing integration in the 1960s and 1970s; George Wallace showed Nixon and Reagan the way, other scholars have written, after the Alabama governor's (apocryphal) epiphany that "the whole United States is southern!"[27]

Historians and journalists have long walked a tightrope between searching for the South's distinctive characteristics and charting the "Americanization" or "northernization" of the region.[28] This analytical confusion is an inevitable result of the balancing act involved in a scholarly tradition that has maintained the faith in southern exceptionalism, as the essential foundation that legitimates the subfield of southern history, while simultaneously chronicling all of the ways in which the traditional South keeps fading away. "For as long as people have believed there was a South, they have also believed it was disappearing," Edward Ayers has noted. "The South has always seemed to live on the edge of extinction, the good as well as the bad perpetually disappearing."[29] In its bicentennial search for the region's essence, *Time* explained that a "New South has been proclaimed in every generation.... The South has changed before—and remained the same, through slavery and secession, independence and defeat, emancipation, reconstruction and integration."[30] Two decades later, the *Washington Post* characterized the South as "a land of oxymorons"—"of danger and decorum, of wealth and want, of growth and stagnation, of promise and compromise, of racial dissonance and racial harmony, of rampant illiteracy and resplendent literature." The *Post* concluded that "the riddle of the South is this: To define what it is, you must first define *where* it is. To define where it is, you must first define *what* it is."[31] Drawing boundaries around cultural identity rather than physical geography, David Goldfield's recent reaffirmation of southern exceptionalism has identified an alternative "historical consciousness," because "there is something different down in Dixie; the difference is real and deep, grounded in the region's distinctive past." Despite dramatic changes in the economy, politics, and race relations of the modern South, "there is a darkness in the southern soul; the time-ticking bomb called history that confounds and burdens the region still."[32]

Regions are culturally constructed spaces of the collective imagination and not simply coherent entities located inside clear lines on a map. Almost every scholar who has pondered the question of southern exceptionalism ends up acknowledging that the region exists less as an actual place than as a symbol, an expression of collective identity, an *idea*.[33] It therefore seems problematic to stake out the boundaries of a historical subfield and a geographic region through circular reasoning; by highlighting paradoxes, riddles, oxymorons, and the constructed nature of memory and identity; by dissolving change and continuity into a single phenomenon; or by citing historical burdens that ought to shape national and not merely regional consciousness. In rejecting the framework of southern exceptionalism, we are not arguing that there are no variations among regions, or that political culture and political economy have become practically identical every place in the nation. But most regional characteristics cited as evidence of differences of kind are really differences of degree—such as rates of unionization or immigration, patterns of religiosity or voting behavior, the pace and scale of urbanization or economic change. Certainly by the second half of the twentieth century, if not before as well, focusing on the South's aberrant qualities compared to the rest of the United States obscures much more than it reveals about the fundamental questions of modern American history. In this volume, we discard the artificial binaries that have governed the relationship between "southern" and "American" history and that have contributed to an idealized national narrative that obscures deep connections across regional boundaries. Our goal is to explore how both southern and American history are transformed when the South is no longer exceptional but, rather, fully integrated into the national narrative.

Regions are so central to the ways in which Americans think about issues of politics, culture, economics, race relations, and identity formation that even scholars trained to be skeptics rarely question the utility of making broad claims about the North and the South, the Midwest and the West, and more recently the Sunbelt and the Rustbelt. Yet a strong case can be made that, of the various interpretative frameworks based on geography, region is the most popular but also the most imprecise scale of analysis. Municipal, state, and national boundaries also define "imagined communities," but at least they have concrete political meanings and exercise actual policymaking powers.[34] The metropolitan area captures a combination of population density and economic integration, while the categories of urban, suburban, and rural encourage comparative analysis across regional and even national borders.[35] Much of the exciting recent research in "southern history," in fact, has been produced by scholars who position themselves in other subfields—such as African-American, urban, political, social, gender, labor, cultural, and Latino history—approaching their projects through comparative frameworks and investigating national or transnational themes that happen to be geographically located, in part, inside the generally accepted parameters of the South. These welcome trends reflect a belated but growing recognition that for most residents of the South, as for most residents of other sections of the United States, regional status is a less salient measure of personal identity than other categories such as race, ethnicity, class, gender, religion, locality, and especially nationality.[36] The greatest works of southern history have always interpreted events in their broader national and international contexts, but if the time has come to rethink the borders of American history in an era of globalization, then there are similar virtues to traversing rather than reinforcing regional boundaries within the United States.[37]

The essays in this volume focus on the second half of the twentieth century, an era of dramatic transformation in the political, economic, and social history of the modern South. In 1938, the Roosevelt administration labeled the South the "Nation's Number One Economic Problem," highlighting the region's intense poverty, relative lack of urbanization and industrialization, overdependence on low wages, and separate labor market.[38] Only two decades later, C. Vann Woodward proposed the label of "Bulldozer Revolution" to capture the South's determined "pursuit of the American Way and the American Standard of Living," marked by the nation's fastest rate of metropolitan growth and the political triumph of the suburban-corporate value system.[39] Scholars have accounted for the changes set in motion by the New Deal, World War II, and the Cold War by emphasizing a regional convergence thesis of steady nationalization and by incorporating the Southeast into a broader Sunbelt region that includes much of the American West. Both the convergence framework and the Sunbelt model emphasize the collapse of the three widely acknowledged pillars of mid-century southern distinctiveness: the one-party electoral system, the cotton-based rural economy, and the legal culture of Jim Crow segregation. The post-1940 period brought the explosion of civil rights protests and racial conflicts in metropolitan regions across the United States, the steady migration of population and resources to the sprawling suburbs throughout the country, and the emergence of the Sunbelt ethos (more than a clearly identifiable and contiguous Sunbelt region) as the nation's political and economic engine.[40] By the end of the twentieth century, the census indicated that the South contained more than one-third of the U.S. population, and the southern and western states associated with the Sunbelt controlled a majority of electoral votes.[41] Evidence of the globalization of the American South could be found almost everywhere, from the boom in foreign investment, to the rise of the Wal-Mart style of international capitalism, to the accelerated immigration patterns that are permanently supplanting the region's binary tradition of black-white race relations.[42]

The arrangement of the essays in this volume represents three main approaches, in terms of methodology and historiography, to overcoming the constraints of southern exceptionalism and reintegrating regional and national history. Each of the contributors emphasizes the importance of comparative analysis that deliberately moves beyond the traditional boundaries of southern—and "northern"—history, ranging from metropolitan developments and Sunbelt trends to projects of national and transnational scope. Many of the chapters also highlight discontinuity over continuity in exploring significant episodes of local, regional, and national transformation, from the militarizing effects of Cold War political economy, to patterns of electoral realignment in a suburbanizing nation, to the demographic changes brought by internal migration and foreign immigration. And most critically, a majority of these essays investigate how the mythology of southern exceptionalism has decisively shaped American identity and national political culture, whether establishing powerful obstacles to civil rights reform, supplying nostalgic tropes for the conservative movement, or distorting the regional narratives of popular culture. The ideas and metaphors of a distinctive South, and the artificial binaries that set the region's past in direct opposition to the national version, have structured the myths of American exceptionalism and hindered the ability to describe United States history on its own terms. As a result of our collective focus on writing American history across regional borders, this volume about the end of southern history spends as much time outside as inside the traditional South, moving from Mississippi to New York City, from South Carolina to Southern California, from Mexico to Atlanta, from Hollywood to the Newport Folk Festival, from the Pentagon to Attica.

Part I, "The Northern Mystique," presents three case studies of the political and racial consequences of the false but powerful dichotomy between an exceptional, reactionary South and a normative, progressive North. During the postwar decades, civil rights activists and liberal reformers most successfully mobilized coalitions to intervene against racial injustice in southern states through laws and policies that exempted the non-South from similar scrutiny. These attempts to nationalize race relations in the South paid many dividends, but they ultimately reinforced a political culture of white innocence and American exceptionalism.

Matthew Lassiter's opening essay historicizes the concept of "de facto segregation" by tracing the rise and fall of the de facto/de jure binary, which mirrored the southern successes and national failures of the civil rights movement. The fiction of de facto segregation defined residential segregation and neighborhood schools as outcomes of the free market rather than as products of a modern state-sponsored system of racial apartheid, an American myth of color-blind individualism that continues to distort collective memory of the civil rights era to this day. The companion essay by Jeanne Theoharis, which builds on her previous work on the nearly forgotten civil rights battles in northern and western cities before 1965, provides a comparative analysis that makes it impossible to retain the dichotomy between a nonviolent southern movement and its militant "northern" counterpart.[43] Activists in Boston and Los Angeles—two very different cities on opposite sides of the country that nevertheless have been subsumed into the "northern civil rights movement"—faced constant challenges to the legitimacy of protest outside of acceptable locations such as Birmingham and Selma. Along a similar path, Heather Thompson's investigation of national criminal justice practices challenges the widespread belief that southern penal institutions and convict labor systems were uniquely barbaric, while showing how the framework of regional distinctiveness adopted by the northern-based prison reform movement facilitated intervention against the brutal excesses of the South but ignored those closer to home.

The essays in part II, "Imagining the South," trace the ideological work done by the idea of southern exceptionalism in the interrelated forums of political discourse and mass culture. Southern narratives of romanticization and demonization have shaped the ways in which national audiences interpreted the civil rights era, while portable metaphors of regional exceptionalism and national convergence have informed the battles over the political uses of the past. Joseph Crespino's critical analysis of the discursive symbolism of "Mississippi" charts the trajectory of three prominent metaphors: the liberal condemnation of the state as an un-American closed society, the New Left recognition that Mississippi might actually be a microcosm of a racist nation, and the segregationist charge that the Magnolia State served as the scapegoat for America's racial sins. Shifting the allegorical focus from Deep South extremism to interracial solidarity, Grace Hale's account of the role of singing in the civil rights movement shows how white northern audiences romanticized the racial innocence and rural authenticity of southern black culture as an imaginative escape from their segregated suburban enclaves, another way to support intervention in Mississippi and Alabama while neglecting conflicts closer to home. White officials in northern and western cities often deflected calls for integration by casting black protesters as angry and "culturally deprived" (as Jeanne Theoharis shows in chapter 2), and the folk music revival drew an implicit contrast between the "militancy" of African-American agitators in the urban North and the deserving masses of the black folk down South. And in a provocative reinterpretation of the thesis of a red-blue national divide, Allison Graham updates her earlier work on how mass culture "frames the South" through analysis of recent Hollywood films about "red America," with cracks only beginning to emerge in the cinematic imagination of an exotic and gothic region that serves as the repository not only of the nation's lost innocence but also of the burdens of history itself.[44]

The contributors to part III, "Border Crossings," address key trends in the political economy of the modern United States by investigating the consequences of federal intervention, the effects of population mobility, and the patterns of suburban development in specific places in the dynamic New South. As James Sparrow argues in "A Nation in Motion," the federal military-industrial complex of World War II and the Cold War worked to nationalize regional economies and brought immense changes to all corners of the United States, not just to the states of the South and the Sunbelt. Sparrow's focus on two war centers in metropolitan Virginia, the Norfolk/Hampton Roads area and the Pentagon location in the D.C. suburbs, reveals how expansive federal power in a permanent warfare state reallocated people and economic resources, promoted landscapes of "decentralized urbanism," and transformed political behavior, race relations, and even personal identity. In a companion piece that views the Cold War from the grassroots, Kari Frederickson's case study of the Savannah River Plant and nearby Aiken, South Carolina, traces the substantial conflicts and changes that accompanied the militarization of a southern landscape, the modernization of local society, and the in-migration of a white-collar suburban workforce. The latter essays in this section take up two of the most important developments in recent America history: the migration of African Americans to the suburbs and the immigration of Mexicans and other Central and South Americans to communities across the United States. Andrew Wiese surveys the evolving regional and national patterns resulting from the suburbanization of 9 million black Americans between 1960 and 2000, with more than half of this population residing in the South and metropolitan Atlanta serving as a national pacesetter. And Mary Odem investigates the recent history of Latin American migration to the Atlanta suburbs and other parts of the multiethnic New South, as Georgia and other traditionally biracial states have rapidly emerged as immigration gateways and flashpoints for conflict.

Part IV, on political realignment, moves beyond misguided models such as the "southern strategy" and misleading metaphors such as the "southernization of America" to offer new national perspectives on issues such as voting rights, grassroots mobilization, and conservative ideology. In our own previously published works, we have argued that southern politics moved firmly into the national mainstream during the era of civil rights and Sunbelt expansion. The racial and class ideologies of white suburbanites from Atlanta and Charlotte increasingly mirrored their counterparts in metropolitan Detroit or Los Angeles, while white conservatives in Mississippi became key contributors to a national backlash against civil rights and a transformed Republican Party that reshaped American politics.[45] In a chapter about the Supreme Court's legislative reapportionment cases of the 1960s, Douglas Smith explains how the pervasive malapportionment of southern states underpinned the one-party politics of white supremacy widely acknowledged as a pillar of regional distinctiveness. But Smith's comparative approach demonstrates that electoral malapportionment had similar effects across the nation, ensuring rural dominance over urban interests until judicial intervention ultimately empowered the suburbs at the expense of both the cities and the countryside. In an investigation of the national origins of the Religious Right, Kevin Kruse moves beyond the conventional wisdom that southern televangelists led working-class fundamentalists into the culture wars of the 1970s. Instead, Kruse emphasizes the grassroots mobilization of Christian nationalism in early Cold War America and the middle-class suburban base of an ecumenical coalition of religious conservatives that wedded moral traditionalism to

Republican politics. Nancy MacLean closes the volume with an exposé of neo-Confederate nostalgia by writers at *National Review* and other vehicles of the conservative movement, as leading intellectuals mobilized a set of Old South myths in their ideological project to dismantle the New Deal legacy and pave the way for the national triumph of unfettered corporate capitalism—the very same conquest of the American Way that C. Vann Woodward anticipated and lamented a half-century ago.

NOTES

1. "Making a Crisis in Arkansas," *Time* (Sept. 16, 1957); "Quick, Hard, and Decisive," *Time* (Oct. 7, 1957); Numan V. Bartley, *The Rise of Massive Resistance: Race and Politics in the South during the 1950's* (Baton Rouge: Louisiana State University Press, 1969), 251–69.

2. "Integration Troubles Beset Northern Town," *Life* (Sept. 2, 1957), 43–46; "War of Nerves," *Time* (Oct. 7, 1957), 29; "Segregation: A Family Moves In," *Newsweek* (Aug. 26, 1957), 27; "Race Trouble in the North: When a Negro Family Moved into a White Community," *U.S. News and World Report* (Aug. 30, 1957), 29–32; *New York Times*, Aug. 17–22, 1957; *Johnson v. Levitt and Sons, Inc.*, 131 F. Supp. 114 (E.D. Pa. 1955). Also see Thomas J. Sugrue, *Sweet Land of Liberty: The Forgotten Civil Rights Movement in the North* (New York: Random House, 2008), 200–28.

3. *Eyes on the Prize: America's Civil Rights Years, 1954 to 1965* (PBS Video, 1987), Episodes 1–6.

4. Gene Roberts and Hank Kilbanoff, *The Race Beat: The Press, the Civil Rights Struggle, and the Awakening of a Nation* (New York: Random House, 2007).

5. Gary Gerstle, "Race and the Myth of the Liberal Consensus," *Journal of American History* (Sept. 1995), 579–86; Jacquelyn Dowd Hall, "The Long Civil Rights Movement and the Political Uses of the Past," *Journal of American History* (March 2005), 1233–63. See also Arnold R. Hirsch, *Making the Second Ghetto: Race and Housing in Chicago, 1940–1960* (Cambridge: Cambridge University Press, 1983); Thomas J. Sugrue, *The Origins of the Urban Crisis: Race and Inequality in Postwar Detroit* (Princeton: Princeton University Press, 1996); Sugrue, *Sweet Land of Liberty*; Jeanne Theoharis and Komozi Woodard, eds., *Freedom North: Black Freedom Struggles Outside the South, 1940–1980* (New York: Palgrave Macmillan, 2003); Martha Biondi, *To Stand and Fight: The Struggle for Civil Rights in Postwar New York City* (Cambridge: Harvard University Press, 2003); Josh Sides, *L.A. City Limits: African American Los Angeles from the Great Depression to the Present* (Berkeley: University of California Press, 2003).

6. *Eyes on the Prize II: America at the Racial Crossroads, 1965 to 1985* (PBS Video, 1990), Episodes 7–14. For the "southernization of America" thesis, see John Egerton, *The Americanization of Dixie: The Southernization of America* (New York: Harper's Magazine Press, 1974); Dan T. Carter, *The Politics of Rage: George Wallace,*

the Origins of the New Conservatism, and the Transformation of American Politics (New York: Simon and Schuster, 1995); Peter Applebome, *Dixie Rising: How the South Is Shaping American Values, Politics, and Culture* (New York: Harcourt Brace, 1996); James N. Gregory, *The Southern Diaspora: How the Great Migrations of Black and White Southerners Transformed America* (Chapel Hill: University of North Carolina Press, 2005).

7. Paul Krugman, *The Conscience of a Liberal* (New York: Norton, 2007), 178, 182.

8. Thomas F. Schaller, *Whistling Past Dixie: How Democrats Can Win without the South* (New York: Simon and Schuster, 2006), 4, 66, 114.

9. Accounts that emphasize the suburban rather than "southern" strategies of Richard Nixon and Ronald Reagan include Lisa McGirr, *Suburban Warriors: The Origins of the New American Right* (Princeton: Princeton University Press, 2001); Matthew Dallek, *The Right Moment: Ronald Reagan's First Victory and the Decisive Turning Point in American Politics* (New York, Free Press, 2000); Matthew D. Lassiter, *The Silent Majority: Suburban Politics in the Sunbelt South* (Princeton: Princeton University Press, 2006). Also see Hodding Carter III, "The End of the South," *Time* (Aug. 6, 1990). Thanks to William H. Frey of the Brookings Institution and the University of Michigan Population Studies Center (http://www.frey-demographer.org/) for providing data on recent in-migration to the South.

10. For a perceptive critique of the red state–blue state framework, see Jonathan Rauch, "Bipolar Disorder," *Atlantic Monthly* (January/February 2005), http://www.theatlantic.com/doc/200501/rauch.

11. For a recent example of a South-driven analysis of racial inequality that understates national culpability, see Ira Katznelson, *When Affirmative Action Was White: An Untold History of Racial Inequality in Twentieth-Century America* (New York: Norton, 2005).

12. Renee Christine Romano and Leigh Raiford, eds., *The Civil Rights Movement in American Memory* (Athens: University of Georgia Press, 2006); Thomas F. Jackson, *From Civil Rights to Human Rights: Martin Luther King, Jr., and the Struggle for Economic Justice* (Philadelphia: University of Pennsylvania Press, 2007); Matthew D. Lassiter, "The 'Color-Blind' Inversion of Civil Rights History," *Revue Francaise D'Etudes Americaines* (Sept. 2007), 65–69; *Parents Involved in Community Schools v. Seattle School District*, 127 S. Ct. 2738 (2007).

13. Gary Orfield and Chungmei Lee, "Racial Transformation and the Changing Nature of Segregation" (Cambridge, Mass.: The Civil Rights Project at Harvard University, 2006), http://www.civilrightsproject.ucla.edu/research/deseg/Racial_Transformation.pdf, and other reports available from The Civil Rights Project at http://www.civilrightsproject.ucla.edu/.

14. Howard Zinn, *The Southern Mystique* (New York: Knopf, 1964), 223.

15. C. Vann Woodward, *The Strange Career of Jim Crow* (New York: Oxford University Press, 1955); Woodward, "The Search for Southern Identity" (1958), republished in Woodward, *The Burden of Southern History* (Baton Rouge: Louisiana

State University Press, 1960, third ed. 1993), 4–5, 13, 25. Also see Woodward, *American Counterpoint: Slavery and Racism in the North-South Dialogue* (Boston: Little, Brown, 1971).

16. Charles Grier Sellers, ed., *The Southerner as American* (Chapel Hill: University of North Carolina Press, 1960), vi. Two decades later, Richard Current argued that "cultural differences between North and South are minimal.... The question is one of basic values, and it seems to me that, in respect to these, both Northerners and Southerners (with few exceptions) have been typically American all along." See Richard N. Current, *Northernizing the South* (Athens: University of Georgia Press), 16.

17. James C. Cobb, *Away Down South: A History of Southern Identity* (New York: Oxford University Press, 2005), 2. Also see Cobb, *Redefining Southern Identity: Mind and Identity in the Modern South* (Athens: University of Georgia Press, 1999).

18. Woodward, "Search for Southern Identity," 3–26 (quotations 16, 17, 20, 13). Also see Woodward, "The Irony of Southern History" (1952), republished in *Burden of Southern History* (third ed.), 187–211. Larry Griffin has argued that Woodward's assertions about southern identity should be considered "factually wrong" because of the exclusion of black southerners from his concept of the "Southern people," and because of the existence of multiple "Souths" and multiple "Americas" rather than a unitary version of each. See Larry J. Griffin, "Southern Distinctiveness, Yet Again, or, Why America Still Needs the South," *Southern Cultures* (Fall 2000), 47–72.

19. David M. Potter, "Depletion and Renewal in Southern History," in *Perspectives on the South: Agenda for Research*, ed. Edgar T. Thompson (Durham: Duke University Press, 1967), 75–89 (quotation 76).

20. James C. Cobb, "An Epitaph for the North: Reflections on the Politics of Regional and National Identity at the Millennium," *Journal of Southern History* (Feb. 2000), 3–24.

21. Larry J. Griffin and Don H. Doyle, "Introduction," in *The South as an American Problem*, ed. Griffin and Doyle (Athens: University of Georgia Press, 1995), 8–9.

22. Nayan Shah, *Contagious Divides: Epidemics and Race in San Francisco's Chinatown* (Berkeley: University of California Press, 2001); David Gutierrez, *Walls and Mirrors: Mexican Americans, Mexican Immigrants, and the Politics of Ethnicity* (Berkeley: University of California Press, 1995); Robert Vitalis, *America's Kingdom: Mythmaking on the Saudi Oil Frontier* (Stanford: Stanford University Press, 2007); David Nathaniel Gelman and David Quigley, *Jim Crow New York: A Documentary History of Race and Citizenship, 1777–1877* (New York: New York University Press, 2003); Davison M. Douglas, *Jim Crow Moves North: The Battle over Northern School Segregation, 1865–1954* (Cambridge: Cambridge University Press, 2005); Robert M. Fogelson, *Bourgeois Nightmares: Suburbia, 1870–1930* (New Haven: Yale University Press, 2005); Charles Abrams, *Forbidden Neighbors: A Study of Prejudice in Housing* (Port Washington, N.Y.: Kennikat Press, 1955); Kenneth T. Jackson, *Crabgrass Frontier: The Suburbanization of the United States*

(New York: Oxford University Press, 1985); David M. P. Freund, *Colored Property: State Policy and White Racial Politics in Suburban America* (Chicago: University of Chicago Press, 2007).

23. See chapter 1 of this volume and the books cited in note 5 above. Scholars who study the civil rights movement "in the North" still tend to flatten the history of places as diverse and distant as Boston (New England), Detroit and Chicago (Midwest), and Los Angeles (West) into a single unified region defined only by its status as the non-South. The new scholarship on the civil rights era "outside the South" also has overemphasized differences between northern/ western and southern places by neglecting new research in southern urban history and drawing contrasts instead with the "classic" textbook version of the "southern movement."

24. Quotations (in sequence) from "Crossing the Red Sea," *Time* (Sept. 2, 1966), 19; Ronald P. Formisano, *Boston Against Busing: Race, Class, and Ethnicity in the 1960s and 1970s* (Chapel Hill: University of North Carolina Press, 1991), 1; George Lipsitz, *The Possessive Investment in Whiteness: How White People Profit from Identity Politics* (Philadelphia: Temple University Press, 1998), 211–33; Griffin, "Southern Distinctiveness," 57 (quoting Mayor Ed Koch).

25. Californians Against Proposition 14, "No Mississippi Here," Folder 7, Box 5, Max Mont Collection, Urban Archives Center, Oviatt Library, California State University, Northridge.

26. Larry J. Griffin, "Why Was the South a Problem to America?" in *South as an American Problem*, 10–32; Griffin, "Southern Distinctiveness."

27. Charles M. Lamb, *Housing Segregation in Suburban America since 1960: Presidential and Judicial Politics* (Cambridge: Cambridge University Press, 2005), 135; Charles M. Payne, " 'The Whole United States Is Southern!': *Brown v. Board* and the Mystification of Race," *Journal of American History* (June 2004), 83–91; Dan T. Carter, *From George Wallace to Newt Gingrich: Race in the Conservative Counterrevolution, 1963–1994* (Baton Rouge: Louisiana State University Press, 1996), 6.

28. For a sampling of this debate, see Harry S. Ashmore, *An Epitaph For Dixie* (New York: Norton, 1958); Woodward, *Burden of Southern History*; Current, *Northernizing the South*; Egerton, *Americanization of Dixie*; Carter, "End of the South"; John Shelton Reed, *The Enduring South: Subcultural Persistence in Mass Society* (Chapel Hill: University of North Carolina Press, 1974); Carl N. Degler, *Place over Time: The Continuity of Southern Distinctiveness* (Baton Rouge: Louisiana State University Press, 1977); Charles Reagan Wilson and William Ferris, eds., *The Encyclopedia of Southern Culture* (Chapel Hill: University of North Carolina Press, 1989); Tony Horwitz, *Confederates in the Attic: Dispatches from the Unfinished Civil War* (New York: Pantheon Books, 1998); Craig S. Pascoe, Karen Trahan Leathem, and Andy Ambrose, *The American South in the Twentieth Century* (Athens: University of Georgia Press, 2005).

29. Edward L. Ayers, "What We Talk about When We Talk about the South," in *All Over the Map: Rethinking American Regions*, ed. Ayers, Patricia Nelson

Limerick, Stephen Nissenbaum, and Peter S. Onuf (Baltimore: Johns Hopkins University Press, 1996), 68–69.

30. "The South Today," *Time* (Sept. 27, 1976), 32.

31. "In Search of the South," *Washington* Post, July 14, 1996.

32. David R. Goldfield, *Still Fighting the Civil War: The American South and Southern History* (Baton Rouge: Louisiana State University Press, 2002), 6, 12–13.

33. See, for example, David L. Carlton, "How American Is the American South?" *South as an American Problem*, 33–56; Current, *Northernizing the South*, 12; Michael O'Brien, *The Idea of the American South, 1920–1941* (Baltimore: Johns Hopkins University Press, 1979); O'Brien, *Rethinking the South: Essays in Intellectual History* (Baltimore: Johns Hopkins University Press, 1988).

34. Benedict Andersen, *Imagined Communities: Reflections on the Origins and Spread of Nationalism* (London: Verso, 1983).

35. Urban historians generally have rejected a distinctive model of southern development, especially for the post-World War II period. See Ronald H. Bayor, *Race and the Shaping of Twentieth-Century Atlanta* (Chapel Hill: University of North Carolina Press, 1996); David C. Perry and Alfred J. Watkins, eds., *The Rise of the Sunbelt Cities* (Beverly Hills: Sage, 1977); Richard M. Bernard and Bradley R. Rice, eds., *Sunbelt Cities: Politics and Growth Since World War II* (Austin: University of Texas Press, 1983); Raymond A. Mohl, ed., *Searching for the Sunbelt: Historical Perspectives on a Region* (Knoxville: University of Tennessee Press, 1990); Mohl, "The Second Ghetto Thesis and the Power of History," *Journal of Urban History* (March 2003), 243–56. For an alternative view that emphasizes "the distinctive characteristics of Southern urbanization," see David R. Goldfield, "The Urban South: A Regional Framework," *American Historical Review* (Dec. 1981), 1009–34 (quotation 1034).

36. Michael O'Brien has suggested that even at the "apogee" of southern distinctiveness in the late 1800s, a majority of the residents of the southern states would not have "accepted 'southern' as the social identity most explanatory of their lives." See O'Brien, "The Apprehension of the South in Modern Culture," *Southern Cultures* (Winter 1998), 3–18 (quotation 12–13).

37. Thomas Bender, ed., *Rethinking American History in a Global Age* (Berkeley: University of California Press, 2002).

38. U.S. National Emergency Council, *Report on Economic Conditions of the South* (Washington: GPO, 1938). Also see Gavin Wright, *Old South, New South: Revolutions in the Southern Economy since the Civil War* (New York: Basic Books, 1986); Nancy MacLean, "From the Benighted South to the Sunbelt: The South in the Twentieth Century," in *Perspectives on Modern America: Making Sense of the Twentieth Century*, ed. Harvard Sitkoff (New York: Oxford University Press, 2001), 202–26.

39. Woodward, "Search for Southern Identity," 4–9.

40. Gregory, *Southern Diaspora*; Numan V. Bartley, *The New South, 1945–1980: The Story of the South's Modernization* (Baton Rouge: LSU Press, 1995); Earl Black and Merle Black, *Politics and Society in the South* (Cambridge: Harvard University

Press, 1987); Bruce J. Schulman, *From Cotton Belt to Sunbelt: Federal Policy, Economic Development, and the Transformation of the South, 1938–1980* (New York: Oxford University Press, 1991); Carl Abbott, *The New Urban America: Growth and Politics in Sunbelt Cities* (Chapel Hill: University of North Carolina Press, 1981).

41. U.S. Census Bureau, "Population Change and Distribution, 1990 to 2000" (April 2001), http://www.census.gov/prod/2001pubs/c2kbr01–2.pdf.

42. James C. Cobb and William Stueck, eds., *Globalization and the American South* (Athens: University of Georgia Press, 2005); Nelson Lichtenstein, ed., *Wal-Mart: The Face of Twenty-First Century Capitalism* (New York: New Press, 2006). Recent studies that evaluate Latino immigration to the South within a national framework include Audrey Singer, Susan W. Hardwick, and Caroline B. Brettell, eds., *Twenty-First-Century Gateways: Immigrant Incorporation in Suburban America* (Washington: Brookings, 2008); Douglas S. Massey, ed., *New Faces in New Places: The Changing Geography of American Immigration* (New York: Russell Sage Foundation, 2008).

43. Jeanne F. Theoharis and Komozi Woodard, eds., *Groundwork: Local Black Freedom Movements in America* (New York: New York University Press, 2005); Theoharis and Woodard, *Freedom North.*

44. Allison Graham, *Framing the South: Hollywood, Television, and Race during the Civil Rights Struggle* (Baltimore: Johns Hopkins University Press, 2001).

45. Lassiter, *Silent Majority*; Joseph Crespino, *In Search of Another Country: Mississippi and the Conservative Counterrevolution* (Princeton: Princeton University Press, 2007).

Part I

THE NORTHERN MYSTIQUE

1

DE JURE/DE FACTO SEGREGATION

The Long Shadow of a National Myth

Matthew D. Lassiter

Two months before Martin Luther King Jr.'s famous "I Have a Dream" address at the 1963 March on Washington, he delivered an early version of the speech in downtown Detroit. In the wake of the epic street demonstrations in Birmingham, only twelve days after President John F. Kennedy finally endorsed a civil rights bill, King arrived in Michigan to support local groups that were organizing marches into the city's overwhelmingly white suburbs to protest housing segregation (figure 1.1). "We've got to come to see that the problem of racial injustice is a national problem," King told a crowd of at least 125,000 people. "I have a dream this afternoon that one day right here in Detroit, Negroes will be able to buy a house or rent a house anywhere that their money will carry them." The nation's preeminent civil rights leader then addressed the matter of de facto vs. de jure segregation, drawing the familiar constitutional contrast and collapsing the prevailing regional distinction at the same time. "Now in the North it's different in that it doesn't have the legal sanction that it has in the South. But it has its subtle and hidden forms, and it exists in three areas: in the area of employment discrimination, in the area of housing discrimination, and in the area of de facto segregation in the public schools. And we must come to see that de facto segregation in the North is just as injurious as the actual segregation in the South."[1]

The narrative of the civil rights era turns out to be much different, and much less triumphant, if we remember Martin Luther King in 1963 in downtown Detroit looking out at the all-white suburbs—not just imprisoned down in Alabama, standing in front of the Lincoln Memorial before

FIGURE 1.1. Martin Luther King, Jr., marches with local civil rights leaders at the front of the "Walk to Freedom" on Woodward Avenue in downtown Detroit, June 23, 1963. King, the head of the Southern Christian Leadership Conference, denounced "de facto segregation in the North" in a speech to 125,000 people, one of the largest civil rights protests in American history. © Bettmann/CORBIS.

heading back to the South, mobilizing a liberal nation to bring a recalcitrant region into compliance with the American Creed. Viewing the civil rights movement before the mid-1960s in its full national context disrupts the linear two-stage story of victory against Jim Crow in the South followed by urban race riots, Black Power, and the rise of white backlash in the North and West. At the same time, King's comparison of "de facto segregation" in the North to "the actual segregation" in the South revolved around an ethical equation rather than a legal argument, more concerned with the effects of racial inequality than the causes. The civil rights movement itself was largely responsible for creating and popularizing the concept of de facto segregation, a strategy designed to appeal to the collective conscience of white liberals and public policymakers, building on the Supreme Court's ruling in *Brown* that "separate educational facilities are inherently unequal."[2] In the long run, this approach proved to be a tactical error because equal protection claims before the federal courts still required evidence of discriminatory state action to trigger legal remedies. According to the established regional dichotomy, enshrined in constitutional law and pervasive in public discourse by the mid-1960s, racial discrimination in the Jim Crow South represented segregation in law (de jure), while residential and educational patterns in the North and West reflected segregation in fact but not enforced by law (de facto). The constitutional opposition of de jure/de facto effectively insulated most northern and western communities from civil rights litigation for nearly two decades after *Brown*, despite ample historical evidence of comprehensive state action in producing deeply entrenched patterns of residential and educational segregation.

The artificial dichotomy between de jure and de facto segregation decisively shaped the trajectory and limited the reach of the civil rights movement between the 1950s and the 1970s. The so-called liberal consensus—the political coalition that produced the landmark civil rights and voting rights legislation of 1964–1965—depended upon the racial construction of an exceptional South and the widespread public denial of the government policies that shaped housing and school segregation in metropolitan regions throughout the United States. Significant popular support for meaningful levels of racial integration never existed at the local level in the urban North or West, but white backlash did not emerge full-blown in national politics until the mid-1960s, primarily because federal civil rights policies until then focused almost exclusively on the South. Federal court decisions during the 1960s also rested on a false binary between de jure school segregation that resulted from deliberate actions by government officials and de facto school segregation caused by housing patterns allegedly beyond their control. When the civil rights movement launched a direct assault on the interlocking patterns of educational inequality and residential exclusion in cities and suburbs across the nation, the tenuous liberal coalition for racial integration disintegrated. A broad spectrum of white actors seized upon the "de facto" rationale through a "color-blind" discourse that defended neighborhood schools and segregated housing as the products of private action and free-market forces alone, a sphere in which government had not caused, and therefore had no right or obligation to remedy, racial inequality. These voices eventually included many northern liberals and intellectuals, the moderate leaders of Sunbelt cities, segregationist politicians from the Deep South, policymakers in the Nixon administration, grassroots organizations that claimed membership in the Silent Majority, and local elected officials in almost every jurisdiction in the country that faced a civil rights lawsuit.[3]

Although the framework of southern exceptionalism leads to distorted interpretations of the past, it is important to historicize the idea of southern distinctiveness as a cultural, political, and legal construction that has been very real in its consequences. The de jure/de facto dichotomy trapped the black freedom struggle within a discourse of regional difference, even as civil rights groups repeatedly emphasized the moral equivalence and challenged the constitutional boundaries between "southern-style" and "northern-style" segregation. National policymakers and liberals in the

North and West generally defined "American-style" segregation through an evasive negation, as the intangible opposite of the Jim Crow system in the South, even as white southerners increasingly depicted their own neighborhoods as de facto landscapes of modernity and progress in synchronicity with the American Dream. Scholars also have played a role in keeping the mythology of de facto segregation alive by failing to confront directly the problem of southern exceptionalism, despite the wealth of recent studies that have explored the government policies that produced racial inequality in the postwar metropolis.[4] The label of de facto segregation is so historically loaded—so wrapped up in artificial binaries between South and North, between the educational and residential arenas, between deliberate state action and private market forces, between white culpability and white innocence—that historians should discard it as an analytical and descriptive category and evaluate it instead as a cultural and political construct. As a constitutional matter, "de facto segregation" does not mean "segregation in the North and West" or "segregation caused by housing patterns" or "institutional racism" or "segregation in areas without Jim Crow laws" or "subtle segregation" or other commonly deployed synonyms. As a legal doctrine, "de facto segregation" means "innocent segregation"—spatial landscapes and racial arrangements that exist beyond the scope of judicial remedy, attributable solely to private market forces in the absence of any historical or contemporary government responsibility.

The NAACP's challenge to state-sanctioned residential segregation predated its much more celebrated campaign against Jim Crow segregation in public schools. Civil rights litigants faced a difficult burden of proof in the area of housing because the Supreme Court's state action doctrine (derived from the *Civil Rights Cases* of 1883) drew a sharp distinction between unconstitutional racial inequality enforced by government policy and permissible acts of racial discrimination undertaken by private individuals. In *Buchanan v. Warley* (1917), the Supreme Court invalidated a Louisville ordinance that mandated housing segregation, holding that "a colored person has the right to acquire property without state legislation discriminating against him solely because of color." Nine years later, in *Corrigan v. Buckley* (1926), the Court dismissed litigation to outlaw restrictive covenants that banned the sale or rental of property to racial and ethnic minorities as "entirely lacking in substance," since nothing in the Constitution "prohibited private individuals from entering into contracts respecting the control and disposition of their own property." Racial covenants proliferated in American cities and suburbs between the 1920s and the 1940s, with deed restrictions enforced by the courts under the doctrine of contract law and simultaneously immunized from challenge under the guise of private property rights. The Federal

Housing Administration (FHA) also encouraged restrictive covenants in residential developments financed by government mortgage programs, with the injunction that "if a neighborhood is to retain stability, it is necessary that properties shall continue to be occupied by the same social and racial classes." In 1950, the U.S. Supreme Court reaffirmed the public/private dichotomy in a case involving the all-white and federally subsidized Stuyvesant Town development, refusing to consider an appeal of a New York Supreme Court ruling that distinguished between illegal racial discrimination by government fiat and permissible racial discrimination in "private enterprise aided by government."[5]

The U.S. Supreme Court expanded the scope of the state action doctrine in *Shelley v. Kraemer* (1948), which overturned two decades of precedent in order to bar the judicial enforcement of private racial covenants as a discriminatory exercise of government power. The justices simultaneously reaffirmed the constitutional principle that the Fourteenth Amendment's equal protection clause applied only to "such action as may fairly be said to be that of the States. That Amendment erects no shield against merely private conduct, however discriminatory or wrongful." Although an important breakthrough in the NAACP's postwar fair-housing campaign, *Shelley v. Kraemer* had a negligible impact on metropolitan patterns of residential segregation, which intensified between the 1940s and the 1960s. A wide array of government policies from the local to the federal levels—exclusionary municipal zoning, pervasive discrimination in mortgage lending programs, public-private collaboration in redlining neighborhoods, open Jim Crow practices in public housing projects, demolition of nonwhite districts through highway construction and urban renewal programs—subsidized the development of segregated suburbs and concentrated minority residents in urban ghettoes. These state-based and publicly subsidized pillars of residential segregation, which came to be clustered under the "de facto" umbrella, shaped the postwar development of cities and suburbs across the nation, resulting in remarkably similar built environments whether metropolitan regions were located inside or outside the South. "What the Ku Klux Klan has not been able to accomplish by intimidation and violence," Clarence Mitchell of the NAACP charged in 1951, "the present federal housing policy is accomplishing through a monumental program of segregation in all aspects of housing which receive government aid."[6]

The postwar tendency to view race relations across a regional chasm obscured the national growth policies that were remaking the metropolitan South, as well as the prominence of modern forms of state-sponsored segregation in every other part of the nation. Gunnar Myrdal's *An American Dilemma*, the influential account of race relations published during World War II, presented a "Negro problem" that was geographically based in the nation's tolerance of the Jim Crow South and psychologically situated within the white liberal conscience and its responsibility to redeem the American Creed of equal opportunity. In 1947, the President's Committee on Civil Rights found that "legally-enforced segregation has been largely limited to the South. But segregation is also widely prevalent in the North, ... [where] segregation in education is not formal, and ... discrimination in housing results primarily from business practices." With few exceptions, mainstream political discourse during the postwar decades simply did not address the question of government culpability in the housing market and instead focused almost exclusively on individual prejudice and private forms of discrimination. "Many Negroes and some whites feel that resistance to real integration in private housing in the North is as stubbornly rooted as the resistance to integrated schooling in the South," an exposé in the *New York Times* charged in 1956. "The final solution of the problem of segregation in the North ... lies in the hearts and minds of people." The white southern defense of Jim Crow represented a "mass commitment to evil," the prominent intellectual Nathan Glazer declared eight years later. "The Southern kind of position just can't be found in the North. ... The American Creed does prevail in the North."[7]

During the 1950s and early 1960s, the southern drama of massive resistance served to obscure the civil rights movement's extensive challenge to Jim Crow housing policies in the metropolitan North and West. "When you get the school cases under control," Los Angeles attorney Loren Miller wrote to NAACP chief counsel Thurgood Marshall in 1952, "we ought to call a meeting of lawyers to consider the increasingly important housing matters to see if we can't fashion some kind of an all out attack on the Levittowns." One year before *Brown*, the NAACP announced that "the eradication of any type of segregated housing that has any form of public financial support must be our first goal." In 1955, however, the federal courts rejected the NAACP's contention that government financing of the all-white Levittown suburb in Pennsylvania constituted official racial discrimination in violation of the state action doctrine. If the FHA did not quickly reverse course, Miller warned, then "the Supreme Court decision on schools will become a dead letter and we will have segregated schools, North and South." The National Committee against Discrimination in Housing likewise denounced "FHA-aided jimcrow Levittowns" and charged that the federal government "has become both the architect and builder of segregated communities." FHA officials responded by pledging to work with the private sector to expand "the market for minority housing," which Miller labeled an official endorsement of a "separate but equal doctrine" on an even greater scale than the Jim Crow system in the South—a "special market in which the Negro must buy housing." "The pattern is the same everywhere," Miller explained. "Residential segregation as we know it today is the end product of more than a half century of intensive government

sanction.... What is needed is an affirmative government policy deliberately designed to undo past discrimination."[8]

During the decade after World War II, the NAACP also launched a
multifaceted campaign against officially authorized school segregation
in northern localities, with special attention to Ohio, New Jersey, and
Pennsylvania. According to a survey by legal scholar Davison Douglas,
"government sponsored school segregation—such as the assignment
of black children to separate 'colored' schools or classrooms—persisted
in open defiance of state law in many northern communities until the
late 1940s and early 1950s." In the Southwest, the de jure segregation
of Latino students remained widespread until the *Mendez* litigation of
1946–1947, when state and federal courts overturned the policies of multiple school districts in Orange County, California. As the Supreme Court
justices contemplated the *Brown* cases, twenty-one states and the nation's
capital still required or permitted formal segregation in public education.
By 1954, most urban and suburban districts outside the southern and border states operated nominally "color-blind" neighborhood schools systems anchored in racially segregated housing patterns and gerrymandered
attendance zones, often combined with "freedom of choice" transfer
policies that allowed white students to escape majority-black or major-
ity-Latino facilities. In 1956, as southern states fought against the *Brown*
decision, the *New York Times* acknowledged that "a Georgian or a Missis-
sippian visiting one of these 'all-Negro' schools...could laugh cynically
at the idea that northern schools are desegregated." This special report
on "the status of the Negro in the North" explained how official integration and accidental segregation co-existed in the absence of Jim Crow:
"Because of the segregation in housing, Negro slums tend to limit Negro
children in slum areas to the neighborhood school. A public school may
thus become 'segregated' in spite of itself, and in spite of the integrated
system of which it is a part."[9]

The case of New York City illustrates the rhetorical commitment to racial
integration by liberal northern policymakers, combined with their insistence on drawing a clear line between government policies that affected
public schools and market forces that shaped urban neighborhoods.
Kenneth Clark, the NAACP consultant whose psychological arguments
had informed the reasoning in *Brown*, observed that the New York City
Board of Education "did not look seriously at the problems of its ghetto
schools until the school segregation cases in the South forced its attention
upon them." In April 1954, a civil rights coalition led by the NAACP and
the Urban League called for an investigation into the "segregation" and
"racial exclusion" of minority students, which the petition attributed to
housing patterns and discussed in the language of psychological damage.
Dr. Clark pointed out that the Supreme Court had not stated that "only
legal segregation is detrimental to the human personality," and then he

leveled the explosive accusation that "Jim Crow" practices existed in the New York City system. School board president Arthur Levitt vehemently denied the southern-style slander of "segregation willfully and designedly imposed," but he also promised to "leave nothing undone to mitigate the evils of school segregation imposed by residential segregation." In December 1954, the board of education passed a resolution pledging to comply with *Brown*, which it characterized as a "challenge to...Northern as well as Southern communities."[10]

The discursive framework of de facto segregation first emerged in the context of New York City's response to the *Brown* decision, at a moment when civil rights activists believed that constitutional law was more concerned with the effects of racial segregation than with the causes, and therefore that politicians and policymakers rather than judges represented the most critical audience. In the public sphere, the earliest mention of "de facto segregation" appears to be a 1955 statement by the Urban League of Greater New York, which demanded "an emergency program to desegregate New York City's public schools" and accused education officials of culpability in the "presently de facto segregated Negro and Puerto Rican schools." Under pressure from local civil rights groups, the New York City Board of Education commissioned a report that proposed modest desegregation techniques, such as the reassignment of teachers to assist "underperforming" (Harlem) schools, the redrawing of a few attendance zones, and "freedom-of-choice" transfers for minority students to attend more integrated facilities. The *New York Times* portrayed these proposals as a reflection of enlightened municipal leadership, because "there is, of course, no official segregation in the city.... There is a de facto form of segregation...caused by the residential pattern. Children go to their neighborhood schools." Unless New York took decisive action, the newspaper explained, "how could we have answered our conscience? What could we have said to our friends in the South?" But the board of education retreated after white neighborhood groups attacked the commission's proposals, and city officials in the decade after *Brown* consistently refused to consider any steps that subverted the educational philosophy of neighborhood schools.[11]

The de facto designation, by defining African-American segregation outside the South as a problem of ethics (the collective white conscience) and a product of markets (economic forces combined with the private right to discriminate), helped to naturalize "neighborhood schools" as a race-neutral policy requiring a political rather than a judicial solution. "The trend of Negro migration to the nation's largest metropolitan areas is bringing about new patterns of segregation of residential areas," the U.S. Commission on Civil Rights concluded in its inaugural 1959 report. "One result, of course, is the *de facto* segregation of many schools. The residential areas, and the one-race schools that result, arise without the force of any legal compulsion." "In the great metropolitan centers of the North," the American Jewish Congress declared, "*de facto* segregation has blighted our communities with a malignancy that is evil and menacing." Instead of being content to "express shock and indignation" about the South, public officials must "take affirmative action" to achieve integration whether northern schools "are segregated by law or in fact." By 1963, civil rights activists had pressured education officials in three states— New York, New Jersey, and California—to announce limited measures to address the problem of "racial imbalance," which the Civil Rights Commission defined as the existence of segregated neighborhood schools, "however innocently caused." Robert Carter, the general counsel of the NAACP, expressed high hopes for "the method of securing state policy decisions outlawing de facto segregation.... Where that fails, we should seek redress in the courts."[12]

In the early 1960s, the NAACP orchestrated a legal and political campaign against public school segregation in dozens of northern and western communities, part of what the organization called an "all-out attack...against Jim Crow schools northern style." An early victory came in *Taylor v. New Rochelle* (1961), a Westchester County suburb of New York City, after civil rights plaintiffs demonstrated that the school board had purposefully gerrymandered (and repeatedly re-gerrymandered) the attendance zone of an overwhelmingly black elementary school. The school district claimed that such "de facto" segregation resulted solely from residential forces beyond its control, but the federal judge ruled that "compliance with the Supreme Court's edict was not to be less forthright in the North than in the South.... It is of no moment whether the segregation is labeled by the defendant as 'de jure' or 'de facto,' as long as the Board, by its conduct, is responsible for its maintenance." The American Jewish Congress labeled *Taylor v. New Rochelle* a "landmark decision in the history of American race relations" and pronounced northern school districts that practiced "unofficial segregation" through administrative devices to "share the same burden of guilt as those in the South." The U.S. Civil Rights Commission concluded that the *Brown* mandate encompassed "racial segregation in the North and West resulting from official action,... [but] *de facto* segregation that results from free private choice, or from residential patterns based on purely private discrimination, is apparently not forbidden."[13]

Civil rights litigation succeeded in proving official culpability in a small number of northern and western suburbs, but the NAACP's pledge to "insure the end of all segregated public education in fact or by law" depended upon the unlikely proposition that federal courts would abandon the longstanding state action doctrine in favor of the abstract "inherently unequal" language of *Brown*. The 1961 report by the Civil Rights Commission did suggest that illegal racial gerrymandering might be far more pervasive in northern and western school districts than the popularity of the de facto designation would indicate. The commission's investigations of northern and western cities also uncovered many of the same freedom-of-choice plans, racially suspect transfer policies, and segregated school construction schemes that were simultaneously marking the era of "token desegregation" in the South. In a 1963 decision, the California Supreme Court found the suburban city of Pasadena guilty of deliberate racial gerrymandering, but then declared housing segregation to be "itself an evil" and charged school boards with the responsibility "to alleviate racial imbalance in schools regardless of its cause." In a 1964 case involving the Long Island suburb of Manhasset, a federal district court labeled as "segregation by law" a neighborhood schools plan that assigned every black student to a single elementary school while 99.2 percent of their white counterparts attended two all-white facilities. The *Manhasset* decision embraced the NAACP's broad interpretation that "segregated schools, be they segregated de jure or 'de facto,' are inferior per se and deprive children of minority groups of equal educational opportunities." The district judge then posed the critical question that remained unresolved a decade after *Brown*: "Can it be said that one type of segregation, having its basis in state law or evasive schemes to defeat desegregation, is to be proscribed, while another, having the same effect but another cause, is to be condoned?"[14]

During 1963–1964, as the nonviolent direct-action movement reached a climax in the Deep South, local affiliates of the NAACP and CORE organized frequent marches and boycotts to protest "de facto segregation" in dozens of northern and western cities, including Boston, New York, Cleveland, Chicago, Denver, and Los Angeles. This chapter of history—before passage of the Civil Rights Act, before the riots in Watts and Detroit, before the media discovery of Black Power—has all but disappeared from the popular memory of the civil rights era. In Chicago, black parents conducted sit-ins and boycotts while charging the district with deliberate gerrymandering, transfer policies permitting white students to avoid majority-black neighborhood schools, and implementation of a token "open enrollment" plan that covered only thirty-four minority students. In Los Angeles, protests by the NAACP and Mexican-American groups resulted in a 1963 commission report that endorsed a race-neutral ideal in educational policy but concluded that "there are no easy answers and no speedy solutions to . . . de facto segregation in our schools, the present segregated housing patterns of the community." In New York City, a series of protests demanding school integration culminated in the largest civil rights demonstration in American history, a one-day boycott in early 1964 by more than 300,000 African-American and Puerto Rican students (figure 1.2). The liberal editorial page of the *New York Times* admonished local activists to remember that "*de facto* segregation . . . is entirely different from that in the South. . . . The root is not in any systematic policy of racial exclusion fostered by law or administrative policy but in neighborhood population patterns." A few months later, a state commission endorsed some modest reforms but asserted bluntly that "total desegregation of all schools...is simply not attainable in the foreseeable future and neither planning nor pressure can change that fact."[15]

FIGURE 1.2. "Fight Jim Crow." The Reverend Milton Galamison walks a picket line in front of a Brooklyn public school on February 3, 1964. Galamison, a longtime leader of the grassroots campaign to integrate the New York City schools, helped organize a massive one-day boycott by African-American and Puerto Rican students to protest racial segregation in the nation's largest school system. © Bettmann/CORBIS.

As the civil rights movement pressed for affirmative action to address the interlinked dilemma of educational and residential segregation, local school boards routinely displaced legal responsibility onto the housing market through the de facto rationale, and federal judges consistently refused to apply the *Brown* mandate to large urban districts outside the South. In the pivotal *Bell* case of 1963, the federal courts accepted the Gary (Indiana) school district's "color blind" defense of its neighborhood schools plan and concluded that "the problem...is not one of segregated schools but rather of segregated housing, either by choice or by design." The reasoning in this highly anticipated ruling reinforced the sharp divide between the housing and educational spheres, with even evidence of state action in the area of residential segregation ("by design") presumed irrelevant to the constitutionality of the neighborhood schools that resulted. The Supreme Court declined to hear the NAACP's appeal that "regardless of the motive or the intent,...there is an affirmative duty on the part of the defendant to integrate the races so as to bring about...a racial balance in each of the various schools." A few months later, in *Webb v. Board of Education*, a federal district court dismissed a similar challenge to Chicago's neighborhood schools plan. The decision recognized the "irreparable harm which could result from segregation under the sanction of law" but concluded that "there is no Constitutional right to be integrated with persons of other Races....De facto segregation resulting from the implementation of a neighborhood school policy, or residential segregation is not enough." A decade after *Brown*, the federal judiciary had reformulated the South-North binary with a second constitutional distinction between illegal "de jure" school segregation resulting from deliberate action by educational officials and permissible "de facto" segregation that encompassed everything else.[16]

On September 14, 1964, Mississippi became the last southern state to begin the process of compliance with the *Brown* decision, when thirty-nine black students entered formerly all-white elementary schools in the capital city of Jackson. The story did not make the front page of the next day's *New York Times*, which instead highlighted a local protest organized by a white group called Parents and Taxpayers: "275,638 PUPILS STAY HOME IN INTEGRATION BOYCOTT." This massive grassroots backlash in New York City came in response to a limited desegregation plan that transferred about 13,000 minority students to identifiably white schools and reassigned about 1,000 white students from Queens and Brooklyn to facilities in adjacent black and Puerto Rican neighborhoods. Civil rights leaders criticized the formula as southern-style gradualism and tokenism, while white parents leveled charges of reverse discrimination with slogans such as "Give us back our neighborhood school" and "Our children also have civil rights." *The New Republic* portrayed the racial attitudes of these working-class white families as a regional inversion of the American Dilemma: "They live in a society accustomed to thinking of itself better than the South, and yet they have feelings not unlike those of white Alabamans." A *U.S. News and World Report* investigation of the resistance to "forced integration" in New York City instead found a genuine attempt to defend the American ideal of color-blind individualism. "Now this is a liberal neighborhood," a white mother from Jackson Heights explained. "We don't object to Negroes or to integration. We believe in civil rights. But we have rights, too, and we will not allow them to steal our rights or to destroy our neighborhood school." Black residents of a segregated enclave nearby believed that the Mason-Dixon line ran right through Queens, the *Times* reported. "It's just as bad here" as in the South, remarked a black parent whose children attended a "de facto segregated" school.[17]

In the summer of 1964, the U.S. Congress finally broke the southern filibuster and passed the Civil Rights Act, but only after liberal sponsors deliberately sought to exempt northern and western communities with the provision that "'desegregation' shall not mean the assignment of students to public schools in order to overcome racial imbalance." Along with furious charges of northern hypocrisy and a regional double standard, politicians in the South immediately began demanding that school districts operating under freedom-of-choice desegregation plans in their states be reclassified as "de facto." In the North and West, many public officials began adopting the label of "racial imbalance," a less pejorative description that took advantage of the escape clause in the Civil Rights Act, to describe neighborhood school systems once conceded to be "de facto" segregated. Although the concepts were synonymous, the NAACP's Robert Carter declared in 1965, "neither usage is satisfactory. *De facto* segregation fosters the misconception that the racial separation it describes is purely accidental, not the responsibility of government and, therefore, outside the reach of the fourteenth amendment." That same year, the Massachusetts legislature passed the Racial Imbalance Act, which cut off funding for urban school districts that did not dismantle majority-black facilities, and *Time* predicted that the evolution of national policy would bring "an all-out Government attack on the racial imbalance of the nation's schools." In 1967, the Department of Health, Education, and Welfare announced that federal oversight of racial patterns in public education, previously restricted to seventeen southern and border states, would henceforth encompass the entire nation. But the Johnson administration promised that northern and western communities would face no penalties for constitutional forms of racial segregation "arising solely from fair and reasonable application of neighborhood school attendance zoning to segregated housing patterns."[18]

The race-neutral defense of segregated neighborhood schools, in combination with the political backlash against the open-housing movement, exposed the hard truth that a national consensus for substantial racial integration had never existed, beyond the difficult enough struggle to intervene against the worst excesses of Jim Crow in the South. The accompanying wave of urban race riots reproduced the rituals of white liberal shock and American innocence lost, the latest nationalization of the regional race problem. "Los Angeles: Why?" asked the cover of *Newsweek* after the explosion of Watts in 1965, one year after three-fourths of white Californians voted to repeal the state's fair-housing law. "Why?" wondered *Time* a year later, following the eruption of violence on Chicago's West Side. Mayor Richard Daley answered the question by blaming the outside agitators in the Southern Christian Leadership Conference, following Martin Luther King's relocation to an inner-city Chicago neighborhood in order to dramatize the issue of residential segregation and pressure Congress to pass a federal open-housing law. "Just as Mississippi stands as the largest bastion of crippling de jure segregation in the South," King responded, "Chicago holds equal status as the most hostile bastion of de facto segregation in the North." During the summer of 1966, the Chicago Freedom Movement conducted marches against housing segregation in several all-white city neighborhoods and in the blue-collar suburb of Cicero, described by *Time* as "Selma without the Southern drawl." But the televised scenes of mob violence that greeted open-housing demonstrations in Chicago did not elicit the same national response as the previous year's voting-rights campaign in Alabama, and a cross-regional alliance in the U.S. Senate killed the fair-housing bill that now represented the top legislative priority of the civil rights movement.[19]

The Johnson administration did endorse federal open-housing legislation as a key pillar in the struggle for racial equality, but public debate about residential segregation continued to focus primarily on private property rights and individual acts of racism rather than the structural role of government programs in shaping the postwar metropolitan landscape. In a 1964 exposé of "Segregation, Northern-Style," CBS television portrayed the barriers to residential integration in the New York suburbs as a hearts-and-minds problem caused exclusively by private market forces, especially the discriminatory practices of the real estate industry and the racial prejudices of white homeowners. At the same time, a secondary strain in liberal discourse did reflect a growing acknowledgment of the role of government policies in structuring the segregated housing market—which civil rights activists had been pointing out for more than two decades. In a 1967 report, the U.S. Civil Rights Commission pinpointed the underpinnings of the national urban crisis: "Negroes who live in slum ghettoes...have been unable to move to suburban communities and other exclusively white areas." While racial discrimination by the real estate industry played a central role, "an important contributing factor to exclusion of Negroes from such areas...has been the policies and practices of agencies of government at all levels." A year later, the Kerner Commission reformulated this assessment into a frontal assault on the intertwined myths of de facto segregation and national "color-blind" innocence: "What white Americans have never fully understood—but what the Negro can never forget—is that white society is deeply implicated in the ghetto. White institutions created it, white institutions maintain it, and white society condones it."[20]

The evolution of civil rights into a full-blown national dilemma corresponded with the southward migration of the de facto/de jure debate. "*De facto* segregation is not yet a major issue in the South," Robert Carter warned in 1965, "but in the urban areas it can be expected to replace formal segregation.... The result could be more racial segregation North and South than existed before 1954 if the Northern pattern of *de facto* segregation becomes the model of school organization." This was already happening in the metropolitan South, in the sense that national rather than regionally distinctive patterns of residential segregation informed school desegregation techniques in the aftermath of *Brown*. By the mid-1960s, most urban districts across the South had adopted "freedom of choice" desegregation formulas and "race-neutral" neighborhood schools plans modeled on techniques that federal judges had explicitly approved as constitutional in response to NAACP litigation in the North and West. The de facto framework, originally devised by civil rights leaders as a strategy to extend the *Brown* mandate beyond the South, turned out to be a road map for southern cities seeking to escape meaningful integration through "northern-style" approaches. In 1966, the Fourth Circuit Court of Appeals cited the Gary, Indiana, precedent in denying the NAACP's challenge to a neighborhood schools assignment plan in Charlotte, North Carolina. "So long as the boundaries are not drawn for the conscious purpose of maintaining segregation," the appellate ruling maintained, "the School Board is under no constitutional requirement that it effectively and completely counteract all of the effects of segregated housing patterns." But the legal climate shifted again with the Virginia case of *Green v. New Kent County* (1968), when the Supreme Court charged southern districts that had operated dual school systems with an "affirmative duty to take whatever steps might be necessary" to eradicate the vestiges of de jure segregation.[21]

In *Swann v. Charlotte-Mecklenburg* (1969), the NAACP achieved a significant victory by convincing a district court to order busing to overcome state-sponsored patterns of housing segregation, a novel and far-reaching extension of the state action doctrine. "The neighborhood school theory has no standing to override the Constitution," stated the opinion by Judge James McMillan, when "superimposed on an urban population pattern where Negro residents have become concentrated almost entirely in one quadrant of a city of 270,000." The *Swann* decision found that school segregation in Charlotte's consolidated city-suburban district resulted from discriminatory housing policies such as municipal planning and zoning, federally funded urban renewal programs, the site selection for low-income projects, and the legacy of restrictive racial covenants. "There is so much state action embedded in and shaping these events," Judge McMillan concluded, "that the resulting segregation is not innocent or '*de facto*.'" In response, white families in suburban Charlotte launched a grassroots revolt that denounced busing for "racial balance" as a violation of the 1964 Civil Rights Act and the constitutional imperative of color-blind nondiscrimination. Under the banner of the Silent Majority, anti-busing movements in Charlotte and other southern cities also established a regional alliance that demanded "the same treatment as northern cities" because neighborhood schools and housing patterns in all metropolitan areas resulted from "de facto as opposed to de jure segregation."[22]

The *Swann* verdict disrupted both the North/South binary and the housing/schools dichotomy by requiring education officials in a southern city to remedy the effects of "northern-style" residential segregation. In January 1970, *Time* attempted to clarify the de jure/de facto question that the Supreme Court had never resolved: "Unlike Southern school segregation, which is the result of official policy, segregation in the North is less purposeful and harder to correct. In most cities, segregation came about accidentally, only to be perpetuated deliberately." This tortured logic highlighted a distinction without a difference to white southern politicians who called for regional fairness and believed, in the words of Senator John Stennis of Mississippi, that "when the North feels the pinch as it has been felt in the South, the harsh regulations and demands will be moderated." In February, Stennis introduced an amendment to establish a uniform school desegregation policy throughout the nation, along with a federal antibusing standard that replicated a law recently signed by Governor Nelson Rockefeller of New York. "Northern liberals were in total confusion," reported *Time*, especially after Senator Abraham Ribicoff of Connecticut endorsed the Stennis measure and accused his home region of "monumental hypocrisy.... We're just as racist in the North as they are in the South." In Richmond, Virginia, the leader of the local antibusing movement drew the obvious conclusion: "If the Supreme Court distinguishes between de jure and de facto segregation, we would like to be placed in the latter category and treated like... the major cities in the North and Midwest."[23]

As the NAACP reopened litigation against neighborhood-schools formulas in urban districts across the nation, the political backlash against court-ordered busing spread from the grassroots to Washington. In the spring of 1970, the Nixon administration released a major policy statement on school desegregation that reinterpreted the de jure/de facto dichotomy by announcing a national standard that treated all regions the same while drawing an explicit line between educational policy and housing markets. "There is a fundamental distinction between so-called '*de jure*' and '*de facto*' segregation: *de jure* segregation arises by law or by the deliberate act of school officials and is unconstitutional; *de facto* segregation results from residential housing patterns and does not violate the Constitution." The White House then extended the latter category to the residentially segregated landscapes of the metropolitan South: "*De facto* racial separation, resulting genuinely from housing patterns, exists in the South as well as the North; in neither area should this condition by itself be cause for Federal enforcement actions." Although Nixon promised that his administration would pursue desegregation remedies in cases of deliberate racial gerrymandering, he also insisted that federal courts could not order "compulsory busing of pupils beyond normal geographic school zones for the purpose of achieving racial balance.... In the case of genuine *de facto* segregation,... school authorities are not constitutionally required to take any positive steps to correct the imbalance." The rejoinder by the U.S. Civil Rights Commission emphasized that "government at all levels invariably is implicated" in patterns of housing segregation, and so there was "little legal substance to the concept of de facto school segregation," which had become an artificial political device masquerading as a legitimate constitutional standard. As if to prove the point, President Nixon personally instructed federal enforcement officials: "When in doubt, call segregation *de facto*, not *de jure*."[24]

In 1971, a unanimous Supreme Court affirmed the *Swann* decree in an ambiguous decision that approved cross-town busing as a remedy for de jure school segregation and jeopardized the de facto defense across the nation without clarifying the housing/education nexus. The justices declined to settle the question of "whether a showing that school segregation is a consequence of other types of state action, without any discriminatory action by the school authorities, is a constitutional violation requiring remedial action." *Time* argued that an exemption for neighborhood schools resulting from housing segregation would mean "the nation was following a racial double standard: nonaction in the North, stern demands for integration in the South." The Civil Rights Commission posed the unresolved question: "What if school segregation results not from administrative decisions of school officials, but from residential segregation for which other State or local government bodies, such as local public housing authorities, urban renewal agencies, zoning boards, and city councils, are responsible?" The commission explained that in the North and West, "it is doubtful that there are many cases in which school segregation actually has resulted solely from accidental factors in which government is not involved.... In such cases, despite the absence of laws expressly requiring or sanctioning it,... school segregation is not *de facto*, but *de jure*." The Supreme Court did abandon the jurisprudence of southern exceptionalism in *Keyes v. Denver* (1973), which found de jure segregation ("intent to segregate") in a large urban district with no statutory history of Jim Crow, but the rationale revolved around racial gerrymandering and other deliberate actions by school officials rather than scrutiny of state-sponsored residential segregation.[25]

Two pivotal cases brought by the NAACP in the early 1970s, one in Michigan and the other in Virginia, produced the most expansive state-action interpretations in the history of school desegregation case law. In *Bradley v. Milliken* (1971), District Judge Stephen Roth labeled Detroit a "de jure segregated public school system" and ordered a metropolitan busing plan through the consolidation of city and suburban districts. The ruling found that "governmental actions and inaction at all levels, federal, state, and local, have combined with those of private organizations...to establish and to maintain the pattern of residential segregation throughout the Detroit metropolitan area." At the same time, Roth dissented from the entire state action exercise with the view that "if racial segregation in our public schools is an evil, then it should make no difference whether we classify it de jure or de facto." In *Bradley v. Richmond* (1972), the NAACP secured another city-suburban busing decree after Judge Robert Merhige found that the "present pattern of residential housing...is a reflection of past racial discrimination contributed in part by local, state and federal government....Negroes in Richmond live where they do because they have no choice." Each lower court decision placed the blame for residential and school segregation on a broad constellation of public and private forces, from the Federal Housing Administration and the real estate industry to municipal agencies inside the cities and exclusionary zoning in the suburbs. Taken together, the two cases represented the culmination of the NAACP's decades-long campaign to puncture the de facto mystique of white innocence by holding both the state and the suburbs responsible for housing and school segregation in the modern metropolis.[26]

But the breakthrough did not last, because the appellate courts soon acted to restore the de facto mythology and reinstate the powerful national narrative that free-market forces alone produced housing segregation. In the summer of 1972, the Fourth Circuit Court of Appeals reversed the Richmond consolidation order, holding that "the last vestiges of state-imposed segregation have been wiped out" and concluding with a remarkable assertion that the "root causes of the concentration of blacks in the inner cities of America are simply not known." In this highly politicized legal climate, the U.S. Supreme Court solidified the de jure/de facto demarcation between educational policies and residential markets by exempting most American suburbs from urban desegregation remedies. In *Milliken v. Bradley* (1974), a narrow majority on the Supreme Court reversed the Detroit consolidation decree but upheld busing within the city limits, a crushing defeat for the NAACP's metropolitan integration strategy. The legal rationale in *Milliken* emphasized the absence of proof that suburban policies had caused urban segregation, but the majority opinion evaded rather than refuted the trial court's substantial evidentiary record that a long history of government programs had shaped residential segregation and therefore neighborhood school segregation throughout metropolitan Detroit. *Milliken* collapsed the regional divide that had pervaded desegregation case law for two decades since *Brown*, but only by erecting a new and equally artificial dichotomy between unconstitutional (de jure) school segregation inside the city and constitutional (de facto) housing segregation in the suburbs.[27]

In political culture and in constitutional law, the reinvigoration of de facto segregation as a description of the metropolitan housing market accompanied a sweeping reclassification of residential segregation as the product of economic rather than racial discrimination. Civil rights litigants secured an important de jure victory in the 1969 *Gautreaux* case, which found the Chicago Housing Authority guilty of a "governmentally established policy of racial segregation" in public housing projects and provided vouchers for seven thousand black families to move into suburban neighborhoods. Responding that "forced integration of the suburbs is not in the national interest," Richard Nixon released a major 1971 statement on "equal housing opportunity" that distinguished between illegal racial discrimination in violation of the Fair Housing Act and legitimate efforts to maintain economic segregation by banning low-income projects and defending property values through exclusionary zoning. The president promised that the federal government would prosecute individual acts of racial discrimination but would "not seek to impose economic integration...[or] federally assisted housing upon any community." Civil rights organizations attacked these "artificial distinctions between racial and economic discrimination" as the latest incarnation of the de jure/de facto fiction, a transparent scheme to recast structural racism in the suburban housing market as a benign form of segregation based solely on class. In a series of cases during the 1970s, the Supreme Court upheld the Nixon administration's position that exclusionary zoning in the suburbs rested on constitutionally permissible economic segregation rather than illegal racial discrimination. In historical context, Nixon's arguments against "forced busing" and "forced housing" revolved around a repudiation of the civil rights agenda of affirmative action that owed as much to the de facto legacies of race-blind liberalism as they did to the 'backlash' of color-blind conservatism.[28]

The mythology of de facto segregation began as a regional binary, separating the South from the nation and statutory discrimination from the free market, and eventually evolved into a deeply politicized method of drawing legal distinctions between schools and housing, cities and suburbs, racism and economics. The consistent thread in this convoluted saga has been the effort to preserve white racial innocence and white spatial privi-lege by shielding a liberal national narrative, an ideology of American exceptionalism that can survive only through the constant renewal of southern exceptionalism, an American Creed of equal opportunity that requires an oppositional region to remain intact, an American national identity that is still discovering itself down in the Jim Crow South. "Sud-denly," claimed *Time* magazine during the antibusing backlash of the early 1970s, "the nation has faltered in its determination to grapple with the toughest moral and political dilemma of the postwar era: how to ensure justice for its blacks." By "heading north" (once again), the civil rights movement's demand for comprehensive integration on a national scale had disrupted (once again) the storyline of the American Creed. "It was not hard to distinguish hero from villain when President Eisen-hower dispatched Screaming Eagle paratroopers to keep Arkansas Gov-ernor Orval Faubus' National Guardsmen from blocking the admittance of nine black children to Little Rock's Central High School in 1957." A quarter century after *Time*'s nostalgic lament for the moral clarity of the southern civil rights era, Kenneth Clark reflected on his own role in pio-neering the "de facto" critique of northern school segregation in the mid-1950s. "I thought the problem of segregation essentially was a southern problem," Clark explained. "At that time, the North rationalized its rac-ism by contending that racially segregated schools were a manifestation of a larger pattern of our racial culture. . . . I did not understand, however, that the maintenance of segregated housing not only excused persistent patterns of school segregation, but that segregated housing itself repre-sented a form of deeply imbedded racism that resisted all attempts at desegregation."[29]

NOTES

1. Martin Luther King, Jr., "Walk to Freedom," June 23, 1963, *MLK: The Martin Luther King Tapes* (Jerden Records, 1995); Stephen Grant Meyer, *As Long as They Don't Move Next Door: Segregation and Racial Conflict in American Neighborhoods* (Lanham, Md.: Rowman & Littlefield, 2000), 173–78.

2. *Brown v. Board of Education*, 347 U.S. 483 (1954), at 495.

3. For the political context of the de facto segregation defense, what I have elsewhere labeled the suburban politics of "color-blind" individualism, see Matthew D. Lassiter, *The Silent Majority: Suburban Politics in the Sunbelt South* (Princeton: Princeton University Press, 2006).

4. Scholars who have directly challenged the concept of de facto segregation include Arnold R. Hirsch, "'Containment' on the Home Front: Race and Federal Housing Policy from the New Deal to the Cold War," *Journal of Urban History* (Jan. 2000), 158–89; Hirsch, "With or without Jim Crow: Black Residential Segregation

in the United States," in *Urban Policy in Twentieth-Century America*, ed. Hirsch and Raymond A. Mohl (New Brunswick, N.J.: Rutgers University Press, 1993), 65–99; Martha Biondi, *To Stand and Fight: The Struggle for Civil Rights in Postwar New York City* (Cambridge: Harvard University Press, 2003), 285; Jeanne Theoharis, "Introduction," in *Freedom North: Black Freedom Struggles Outside the South, 1940–1980*, ed. Theoharis and Komozi Woodard (New York: Palgrave Macmillan, 2003), 8; Thomas J. Sugrue, *Sweet Land of Liberty: The Forgotten Civil Rights Movement in the North* (New York: Random House, 2008).

   5. *Buchanan v. Warley*, 245 U.S. 60 (1917); *Corrigan v. Buckley*, 271 U.S. 323 (1926); *Dorsey v. Stuyvesant Town Corp.*, 299 N.Y. 512 (1949), 339 U.S. 981 (1950); Michael J. Klarman, *From Jim Crow to Civil Rights: The Supreme Court and the Struggle for Racial Equality* (New York: Oxford University Press, 2004), 79–85, 90–93, 142–46; Clement E. Vose, *Caucasians Only: The Supreme Court, the NAACP, and the Restrictive Covenant Cases* (Berkeley: University of California Press, 1959); Robert M. Fogelson, *Bourgeois Nightmares: Suburbia, 1870–1930* (New Haven: Yale University Press, 2005); Kenneth T. Jackson, *Crabgrass Frontier: The Suburbanization of the United States* (New York: Oxford University Press, 1985), 203–18.

   6. *Shelley v. Kraemer*, 334 U.S. 1 (1948); Lassiter, *Silent Majority*; Klarman, *From Jim Crow*, 212–17, 261–64; David M. P. Freund, *Colored Property: State Policy and White Racial Politics in Suburban America* (Chicago: University of Chicago Press, 2007). Mitchell quoted in Davison M. Douglas, *Jim Crow Moves North: The Battle over Northern School Segregation, 1865–1954* (Cambridge: Cambridge University Press, 2005), 268.

   7. Gunnar Myrdal, *An American Dilemma: The Negro Problem and Modern Democracy* (New York: Harper and Bros., 1944); *To Secure these Rights: The Report of the President's Committee on Civil Rights* (Washington: GPO, 1947), xi, 65–67, 79, 166; *New York Times* [hereinafter *NYT*], April 25, 1956; "Liberalism and the Negro: A Round-Table Discussion," *Commentary* (March 1964), 28–29. For an early critique of public and private housing discrimination, see Charles Abrams, *Forbidden Neighbors: A Study of Prejudice in Housing* (Port Washington, N.Y.: Kennikat Press, 1955).

   8. Loren Miller to Thurgood Marshall, Oct. 3, 1952, Folder 2, Box 38, Miller Speech, "For Free Men: Freedom," Oct. 7, 1962, Folder 2, Miller Speech, "How Firm a Foundation: Governmental Responsibility for Residential Segregation," n.d. [early 1960s], Miller, "Speech to the Housing Conference of the National Committee against Discrimination in Housing," March 14, 1955, Folder 8, Box 44, National Committee against Discrimination in Housing, "Housing and Civil Rights," July 1960, Folder 15, Frances Levenson, Testimony to Housing Subcommittee, March 28, 1956, Folder 19, Norman P. Mason [FHA Commissioner], Speech to National Committee against Discrimination in Housing, May 21, 1954, Folder 16, Box 26, Loren Miller Papers, The Huntington Library; Meyer, *As Long as They Don't Move Next Door*, 141; *Johnson v. Levitt and Sons, Inc.*, 131 F. Supp. 114 (E.D. Pa. 1955).

9. Davison M. Douglas, "The Limits of Law in Accomplishing Racial Change: School Segregation in the Pre-*Brown* North," *UCLA Law Review* 44 (Feb. 1997), 681; Douglas, *Jim Crow Moves North*, 237–73; *Mendez v. Westminster*, 54 F. Supp 544 (1946); *Westminster v. Mendez*, 161 F.2d 774 (1947); Klarman, *From Jim Crow*, 304; *NYT*, April 25, 1956, Aug. 26, 1957.

10. Kenneth B. Clark, *Dark Ghetto: Dilemmas of Social Power* (New York: Harper & Row, 1965), 118; Nathan Glazer, "Is 'Integration' Possible in the New York Schools?" *Commentary* (Sept. 1960), reprinted in *Integration vs. Segregation*, ed. Hubert H. Humphrey (New York: Thomas Y. Crowell Co., 1964), 186; *NYT*, April 25, July 14, 1954; June Shagaloff, "NAACP Public School Desegregation Front in the North and West," June 1962, Frames 0032-53, Reel 23, Part 22, Papers of the NAACP.

11. *NYT*, Dec. 24, 1954, Nov. 10, 1955, July 24, 1956, Feb. 10, March 4, Oct. 31, 1957; Biondi, *To Stand and Fight*, 241–47. The phrase "segregation-in-fact" appeared in some judicial forums at least as early as 1954. See Jack Greenberg, *Race Relations and American Law* (New York: Columbia University Press, 1959), 252.

12. *Report of the United States Commission on Civil Rights, 1959* (Washington: GPO, 1959), 258; American Jewish Congress, "From Color Blind to Color Conscious: A Study of Public School Integration in New York City" (1959), Folder 6, Box 86, American Civil Liberties Union of Southern California Records, Department of Special Collections, Charles E. Young Research Library, University of California, Los Angeles [hereinafter ACLU-UCLA]; *Civil Rights '63: 1963 Report of the United States Commission on Civil Rights* (Washington: GPO, 1963), 65–72; Robert Carter, "De Facto School Segregation," n.d. [early 1960s], Frames 0560-62, Reel 23, Part 22, Papers of the NAACP.

13. *Taylor v. New Rochelle*, 191 F. Supp. 181 (1961), at 187, 194; *Taylor v. New Rochelle*, 195 F. Supp. 231 (1961); Shagaloff, "NAACP Public School Desegregation Front"; Will Maslow and Richard Cohen, "School Segregation, Northern Style" (Public Affairs Committee, 1961), Folder 15, Box 86, ACLU-UCLA; *Education: 1961 Commission on Civil Rights Report* (Washington: GPO, 1961), 100, 103.

14. June Shagaloff, "Public School Desegregation in the North and West," Feb. 21, 1963, Frames 0029-62, Reel 24, Shagaloff to Robert Carter, April 8, 1964, Frames 0172-73, Reel 23, Part 22, Papers of the NAACP; *Education: 1961 Commission on Civil Rights Report*, 99–115; *Jackson v. Pasadena City School District*, 59 Cal. 2d 876 (1963); *Blocker v. Board of Education of Manhasset*, 226 F. Supp. 208 (1964).

15. Shagaloff, "Public School Desegregation"; "Report of the Ad Hoc Committee on Equal Educational Opportunity," Sept. 12, 1963, Frames 0063-85, Reel 124, Part 22, Papers of the NAACP; "The Facts of De Facto," *Time* (Aug. 2, 1963), 30–31; "Public Schools: The Spreading Boycott," *Time* (Feb. 14, 1964), 40; *NYT*, Sept. 4, 1963, Feb. 4, 1964; State Education Commissioner's Advisory Committee on Human Relations and Community Tensions, "Desegregating the Public Schools of New York City" [Allen Report], May 12, 1964, quoted in Clark, *Dark Ghetto*, 119. Recent scholarship that explores these events includes Theoharis and Woodard, *Freedom North*; Sugrue, *Sweet Land of Liberty*.

16. *Bell v. School City of Gary, Indiana*, 213 F. Supp. 819 (1963), at 822, 827–28, 324 F.2d 209 (1963), 377 U.S. 924 (1964); *Webb v. Board of Education of City of Chicago*, 223 F. Supp. 466 (1963), at 468.

17. *NYT*, Sept. 15, 1964; Murray Kempton, "New York School Boycott," *New Republic* (Sept. 26, 1964), 6–7; "Says a White Mother, 'We Have Rights, Too,'" *U.S. News and World Report* (Oct. 26, 1964), 71–79; Fred Powledge, " 'Mason-Dixon Line' in Queens," *NYT Magazine* (May 10, 1964).

18. Civil Rights Act of 1964, http://usinfo.state.gov/usa/infousa/laws/majorlaw/civilr19.htm; Robert L. Carter, "De Facto School Segregation: An Examination of the Legal and Constitutional Questions Presented," in *De Facto Segregation and Civil Rights: Struggle for Legal and Social Equality*, ed. Oliver Schroeder, Jr., and David T. Smith (Buffalo: William S. Hein, 1965), 29; "Another First for Massachusetts," *Time* (Aug. 27, 1965), 56; "Segregation Means Unequal," *Time* (July 22, 1966), 54; *Washington Post*, Sept. 15, 1967; Joseph Crespino, "The Best Defense Is a Good Offense: The Stennis Amendment and the Fracturing of Liberal School Desegregation Policy, 1964-1972," *Journal of Policy History* No. 3 (2006), 306–10; Gary Orfield, *Must We Bus? Segregated Schools and National Policy* (Washington: Brookings, 1978), 279–318.

19. "Los Angeles: Why?" *Newsweek* (Aug. 30, 1965); "Battle of Roosevelt Road," *Time* (July 22, 1966), 18–19; "West Side Story." *Newsweek* (July 25, 1966), 17–18; "Crossing the Red Sea," *Time* (Sept. 2, 1966), 19; "Voter Backlash over Race Issue?" *U.S. News and World Report* (Sept. 19, 1966), 34–36; *NYT*, Aug. 11, 1966; Meyer, *As Long as They Don't Move Next Door*, 83–211.

20. CBS Reports, *Segregation, Northern-Style* (Princeton, N.J.: Films for the Humanities and Sciences, 2003); U.S. Commission on Civil Rights, *A Time to Listen…A Time to Act* (Washington: GPO, Nov. 1967), 60, 90; *Report of the National Advisory Commission on Civil Disorders* (New York: New York Times Co., 1968), 2; Charles M. Lamb, *Housing Segregation in Suburban America since 1960: Presidential and Judicial Politics* (Cambridge: Cambridge University Press, 2005), 26–50.

21. Carter, "De Facto School Segregation," 28; *Swann v. Charlotte-Mecklenburg*, 369 F.2d 29 (1966); *Green v. New Kent County*, 391 U.S. 430 (1968), at 437–38; Lassiter, *Silent Majority*, 23–174.

22. *Swann v. Charlotte-Mecklenburg*, 300 F. Supp. 1358 (1969), 306 F. Supp. 1299 (1969); Unified Concerned Citizens of America, "General Statement," Aug. 1970, sect. 2, James L. Doherty Papers, Virginia Historical Society, Richmond, Va.

23. "What about the North?" *Time* (Jan. 19, 1970), 16; "Turn-Around on Integration," *Time* (March 9, 1970), 9–16; *Jackson Clarion-Ledger*, Oct. 18, 1969; *NYT*, Feb. 5–6, 10–13, 19–20, March 1, 1970; Crespino, "Best Defense," 312–20; James L. Doherty to Virginia Crockford, Sept. 21, 1970, Box 1, Virginia Crockford Papers, M283, Special Collections and Archives, James Branch Cabell Library, Virginia Commonwealth University.

24. Richard Nixon, "Desegregation of America's Elementary and Secondary Schools," March 24, 1970, *Weekly Compilation of Presidential Documents*, 424–40;

NYT, April 12, 1970; John Ehrlichman, *Witness to Power: The Nixon Years* (New York: Simon & Schuster, 1982), 233.

25. *Swann v. Charlotte-Mecklenburg*, 402 U.S. 1 (1971); "A Supreme Court Yes to Busing," *Time* (May 3, 1971), 13–14; U.S. Civil Rights Commission, *Understanding School Desegregation* (Washington: GPO, 1971); *Keyes v. Denver*, 413 U.S. 189 (1973).

26. *Bradley v. Milliken*, 338 F. Supp. 582 (1971), 345 F. Supp. 914 (1972); *Bradley v. Richmond*, 338 F. Supp 67 (1972).

27. *Bradley v. Richmond*, 462 F.2d 1058 (1972); *Milliken v. Bradley*, 418 U.S. 717 (1974).

28. *Gautreaux v. Chicago Housing Authority*, 296 F. Supp. 907 (1969); Leonard S. Rubinowitz and James E. Rosenbaum, *Crossing the Class and Color Lines: From Public Housing to White Suburbia* (Chicago: University of Chicago Press, 2000); Richard Nixon, "Federal Policies Relative to Equal Housing Opportunity," June 11, 1971, *Weekly Compilation of Presidential Documents*, 892–905; *NYT*, Dec. 11, 1970, July 14, 1971; *James v. Valtierra*, 422 U.S. 490 (1971); *Warth v. Seldin*, 422 U.S. 490 (1975).

29. "Turn-Around on Integration," *Time* (March 9, 1970), 9–16; Kenneth B. Clark, "Forum: In Pursuit of a Dream Deferred: Linking Housing and Education," *Minnesota Law Review* (April 1996): 745–48.

2

HIDDEN IN PLAIN SIGHT

The Civil Rights Movement outside the South

Jeanne Theoharis

In the spring of 1963 in Birmingham, Alabama, after months of nonviolent demonstrations met with fire hoses, police dogs, and hundreds of arrests, civil rights activists reached an agreement with business and city leaders to desegregate the downtown facilities. Then, on the evening of May 11, 1963, a group of white segregationists angered by the agreement threw a bomb into the house of Rev. A. D. King and another bomb into the Gaston Motel, where Rev. Martin Luther King Jr. and other members of the Southern Christian Leadership Conference had been staying during the Birmingham campaign. Upon hearing of the attacks, more than two thousand African Americans gathered outside the damaged motel, throwing rocks and bricks, looting commodities, and setting a nearby grocery store on fire. Police began to assault the angry crowd, beating people fiercely. By the end of the night, seventy people had been hospitalized and a number of businesses had been looted and burned down.[1]

Three thousand miles away, from 1962 to 1964, black Angelenos also took to the streets to protest racial inequality. They held regular demonstrations demanding desegregation and equity in Los Angeles's public schools, protested the police murder of the unarmed Nation of Islam secretary Ronald Stokes, and fought to oppose racially exclusive housing developments and the segregationist state ballot initiative Proposition 14 (which sought to repeal the hard-won 1963 Fair Housing Act). They were met with city intransigence around school inequality, no reform of police practices or charges brought against the officers who killed Stokes, and the decisive victory of Proposition 14 in November 1964. Then, on August 11,

1965, a California Highway Patrolman pulled over 21-year-old Marquette Frye for drunk driving. As a crowd gathered on the scene, another police officer began hitting Frye and his mother. Some of the African-American onlookers started throwing stones and bottles, and the unrest escalated to the looting and burning of buildings. In response, the police cracked down on rioters and the black community at large. The city instituted a curfew restricted to the black neighborhoods of South Los Angeles. At the end of seven days of violence, thirty-four people had died and hundreds more were injured, many at the hands of the local police or the California National Guard. Four thousand black residents had been arrested, and $45 million in property had been damaged.

In most history textbooks and in the public imagination, the Watts riot of 1965 commands a prominent spot, often the first black political action chronicled outside of the South. Watts often serves as the introduction to the northern racial landscape, the dividing line between the heroic southern freedom struggle and the civil rights movement's militant and northward turn. Conversely, the Birmingham riot two years earlier barely merits a mention in the epic narrative of the southern struggle, even though the outbreak of black militancy in Alabama helped spur President Kennedy to endorse the Birmingham agreement a day later and the Civil Rights Act the next month. The parallels between the racial politics of Birmingham and Los Angeles—longstanding grassroots civil rights movements; police brutality and cooperation with white vigilantism; racial inequality in jobs, schools, and housing; and growing black frustration with the lack of progress—have been lost to a strict binary between a nonviolent black movement in the South and the rise of black frustration and violence in the North. The presence of a vibrant nonviolent civil rights movement in Los Angeles in the decades before 1965, like the black uprising in Birmingham in 1963, has become hidden in plain sight—chronicled on the front pages of newspapers at the time but largely absent in the historical memory of the era.

The prominence of the Watts story, and the absence of the pre-1965 northern civil rights movement in the historical imagination, has helped further a clear opposition between what happened in "the South" and what transpired in the rest of the country called "the North." Placing Watts, a neighborhood in Southern California, in "the North" turns on a long-imagined dichotomy between legalized Jim Crow segregation in the South and the allegedly non-state-sponsored segregation that existed outside of the South. This form of southern exceptionalism distinguishes the "southern race problem" from the "racial tensions" plaguing northern ghettoes, drawing a bright line between a righteous nonviolent movement that flowered in the South and the various forms of black anger and Black Power politics that arose *not in the South*. Indeed, the Watts riot from the outset was linked to ghetto frustration in Harlem, Detroit,

Newark—"the North"—and was not understood either as a western or as a national phenomenon. Distinctive regional histories (among and within the Northeast, Midwest, Sunbelt, and Northwest, not to mention within the South itself) and varying processes of racial stratification have receded into a potent binary between a racial system found in the South and a supposedly nonracial system found everywhere else.

The North has consequently derived its meaning not as a regional designation but as a vague though powerful evocation of the supposed racial liberalism of northern whites (descending from the role of the North in the Civil War) and the opportunities that southern black migration to northern and western cities were supposed to have opened. Racism is thus understood as a relic of a backward premodern system entrenched in the South—and the aspects of this system that made their way to the North are seen as flaws in an otherwise liberal land of opportunity, rather than as a constitutive element of the northern political economy. Thus, the phrase "the North" is deployed throughout this essay in its ideological and symbolic sense to refer to all the many places in the nation imagined *not to be* the Jim Crow South.

Dominant explanations of the civil rights movement, then, have turned on the evils of southern whites and the goodness of southern blacks, and on the liberalism of northern whites and the alienation of northern blacks. Through this lens, the northern struggle is seen as born out of fire and anger from an alienated community with little political organization. Many historians treat white northern opposition to homegrown civil rights movements differently from scholars who study southern resistance. While "southern segregationists" seek to prevent school desegregation, similar movements in the North are often described as "white backlash" or "antibusing movements" and rarely are termed "segregationist."[2] Anti-civil rights organizing in the North is often cast as a reaction to the riots and the black militancy that developed afterward, rather than revealed for what it was—a "frontlash"—as white residents sought to block African-American educational, job, and housing opportunities. When southerners talk about the uncouth behavior and separate culture of blacks, is it recognized as an aspect of their racism, but when sociologists or other northern liberals use similar explanations of "cultural deprivation" to describe black educational underachievement, it is treated as a legitimate explanation of "black cultural responses" to structural conditions. Historians have treated as calculated and contrived the southern "surprise" when the sit-ins erupted in 1960, but not used a similar perspective when describing northern "surprise" over the Watts riot. The attempts to "understand" northern white residents' overt opposition to desegregation—as Ronald Formisano writes, "thousands of decent, moderate whites across the city [of Boston] cannot be said to have been racists"[3]—reflect the problematic assumption that racism did not pervade the northern consciousness as it did the southern.

The idea of state-sponsored racism as a problem of the South—and thus the civil rights movement as a southern movement—takes its cue from the political and media discourses of the time. By the time of the 1963 Birmingham protests, the national media (based outside of the South) had grown increasingly sympathetic to the nonviolent southern struggle. Conversely, while northern protests often made front-page news in the *New York Times, Los Angeles Times,* and *Boston Globe* (among others), they were not framed as part of the same struggle as the southern movement. At the beginning of the 1974 school year, the *Globe* editorialized that Judge W. Arthur Garrity's decision ordering the desegregation of the Boston Public Schools came from "out of the blue," erasing the local movement for desegregation and equity that had been covered in its pages for two decades. Similarly, despite numerous local civil rights protests against segregated schools and housing in the early 1960s that made its front pages, in 1967 the *LA Times* claimed that it was "the summer of 1965,...when the white community abruptly discovered what Negroes already knew—that Negro area schools were less than equal."[4] The treatment of the race problem as necessarily southern (rather than a constitutive national flaw) was also a strategic Cold War formulation that framed racism as a southern anachronism, held up the southern movement as proof of the perfectibility of American democracy, and treated northern movements as dangerous and deviant.[5]

Recent scholarship has demonstrated how misguided this view of American racial politics is.[6] American apartheid was not just left over from slavery and the demise of Reconstruction in the South; it also has modern and liberal roots in the changes that took place in American citizenship, wrought in part by the New Deal and the GI Bill. This social citizenship—union rights, access to home loans and higher education, Social Security, unemployment insurance, and welfare—widened the American middle class but was deeply exclusionary in its provisions. Its ostensible universality, however, obscured its biases and ensured that those left behind would be blamed for their second-class status. As community activists sought to challenge these exclusions in the postwar period, Los Angeles, like Birmingham (and most American cities), became home to a vibrant array of movements for racial justice. And the preponderance of white Angelenos (like their compatriots in Birmingham and across the country) resisted these movements and fought for their right to live in white communities, attend white schools, and reserve the best jobs for white people—sometimes alongside their support of the southern civil rights struggle.

An examination of black activism for school desegregation and educational equity in Boston and Los Angeles from 1954 to 1965 complicates popular notions of the heroic period of the civil rights movement. Boston, like Watts, played a starring role in the national imagination of northern racial conflict when violent white protests erupted against court-ordered school desegregation in 1974. And as in Los Angeles, the organized black activism that preceded the events of 1974 and 1975 that captured the national spotlight have largely disappeared from Boston's civil rights history, in favor of a story of a naïve liberal judge from suburban Wellesley, who foisted busing on white working-class ethnics. Despite a three-decade struggle in the city for racial desegregation and educational equality, African Americans became bit players in the dramatic story of "Boston's busing crisis."

The idea of the South and of the movements unfolding there—and its presumed *difference from* the North—served as a constant reference point that bedeviled these northern civil rights activists. This notion of the South also made Boston and Los Angeles, with their significantly different histories (the Revolutionary War versus westward expansion, a hotbed of abolitionist activity and a multiracial city with a Mexican past), curiously similar in postwar race relations. Boston and Los Angeles became "the North" in their construction of racial innocence—in their public investment in *not* being the South. In both Boston and Los Angeles, city and school board officials refuted black demands with the charge that "this is not Birmingham." White leaders and political institutions in both cities attempted to preserve racial segregation while simultaneously denying its existence, casting urban black and Latino communities as lacking the cultural values, work ethic, and behavior necessary for success, and suggesting these factors explained existing inequities in jobs, schools, housing, and policing.

These local civil rights movements were continually forced to prove that racial segregation and resource inequity in the public schools of these liberal cities were real, harmful, and products of official policy. In both cities, local school officials used attendance boundaries, feeder patterns, transportation policies, teacher hiring practices, and other methods to ensure that the vast majority of black and Latino students attended segregated, under-resourced schools. (Notably, federal courts would ultimately rule on the "intentional" segregation found in both Boston and Los Angeles.) Despite years of organized protests in both places, public officials and journalists repeatedly forgot black grievances, constantly offered to "study the issue," and persistently claimed that systematic segregation did not exist in these racially progressive cities. While their white southern counterparts in the 1950s and early 1960s were largely willing to defend segregation and states' rights, a different lexicon of race emerged in the North—one that celebrated "color-blindness" and was "surprised" by black anger; that cast African-American and Latino youth as "problem students" whose "cultural deprivations" (along with those of their parents) hampered their educational success; and that framed white resistance to racial integration in a language of "neighborhood control," "taxpayer's rights," and "forced busing." With public support of racial segregation viewed as the distasteful purview of southern racists, this culturalist discourse provided a socially acceptable rhetoric to harness many northern whites' virulent opposition to desegregation.

Deriving partly from the mid-century sociological theories of E. Frank-lin Frazier and Gunnar Myrdal (and gaining further prominence with the 1965 Moynihan Report), this formulation cast "northern blacks" as undone by the structural landscape of northern cities, untethered from the values of religion, family, and community that anchored southern black communities. The adjective "North," when used to describe blacks (as in "northern blacks"), thus came to signify this kind of community dissolution and dysfunction. Arguing that the structures of American racism and urban political economy produced black cultural responses that led to black educational (and job) underattainment, white liberals in both cities, with support from some black middle-class leaders, sponsored programs to address juvenile delinquency and provide cultural remedia-tion to facilitate black educational progress. Many northern liberals could thereby claim attention to race, while maintaining that the structures of schooling, housing, and jobs in these cities were open and that success was determined by a combination of community norms, parenting, and student work ethic.[7]

Attempting to counter this discourse of cultural pathology, black civil rights activists in Boston and Los Angeles regularly pointed to the similari-ties between their protests and those of the southern movement. Scholars have tended to interpret northern black attention to the southern strug-gle as proof that northern blacks saw the southern movement as more urgent—and consequently they miss the strategic aspect of this interest. As they reified the righteousness of the southern struggle, activists in both cities did so not only because they were inspired by the bold actions of southern black activists but also because they were trying to elevate their own campaigns and challenge the cultural framework that rendered the problems of their communities so very different from southern ones. Indeed, the hidden nature of the northern black freedom struggle was, in part, a strategic response by northern white officials and residents to deny black grievances. The idea of "the South," then, was a constant hurdle for movement activists who often sought to highlight the national race problem. For community leaders in Boston and Los Angeles, the nation's focus on the South—where the "real struggle" was going on—was a foil that eclipsed their own movements and simultaneously served as a site through which they anchored the morality of their own struggle.

BOSTON: FIGHTING SEGREGATION IN THE HOME OF ABOLITIONISTS

In 1950, Ruth Batson realized that her daughter, who attended a black school in Boston, did not have a science class like her white friend's son did in his school. Having seen an advertisement for the NAACP in which local blacks were told to bring their complaints to the organization, Batson called the Roxbury office. The next day, the NAACP called back to ask her to chair a new subcommittee on schools. In assuming this position, Batson recalled, "my life changed profoundly." She faced a mixed response to her role as a civil rights activist. "Some black citizens scolded me for raising the issue of segregation and discrimination in Boston, the seat of culture and the home of abolitionists....Some white citizens—usually officials and press representatives—argued my declarations to be without foundation."[8] Furthermore, like their southern counterparts, white officials and residents accused Batson and other Bostonians who were pushing for racial desegregation of being communists.

From its formation in 1950, the NAACP's public school subcommittee, composed of parents and other community activists, focused on educational equity and the fair allocation of resources within the Boston Public Schools (BPS). From the outset, the NAACP faced opposition from both blacks and whites over whether segregation even existed in this northern city. As Batson explained, "We were 'raising a false issue.'"[9] Yet, the subcommittee saw firsthand that keeping black students in separate facilities was a way for the Boston School Committee (the elected body that ran the BPS) to provide them with an inferior education. Their studies revealed that six of the city's nine black elementary schools were overcrowded. Four of the district's thirteen black schools had been recommended for closure for health and safety reasons, while eight were in need of repairs to meet present city standards.[10] Per pupil spending averaged $340 for white students but only $240 for black students. Teachers at predominantly black schools were less permanent and often less experienced than those assigned to white schools. The curriculum at many black schools was outdated and often blatantly racist, and the school district overwhelmingly tracked black students into manual arts and trade classes rather than college preparatory ones. According to Batson, the subcommittee found a "general consensus" among principals who claimed that black students did not do as well as white students because "the parents did not seem to care." School officials thus did not defend segregation in itself, but blamed the problems with black schools on black children's motivation and their parents' values.[11]

The school district also segregated individual facilities through pupil assignment policies that fed black students into high school in ninth grade but whites in tenth—and often into different junior high schools before that. As parent activist Ellen Jackson explained, "you could live on the same street and have a white neighbor, as I did, and you went to one junior high school and she went to another junior high school....It was not de facto at all."[12] In addition to the racial gerrymandering of attendance zones (many schools were located at the edges of districts with

irregular shapes), the Boston School Committee reserved the overwhelming majority of jobs for white employees through racially discriminatory
hiring and promotion practices. Many schools had no black members on
the faculty (blacks made up only 0.5 percent of the city's teachers), and
there were no black principals in the system.[13]

The NAACP public school subcommittee was heartened in 1954, when
the Supreme Court issued its landmark decision in *Brown v. Board of Education*, believing that the ruling would mean significant change in BPS.
But in the years following *Brown*, partly because the national NAACP was
focusing its efforts on the South, the subcommittee found it "difficult to
keep the momentum going on the education issues [in Boston]"[14] and
to overcome the sense that school segregation was "a southern problem." According to Batson, "northern states were very smug."[15] In the
early 1960s, the NAACP tried to persuade the Massachusetts Commission Against Discrimination (MCAD) to recognize the existence of racial
segregation in Boston's schools. But MCAD refused, claiming that racial
segregation was not a problem in the city. While the existence of public
commissions such as MCAD seems to attest to a different racial climate
in Massachusetts, its unwillingness to investigate institutions such as the
Boston Public Schools—and indeed its willingness to proclaim them as *not
segregated*—protected the district's discriminatory practices.

The NAACP responded by taking its case en masse to the School Committee in June 1963, part of the larger wave of school segregation protests
across the country at the same time that the nation's attention focused
on the dramatic civil rights protests in Birmingham. Supporters packed
the Boston hearing. More than eight hundred more were turned away
and instead congregated outside the building, singing freedom songs.[16]
Saying it was "too late for pleading," Ruth Batson laid out the NAACP's
fourteen-point program, decrying the existence of "de facto segregation,"
curriculum bias, tracking and hiring discrimination in BPS.[17] In response,
according to Batson: "We were insulted. We were told our kids were stupid
and this was why they didn't learn."[18]

To continue the pressure on the School Committee, black community
leaders turned to direct action. A week after the hearing, they organized
a school boycott. Nearly half of the city's black high school students participated and attended Freedom Schools.[19] The School Committee then
agreed to a second hearing with the NAACP, but shut the meeting down
when civil rights leaders used the phrase "de facto segregation." Calling
it "a horrible time to live in Boston," Batson later explained, "The press
came out: NAACP is wrong....We got very little public support and we
got absolutely no political support....All kinds of hate mail. Horrible
stuff. I also got calls from black people in Boston. They would call up and
they'd say, 'Mrs. Batson, I know you think you're doing a good thing.
And maybe where you came from there was segregation, but we don't

have segregation in Boston.'...Of course, now I was born in Boston. So there were people who could not accept the fact that this horrible thing was happening in Boston."[20] The NAACP chapter, under the leadership of 68-year-old Melnea Cass, carried out numerous sit-ins and pickets against the School Committee. Cass viewed the city's intransigence as "a calamity happening to us as black people trying to get something done, and couldn't impress anybody."[21]

Local activists called a second boycott of schools for February 26, 1964, to coincide with a nationwide campaign organized by the Student Non-violent Coordinating Committee to dramatize segregation in the nation's schools. The School Committee met with the Boston NAACP with the hope of derailing the boycott, but the group refused. On February 24, Martin Luther King endorsed Boston's boycott and highlighted the intentional nature of Boston's segregation: "de facto segregation in the North is as evil as open segregation in the South....The tactics may differ, but the intent is the same."[22] The boycott succeeded in drawing nearly 20,000 participants and prompted Governor Owen Peabody to convene a blue-ribbon committee to study racial discrimination in the schools.[23] The committee's report found that Boston's schools were indeed racially imbalanced and that such imbalance was harmful to students' educations. ("Racial imbalance" was the more palatable northern term for segregation to describe schools with more than a 50 percent nonwhite student body; an *all-white* school was still considered a *racially balanced* school.) The lobbying efforts of the black community and its white allies led to the state legislature's passage of the Racial Imbalance Act of 1965, which forbade the commonwealth from supporting any school more than 50 percent nonwhite. The law provided that a district denied funding could seek judicial review of its situation. Unsuccessfully challenging the act's legality in court, the School Committee fought to get it repealed by the legislature and then used the judicial review process to delay obeying the law for the next decade.

Boston had implemented an open enrollment policy in 1961 that allowed students to attend any school as long as open seats existed. But the School Committee forbade the use of school funds to bus children to the seven thousand open seats throughout the city.[24] Open enrollment in many ways functioned like the "freedom of choice" plans used in many southern cities to minimize compliance with the *Brown* decision. By the mid-1960s, the School Committee was taking more deliberate and costly actions to avoid desegregation, yet its members continued to maintain their public stance that Boston's schools were not segregated. The district decided to buy an old synagogue to use as a new school—which cost $125,000 to purchase and renovate, and $90,000 a year to operate—rather than bus 150 to 200 black students from the crowded black Endicott school to under-enrolled white schools (which would have cost $40,000 per year). Claiming that busing was an infringement on the rights of (white) taxpaying families, the School Committee then moved to institute double-session days in black schools rather than bus minority students from overcrowded schools to white schools, even as the district bused white pupils to other white schools to eliminate overcrowding.[25]

School and city officials in Boston sought to deflect charges of racial injustice by blaming black parents and students for their culture and values. In January 1964, School Committee chair William O'Connor declared: "We have no inferior education in our schools. What we have been getting is an inferior type of student."[26] While Boston officials did not feel comfortable publicly embracing segregation, they did not mind calling black students inferior, unmotivated, and unintelligent. It was more palatable in a liberal city such as Boston to use a sociological language of "culture" to justify the segregation of black students. School Committee member Joseph Lee placed responsibility for improving black schools on the black community itself: "The Negro can make their schools the best in the city if they attend more often, on time and apply themselves." After identifying the problem as the deficiencies within individual students, BPS created a special program, Operation Counterpoise, for "culturally deprived" students; according to School Committee chair William O'Connor, "the Roxbury area of Boston requires 'a different type of education' to meet the education capacity of the residents."[27] While many Bostonians could easily identify the hypocrisy of white southerners who claimed that blacks had their own culture and preferred separation, "many of the staunchest bigots of the city," according to former BPS teacher Jonathan Kozol, "could convince themselves that they were acting and speaking out of decent feelings."[28]

"Forced busing" also emerged as the covert language through which many whites expressed their opposition to racial desegregation, despite the fact that BPS bused increasing numbers of white students to maintain white schools or to improve educational quality in the district. Indeed, before court-ordered busing began in 1974, 90 percent of high school students in Boston took a bus to school. Louise Day Hicks, a School Committee member who later won a city council seat and became the public leader of the anti-desegregation movement, played on fears of "forced busing" while asserting that "there has never been any discrimination in the city of Boston and those who say there is are doing a great disservice to this great city."[29] Civil rights activists tried to run School Committee candidates committed to addressing racial inequality, and held a march 10,000 strong to highlight the need for electoral change. But when all but one of their candidates lost, civil rights activist Mel King (who ran unsuccessfully for School Committee three times) explained, "we were forced to abandon our naïve notion that Boston whites wanted integration."[30]

In 1965, a group of black parents led by Ellen Jackson, a mother of five children in BPS, decided to transport their children themselves, since the district refused to provide buses for black students to fill the open seats in majority-white schools. They called their program Operation Exodus— and believed that busing their children would shame BPS into taking over the operation. Holding bake sales, benefit concerts, and dances to keep their efforts afloat, Operation Exodus bused 250 black students in 1965, 450 in 1966, and 600 in 1967 (figure 2.1). But BPS never took over the responsibility for operating the transportation program, although the district later attempted to use Operation Exodus to prove its compliance with federal and state desegregation orders.[31]

In order to continue to bring pressure on the School Committee, civil rights activists invited Martin Luther King to Boston twice in 1965. The first time, King attempted to meet with the School Committee, which rebuffed his efforts in a meeting that Ellen Jackson termed "such a disaster."[32] The

FIGURE 2.1. On September 9, 1965, black students in the Roxbury section of Boston register for transportation to white schools as part of "Operation Exodus." A group of black parents established the voluntary program to utilize Boston's open enrollment policy, which resembled "freedom of choice" desegregation plans in the South, after the Boston School Committee refused to provide the buses that would enable black students to transfer out of overcrowded and segregated facilities. © Bettmann/CORBIS.

second time, he led a march 22,000 strong to protest Boston's school segregation. At that rally, Batson proclaimed: "This cradle of liberty has lulled too many into a state of apathy—into a state of smug false security where we had really come to believe that all was well. But all was not well and all is not well—but unlike our co-workers in Selma, we were never too sure of what and how to fight, for our enemy was not visible and what opposition we had was polite and tactful." Even in 1965, after years of marches and rallies, freedom schools and school boycotts—indeed, right in the middle of an organized nonviolent protest similar to that being waged concurrently in Selma—Batson still had to justify the need for a movement in Boston. Comedian Dick Gregory highlighted the contradictions of Boston's racial liberalism: "Here is the only city in the country where there is a big statue of Negroes fighting for their country,... and now it is a place where they feel they are doing the Negro a favor to grant his Civil Rights."[33]

The movement for school desegregation in Boston would continue for the next decade, as black high school students walked out of classes, black community leaders built independent schools, and local parents affiliated with the NAACP filed a federal lawsuit against the School Committee in 1972. Throughout this period, civil rights activists continued to face deep resistance to their argument that segregation flourished in the city of Boston, the home of nineteenth-century abolitionists and a leading center of northern liberalism in the twentieth century. In 1973, in a lengthy article on the Boston schools entitled "More Segregated than Ever," the *New York Times* still cast a benign eye: "The Boston area can boast a long record of good race relations.... It is a spirit of tolerance that can be traced as far back as the eighteen-thirties, when the abolitionist movement took root in Boston.... The effects of segregated schools can only be surmised. For the most part, they [black students] attend overcrowded and run-down schools, but the sociological evidence suggests that the quality of school buildings and facilities is not overly important to learning."[34] This culturalist explanation allowed the *Times* to frame the educational issues of black students in Boston as somehow different and thus outside of the mandate of *Brown*, which had decisively linked the quality of facilities to effective learning and constitutional equality.

LOS ANGELES: STRUGGLE IN THE PROMISED LAND

After moving to Los Angeles in 1941, African-American novelist Chester Himes lamented the city's racial climate: "Los Angeles hurt me racially as much as any city I have ever known—much more than any city I remember from the South. It was the lying hypocrisy that hurt me. Black people were treated much the same as they were in any industrial city of the South.... The difference was the white people of Los Angeles seemed to be saying, 'Nigger, ain't we good to you?' "[35] School segregation had been upheld in the California courts in 1924 (encompassing Latinos as well as African Americans); by the 1920s the rejuvenated Ku Klux Klan had solidified a supple base of supporters in L.A.; many hotels, swimming pools, and other business establishments barred black patrons; and restrictive covenants formed a legal wall around South Los Angeles that black Angelenos could rarely scale. As Reverend H. H. Brookins explained, "a person coming out of the South with a vision of the Promised Land...finds that Los Angeles is not the Promised Land he had expected."[36]

Indeed, Marnesba Tackett, who migrated to L.A. in 1952 and soon became a leading civil rights activist, "found...very little better than what I found in the South."[37] In the early 1950s, Tackett led the NAACP's Education Committee, which began attacking segregation in the city's schools, the lack of black teachers, and the racial "stereotypes" in the curriculum.[38] The board of education of the Los Angeles Unified School District (LAUSD) vehemently denied the charge, claiming that they maintained a color-blind policy and kept no records of the racial distribution of students or teachers. As in Boston, the need to *prove* the existence of segregation would be a persistent challenge for civil rights groups like the NAACP, Congress of Racial Equality (CORE), and American Civil Liberties Union (ACLU), which demanded on countless occasions that LAUSD administer a racial census to determine the obviously segregated nature of its schools. The board resisted calls for a school census (until forced by the state in 1966), claiming that black parents would object to the inscribing of race on individual student records. Subsequent access to school records in the *Crawford* desegregation lawsuit, according to ACLU activist John Caughey, showed that the board of education had been "reliably informed about where Blacks were" and thus had purposefully, if unsurprisingly, "misrepresented its own knowledge of school segregation in LAUSD."[39]

School segregation worsened in Los Angeles after the *Brown* decision. Civil rights leaders always made the comparison with the South—in order to prove the degree of segregation in Los Angeles. As the black newspaper *California Eagle* reported, "More Negro children attend all-Negro schools in Los Angeles than attend such schools in Little Rock."[40] LAUSD tracked the overwhelming majority of black students into manual and vocational programs rather than for college, and the curriculum reflected racial biases and "happy slave tales." Patterns of segregation in the public schools did not simply derive from racialized housing patterns, as LAUSD claimed, but instead resulted from systematic methods employed by local and state officials to solidify residential segregation and to distribute educational resources through gerrymandering school districts, restrictive hiring, and other bureaucratic measures. As Tackett explained, LAUSD divided its vast system into racially segregated neighborhood schools that could easily have been drawn to create racially heterogeneous schools. "In the Wilshire Olympic corridor,...if the line had been drawn east and west instead of north and south, they would have integrated the schools in that area automatically."[41] This racial gerrymandering caused black schools to become increasingly crowded in the postwar period; as black migration to Los Angeles increased, the board of education readjusted the lines to keep black students ensconced in black schools. As minority schools grew impossibly overcrowded, the board simply changed them to double-session days instead of transferring some black students to less crowded, predominantly white schools.

In 1961, the Southern California chapter of the American Civil Liberties Union joined the NAACP and CORE in pressuring the board to address issues of school segregation, particularly highlighting the dramatic overcrowding plaguing many black and Latino schools in the city. Black students were predominantly segregated in South L.A., while East L.A. schools were overwhelmingly Latino.[42] Black parents and students also picketed the all-white Baldwin Hills Elementary School and Huntington Park High School to call attention to these inequalities. In 1961, Martin Luther King made the first of many trips to the city to speak to an L.A. Freedom Rally. More than 28,000 people heard King highlight the issues facing African Americans in Los Angeles and draw connections between southern struggles and the L.A. movement. Shortly after getting out of a Birmingham jail in May 1963, King returned to L.A. and spoke to crowd of more than 35,000 people at Wrigley Field. "You asked me what Los Angeles can do to help us in Birmingham," he told the audience. "The most important thing that you can do is to set Los Angeles free because you have segregation and discrimination here, and police brutality."[43] The turnout at these events and the tenor of the coverage in the local black newspapers indicate that African Americans in Los Angeles viewed themselves as part of a national freedom movement. In the years before the Watts uprising, King repeatedly highlighted the racism rampant in Los Angeles and the civil rights struggles of black Angelenos. While journalists and some historians have painted a picture of a naive King, out of touch with racial issues in the North before Watts erupted, his repeated appearances in the early 1960s on behalf of education, housing, and police injustice in Los Angeles dispel this myth.

As for local civil rights leaders, the NAACP's Marnesba Tackett critiqued the idea that blacks in Los Angeles had largely viewed the civil rights movement from afar.

Of course, Los Angeles was very sympathetic toward what was going on in the South. We did raise money that we sent to the South....I was not as active in that phase of it because my priority was in trying to get equal education right here in Los Angeles, where we had a lot of discrimination, a lot of work done in terms of the way boundaries were drawn.... It all needed to be worked on at one and the same time.[44]

Inspired by King's visit to create a unified front in Los Angeles, seventy-six community and political groups formed the United Civil Rights Council (UCRC) in June 1963. Tackett was unanimously selected as the UCRC's education chair.[45] Attacking the board of education's claim of color-blindness, she compared Los Angeles schools to "those of Alabama and Mississippi."[46] The UCRC drew up a list of demands for the board: redraw district lines to achieve racial desegregation; transfer black students attending overcrowded schools on half-day sessions to underenrolled majority-white schools; diversify the curriculum to rid textbooks of damaging stereotypes and include black and Latino history and culture; and change the transfer and promotion process to distribute black teachers throughout the entire district and enable career advancement for them.

Most members of the board of education actively opposed desegregation while maintaining publicly that the problem did not exist. Board member Charles Smoot declared: "No de facto segregation exists.... I resent pressure put on the board.... We represent majorities."[47] His colleague J. C. Chambers asserted that if not much black history was being taught in LAUSD, that was because there was "not much of it to teach," and he also accused Tackett (a real estate broker) of being a communist. But board member Georgiana Hardy, a white liberal, called for the convening of a special Ad Hoc Committee to investigate the issues. That committee would "study" the problem for the next eighteen months, amid continuing pressure from civil rights groups for the Board to take decisive action.[48]

Black leaders continued to make many direct comparisons between Los Angeles and Birmingham—to the toxic racial climate that existed in both cities and the confrontational direction in which local movements in Alabama and Southern California were now moving. Such comparisons were strategic attempts to demonstrate the gravity of the situation in Los Angeles and to highlight the righteousness of the struggle being waged by black Angelenos. Rev. Maurice Dawkins, the former president of the NAACP chapter, threatened Birmingham-style demonstrations if city officials did not take decisive action around schools, jobs, and policing. "We are not just asking for a small specific adjustment," Dawkins explained, "but a total community integration." Yet liberal board of supervisors member Kenneth Hahn (not unlike clergy in Birmingham) asserted that such confrontational tactics were unnecessary and alienating in a progressive city like Los Angeles.[49]

Seeking to distinguish L.A.'s liberal racial politics from those of Birmingham, Hahn held a conference of city and county officials, businesspeople, and black leaders in early June of 1963 "to avert any violent demonstrations similar to those that have torn cities apart in the South."[50] Purposefully echoing King's "Letter from Birmingham Jail," a group of L.A.'s black leaders then issued a statement "To Men of Good Will": "All deliberate speed has meant no speed at all. The spirit of Birmingham means integration now in every way."[51] At a press conference, writer James Baldwin further elaborated, "I doubt that a single Negro in Los Angeles would agree that conditions are improving.... The real Negro leaders have been trying to speak to you for years.... You won't listen."[52]

On June 24, 1963, just months after the Birmingham protests had captured national headlines, and despite criticisms from many white politicians and some black residents, more than one thousand people joined the UCRC in a Freedom March through downtown Los Angeles to the headquarters of the board of education. This was the first in a series of marches that continued all summer to pressure the board to address school segregation and inequality. As in Birmingham, confrontational direct action tactics were on full display in Los Angeles—and the *Times* ran front-page stories announcing "Negroes State Race March on School Board Hearing" and "L.A. Declared Target for Total Integration." As Tackett recalled, "there was so much resistance [in Los Angeles] that I really did not have time to work actively [on behalf of the movement in the South]."[53] Increasingly frustrated with the board's lack of action, the UCRC held a silent protest in July to dramatize their belief that further talks with LAUSD officials were fruitless. National civil rights leaders then joined the UCRC's fight. James Farmer of CORE and James Forman of SNCC came to Los Angeles in August to lead a march of more than six hundred people to the board of education building.[54]

The UCRC highlighted the examples of two South L.A. high schools, Jordan High School (98 percent black) and South Gate High School (less than 1 percent black), which were less than two miles apart, to demonstrate the intentionality of school segregation in Los Angeles. Five black students had desegregated South Gate High School in June and faced eggs, bricks, Confederate flags, and racial epithets.[55] Despite the board's claims that Jordan and South Gate were simply "neighborhood schools," Jordan sat at its own eastern boundary line, many black students lived closer to South Gate than Jordan, and many whites closer to Jordan than South Gate. Black community leaders pressed the board to rezone the two schools using geographic distance as the sole determinant. Tackett explained that "the education at South Gate was so much better, there was no comparison. Alameda Street, the boundary which separated them, was called 'the line.' ... The school board kept expanding Jordan's boundary as more black children moved into it instead of sending them to South

Gate." Indeed Alameda served as a "natural boundary" separating segregated high schools at 103rd, Manchester, and Slauson Streets, but not at the Vernon intersection, where black elementary schoolers were expected to cross this major thoroughfare to get to school.[56] Then in August 1963, in response both to the city's continued intransigence around equity issues and news that the city was about to commit $1 million to upgrade the segregated Jordan High School, activists went to the courts in *Crawford v. Los Angeles Board of Education*. The case was expanded to the whole district, and in 1970, Judge Alfred Gitelson found LAUSD to be substantially and intentionally segregated.[57]

Instead of desegregation, Los Angeles school officials proposed a solution of increased funding to "culturally disadvantaged" schools, including money for a new anti-dropout program at Jordan. Board members also continued to assert that racial inequality was not an issue, with conservative J. C. Chambers claiming that Los Angeles had moved faster than any other city to address any issues of de facto segregation.[58] On September 12, 1963, the board's Ad Hoc Committee finally issued its report. After fifteen months of hearings, the report rejected most of the UCRC's demands and placed responsibility for any school problems that did exist outside the board's purview, notably segregation in housing patterns, high rates of black poverty, and "the lack of hope and motivation among some of these families which leads them into negative attitudes toward education and the demands the school makes on their children."[59]

The language of "negative attitudes toward education" provided school officials a way to evade responsibility for any racial patterns within the LAUSD and strategically to turn the table on the growing movement by black (and Latino) parents for desegregation and educational equality. By blaming black and Latino families for their poor values and lack of motivation, the report suggested that cultural pathologies rather than public policies caused minority student underachievement. The board thus offered a palatable justification for liberal white sensibilities regarding the existence of racially divided schools: a group of culturally deficient students, not a segregated system. Simultaneously, by portraying black parents as evading their own responsibilities for their children's attitudes toward school, the Ad Hoc Committee's report worked to delegitimize civil rights protests. Like in Boston, the district would raise the budget for compensatory programs for black children but refused to address segregation.[60]

The UCRC and CORE attacked the board's "failure to obey the law of the land" [*Brown*] and held sit-ins, sleep-ins, and study-ins throughout the fall of 1963. Hundreds of student protesters marched, lined the halls of the board of education building, and disrupted one meeting with a sing-in.[61] These confrontational tactics were not popular in a city proud of its liberalism. In November, the dean of the University of Southern California (located at the edge of South L.A.) barred James Farmer of CORE from speaking on campus because he was "too controversial."[62]

In 1964, the burgeoning civil rights movement in Los Angeles had to shift its organizational energies in an effort to defeat a menacing ballot initiative. Proposition 14 sought to repeal the Rumford Fair Housing Act, a long-fought 1963 state law that banned racial discrimination in the sale and rental of property. The NAACP, UCRC, and CORE conducted voter registration workshops, held marches, and lobbied liberal Governor Edmund Brown to be vocal in his opposition to Proposition 14.[63] Martin Luther King returned to the city on two occasions to join the fight against Proposition 14, warning that its passage would "be one of the most shameful developments in our nation's history."[64] Only four months after Lyndon Johnson signed the Civil Rights Act, voters in California helped return the president to the White House with nearly 60 percent support and authorized Proposition 14 by a two-to-one majority. While the courts ultimately overturned the referendum, the message behind Proposition 14's overwhelming approval was clear: many neighborhoods in California were not open to black residents, and liberal politicians such as Lyndon Johnson and Edmund Brown who had publicly committed themselves to pressing for civil rights in the South were not as vigorous in fighting for equality in the rest of the nation.

As Celes King, who served as vice president of the Los Angeles NAACP from 1964 to 1966, observed: "[With] the models in the other part of the country where they appeared to be making progress, here in Los Angeles we were supposed to be the satisfied blacks. Well, [we] really weren't satisfied."[65] Nine months later, the arrest of Marquette Frye sparked seven days of rioting in the largely black neighborhoods of South Los Angeles. Despite an active black freedom movement in the city for decades, local and state officials were astonished by the anger evident in the Watts riots. Governor Brown, on vacation when the riot started, flew home immediately and informed reporters that "nobody told me there was an explosive situation in Los Angeles."[66] Mayor Sam Yorty had recently testified to the U.S. Civil Rights Commission that Los Angeles had "the best race relations...of any large city in the United States." Los Angeles Police Chief William Parker concurred, even though CORE and the UCRC had been calling for his resignation for more than a year.[67]

In an essay for the *Los Angeles Times* opinion page, well-known political commentator Theodore White summed up the "surprise" at the riots: "One must start, of course, with the beginning mystery, the most puzzling of all—why Los Angeles? For, in Los Angeles, Negroes have lived better than in any other large American city, with the possible exception of Detroit...and, up to now, treated better by their white fellow citizens than in any other city in the nation." White described the city's "open and easy tolerance," where black people had made "spectacular" progress.[68] While endorsing dialogue between the black community and

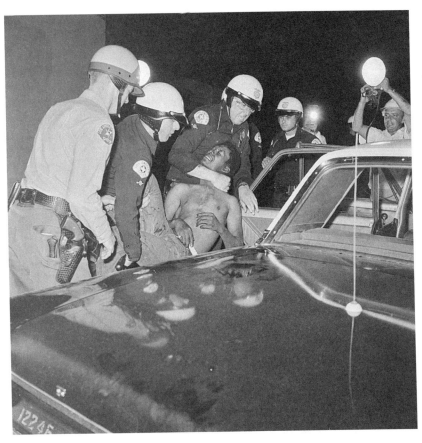

FIGURE 2.2. Members of the Los Angeles Police Department force an African-American man into a squad car on August 12, 1965, during the second night of racial violence in Watts—which many black residents viewed as an extension of longstanding practices of police violence in the city. Local and national expressions of shock at the seven-day black uprising ignored decades of civil rights protest against entrenched patterns of racial discrimination, police brutality, and residential and educational segregation in metropolitan Los Angeles. Historical memory of the civil rights era in L.A. has replicated this erasure, replacing a long history of black activism with images of young men clashing with police. © Bettmann/CORBIS.

the police department, a *Los Angeles Times* editorial similarly minimized black concerns: "It is likely that Negro complaints hinge more around their resentment of alleged police attitudes and procedure, than outright brutality.... Certainly such a condition [of a double standard between the policing of white and black communities], if indeed it exists, is not the result of a deliberate code." The *Times* previously had covered the protest movement that emerged in 1962–1963 after the police killing of Ronald Stokes, the unarmed secretary of the Nation of Islam. Activists documented a widespread pattern of police abuse in Los Angeles that, as the *Times* had reported, resulted in the creation of a blue ribbon committee but little change in police practices. In 1964, the *Times* also recounted the calls for Chief Parker's resignation by CORE and the UCRC. Yet despite years of civil rights activism and a six-day uprising, the *Times* was unwilling to acknowledge a pattern of police brutality in Los Angeles.[69]

The surprise expressed by many white citizens, city officials, and the mainstream news media after the Watts uprising should be understood in part as the surprise of intransigence—a willful shock. While Los Angeles had been home to a multitude of movements that persistently challenged the racial injustice at the city's core, the frame of surprise worked to deny the longstanding nature and significance of those grievances and to obscure the history of a protracted struggle within the city. The framework of southern exceptionalism, evident in the widespread notion that the civil rights movement was taking place in Birmingham but not also in Los Angeles, enabled this blind spot. As Martin Luther King would point out later that fall, the leaders of Los Angeles could have anticipated the riot given the conditions in the city and white intransigence to civil rights demands.[70] But the news media did not force public officials to account for why a decade-long civil rights movement in the city had produced almost no change in schools, housing, job structures, or police practice (which certainly fueled the frustration that spurred the riot), because they too had constructed Los Angeles's movement as different from the righteous southern movement. Without this history of struggle, the view that black people possessed an alien culture with separate values—already present in public discourse—gained even more currency after Watts.[71] The erasure of this history of L.A.'s pre-1965 civil rights movement constructed the city's black residents as an angry and foreign people who had courageously escaped Jim Crow but lost their way in the promised land.

SOUTHERN EXCEPTIONALISM AND AMERICAN REDEMPTION

Understanding the civil rights movements in Boston and Los Angeles requires reexamining many of the moral truisms at the heart of the southern civil rights narrative. The belief in southern exceptionalism has been strangely comforting for it provides now—as it did in the 1950s and 1960s—a moral version of history, of "good guys" (gutsy southern blacks and their northern white allies), "bad guys" (racist southern whites and alienated northern blacks), and happy endings. On one side of the Mason-Dixon line, a courageous black people held together by longstanding cultural traditions fought systematic racial inequality forged under an anachronistic plantation system and organized a broad-based nonviolent movement that changed the hearts and minds of the nation. On the other side, having made it to "open and tolerant" cities like Boston and Los Angeles, a beleaguered black people lost those moral and family traditions and, confounded by anger and structural inequality, turned toward riots and racial separatism.

The disruption of this binary leaves a much messier version of history. The nonviolent civil rights movement did flourish in *all* regions of the country from 1954 to1965 and beyond, but it did not succeed fully in producing desegregated schools, fair hiring practices, open housing, an end to police brutality, or even a widespread recognition that state-sponsored racial discrimination pervaded the nation and not just the Jim Crow South. Northern liberals may have pushed for certain kinds of change in the South, but they often maintained and erected new barriers to desegregation and structural change in their own backyards. Using the example of their northern counterparts, southern segregationists moved from a defense of Jim Crow and states' rights to an opposition to "forced busing," a lamentation about the "decline of values" among black people, and an insistence on "taxpayer rights."[72]

During the 1950s and 1960s, and increasingly since, a public record of civil rights movements outside the South receded from view because it did not fit with the political advantages of a southern-centric narrative. By holding up the evils of the Jim Crow South and celebrating the courageous folks who defeated it, the nation cast state-sponsored racial segregation as a relic of an antiquated regional system. This distorted history thus immunized America's modern system of racial privilege, embracing a language of culture and values that grew popular in the postwar period to justify the discrimination and inequality that still holds sway. Thus, today, when public figures lament a newly urgent crisis of declining value for education in the African-American community, they are actually taking up the discourse northern public officials have used for more than fifty years to preserve segregation and frame black behavior as the key to black educational success or failure. Looking squarely at the civil rights movements that took place in Boston, Los Angeles, and other cities across America in the 1950s and 1960s forces us to move past the morality tale of South versus North to a more sober examination of the nation's race problem.

NOTES

Portions of this essay have appeared in "Alabama on Avalon," in *The Black Power Movement*, ed. Peniel Joseph (New York: Routledge, 2006), 27–54; and "They Told Us Our Kids Were Stupid," in *Groundwork: Local Black Freedom Movements in America*, ed. Jeanne Theoharis and Komozi Woodard (New York: New York University Press, 2005), 17–44.

1. Robin Kelley, "Birmingham's Untouchables," *Race Rebels: Culture, Politics, and the Black Working Class* (New York: Free Press, 1994), 77–101; Diane McWhorter, *Carry Me Home: Birmingham, Alabama* (New York: Simon & Schuster, 2001).

2. Most books on Boston school desegregation aim "to portray organized anti-busing with understanding." See Ronald P. Formisano, *Boston against Busing: Race, Class, and Ethnicity in the 1960s and 1970s* (Chapel Hill: University of North Carolina Press, 1991), quotation xii; Alan Lupo, *Liberty's Chosen Home: The Politics of Violence in Boston* (Boston: Little, Brown, 1977); Louis Masur, *The Soiling of Old Glory: The Story of a Photograph That Shocked America* (New York: Bloomsbury, 2008); and J. Anthony Lukas, *Common Ground: A Turbulent Decade in the Lives of Three American Families* (New York: Knopf, 1985).

3. Formisano, *Boston against Busing*, xi.

4. Jack Jones, "The View from Watts Today: Parents and Children Hunger for Knowledge," *Los Angeles Times*, July 20, 1967.

5. Mary Dudziak, *Cold War Civil Rights: Race and the Image of American Democracy* (Princeton: Princeton University Press, 2000).

6. See the work of Matthew Countryman, *Up South: Civil Rights and Black Power in Philadelphia* (Philadelphia: University of Pennsylvania Press, 2005); Thomas J. Sugrue, *Sweet Land of Liberty: The Forgotten Struggle for Civil Rights in the North* (New York: Knopf, 2008); and Craig Wilder, *A Covenant with Color: Race and Social Power in Brooklyn* (New York: Columbia University Press, 2000). For further elaboration of this argument, see Jeanne Theoharis and Komozi Woodward, eds., *Freedom North: Black Freedom Struggles Outside the South, 1940–1980* (New York: Palgrave Macmillan, 2003).

7. Daryl Michael Scott and Nikhil Pal Singh provide elaboration of the ways this culturalist discourse recast longstanding conservative ideas of black inferiority within the new paradigms of urban sociology. See Scott, *Contempt and Pity: Social Policy and the Image of the Damaged Black Psyche, 1880–1996* (Chapel Hill: University of North Carolina Press, 1997); Singh, *Black Is a Country: Race and the Unfinished Struggle for Democracy* (Cambridge, Mass.: Harvard University Press, 2005).

8. Ruth Batson, *A Chronology of the Educational Movement in Boston*, 9–10, unpublished manuscript in Box 1, Ruth Batson Papers, 2001-M194, Schlesinger Library, Radcliffe Institute.

9. Interview of Ruth Batson, Civil Rights Documentation Project, Moorland Spingarn Research Center, Howard University, 3.

10. Ruth Batson, "Statement to the Boston School Committee," in *The Eyes on the Prize Civil Rights Reader*, ed. Clayborne Carson, et al. (New York: Penguin, 1991), 598.

11. Batson, *Chronology*, 48.

12. "Interview with Ellen Jackson," in *The Black Women Oral History Project*, ed. Ruth Hill (Westport, Conn.: Meckler, 1991), 235.

13. Steven J. L. Taylor, *Desegregation in Boston and Buffalo: The Influence of Local Leaders* (Albany: SUNY Press, 1998), 49.

14. Batson, *Chronology*, 58.

15. Ruth Batson, "Presentation on Mental Health and Desegregation," School Desegregation Conference (November 1, 1978), Box 1, Batson Papers.

16. Mel King, *Chain of Change: Struggles for Black Community Development* (Boston: South End Press, 1981), 33.

17. Batson, "Statement to the Boston School Committee," 597–98.

18. Henry Hampton and Steve Fayer, *Voices of Freedom: An Oral History of the Civil Rights Movement from the 1950s through the 1980s* (New York: Bantam, 1991), 589.

19. J. Michael Ross and William M. Berg, *"I Respectfully Disagree with the Judge's Order": The Boston School Desegregation Controversy* (Washington: University Press of America, 1981), 49.

20. Batson, *Chronology*; Hampton and Fayer, *Voices of Freedom*, 590–91.

21. "Interview with Melnea Cass," *Black Women Oral History Project,* 350.

22. Batson, *Chronology*, Addendum 152b; 150.

23. Ross and Berg, *I Respectfully Disagree*, 49; J. Brian Sheehan, *The Boston School Integration Dispute: Social Change and Legal Maneuvers* (New York: Columbia University Press, 1984), 70.

24. U.S. Commission on Civil Rights, *Desegregating the Boston Public Schools* (Washington: GPO, 1975), xiv; Taylor, *Desegregation in Boston and Buffalo*, 43–44.

25. In 1973, the School Committee willingly gave up $65 million in state and federal funds rather than desegregate BPS. Judge Garrity's 1974 decision in *Morgan v. Hennigan* affirmed the intentionality of Boston's school desegregation. The Boston School Committee had "knowingly carried out a systematic program of segregation affecting all of the city's students, teachers, and school facilities"; 379 F. Supp. 410 (1974).

26. Batson, *Chronology*, 134.

27. Batson, *Chronology*, 117, 141.

28. Jonathan Kozol, *Death at an Early Age: The Destruction of the Hearts and Minds of Negro Children in the Boston Public Schools* (New York: Bantam Books, 1968), 136.

29. Berkeley Rice, "Boston: 'I Am a Symbol of Resistance'—Hicks," *New York Times Sunday Magazine* (November 5, 1967).

30. King, *Chain of Change*, 36.

31. James Teele, *Evaluating School Busing: Case Study of Operation Exodus* (New York: Praeger, 1973); Interview of Ellen Jackson by Peggy Lamson, on file at the Schlesinger Library for Research on Women, Radcliffe Institute for Advanced Study.

32. "Interview with Ellen Jackson," *Black Women Oral History Project,* 146.

33. Ruth Batson, "Statement made at King March on April 23, 1965," Batson Papers; Batson, *Chronology*, 128.

34. Robert Reinhold, "More Segregated than Ever," *New York Times*, September 30, 1973.

35. Chester Himes, *The Quality of Hurt: The Early Years* (New York: Paragon House, 1990), 74.

36. Gerald Horne, *Fire This Time: The Watts Uprising and the 1960s* (New York: Da Capo Press, 1997), 37.

37. Marnesba Tackett Interview by Michael Balter, 1988, Oral History Program, Department of Special Collections, University of California at Los Angeles, 75.

38. Tackett Interview, 80.

39. John Caughey, *To Kill a Child's Spirit* (Itasca, Ill.: Peacock Publishers, 1973), 15–16.

40. John and LaRee Caughey, *School Segregation on our Doorstep: The Los Angeles Story* (Los Angeles: Quail Books, 1966), 10. See also John Caughey Papers, Department of Special Collections, UCLA.

41. Tackett Interview, 128–29.

42. Latino parents successfully filed suit in *Mendez v. Westminster* in 1945 against four districts in Orange County regarding school segregation; their case became an important precedent for the *Brown* decision; 54 F. Supp 544 (1946).

43. Tackett Interview; "Greatest Freedom Rally Here Nets Heroes Over $75,000," *Los Angeles Sentinel*, May 30, 1963.

44. Tackett Interview, 128–29.

45. Josh Sides, *L.A. City Limits: African American Los Angeles from the Great Depression to the Present* (Berkeley: University of California Press, 2003), 163; Tackett Interview, 106–7.

46. Caughey, *School Segregation on our Doorstep*, 16.

47. Becky Nicolaides, *My Blue Heaven: Life and Politics in the Working-Class Suburbs of Los Angeles, 1920-1965* (Chicago: University of Chicago Press, 2001), 291.

48. Tackett Interview; Theoharis, "Alabama on Avalon," 41–44.

49. Quotation from "L.A. Declared Target for Total Integration," *Los Angeles Times*, May 31, 1963; Theoharis, "Alabama on Avalon," 41–42.

50. "L.A. Meeting Proposed to Avert Racial Strife," *Los Angeles Times*, June 4, 1963.

51. "Los Angeles Choice: End Segregation or Face Mass Action," *California Eagle*, June 13, 1963.

52. "Baldwin Tells L.A. Bitter Facts on Bias," *California Eagle*, May 16, 1963.

53. Tackett Interview, 128–29.

54. "3 of 'Big Four' Will Lead School March," *California Eagle*, August 8, 1963.

55. "Negro Students Dodge Eggs During Last Week At South Gate High," *Los Angeles Sentinel*, July 4, 1963.

56. "Dymally Hits Inequal School Boundary Lines," *Los Angeles Sentinel*, September 6, 1962.

57. *Crawford v. Los Angeles Board of Education*, Superior Court of Los Angeles County, No. 822854 (1970).

58. "Los Angeles Schools Called Best on Rights Issue," *Los Angeles Times*, September 11, 1963.

59. Report of the Ad Hoc Committee on Equal Education Opportunity, September 12, 1963, Box 164, John Caughey Papers, Department of Special Collections, UCLA.

60. Caughey, *School Segregation on our Doorstep*, iii.

61. Nicolaides, *My Blue Heaven*, 303.

62. "USC Dean Won't Let Farmer Speak," *California Eagle*, November 7, 1963.

63. "March To Save Fair Housing," *Los Angeles Sentinel*, January 9, 1964; "UCRC Backs Boycott," *Los Angeles Sentinel*, November 21, 1963.

64. "Housing Foes Picket King, CRB Banquet," *California Eagle*, February 20, 1964.

65. Celes King Interview, 1988, by Bruce Tyler and Robin Kelley, Oral History Program, Department of Special Collections, UCLA.

66. Kirse Granat May, *Golden State, Golden Youth: The California Image in Popular Culture, 1955–1966* (Chapel Hill: University of North Carolina Press, 2002), 160.

67. Sides, *L.A. City Limits*, 169.

68. Theodore H. White, "Lessons of Los Angeles," *Los Angeles Times*, August 22, 1965.

69. "Times Editorial: We Must Speak to Each Other," *Los Angeles Times*, August 29, 1965.

70. Martin Luther King, Jr., "Beyond the Los Angeles Riots: Next Step, The North," *Saturday Review* (November 13, 1965), 33–35, 105.

71. The UCLA Los Angeles Riot study found that 64 percent of blacks surveyed after the Watts riot thought the riot was justified.

72. For elaboration of this argument, see Matthew D. Lassiter, *The Silent Majority: Suburban Politics in the Sunbelt South* (Princeton: Princeton University Press, 2006); and Kevin M. Kruse, *White Flight: Atlanta and the Making of Modern Conservatism* (Princeton: Princeton University Press, 2005).

3

BLINDED BY A "BARBARIC" SOUTH

Prison Horrors, Inmate Abuse, and the Ironic History of American Penal Reform

Heather Ann Thompson

Crime and punishment in the South has long been the subject of public fascination. Like gawkers who just can't seem to avert their eyes from a bloody roadside wreck, Americans have flocked to prison movies in the popular genre of southern Gothic. *Cool Hand Luke* (1967) captured the horrors of life on a southern chain gang in the late 1940s, while *Brubaker* (1980) exposed the brutality of an Arkansas prison farm in the 1960s. More recently, *The Green Mile* (1999) chronicled the saga of an innocent black man facing the death penalty in Depression-era Louisiana, and the blockbuster *O Brother, Where Art Thou?* (2000) followed the exploits of three white men who escape from a chain gang in the sweltering sun of the Mississippi Delta. A national audience has been equally riveted by numerous books about the South's particularly barbaric criminal justice system, such as Robert Burns's classic 1932 memoir *I Am a Fugitive from a Georgia Chain Gang!* and Tom Murton's grisly 1969 exposé *Accomplices to the Crime: The Arkansas Prison Scandal* (which inspired the film *Brubaker*).[1] While the most sadistic aspects of the South's penal system have never ceased to enthrall, they also have never seemed to surprise. After all, the region's economic and political system had formerly revolved around slavery, an institution so barbaric, so heinous, that it assuredly would have tainted southern culture long after it ended.

Unlike film executives, historians have worked very hard to complicate how Americans view the South and understand its past. As their research has made clear, this region was neither the fantasyland of moonlight and magnolias portrayed in *Gone with the Wind* (1939) nor was it the living nightmare of *Deliverance* (1972). While scholars have challenged Hollywood's stereotypes of the South, few historians of crime and punishment really have questioned the popular premise that the southern justice system was uniquely brutal because of the region's ugly past.[2] Without question, very real differences existed between northern and southern penal practices throughout most of the twentieth century—differences that have clear connections to the antebellum period and to the role that slavery played in shaping southern law and society. Long after the Civil War, southern states favored prison farms over penitentiaries, and those farms looked and operated very much like the plantations of old. In addition, racially biased criminal justice policies across the South resulted in the disproportionate incarceration of African Americans, and black inmates also suffered far worse abuse than did white prisoners. Although the era of Reconstruction had the potential to bring southern blacks greater protection from white racial brutality, and also might have created brand-new penal institutions that had no physical or cultural resemblance to those of the antebellum period, it did neither. Nevertheless, it is problematic to view the southern criminal justice system as exceptionally cruel compared to the rest of the nation.

First and foremost, interpretations that emphasize the "exceptional" nature of the southern justice system obscure the extent to which historical penal practices in northern and western states also have been inhumane and deeply racialized. Seeing criminal justice practices in the South as divergent from national standards fundamentally distorts understandings of how race and power played out across the United States after the Civil War. The recognition that southern penal systems did not have a monopoly on working their inmates to death, or on meting out much harsher punishments to black lawbreakers than to white ones, does not diminish the region's history of vicious racism. Rather than somehow muting the South's seemingly insatiable desire to cling to white supremacy, or its most horrific practices of racial subjugation such as lynching, reckoning more deliberately with the North's penal practices dramatically expands our historical appreciation of just how devastating a role cruelty and racism have played in the making of modern America writ large.

While the belief that the southern justice system was uniquely harsh has blinded scholars and public opinion alike to the ways in which the politics of race and punishment intersected across the nation after the Civil War, the *construct* of southern exceptionalism nevertheless must be taken seriously. In short, the very fact that most Americans viewed the penal system of the South as exceptional *itself* shaped the ways in which criminal justice policies evolved, not only within the region but also across the entire nation. In the 1960s, for example, the widespread belief that the South was especially barbaric directly facilitated northern liberal efforts to improve penal conditions in that region. However, the very same notion of southern distinctiveness directly hindered northern prisoners' efforts during the same decade to end the abuses that also flourished in the institutions where they were confined. The hard reality was that, while white northerners could understand why black prisoners in the South needed to protest the conditions of their incarceration, most never felt that those held in the penal institutions of the North had much to complain about. This regional double standard ultimately mattered a great deal, not only to the ways in which some of the North's most dramatic prison rebellions played out during the 1960s and 1970s but also to the ability of the American penal reform movement to survive the last decades of the twentieth century.

Because liberal support for prison reform was so intimately tied to the desire to save southern prisoners from a criminal justice system still locked in the inhumane practices of the antebellum era, once Americans came to believe that the South finally had modernized, they had little desire to intervene any further on behalf of inmate rights anywhere. The consequences of this wholesale disinterest in what went on behind bars in the United States were vast. In short, what followed southern penal reform was a new era of punitive prison policy—one that came to haunt inmates no matter which state had incarcerated them. By the end of the twentieth century, prisons and penal practices across the nation had become uniformly harsh, and few reformers cared to scrutinize them any longer. State officials from Mississippi to Michigan to California enjoyed carte blanche to run their prisons in any way they wished.

Virtually every argument about southern exceptionalism begins with the inescapable fact that slavery dominated the region's political economy during the antebellum period and led directly to the Civil War. In the eyes of white northerners, the region's unequivocal embrace of human bondage and its willingness to defend slavery at all costs proved that white southerners were a different breed altogether. Not only did southern whites seem to have absolutely no qualms about treating other human beings with extreme cruelty, they did so on a regular and most ordinary basis. At base, northerners believed that this comfort with violence and abuse was unlikely to evaporate just because outsiders abolished the institution of slavery. Inhumane social practices were too engrained, too tied to regional identity, and frankly too useful to those southern whites who put a premium on maintaining their political and economic power simply to fade away over time.[3]

But had white northerners taken even a cursory look at penal practices in their own region during the antebellum period, they might have been surprised to learn how shockingly brutal northern institutions also could be to inmates over whom they had ultimate control. Even though slavery in northern states had existed in the much more distant past, white northerners also seemed disinclined to provide humane treatment for prisoners as the nineteenth century unfolded. Take, for example, the "model" Eastern State Penitentiary that the Quakers had built in Philadelphia in 1832. When prison officials were not locking inmates up for years at a time in solitary confinement, they kept convicts in a dank cement dungeon for days, weeks, and months without heat, bedding, light, or clothing. Guards also subjected certain prisoners to "shower baths," which consisted of stripping off their clothes, tying them to a wall outside, and then dousing them with buckets of freezing water until shells of ice formed on their skin. Worse, some inmates at Eastern State Penitentiary also suffered the "iron gag," a five-inch long device that clamped over their tongues. Guards would force a prisoner to wear leather gloves, cross his hands behind his back, and then link chains from the gloves back up to a choking mouth gag so that any movement at all would cause excruciating pain. And if these "treatments" did not exact the result that officials hoped for, a prisoner might find himself in the "Tranquilizing Chair," bound to the seat with chains, leather straps, and locks so that he was completely immobilized. While in this chair, he would be beaten as well as restrained for such a long period of time that his legs became severely swollen and unusable.[4]

Northern prison officials not only felt comfortable with torture but, like the many white officials who meted out punishment to black lawbreakers in the South, they also reserved some of their most vicious and capricious treatment for the African-American inmates under their control.[5] One prison doctor, Dr. Chauncey Beldon, was so disturbed by how the warden of a Connecticut prison treated the "colored men" in his charge in the 1830s that he testified publicly to the brutality. Hylas Styles, the so-called overseer of that prison's shoe shop, had his own horrific stories of abuse to report. This guard reported that one African-American "boy" in his shop was so sick that he was "much swollen in his limbs and bowels and had great difficulty breathing." But when this inmate "begged in tears" to return to his cell, the deputy warden forced him to work hard all day, after first "grabbing him by the hair and violently shaking him about the room." The prisoner then died in his cell.[6]

Yet as brutal as northern penal practices were in the antebellum era, Americans seemed to know virtually nothing about them. And thus, when terrible stories of prisoner abuse began coming out of the South after the Civil War, it seemed obvious, at least to most northerners, that white southerners must still be locked in the cruel ways of their slave past. Indeed, no sooner had African Americans been freed than white southerners seemed to have found an insidious new way to treat them like chattel: the convict leasing system. Southern states, which incarcerated blacks in record numbers after 1865, began leasing these prisoners out to private employers in mines, railroad yards, and turpentine forests. Many of these private parties tortured black convicts and sometimes worked them literally to death.[7]

Few critics of this practice realized, however, that the system of leasing convicts out to private employers was actually a northern invention that began long before the Civil War. In fact, the demand for convict labor was such an important feature of northern penitentiaries in the antebellum period that politicians went to extraordinary lengths to make sure that prisons met the needs of private companies. When an influenza epidemic gutted the leased-convict labor force at one northern state prison in 1831–1832, for example, the state legislature received a petition from Benjamin Grannis & Son, a shoe company, "praying for relief from the losses sustained as contractors at the prison."[8]

Leased convicts in northern prisons also endured barbaric punishments when employers felt that they were failing to meet production quotas. Officials at the Maine State Prison were so determined to deliver shoes made in their prison shop that a few lone prison employees felt the need to report their bosses' cruel treatment of inmates. According to the testimony of one, Charles G. Chase, the prison confined inmate Albert Peters to the dungeon for not working hard enough, and he then "had a ball and chain put on him" that caused him to die.[9] The prison's night watchman, Sylvester B. Hahn, reported that officials ordered other convicts who failed to produce enough to be locked indefinitely in so-called lazy cells and to be given no water during their stay there. Hahn was particularly haunted by the vision of these prisoners in the lazy cells sticking out their raw and swollen tongues to show him how desperately thirsty they were.[10]

A key reason that convict leasing became such a fixture in the postbellum South was that the northern capitalists who underwrote a large percentage of that region's infrastructure projects thought it the best way to secure a massive amount of labor quickly and cheaply. Recruiting immigrant laborers to the region would have been another possibility, but northern businessmen knew firsthand the potential perils of employing union-savvy foreigners, and they made it clear to their southern counterparts that labor unrest was the last thing any of them wanted. While the white southerners who sought to modernize their region in the wake of the Civil War swiftly embraced the idea of leasing prisoners out to private companies, and clearly relished the ways in which this labor system reinforced white supremacy in the region, they nevertheless were largely following the lead of northern venture capitalists who were already familiar with the economic benefits of utilizing a captive workforce.[11]

As practiced in the South, convict leasing turned out to be a much uglier affair than it ever was in the North. The sheer number of men who died while working for private companies in the South reveals that the practice took particularly brutal forms in that region. And yet, the fact that white southerners previously had embraced chattel slavery does not, in itself, offer the best explanation for why convict leasing was so particularly deadly in the region. While the southern turpentine industry netted far more casualties than did northern shoe shops, an exceptionalism explanation for this comparative reality tends to obscure the most significant reasons that convict leasing was particularly devastating for prison populations in states such as Florida and Alabama. What really was unique about convict leasing in the South was the nature of the labor that employers required convicts to do, and how many of them were needed to do it, as this region sought to rebuild and to modernize itself.[12]

Building entire railroad systems, excavating dangerous mines, and tapping trees for turpentine required many more workers than did producing machine parts or garments. Forced labor in the swamps of Florida, in the coal caverns of Tennessee, or on the railroad tracks of North Carolina clearly represented a much more treacherous proposition than did toiling in a northern manufacturing facility. But the paths that conscripted labor took in southern and northern states were a difference of form but not necessarily of substance. For those inmates in the North who died after being "strapped to the floor of their cells for three weeks at a time without being released for any purpose," or after enduring "that relic of the Spanish Inquisition, suspension by the hands," or from other "cruel punishments inflicted," even small-scale convict leasing proved to be far more barbaric than the region's significantly lower fatality rate implied.[13]

States in both the South and the North began to move away from the practice of leasing convicts to private companies at the end of the nineteenth century. In the South, nonconvict workers increasingly spoke out against the inmate labor contracts entered into by employers and state governments, which took paying jobs and living wages away from the regular workforce.[14] As a result of labor activism by wage workers, including dramatic confrontations with employers in states such as Tennessee, southern states largely had abandoned convict leasing by the turn of the century.[15] The labor movement also severely curtailed the practice of leasing convicts out to private employers in the North. In 1929, union leaders and small manufacturing interests pressured Congress to pass the Hawes-Cooper Convict Labor Act, which gave states the power to keep prisoner-made products off the shelves of their local stores. With the collapse of the entire U.S. economy in the 1930s, even the federal government had a significant interest in keeping convicts from working, and Congress passed two more laws that placed additional restrictions on the use of prisoner labor across the country.[16]

What followed convict leasing in the South, however, hardly secured that region a more favorable national reputation. In the 1920s, white southern leaders increasingly embraced an even more public and degrading way to exploit their overwhelmingly black inmate population, and simultaneously to earn the moralistic scorn of their northern counterparts: the chain gang. The sight of southern prisoners chained together in striped uniforms, forced to labor in the baking sun, seemed to provide a seamless connection to antebellum slave society and a visibly modern representation of white supremacy. In 1932, Warner Brothers took moviegoers into the netherworld of the southern penal system with a gritty melodrama, *I Am a Fugitive from a Chain Gang*. The film capitalized on a new spirit of penal reform in the North and contributed to the popular equation of chain gangs with the spectacle of racial degradation. Notably, even the chain gang was not a southern invention, as it had first surfaced in the North during the 1700s.[17] Still, in the twentieth century, northern states did not utilize this form of forced labor, and it therefore became synonymous with "the bigotry and racism that prevailed in the Old South."[18] The fact that the labor exploitation of inmates in northern prisons was much more invisible meant far less public scrutiny and concern in that region.

Equally important in terms of public opinion, northern prison reformers during the early 1900s seemed genuinely committed to introducing meaningful rehabilitation programs in their penal facilities. In 1932, a prison commission in the state of New York called for "academic instruction" for convicts that would include the "eradication of illiteracy" and the teaching of skills necessary to function in mainstream society.[19] But even the most well-intentioned prison reforms in the North were routinely undermined by everyday and egregious acts of barbarism against the inmates who were supposed to benefit from them. Perhaps the worst Depression-era incident occurred in 1938, after inmates at the Holmesburg prison in Pennsylvania began a hunger strike to protest their deplorable conditions. Prison officials broke the strike and placed four alleged ringleaders into "the Klondike," a small brick punishment unit lined with a bank of radiators that they then turned on full blast. The four men "cooked to death in a simulated oven," according to an exposé of the Pennsylvania "torture chamber."[20]

Prisoners did not necessarily fare better when confined inside northern institutions rather than being chained to one another in the South. This was particularly true of black inmates. Although white northerners did not have Jim Crow laws to bolster their practices, there is little question that they were also deeply invested in the defense of white privilege and power, and their criminal justice systems continued to reflect that commitment. The gap between the rhetoric of reform and the realities of prison practice became clear to increasing numbers of black southerners who took part in the Great Migration and then found themselves dealing with northern-style justice. In 1933, a black man named Romaine Johnson was hounded while locked inside a New Jersey jail by "a crowd of 500 persons" that had assembled and "threatened to lynch the prisoner."

Even though state officials held the mob at bay, to Johnson the shouts and jeers filling the air were as horrifying in this northern state as they would have been in any southern locale.[21] That same year, a white prison guard murdered James Matthews, an African-American inmate from New York, by kicking and punching him for being "too sick to work at an assigned task."[22] But unlike the inmates paraded before the public on the southern chain gang, prisoners such as Johnson and Matthews drew little attention, and the northern idea that southern justice was uniquely barbaric grew even more entrenched during the twentieth century.

Although the institution of slavery followed by the practices of convict leasing and chain gangs had each done its part to make northerners believe that the South was exceptional in the area of crime and punishment, the stories that came out of the region during the 1960s particularly served to cement this view. The events of that decade focused the attention of many Americans, from the grassroots to the federal levels, on the eradication of the racial discrimination that plagued the educational institutions and public spaces of the South. In the process, southern penal practices, almost accidentally, came under a new kind of scrutiny.

Ironically, it was because segregationist leaders decided to deal with the new reform spirit of the civil rights era by locking up anyone who dared criticize the South's politics of white supremacy that the southern criminal justice system received more attention than ever before. After Mississippi officials imprisoned prominent civil rights leaders such as Stokely Carmichael and James Farmer in the state's notorious Parchman Farm, for example, the NAACP and a group called the Lawyers' Committee for Civil Rights under the Law decided to conduct interviews with scores of other inmates being held there. Activists had heard horror stories while in prison, and the civil rights groups were shocked by what they learned. One "fourteen-year-old black youth who had been serving ninety days for shoplifting," for example, "had been shot in the face by a trustee, . . . causing total blindness and permanent brain damage." An adult inmate, George Humes, had been "handcuffed to bars, on tiptoes for 2 days without food, water, or bathroom facilities," while another named Walter Nathan had been "handcuffed and hung from tree." Equally as disturbing, a Parchman guard, J. D. Gilmer, had forced prisoner Donald Waldie "to maintain a mid-suspended position which one assumes during the course of doing push-ups" while shooting bullets "above or below him if he moved."[23]

The accounts from Parchman were bad enough, but the reports from Arkansas were arguably even worse. Tom Murton, a former criminology professor and the acting Chief of Corrections in Alaska, came to Arkansas in 1967 to run two of its most notorious prison farms that sat together on a huge tract of state land: Cummins and Tucker. Conditions on these farms were so brutal that Governor Orval Faubus, an outspoken segregationist, felt compelled to order a formal inquiry that was completed in 1966. The findings by the state's Criminal Investigation Division were so horrific, however, that Faubus decided to keep the report under wraps until 1967, when his successor, the reform-minded Winthrop Rockefeller, was ready to assume office. Rather than crumbling under the weight of the prison farm scandal, as his opponents hoped, Rockefeller instead decided to hire Murton to overhaul the Arkansas criminal justice system from the ground up.[24]

Although Murton was optimistic that he could reform these two prison farms, when he arrived at the 21,000-acre complex on which they sat, he

FIGURE 3.1. A black inmate in 1968, walking on a makeshift crutch at Cummins State Farm in Arkansas, which became a national symbol of the "barbaric" South. Prison reformer Tom Murton chronicled the brutal treatment and corruption scandals in the Arkansas penitentiary system in the best-selling expose *Accomplices to the Crime* (1969), which inspired the Robert Redford film *Brubaker* (1980). © JP Laffont/Sygma/CORBIS.

was taken aback by how frozen in time it seemed (figure 3.1). To Murton, it appeared that "slavery was never really abolished in Arkansas."[25] Not only was the warden's dwelling still called "the Big House," but the prison guards reveled in the personal customs and punishment practices of the antebellum era with impunity. As one Tucker guard told Murton, "you may know quite a bit about penology, but you have a lot to learn about Arki-ology." When Murton pressed the guard about what he meant, he explained that the prisoners and culture in the state were different from other places. As the guard put it, "There's no logic to us'ns.... Arkies are tough and we think different from other folk."[26] Thus, from his first day at Tucker Farm, Murton interpreted virtually everything he heard and saw as the product of a slavery-scarred past.

Seeing the conditions at Tucker Farm through this lens seemed to help Murton, a seasoned professional, to make sense of prison horrors that exceeded any he had previously witnessed. At the Tucker and Cummins farms, the most violent and aggressive inmates actually ran the institutions and made sure that other prisoners worked from dawn to dusk in the fields without rest. Of course, the southern plantation owners of the previous century also had used particularly brutal men to drive production in the fields, and so the use of trustee guards made some kind of sense to Murton. These prison farms also had actual "overseers" responsible for disciplining anyone whom they felt was not working hard enough. These modern-day overseers used everything from "Black Annie" (a thick strapped whip) to the notorious "Tucker Telephone" (with live electric wires to be attached to inmates' genitals) to keep their captive workforce in line.[27]

Murton devoted much of his first year as the new warden to improving conditions at Tucker Farm, and he was slated to take over Cummins Farm and head up a new Department of Corrections the following year. But many Arkansas residents and state officials soon tired of his reformist zeal, which made Governor Rockefeller increasingly lukewarm toward Murton's plans to modernize the penal farms. When Murton decided to investigate inmate rumors that there were actually dead bodies buried at Tucker—ostensibly murdered by trustee guards or line overseers—Rockefeller dramatically distanced himself from the reformer he had hired so enthusiastically less than a year earlier. When Murton, surrounded by reporters from across the United States, then dug up three bodies, the governor fired him.[28]

By 1969, Murton had written a graphic account of his time in Arkansas, *Accomplices to the Crime*, and northern readers were flocking to buy his sensational memoir. As a result of his revelations, as well as those brought to light by civil rights activists during the same period, the northern fascination with southern crime and punishment, and the widespread belief that the South was the nation's most sadistic region, reached an all-time high. Barbaric practices certainly abounded in southern prisons during this period, and these institutions still borrowed much from the language and punishment styles of the region's past. And yet, as in earlier decades, even a cursory look at what was happening in northern prisons in the 1960s should have raised serious questions about the uniqueness of the brutality that flourished in southern penal institutions.

Sociologist Bruce Jackson was one of many who had been stunned by the abuses that took place in southern prisons. In fact, Jackson gained firsthand knowledge when he conducted extensive research at the infamous Louisiana State Penitentiary at Angola in 1968. Jackson also decided to visit a number of penal institutions in the North. After seeing prisons at work in both regions, he was no less appalled by how cruelly the South treated its inmates, but, he pointed out, "so does the North, and no one likes to talk about it." In Jackson's view, the Massachusetts Correctional Institution at Bridgewater was "one of the most wretched" prisons in the country, the "worst place" he had "visited, North or South." While touring this New England prison, Jackson happened upon one building "with row on row of door-lined corridors, and board floors and brick walls. Every few feet there was a wooden door braced shut by a beam and a Judas-hole to peek through. Some of the rooms had a bed and a pan, none had running water, some had nothing at all but a naked man wrapped in an army blanket." One of these men, he later learned, had been there since the age of seven for the crime of running away from home. He was now sixty years old.[29]

The Massachusetts Correctional Institution was by no means the only place where northern prison brutality flourished in the 1960s. Although media attention zeroed in almost exclusively on the South, African-American inmates in Philadelphia were routinely used for a series of medical experiments that, for any other population, would have been deemed outrageous. Officials at the Holmesburg Prison—inspired by the successes of medical experimentation on the insane and the incarcerated in other states, such as Ohio, Michigan, and California—had granted the University of Pennsylvania Medical School carte blanche with its wards since the 1950s. During the Vietnam War, the concentration of large numbers of test subjects at Holmesburg Prison attracted additional researchers from pharmaceutical and chemical companies and the U.S. Department of Defense. According to the official photographer for Dr. Albert Kligman, one of Holmesburg's primary experimenters, "They were just preying on people. Using an inmate was cheaper than buying a chimpanzee, and the results were better."[30] Since inmates were usually desperate to make money for bail or to buy soap from the commissary, they made easy victims.

To many inmates at Holmesburg, $10 for every twenty-four-hour period of injections with previously untested "mind control" drugs, or $35 each time they agreed to immerse their testicles in radioactive liquid for a few hours a month, was a "king's ransom." But no amount of money could undo the severe medical and psychological damage caused by some of these prison experiments. After enduring mind-control tests run by the U.S. Army, one inmate reported that "guys came back to population and didn't remember their names. Guys would fade in and out of consciousness....Some guys beat themselves up and punched themselves in the head. Some of the guys told me they had violent, ugly trips. Being eaten by giant spiders, living in the 13th century. One guy said he was hung and killed."[31] Perhaps the most barbaric experiments at Holmesburg were conducted at the behest of Dow Chemical Corporation, which contracted with Dr. Kligman in 1965 to test Dioxin, later disclosed to be the central ingredient in Agent Orange. Neither the company nor the doctor seemed troubled by the fact that they conducted this testing disproportionately on African-American inmates ("47 to 9 in the first protocol"), or by the fact that the scientists told these human subjects they were testing "skin softeners."[32]

So absorbed was the nation by the horror stories coming out of southern prisons in this period that few Americans even bothered to ask what might also be going on in northern penal institutions such as Holmesburg. At the same time, there was a real upside to the single-minded focus of national attention on the barbarism of the southern criminal justice system, particularly for those imprisoned in the region. By the 1960s, tales of southern abuse and racial backwardness no longer simply made white northerners feel smug about how comparatively enlightened they were. Instead, the tales told by reformers such as Tom Murton motivated key reforms to this regional bastion of brutality.

Because so much new light shone on the southern criminal justice system in the 1960s, civil rights activists were able to secure significant legal breakthroughs in the area of prisoner rights, building on their successful judicial attack against Jim Crow segregation laws. Not coincidentally, several of the most important legal cases of the decade, which dramatically improved life for inmates across the South, stemmed directly from the gruesome revelations from Tucker and Cummins Farms in Arkansas and Parchman Farm in Mississippi.

After the Murton exposé brought attention to their cause, and with the help of a group of northern attorneys, Arkansas inmates filed a lawsuit against the state correctional system. In *Holt v. Sarver* (1969), District Judge J. Smith Henley declared that the Arkansas prison system had "failed to discharge a constitutional duty" to protect the inmates under its care and to ensure that they might have the most basic protection to "fall asleep at night without fear of having their throats cut before morning," and he instructed the system to reform itself. In 1970, after the state made insufficient progress in complying with the initial *Holt* ruling, Judge Henley placed the entire prison system under an injunctive order and forbade it from acting independently of the court until such time as it could manage itself. Judicial supervision ultimately led to a complete overhaul of the Tucker and Cummins prison farms.[33]

The *Holt* rulings provided an important precedent for inmates in many states beyond Arkansas. According to a legal analysis, "beginning with *Holt v. Sarver*, federal courts found prisons or entire prison systems violative of the cruel and unusual punishments clause, and broad remedial orders directed to improving prison conditions and ameliorating prison life were imposed in more than two dozen States."[34] And just as the attention that Murton brought to Tucker and Cummins led to a landmark prisoner rights decision, the brutality at Parchman Farm eventually resulted in a number of significant legal victories for the prisoner rights movement.

In *Anderson v. Nosser* (1971), a federal court found that Parchman's superintendent had violated the Eighth Amendment's ban on cruel and unusual punishment and made it clear that such abuses would no longer be tolerated. As one judge reprimanded the prison officials: "We deal with human beings not dumb driven cattle."[35] The second major Parchman case, *Gates v. Collier* (1972), led to an equally important indictment of the barbaric treatments meted out by Mississippi prison officials. Armed with powerful statements from inmates, lawyers were able to prove that countless "murders, rapes, beatings, and tortures" had taken place at Parchman between 1969 and 1971. The evidence against Mississippi's prison system proved so overwhelming that when the plaintiffs' attorneys compiled every account of abuse they had gathered into one document for the court, it ran "to more than fifty single-spaced pages."[36]

The birth of a committed penal reform movement in the 1960s should have been good news for all of America's prisoners, including those locked in institutions outside of the South. And to the extent that northern and western inmates benefited from legal precedents set in southern cases such as *Holt v. Sarver*, it definitely was. Even if the media took far less note of it, northern prisoners also filed a number of critically important lawsuits on their own behalf in the 1960s and 1970s. But whenever northern inmates tried to wage a more public fight to reform their penal institutions, most notably by launching civil rights protests within them, they got nowhere. Indeed, the staying power of the southern exceptionalism paradigm not only ensured that northern prison officials would be immunized from public scrutiny and condemnation but also virtually guaranteed that northern inmates would have no support—and, indeed, would face substantial backlash—when they tried to improve the way that officials ran their facilities.

The nation's commitment to penal reform was seriously tested when northern inmates began demonstrating that deep-seated racism, unconscionable neglect, and outright cruelty were not the problem of southern prisons alone. Most Americans were indisposed to seeing northern prisoners as victims of ill treatment and therefore were suspicious of, if not outright hostile toward, their motives whenever they decided to protest. The fact that poor urban minorities had become increasingly outspoken during the 1960s, and had been arguing that they suffered mistreatment at the hands of police officers and discriminatory employers and lenders, made many white northerners fear that they were becoming the victims of some larger left-wing or "Black Power" plot to destabilize mainstream American society. As one white man opined about African Americans in Detroit, "the blacks won't be satisfied until they get complete control of our country by force if necessary."[37] Thus, in the 1960s and early 1970s, whenever northern inmates sought to improve their conditions by using the same strategy that had worked for prisoners in the South—that of simply getting the word out regarding how bad things really were—they netted extraordinary repression.

In 1969, the same year that Tom Murton published his exposé of Arkansas, fifty inmates at the Bridgeport Correction Center tried to call attention to the deplorable medical care that sick prisoners received from the state of Connecticut. For their troubles, they received a one-inch column mention in the *New York Times*, and then only after correctional officials mobilized a battalion of extra guards and a contingent of the Connecticut State Police to storm the prison and lock the inmates down.[38] Later that summer, when two-thirds of Holmesburg Prison's 1,325 inmates launched a hunger strike in an effort to attract publicity to serious problems there, their cries for support also secured little more than a brief mention by the media and an unsympathetic response from prison administrators.[39]

Northern inmates nevertheless clung to the hope that, if Americans just knew about the conditions that they endured, then the public would demand reforms. In 1971, this was exactly what 2,500 men at one of New York State's most infamous maximum security prisons, the Attica State Correctional Facility, were counting on. The inmates at Attica never had enough food, clothing, or even toilet paper, and to get what they needed, they were forced to hustle and barter in ugly and exploitive ways. For the black inmates, the conditions were particularly bad. Attica employed no black guards, and the poorly trained and jaded white correction officers sometimes dished out racial epithets as well as beatings when they became frustrated.[40] The state-issued baton carried by every Attica guard was known throughout the prison as a "Nigger stick." Finally, as was the common case in southern penal institutions, Attica's doctors were openly dismissive of inmates' medical complaints and particularly minimized the sufferings of African-American and Puerto Rican prisoners. The health of sick inmates deteriorated because prison physicians viewed them as manipulators and malingerers, and at least one inmate died in his cell in 1969 after doctors disregarded his medical complaints as fabrications.[41]

In early summer 1971, a group of Attica's inmates decided to try to publicize their own story, largely because of inspiration by the activism erupting in urban centers as well as by the pathbreaking legal cases coming out of places such as Arkansas and Mississippi. African-American inmate Herbert Blyden wrote a detailed letter to John Dunne, chairman of the New York State Senate Committee on Crime and Correction, asking for an investigation of Attica that would bring reforms to the facility. But the hoped-for inquiry, let alone improvements, never came. Undaunted, another group of inmates wrote a letter to the new state commissioner of corrections, Russell Oswald, who had a reputation for being sympathetic to inmate needs. Attica's prisoners assured Commissioner Oswald that they merely wanted him "to be aware of our needs and the need for prison reform," and they also stressed that they wanted to achieve such improvements "in a democratic manner." They specifically asked for "legal representation before the Parole Board; improvement in medical care, visiting facilities, food and sanitary conditions in the mess hall, personal hygiene, clothing, recreational facilities, and working conditions in the shops; a uniform set of rules in all prisons; adjustment of commissary prices."[42]

After months of waiting resulted in little more than the vague promise that Oswald would look into their concerns, inmate Frank Lott sent a final letter to the commissioner on August 16, 1971. Sounding desperate, he wrote that "we are anxiously awaiting your evaluation of our manifesto. I realize that you are a busy man, T.V. and all that, but I do hope that you will drop me a few lines and let me know what is happening."[43] But neither Commissioner Oswald nor New York's governor, Nelson Rockefeller, was eager to respond to Attica's prisoners or their grievances, as they suspected the former to be Black Nationalists and white leftist troublemakers and the latter to be red herrings for a broader revolutionary agenda.[44] Ultimately, no state official took sufficient steps to defuse the crisis that was clearly brewing at the Attica State Correctional Facility.

Frustration bubbled over on the morning of September 9, 1971, after an altercation the night before between guards and two inmates that had left every prisoner unnerved and jumpy. A full-scale riot began when a small group of Attica's inmates broke free of corrections officers. Within hours the majority of prisoners were in control of the facility and had taken forty-two men, a mix of guards and prison employees, hostage. By mid-morning, these inmates had gathered in one of the main exercise areas known as D Yard, and from that point forward the riot became a rebellion. Although the riot had been spontaneous, prisoners quickly realized that they had an extraordinary opportunity to call national and even international attention to what life was like behind bars at this northern prison. And indeed, by the end of the day every major television network was broadcasting live from Attica. It was hard to ignore this particular inmate protest, not only because of the hostage taking but also because this time prisoners had demanded that reporters cover their cause. Over four days, a parade of unknown, overwhelmingly black men took to the megaphone and broadcast their grievances, loud and clear. Their demands for more humane treatment were transmitted to homes around the country, and Americans could no longer pretend that everything was just fine in the prisons of the North.[45]

Viewers at home could, however, decide that any problems facing penal institutions such as Attica had been largely created by the inmates themselves, men who had little to complain about but wanted nevertheless to further a radical agenda. Pleas for better prison conditions never provided Attica's inmates with the sympathy enjoyed by their counterparts locked up in the South. Quite the opposite. In the early hours of September 13, Governor Rockefeller approved the forcible retaking of the prison by more than five hundred New York state troopers, and scores of corrections officers joined in the assault. Attica became a bloodbath over the course of ten frenzied minutes that morning, as these heavily armed men shot more than 2,500 hollow-tipped and deer-slug bullets down into the confines of the 50- by 50-yard enclosure where inmates and hostages alike had congregated. When the smoke cleared, thirty-nine people lay dead or dying (ten of whom were hostages), and almost a hundred others had been severely wounded (figure 3.2).[46]

Even if mainstream Americans had been hostile toward, or even skeptical of, the inmates at Attica during their protest, the sheer brutality of the state's assault on the prison might well have generated some substantial sympathy on their behalf—at least as much as the unarmed inmates at Cummins and Tucker Farms had enjoyed when correctional personnel shot and killed them. But it did not. Instead, the public looked to New York state officials to explain what had gone so wrong at Attica. The officials responsible for ordering the assault stood in front of the prison and announced that all of the hostages had died because inmates had slit their throats, that some of the hostages had been killed days earlier, and that an inmate had cut off one hostage's penis and stuffed it into his mouth. Within hours, the front pages of the *New York Times*, the *Los Angeles Times*, and countless other newspapers across the nation ran this version of events. The Attica uprising revealed "a barbarism wholly alien to civilized society," recounted the *New York Times*. "Prisoners slashed the throats of utterly helpless, unarmed guards [as they] held out for an increasingly revolutionary set of demands."[47]

Within a few days, a local coroner who performed autopsies on all of the dead hostages corrected this distorted account of the Attica riot and made clear that each had been killed by troopers rather than prisoners. His findings, however, seemed to make little difference to those who already had decided that the inmates were to blame for the ugliness at Attica. The harsh reality was that even before troopers stormed the prison,

FIGURE 3.2. September 13, 1971: at the end of a four-day rebellion, inmates at the Attica state prison in New York lie on the ground at left, while others stand stripped for search at right. Earlier in the day, Governor Nelson Rockefeller ordered state troopers to retake the prison by force. Thirty-nine people died in the assault, and subsequent investigations determined that the police began firing on the prisoners four minutes before issuing an appeal that they surrender. © Bettmann/CORBIS.

the public seriously doubted northern inmates' claims of bad treatment, and even after so many prisoners had been wounded or killed by trooper bullets, many Americans assumed that these criminals must have done something to deserve what they got. Attica's inmates had not suffered at the hands of southern racists or faced penal practices that harkened back to slavery. Thus, they must have caused problems in a place where none existed. As one California resident, W. T. Combs, declared in a telegram to Attica's warden on September 14, "there should have been no surviving inmates after the cellblock was cleared."[48]

The long-held belief that the South's criminal justice system was uniquely racist and brutal, because of the legacy left by slavery and continued by Jim Crow segregation, mattered well beyond the specific prison protests that erupted in the North during the 1960s and 1970s. The fact that most Americans understood the barbaric treatment of inmates through the lens of regional exceptionalism proved very costly, not only to those locked in northern prisons but, eventually, to southern inmates as well. By the end of the 1970s, the judicial branch had been monitoring southern states and reforming the policies of their penal institutions for almost a full decade with notable results. And by the 1980s, such judicial activism south of the Mason-Dixon line had led most Americans to believe that the problem of inmate abuse in the United States was solved. The South, having finally thrown off the shackles of its slave past, now ran modern penal institutions that, by definition, no longer needed special scrutiny or intervention.

The problem, however, was that modernizing prisons did not necessarily humanize them. In fact, in the wake of the penal reform efforts that brought needed attention to the South, an even more powerful "law and order" fever gripped the nation as a whole.[49] By the 1980s, legislators were passing much tougher laws, judges were mandating much longer sentences, and politicians and prison officials were attempting to abolish incentives like parole altogether. The consequences of this new and seemingly endless "war on crime" were vast. Not only did the nation's justice system become much more punitive, but its prison population grew at an explosive rate. By the close of the twentieth century, the United States was incarcerating a larger percentage of its citizenry than any other country in the world. Indeed, even before the first decade of the twenty-first century had ended, over 7 million Americans were living behind bars or were on parole or on probation.[50]

In key ways, the "get tough on crime" sentiment that came of age in the final decades of the twentieth century was a return to a much earlier era. Once again, penologists as well as politicians were touting the necessity for, and societal merits of, locking prisoners up in complete isolation for twenty-four hours a day—this time in futuristic supermax prisons for the duration of their sentence. Despite the fact that national as well as international human rights organizations routinely condemned supermax prisons as barbaric, every state had built at least one by the start of the twenty-first century, and most were planning to construct even more. It is no secret that such institutions rely heavily on sensory deprivation as well as physical abuse to control their inmate populations, but even when those nightmarish places were opened in the South, there was no public outcry.[51]

The ultimate irony for the history of modern penal reform was that the more like the North that the South became the more comfortable the nation was letting the states of that region, like those everywhere else in the country, do pretty much as they pleased with their own penal systems. Given the North's very real, albeit largely hidden, history of dehumanizing prisoners and treating them with serious cruelty, this regional convergence is not at all good news.

NOTES

1. Robert E. Burns, *I Am a Fugitive from a Georgia Chain Gang!* (Athens: University of Georgia Press, 1997 [reprint of 1932 edition]); Thomas O. Murton and Joe Hyams, *Accomplices to the Crime: The Arkansas Prison Scandal* (New York: Grove Press, 1969).

2. Edward L. Ayers, *Vengeance and Justice: Crime and Punishment in the Nineteenth-Century American South* (New York: Oxford University Press, 1984); Mary Ellen Curtin, *Black Prisoners and their World, Alabama, 1865–1900* (Charlottesville: University Press of Virginia, 2000); Alex Lichtenstein, *Twice the Work of Free Labor: The Political Economy of Convict Labor in the New South* (New York: Verso, 1996); David M. Oshinsky, *Worse than Slavery: Parchman Farm and the Ordeal of Jim Crow Justice* (New York: Free Press, 1996); Karin Shapiro, *A New South Rebellion: The Battle Against Convict Labor in the Tennessee Coalfields, 1871–1896* (Chapel Hill: University of North Carolina Press, 1998).

3. On the inability of white southerners to escape the social practices of the slave past, see, in particular, Ayers, *Vengeance and Justice*; Oshinsky, *Worse than Slavery*.

4. Norman Johnson, with Kenneth Finkel and Jeffrey Cohen, *Eastern State Penitentiary: Crucible of Good Intentions* (Philadelphia: University of Pennsylvania Press, 1994), 61.

5. Charles Dickens, *American Notes* (1842), 120. Online version edited by John Lance Griffith, 1996, http://xroads.virginia.edu/~HYPER/DICKENS/titlepg.html.

6. "Minutes of the Testimony Taken before John Q. Wilson, Joseph Eaton, and Morris Woodruff, Committee from the General Assembly, to inquire into the condition of Connecticut State Prison Together with their Report and Remarks upon the Same" (Hartford, Conn., 1834), reprint edition by Arno Press (New York: 1974), 47–49.

7. See Lichtenstein, *Twice the Work of Free Labor*, for a persuasive argument that the New South was built on the foundation of convict labor.

8. "Minutes of the Testimony Taken before John Q. Wilson," 5.

9. *Report of the Joint Special Committee on the Investigation of the Affairs of the Maine State Prison* (Augusta, Maine: Sprague, Owen and Nash, 1874), reprint by Arno Press (New York: 1974), 66.

10. Ibid., 87.

11. Lichtenstein, *Twice the Work of Free Labor*.

12. For more data on the extraordinary death and injury toll of convict leasing in the South see Lichtenstein, *Twice the Work of Free Labor*; Curtin, *Black Prisoners and their World*.

13. Henry Elmer Barnes, *A History of the Penal, Reformatory and Correctional Institutions of the State of New Jersey: Analytical and Documentary* (Trenton, N.J.: MacCrellish and Quigley, 1918), reprint by Arno Press (New York: 1974), 133.

14. Shapiro, *New South Rebellion.*

15. For more on the dramatic labor actions against convict leasing in Tennessee, see Shapiro, *New South Rebellion.*

16. The Hawes-Cooper Act, Public Law 669, 70th Congress (1929); Henry Bartow Hawes, *Power of Congress To Protect State Laws: Two Unanimous Supreme Court Decisions Defining Federal Authority under Interstate Commerce Clause. The Laws and Briefs of Counsel Prevailing in Test of Federal and State Convict-Labor Statutes* (Washington: W. F. Roberts Co., 1938); The Ashurst-Sumner Act, Public Law 215, 74th Congress (1935); Hermon Murphey, *Regulation of Conditions of Employment under the Walsh-Healey Act* (New York: National Industrial Conference Board, 1936).

17. Marylee Reynolds, "Back on the Chain Gang," *Corrections Today* (April 1996).

18. Ibid.

19. New York (State) Commission on Prison Administration and Construction, *An Educational Program for New York State's Penal System: Special Report by Commission to Investigate Prison Administration and Construction* (New York: January 1932), 24.

20. Allen M. Hornblum, *Acres of Skin: Human Experiments at Holmesburg Prison: A True Story of Abuse and Exploitation in the Name of Medical Science* (London: Routledge, 1998), 31.

21. "Jersey Lynching Averted," *New York Times*, August, 31, 1935.

22. "Prisoner's Death," *New York Times*, September 14, 1933.

23. Oshinsky, *Worse than Slavery*, 238, 243.

24. Murton and Hyams, *Accomplices to the Crime.*

25. Ibid., 43.

26. Ibid., 28.

27. Ibid.

28. Ibid.

29. Bruce Jackson, "Our Prisons are Criminal," *New York Times*, September 22, 1968.

30. Hornblum, *Acres of Skin*, 24.

31. Ibid., 7.

32. Ibid., 166, 171, 172.

33. As quoted in Bruce Jackson, *Killing Time: Life in the Arkansas Penitentiary* (Cornell University Press, 1977), 22. Also see *Holt v. Sarver*, 300 F. Supp. 825 (1969); *Holt v. Sarver*, 309 F. Supp. 362 (1970).

34. Find Law: Guide to Government, "U.S. Constitution: Eighth Amendment," http://conlaw.usatoday.findlaw.com/constitution/amendment08/08.html.

35. Oshinsky, *Worse than Slavery*, 238–39; *Anderson v. Nosser*, 438 F.2d 183, 205 (1971).

36. Oshinsky, *Worse than Slavery*, 252; *Gates v. Collier*, 501 F. 2d 1291 (1972). Regarding *Gates v. Collier*, Oshinsky notes that "never before had the federal government intervened in a prison reform case on the state level," 241.

37. Joel D. Aberbach and Jack L. Walker, "The Meanings of Black Power: A Comparison of White and Black Interpretations of a Political Slogan," *American Political Science Review*, 64, no. 2 (June 1970), 64.

38. "Prison Protest in Bridgeport," *New York Times*, July 1, 1969.

39. "Hunger Strike in Prison," *New York Times*, June 3, 1969.

40. Interview with former Attica guard John Stockholm by author, July 1, 2005, Lehigh Acres, Florida.

41. Handwritten note from guard BJ Conway, on file at the Attica State Correctional Facility, Attica, New York.

42. *Attica: The Official Report of the New York State Special Commission on Attica* (New York: Praeger, 1972), 135, 134.

43. Ibid., 110.

44. On Oswald's suspicions of Attica inmates' grievances, see Russell Oswald, *Attica: My Story* (New York: Doubleday, 1972), 40. For Rockefeller's suspicions, see speech draft in Folder 3471: 9/2471, "New York State Bar Association. Dedication of New Center. Albany, N.Y., Friday September 24, 1971," Nelson Aldride Rockefeller Papers, Research Group 15, Series 33: Speeches, Box 85, Rockefeller Archive Center, Pocantico Hills, New York.

45. Material on Attica is from the author's forthcoming study of the Attica prison uprising and its legacy, to be published by Pantheon Books. Many other books cover the Attica rebellion in journalistic or memoir form. See, for example, Tom Wicker, *A Time to Die* (New York: Quadrangle Press, 1975); Milton Haynes and Herman Badillo, *A Bill of No Rights: Attica and the American Prison System* (New York: Dutton, 1972); Oswald, *My Story*; Richard X Clark, *The Brothers of Attica* (New York: Links, 1973).

46. There are numerous accounts of the retaking of Attica, including the four listed above. Also see the investigative report by the McKay Commission, *Attica: The Official Report of the New York State Special Commission on Attica* (1972). Much of the horror of the assault did not come to light, however, until the inmates filed civil suit against the State of New York for the role that it had played. This case took almost thirty years to reach resolution, and the court records specifically addressing the retaking are invaluable historical documents.

47. "Massacre at Attica," *New York Times*, September 14, 1971. Also see coverage stating that "nine hostages were killed by inmates" in the *Los Angeles Times*, September 13, 1971.

48. Telegrams on file at the Attica State Correctional Facility, Attica, New York.

49. On the nation's post-1960s "war on crime" and embrace of a much more punitive justice system, see Michael Flamm, *Law and Order: Street Crime, Civil Unrest, and the Crisis of Liberalism in the 1960s* (Columbia University Press, 2007); Jonathan Simon, *Governing Through Crime: How the War on Crime Transformed American Democracy and Created a Culture of Fear* (Oxford University Press, 2007).

50. U.S. Department of Justice, Bureau of Justice Statistics, "Adult Correctional Populations, 1980–2006," http://www.ojp.usdoj.gov/bjs/glance/corr2.htm.

51. Human Rights Watch, "Cold Storage: Super-Maximum Security Confinement in Indiana," (October 1997), 30, http://www.hrw.org/legacy/reports/1997/usind/.

Part II

IMAGINING THE SOUTH

4

MISSISSIPPI AS METAPHOR

Civil Rights, the South, and the Nation in the Historical Imagination

Joseph Crespino

The American South has existed never so much as a literal place than as a figurative one. Yes, it is a location on the map, a collection of states and localities that historically have shared an economic, political, and cultural logic, one that in the nineteenth century was sufficient to lead eleven of those states to secede from the Union and wage the bloodiest and most destructive war that the United States has ever known. Yet that fact says as much about the power of the imagination as it does about the "reality" of the South. The truth of the South as an imagined place always is revealed when one tries to define the edges of the region. Is Texas really southern? It was part of the Confederacy. What about Florida? The panhandle, yes; Miami, no. Oklahoma? It depends. The other great indicator, of course, is race. African Americans have lived in the South for as long as people have discussed such a thing, yet it was only with the civil rights movement that Americans could begin to imagine African Americans as southerners, too.

As an imagined space, the South has long played a key role in how Americans have thought about their nation. Edward Ayers has pointed out that at various moments the South has represented "evil tendencies overcome, mistakes atoned for, progress yet to be made."[1] In the civil rights era, the American South was all of those things and more. It was an iconic space that Americans argued over as a way of making sense of the nation's formal commitment to equality and what that commitment would mean for the country's present and future. Countless Americans who otherwise had no connection to, or interest in, southern politics became wrapped up in the struggle of southern blacks to overturn de jure segregation laws. There were other fights over democracy and equality taking place across the nation in the 1950s and 1960s, yet those that occurred in the South were the quintessential ones—the most dramatic, symbolic and telegenic. The novelist Walker Percy noted this phenomenon in a 1965 review of several books on the South's racial crisis. "There is something wrong with Los Angeles too, but where is it? How does one get hold of it?" Percy wondered. Referring to the Mississippi county where three civil rights workers had been murdered a year earlier, he added, "There is nothing unlocated about [the white racists] of Neshoba County."[2]

There are numerous ways to discuss this imagined South, but no place has seemed more distinctive than Mississippi, the state, at least a portion of which, historian James Cobb has called the "most southern place on earth."[3] The poorest, least industrialized southern state with the highest percentage of African-American residents in the nation, Mississippi has long been imagined as the South on steroids, the South in all of its gothic horror and campy, absurdist charm, the center of what the journalist Robert Sherrill called the "super South," that "nerve strand that has been peeled slick, stretched taut between the poles of Black and White, and twanged."[4]

If Mississippi has been the most southern place on earth, it also has been several other things. At least three distinct tropes involving Mississippi and the nation emerged during the civil rights era. First is the metaphor of Mississippi as a "closed society." This was the title of James Silver's influential book published during Freedom Summer 1964. It was the metaphor of Mississippi exceptionalism, of Mississippi as the singular site of political authoritarianism and racial extremism in 1960s America.[5] Second is the inverse trope of Mississippi as synecdoche, or America as Mississippi Writ Large. In the 1960s, this trope emerged among African Americans in Mississippi and other civil rights activists who saw firsthand the abuses of Mississippi law enforcement and the unwillingness of federal authorities to intervene. It would later be adopted by the New Left, particularly among student activists who volunteered during Mississippi Freedom Summer but subsequently found comparable abuses elsewhere. Finally, there is the metaphor of Mississippi as scapegoat, the favorite trope of southern segregationists who portrayed themselves as the victims of northern hypocrites who heaped the sins of the nation on the heads of white Mississippians while ignoring the racism of their own cities and suburbs. In the 1950s and 1960s, the scapegoat defense was a staple of southern segregationist rhetoric.

Each of these three tropes reveals important aspects about the history and memory of the modern civil rights movement. None is sufficient alone as a description of the forces at work or the stakes involved in the black freedom struggle. Importantly for this volume, however, the trope of

Mississippi as a closed society exemplifies both the contributions and the limitations of a southern exceptionalist framework. The other two tropes—Mississippi as synecdoche and the scapegoat metaphor—challenge the conventional wisdom about Mississippi in the 1950s and 1960s as a place set apart from the rest of America. They cast suspicion, from opposite ends of the political spectrum, on what has become the dominant triumphal narrative of the civil rights era as a period when nonviolent activists used the power of moral persuasion to bring retrograde racist southerners into line with the rest of modern, open America. Considered together, these three tropes reveal the politics implicit in various historical narratives about the southern civil rights movement and how these narratives continue to shape our understanding of the South and the nation.

James Silver's *Mississippi: The Closed Society* was published the day after three civil rights workers disappeared in Neshoba County in June 1964. Silver was an eyewitness to the white racist hysteria that gripped Mississippi from the 1954 *Brown* decision through the mid-1960s. His outspoken denunciation of racial authoritarianism in the state led Mississippi officials to make repeated attempts to have him removed from his position in the History Department at the University of Mississippi. As a historian of the nineteenth-century South, Silver argued that white racial orthodoxy in 1950s Mississippi had a lot in common with the fire-eating radicalism of the 1850s that drove the state to secede from the Union. "It wasn't called propagandizing in those days," Silver wrote, "and the modern totalitarians hadn't refined and classified the Big Lie technique, but ante-bellum Mississippians had swallowed a remarkably unstable mixture of noxious home brews."[6]

Silver framed Mississippi's racial crisis in terms of the South's unique history of rebellion and war. His metaphor of the closed society can be placed alongside other metaphors of that time that viewed civil rights conflicts as the culmination of battles over freedom and equality for African Americans that first began with emancipation. Thus, the federal civil rights legislation of the mid-1960s represented "America's Second Reconstruction." Or, the 1962 showdown between Mississippi Governor Ross Barnett and the Kennedy administration over the enrollment of James Meredith at the University of Mississippi has been called "the last battle of the Civil War" (figure 4.1). Yet Silver's description of authoritarian leaders in Mississippi also resonated with an American public engrossed in the Cold War struggle against that other closed society; charges of totalitarianism, suppression of free speech, and state-directed mind control tactics in Mississippi were also the accusations that sprung to mind when Americans considered the political life of the Soviet Union.[7]

In the summer of 1964, Silver's book appeared on the best-seller lists of the *New York Times* and *Time* because it helped explain a state that seemed

FIGURE 4.1. Ross Barnett, governor of Mississippi from 1960 to 1964, cheering on the Ole Miss Rebels in Jackson on October 6, 1962. The football game took place less than a week after white riots on campus following the enrollment of James Meredith, the first African-American student to attend the University of Mississippi. Barnett, who faced contempt charges for his defiance of federal authorities, personified what the author James Silver referred to as Mississippi's "closed society" during the early 1960s. © Bettmann/CORBIS.

so out of step with the rest of the country. In the early 1960s it was a common view that Mississippi was a land apart. Many Americans outside of Mississippi identified with Phil Ochs's song "Here's To the State of Mississippi," which urged the state to find "another country to be part of." One visiting journalist recalled his sense of relief after he had "slipped across" the Mississippi-Tennessee border to return to his Memphis hotel room. The Syracuse University football team, a participant in the 1965 Sugar Bowl in New Orleans, snubbed the hotel on the Mississippi Gulf Coast where visiting teams traditionally stayed out of fear "for the safety of their Negro players if they came to Mississippi." No act of protest was too small to voice disgust at Mississippi: a man in Berkeley, California, wrote Mississippi officials to inform them that he had refused to buy a chicken at his local grocery marked with the sticker "Raised in Mississippi."[8]

By the time that Silver's book appeared in 1964, public outrage against white racism in Mississippi found expression in what one New York publisher called a "surfeit of books on the civil rights problem." Written by civil rights workers, journalists, and lawyers who traveled the South to cover or assist in the civil rights effort, the books all puzzled over Mississippi's racial peculiarity. The eagerness to consume these accounts of southern racism seemed proportional to the outlandishness of the tales themselves: the more vulgar the racism in Mississippi, the more interesting it was to American readers. This market effect was not lost on Silver. When he found sales of *The Closed Society* flagging, he would wire friends still living in Mississippi with the facetious admonition: "Burn another church."[9]

The closed-society metaphor juxtaposed not only the South with the nation but also the rural Deep South with the moderate urban South. National observers applauded when white leaders in Greensboro, North Carolina, adopted a school desegregation plan that made the city one of the first in the South to desegregate its schools. Similarly, President John Kennedy went to great lengths to praise the moderation of white Atlantans who helped implement a token school desegregation plan in 1961. The conventional wisdom at the time was that white moderates such as these were the key to the region's transformation. The problem in a closed society like Mississippi was that none of the "good white folks" had stepped up to denounce extremism. James Silver, who by 1965 had abandoned his teaching post at Ole Miss at least in part because of the constant harassment he experienced from state officials and hard-line segregationists, was living proof of how dangerous such moderation could be in the Deep South.[10]

Critics of Silver must be mindful of the liberal journalist Ronnie Dugger's admonition: "Holding [Silver] up against ordinary standards of 'book reviewing' is trivial.... As well criticize *Common Sense*, when it came out, for an excess of fervor."[11] Yet by the time *The Closed Society* appeared in 1964, the forces of white racial authoritarianism that had arisen in the aftermath of the *Brown* decision were already in decline. When the revised edition of the book appeared in 1966, the additional chapter, "Revolution Begins in the Closed Society," was more than two-thirds as long as the original text. Silver's account of a closed society resonated with many Americans at a time when the racial crisis still seemed like a southern problem. By decade's end, however, Mississippi racism seemed less like a blight on America's character than a symbol for all that was wrong with the nation. "The ghetto riots of the mid-1960s have weakened public belief in Mississippi's singularity as a rural cancer-spot of bigotry isolated from an urbanizing, progressive America," wrote one reviewer of the 1966 revised edition. "It is now clear that there is a bit of Mississippi in the heart of every metropolis, that the suburbs are still 'closed societies.'" By 1971, Phil Ochs had stopped singing "Here's To the State of Mississippi." He rewrote the song and titled it "Here's To the State of Richard Nixon."[12]

The metaphor of the closed society had an important political impact in the mid-1960s because it helped explain the violent images of white racism that seemed to be pouring out of the Deep South on a daily basis. The failure of the closed society metaphor was not so much in its description of Mississippi, but in the refracted image of America. If Mississippi was a closed society, America was by implication an open one. It was an America committed to a creed of equality and justice, an America whose dilemma was to open up the recalcitrant strongholds of the Deep South, to more fully integrate them into the social and political life of the nation.[13]

Black Mississippians knew better than anyone how closed Mississippi society was, but they held no illusions about white Mississippians being distinctive in their racism. Throughout the early 1960s, African Americans in Mississippi who suffered the economic harassment of the Citizens' Councils or the violent repression of the Klan appealed to federal authorities for help but received very little in return. Civil rights activists who had come to the state to help local African Americans register to vote or achieve basic educational opportunities not afforded by Jim Crow schools were appalled by the federal government's unwillingness to afford basic protections to African Americans who risked their lives in challenging local racists. The exasperation with the callousness of federal officials found expression in a poster that hung in the Mississippi offices of the Student Nonviolent Coordinating Committee (SNCC). "There's a street in Itta Bena called Freedom," it bitterly observed. "There's a town in Mississippi called Liberty. There's a department in Washington called Justice."[14] After the 1964 Democratic National Convention, when the Mississippi Freedom Democratic Party (MFDP) failed to unseat the state's all-white traditional Democratic delegation, this frustration led to disillusionment among many activists. MFDP members had no problem accepting the fact that Mississippi was a closed society; they were quick to add, however, that America was a closed society as well.[15]

An interesting counterpoint to James Silver's *Mississippi: The Closed Society* was published that same year. *The Southern Mystique* (1964) was a collection of essays by Howard Zinn, a white professor at historically black Spelman College in Atlanta and, like Silver, a professional historian who witnessed the South's racial troubles firsthand. The thrust of the essays was an attack on southern exceptionalism, on the idea of that "mysterious and terrible South." When he first came south to teach, Zinn took for granted the uniqueness of the region, its unusual history of slavery and war that had distilled into the peculiar set of Jim Crow laws and social relations. His experience living in the South, however, changed his view. "It's time to clear from our minds that artificial and special mystique, so firmly attached to the Southern white, that has long served as a rationale for pessimism and inaction," Zinn wrote.[16] The inaction was the important point for Zinn. He combated the fatalistic notion that white southerners were beyond the reach of reason, impervious to change. It was the same sensibility that C. Vann Woodward had attacked in *The Strange Career of Jim Crow* (1955), published nearly a decade earlier. Woodward searched for a "usable" southern past, one that showed that strict segregation had not always been the rule in post-emancipation southern society.[17]

Zinn used sociological and psychological evidence to suggest that white southerners could change given the proper circumstances, the right mix of pushes and pulls. He argued that the South's "mystic germs of prejudice" were not so mysterious after all. Zinn also worked closely with members of the Student Nonviolent Coordinating Committee and wrote extensively about them. He was well aware of the growing unrest within the movement about framing racial prejudice as a regional, rather than a national, issue. "The South,... far from being utterly different, is really the essence of the nation," Zinn wrote. The region had merely "taken the national genes and done the most with them. It contains, in concentrated and dangerous form, a set of characteristics which mark the country as a whole."[18]

The Southern Mystique received a muted reception compared to that of Silver's *Closed Society*. Zinn's sociological and psychological evidence seemed naïve to some critics. A recurring complaint was that as an outsider to the region, Zinn simply underestimated the racism of white southerners. The stalwart southern liberal Lillian Smith believed that Zinn presented a "curiously distorted picture of the contemporary South." Racism in the North was a neurosis, Smith wrote; in the South, it was on the order of a psychosis, the root of "terrifying splits, loss of the realities of a democratic government based on law, a regression to primitive thinking and acting."[19] The critic Charles Raines dismissed Zinn's assertions about the similarities between the North and South as evidence that the author "has not experienced the Southern sun from the time of his birth, nor the Southern sense of guilt and defeat as did Faulkner and many others." "The South is different," Raines argued; "its people are different. Practically everything Faulkner, Williams and Wilbur Cash has said, Zinn's argument to the contrary notwithstanding, is true for better or for worse."[20]

Zinn's formulation did not catch on among academic critics and longtime southern liberals, but it reflected a growing consensus among young activists in what would come to be called the New Left. An increasing number of politically active American youths had come to question the image of the innocent America that was implicit in a metaphor such as the closed society. Mississippi was not *sui generis* but, rather, the demented heart of an America gone wrong. This view could be seen most clearly in the student protests that rocked American campuses, beginning with the Berkeley Free Speech Movement in the fall of 1964. Mario Savio was a Freedom Summer volunteer who returned to Berkeley to draw direct parallels between how political power operated in Mississippi and in California.

"The two battlefields may seem quite different to some observers," Savio wrote, "but this is not the case."

> The same rights are at stake in both places—the right to participate
> as citizens in democratic society and the right to due process of law.
> Further, it is a struggle against the same enemy. In Mississippi an
> autocratic and powerful minority rules, through organized violence,
> to suppress the vast, virtually powerless majority. In California, the
> privileged minority manipulates the university bureaucracy to suppress
> the students' political expression. That "respectable" bureaucracy
> masks the financial plutocrats; that impersonal bureaucracy is the
> efficient enemy in a "Brave New World."[21]

Berkeley student activists privately circulated a political cartoon that had been redrawn from one originally created in Mississippi. The image showed two men, one dressed as a Klansman and the other as an overweight good old boy draped in a Confederate flag. In the original, the good old boy was depicted as raping a blindfolded female figure meant to represent Justice. In the Berkeley version, the two male figures were recast, one wearing an academic cap and gown and the other representing university president Clark Kerr.[22]

The writer Godfrey Hodgson later posited a formula that synthesized the political ideology of the emerging New Left: "Berkeley equals Mississippi equals Vietnam." Policemen in Berkeley who hauled off nonviolent demonstrators resembled the storm troopers of the Mississippi Highway Patrol. White student activists could imagine themselves as disenfranchised African Americans, and university administrators as racist administrators defending the old guard. Berkeley protesters followed the example of civil rights leaders in discussing a boycott on Mississippi. They began to talk about university investments in corporations such as Mississippi Power and Light, investments that were propping up the racist regime, before they moved on to talking about university investments in the tools of war. In this formulation, Mississippi was the imaginative ground, the political primer for the radical movements that were to come in the 1960s.[23]

The trope of America as Mississippi Writ Large did not begin at Berkeley in 1964. For example, it was at the center of C. Vann Woodward's analysis of American racial politics at the turn of the twentieth century. One of the key parts of Woodward's classic book *The Origins of the New South* (1951) was a chapter titled "The Mississippi Plan as the American Way," which described how the disfranchisement and segregation campaigns pioneered by the state's 1890 constitution became a model, not merely for similar campaigns of exclusion across the South but also for white Americans, northerners and southerners alike, who had taken up the "White

Man's Burden" in the Philippines. In *Williams v. Mississippi* (1898), the Supreme Court adopted the view of the Mississippi Court, declaring that there was nothing objectionable in the voting provisions of Mississippi's Constitution; it was merely the case that "evil was possible under them." Commenting on the decision in light of the nation's dilemma in the Philippines, the *Nation* found it "an interesting coincidence that this important decision is rendered at a time when we are considering the idea of taking in a varied assortment of inferior races in different parts of the world"—races "which, of course, could not be allowed to vote." The irony for Woodward was that at the dawn of the twentieth century Mississippi, far from an isolated backwater, actually set the pace for American racial policy at home and abroad.[24]

A similar kind of ironic framework—a neo-Woodwardian interpretation—has emerged in historical analyses of the Deep South's role in the origins of the modern right. The southern way has once again become the American way for journalists and scholars who have analyzed the success of the Republican Party since the 1960s. They have argued that the achievement of the modern right has been in channeling the fury of white southerners and repackaging the message in racially coded appeals. This was the Republicans' "southern strategy," which journalists at the time hailed as being key to Republican success and which scholars since have used to connect the politics of the massively resistant white South with the politics of the modern Republican Party. The southern strategy thesis has at its core the same ironic formulation that drove the America Writ Small metaphor. Instead of the recalcitrant Deep South becoming more like America, in fact, the reverse happened: America was "southernized."[25]

As powerful as the southern-strategy thesis has been in explaining the lingering problems of racial division in American politics, this formulation obscures important changes that have occurred in the Deep South in the past half-century. By the 1960s, the plantation economy that had been preserved in Reconstruction and that had provided the economic rationale for the legalized subjugation of southern blacks was in dramatic collapse. The South's "bulldozer revolution," the post-World War II industrialization and urbanization of the region, certainly did not end racial discrimination, but it changed the dynamics. White conservatives from the rural Black Belt that long dominated the politics of a state like Mississippi played a role in the growth of the Republican Party across the South, but by the 1980s the party's most fertile ground was not the Black Belt—the former stronghold of the Dixiecrats—but expanding metropolitan areas. Republicans started winning presidential votes in the urban South as early as the Eisenhower campaigns of the 1950s. But as political scientists Merle and Earle Black have shown, the party identification of southern whites did not shift significantly until the 1980s, and GOP expansion always came first and most impressively in the upper South and in metropolitan areas.[26]

From the 1950s to the 1980s, Mississippi underwent a dramatic economic and social transformation. Political power shifted away from the rural Black Belt agricultural elite that had been tied to the national Democratic Party through New Deal agricultural policy and an atavistic cultural aversion to the party of Reconstruction. Supplanting this Black Belt elite was a group that historian Bruce Schulman has described as the "new Whigs," a modern, industrially oriented, urbanized (and suburbanized) business class that aggressively sought federal dollars and advocated a pro-corporate, anti-union politics of small government and low taxes. While it hardly suggests the full story, it is telling that as late as 1951, farmers outnumbered businessmen in the Mississippi state legislature nearly three to one. By 1983, the legislature contained ninety-five businessmen compared to only twenty-one farmers.[27]

A southern strategy thesis that draws a bold line connecting the politics of massive resistance and the politics of the modern Republican Party fails to appreciate the extent of these economic and political changes. It takes the rural Deep South experience as representative of the entire region and ignores the more populous and increasingly important political experience of the Sunbelt South—an experience that had much less to do with the old politics of massive resistance than with a new, color-blind meritocratic rhetoric of rights and responsibilities that stretched far beyond the states of the former Confederacy.[28] Those who figure the South as synecdoche, in essence, posit the continuity of southern white racism from the massive resistance era through to the racial conservatism of the modern Republican Party. Certainly in a state like Mississippi, race remains a central division—politically, culturally, and spatially. The challenge for scholars, however, is to reconcile the continuity of white racism in the South with both the evolution of its expression and the dramatic changes that have swept the state and the region.

In 1964, James J. Kilpatrick, the editor of the *Richmond News Leader* and a regular commentator on the South for *National Review*, wrote an article titled "In Defense of Mississippi." At the moment of the civil rights movement's greatest triumph, the contrarian Kilpatrick believed that the real problem was not Mississippi racism but northern hypocrisy: "We will pile all our sins on the head of the scapegoat, and drive her into a Dixie wilderness." The "blunt truth," Kilpatrick argued, was that compared to the "jungles of Harlem and Central Park, Jackson [Mississippi] is an oasis of pure tranquility." Kilpatrick's scapegoat thesis was the stuff that Mississippi segregationists loved. It assured them that they were not alone— that, in fact, there were many good, decent Americans who understood their plight, who felt the same way that they did.[29]

The problem, at least according to one literary-minded segregationist, was that what most Americans read about the South had been filtered by "false image-makers." This was the characterization by Medford Evans, a Citizens' Council executive with a Ph.D. in literature from Yale. Evans was a right-wing gadfly who had been a John Birch Society organizer and coordinator, a special aide to General Edwin Walker (who was reprimanded by the Defense Department for indoctrinating his troops with far right anti-communist material), and author of *The Secret War for the A-Bomb*, which attacked left-wing intellectuals for endangering American national security. American tastemakers were obsessed, Evans believed, with the Southern Renaissance's vision of the gothic South. According to Evans, Erskine Caldwell, Tennessee Williams, and most especially William Faulkner were not representative of the South—they were "neurotics." The success of their literature, he argued, was explained by the fact that "their own quite evidently neurotic approach to any sort of material whatever…finds a responsive chord in the neurotic New York critics who for reasons of their own find satisfaction and hope for profit in the distribution of prurient, macabre, or otherwise shocking pictures labeled 'South'." Plays and novels allegedly about the South were "simply pornography disguised as regional literature." For these writers and critics, Evans argued, the South was a "Shangri-La for Freudian fantasies."[30]

The scapegoat metaphor had its roots in a regional rhetorical wrangle that dated back to the first half of the nineteenth century, when southern slaveholders, stung by what they considered to be the abolitionist posturing of New Englanders, pointed out that it was Yankee traders who had sold them their slaves in the first place.[31] In the 1950s, a variation of the scapegoat thesis involved conservative southern newspaper editors who charged that their northern counterparts sent teams of reporters to cover racial strife in the South while ignoring or minimizing racial disturbances in their own cities. This is what Thomas R. Waring, editor of the *Charleston News and Courier*, described somewhat awkwardly in 1955 as the "paper curtain," one that "shuts out the Southern side of race relations from the rest of the country." Back and forth charges of bias led to a heated discussion between northern and southern editors at the 1956 meeting of the American Society of Newspaper Editors. In 1960, William D. Workman, an editor at the *Columbia* (South Carolina) *State*, wrote a chapter-long defense of Waring's thesis in his book *The Case for the South*.[32]

The charge that northern newspapers ignored racial strife in their own backyards was not baseless. There were a variety of reasons that the major dailies stayed away from stories of racial conflict. One had to do with a sense of civic responsibility, the feeling that covering struggles over housing integration would only "inflame" racial hostilities. In Chicago in the late 1940s, when postwar housing shortages were at their peak, it was the job of the mayor's Commission on Human Relations to make sure that racial bombings or arson committed by whites, estimated at about one every three weeks, did not make it into the papers. Another involved the growing northern civil rights movement in the postwar period. James Gregory argues that twenty-five years earlier, white-owned northern newspapers would surely have sided with white homeowners in their fight against neighborhood encroachment by African Americans. By the 1950s, however, the presence of increasingly organized and politically influential black communities in northern cities led editors to take a more neutral stance. The easiest thing became to ignore the racial struggles over neighborhoods, or at least to bury them in the back pages. The silence was so pervasive that scholars of the urban North have had to turn to small weekly papers published by African Americans or by white neighborhood groups in order to recover this history.[33]

No southern editor pushed harder the idea of a northern paper curtain on civil rights issues than Grover C. Hall, Jr., editor-in-chief of the *Montgomery* (Alabama) *Advertiser*. In the mid-1950s, Hall opened his newspaper's offices to visiting northern journalists who came to his city to cover the Montgomery Bus Boycott. He pitched his complaints about northern bias to reporters from such papers as the *New York Herald Tribune*, *Le Figaro*, and the *London News Chronicle*. One of the more sympathetic listeners was Murray Kempton of the *New York Post*, who conceded that he had been planning to write a series on northern racial discord. Hall sent an open letter to Kempton's editor at the *Post*, James A. Wechsler, proposing that Hall and Kempton make the rounds in New York, surveying the racial scene there. Hall was less enthused when Wechsler countered with the offer of sending him around with Ted Poston, an African-American reporter at the *Post* already at work on a similar story.[34]

Hall, however, kept up his campaign for much of 1956. The *Advertiser* ran a series of articles, many written by Tom Johnson, that reported on incidents of racial conflict outside of the South. Titled "Tell It Not in Gath, Publish It Not in the Streets of Askelon," these articles included reports on the racial strife at the Trumbull Park Homes in Chicago, which began in 1953 after an African-American family moved into the previously all-white Chicago Housing Authority complex.[35] Johnson also attacked Michigan governor G. Mennen (Soapy) Williams, who canceled a speech in Birmingham because of the city's segregation statutes, and Congressman Charles C. Diggs of Detroit, who addressed the NAACP in Montgomery. Both men must have had their hands full, Johnson scoffed, given Detroit's large black population and surrounding suburbs such as Dearborn, Wyandotte, and Royal Oak, none of which (according to Johnson) had a single African-American resident.[36] Appearing most regularly in the pages of the *Advertiser*, however, were letters to the editor from ex-Alabamians, traveling salesmen from the North, or northern white housewives, all of whom found little difference in the racial attitudes and practices of white northerners compared to those of white southerners.[37]

Hall was a confidante of George Wallace, and few southern politicians made more of the region's victimology than the governor of Alabama. On his campaign swings north, George Wallace compared crime rates in northern cities to those in Alabama. A pet project of southern senators and congressmen in the 1960s was to sponsor protest bills that recommended redistributing the African-American population of the South. Let white liberals get a taste of racial diversity, segregationists argued, then let us see how eager they are to integrate. In 1964, Representative George W. Andrews of Alabama proposed a government-sponsored resettlement commission that would move African Americans out of the South and find new homes for them in the North.[38] That same year, Senators John Stennis of Mississippi and Richard Russell of Georgia introduced an amendment to civil rights legislation that would have redistributed the African-American population evenly throughout the nation.[39] This had been a segregationist ploy for years. In the 1950s, the Citizens' Council printed a map that calculated how many African Americans each state would have to absorb to equalize the percentage of black residents across the country (figure 4.2).[40]

As rhetorical strategy, the metaphor of the Deep South as scapegoat was morally offensive. Scapegoats are innocent proxies for the sins of others; if anything is clear from the historical record, it is that white southerners were not innocent. Even Kilpatrick had to admit there was a "terrible sickness" in Mississippi in 1964, "made all the more tragic by the unwillingness of so many Mississippians publicly to acknowledge the cancer that exists."[41]

By the late 1960s, however, the scapegoat metaphor had moved beyond mere rhetoric to become the basis for a segregationist attack on federal school desegregation policy. In 1964, southern politicians had objected to provisions in the Civil Rights Act on the grounds that it created a "regional" bill directed solely at white southerners, one that ignored "de facto segregation" in the North. Southern segregationists complained that language in Title IV that prohibited the civil rights bill from being used to correct "racial imbalances" was inserted in order to protect de facto segregation in northern cities and suburbs. During debate on the Senate floor, for example, John Stennis of Mississippi found it "strikingly strange" that Emmanuel Celler, the New York representative who chaired House Subcommittee #5—the committee generally thought to be the most aggressive in strengthening the legislation—accepted an amendment that provided that "desegregation" would not mean "the assignment of students to overcome racial imbalance." Stennis noted the broad opposition in New York to efforts to correct racial imbalances in public schools, and he suggested that Celler's vote came because of the "strong reaction" in New York "against the proposal to overcome a State racial imbalance by disturbing the children and transporting them out of their community."[42]

Negro Surplus Or Deficit For Each State

FIGURE 4.2. Following the *Brown* decision, the Citizens' Councils of America produced a map that alleged to show the "Negro surplus or deficit" if the nation's African-American population were spread equally across all fifty states. The Citizens' Council was one of several southern groups that urged "voluntary migration" and resettlement of African Americans outside of the South. These segregationist organizations believed that white southerners served as the "scapegoats" of white northern and western supporters of civil rights reforms, and by the late 1960s, white southern politicians such as Senator John Stennis of Mississippi pushed for desegregation in the North and West with the intent of sparking a national white backlash against busing.

Southern segregationists claimed that it was "northern hypocrisy" that led to the racial imbalance language in Title IV of the 1964 Civil Rights Act. Certainly there was plenty of hypocrisy to go around in both the North and the South on the issue of school desegregation. The architects of the "racial imbalance" language knew how controversial the issue of school desegregation was in their own districts. They also knew, however, that southern segregationists had successfully diluted civil rights legislation in 1957 and 1960, just as they had used southern seniority and the filibuster to frustrate every effort at civil rights reform since a liberal bloc first emerged in Congress in the 1930s. Civil rights sponsors understood that in order to get meaningful legislation past the southern bloc in the Senate, moderates and liberals must stand united.[43]

Southern segregationists fought federal school desegregation efforts in a variety of ways, but none was stranger than the strategy pioneered by southern segregationists by the end of the 1960s. In December 1969, Mississippi governor John Bell Williams proposed a $1 million program financed by the Mississippi state legislature to file school desegregation suits in northern states with patterns of de facto segregation.[44] In January 1970, the attorneys general in Mississippi, Louisiana, and Florida announced plans to intervene as friends of the court in a Pasadena, California, school desegregation case in order to argue for the removal of de facto racial segregation.[45] And in February 1970, Senator John Stennis introduced an amendment to a federal education bill that called for equal desegregation efforts in both the North and the South, regardless of whether the segregation resulted from state action or residential patterns. Stennis's ostensible goal was to bring about "one uniform policy" on school desegregation, "applicable nationwide." But the real motivation, which every southern official conceded, was the hope that accelerated desegregation in the North and West would spark a broader, national backlash against school desegregation.[46]

These efforts would likely have been ignored as just the latest southern lost cause had it not been for the intervention of Abraham Ribicoff, U.S. Senator from Connecticut and a former secretary of the Department of Health, Education and Welfare in the Kennedy administration. Ribicoff gave a rousing speech on the Senate floor vindicating southern claims to martyrdom. He charged his fellow northern liberals with "monumental hypocrisy" in pursuing vigorous enforcement of southern desegregation while ignoring the racial separation between all-white suburbs and all-black inner cities. For too long, Ribicoff believed, liberals had led the attack on southern segregation while ignoring the glaring and growing racial divide in American metropolitan areas.[47]

The public debate that ensued over federal school desegregation policy was unlike any that had taken place in the sixteen years since the *Brown* decision.[48] Liberals quickly denounced Ribicoff and the Stennis amendment for converting "liberal guilt into segregationist glee." "Segregation is far too important a subject to be left to the segregationists," the *Washington Post* reasoned.[49] Dissenters rightly worried that the Stennis amendment was merely trying to use liberal confusion to win concessions for southern public schools. Ribicoff understood how his words confirmed long-held accusations of the most committed southern opponents of school desegregation, but his concern was with the crisis in urban America. He argued that policies designed to desegregate school districts in the rural South were insufficient to deal with the challenges of segregation in metropolitan areas. "The suburbs are the new America," Ribicoff argued; millions of white Americans were moving out of the cities, leaving behind a hollowed shell where poor minorities faced limited employment and educational opportunities. Ribicoff pointed out that 80 percent of the new jobs created in the past two decades were located in the suburbs. The dual school system of America's metropolitan centers was only one manifestation of the more fundamental problem: "the dual society that exists in every metropolitan area—the black society of the central city and the white society of the suburbs."[50]

The Stennis amendment controversy was deeply troubling to white liberals—particularly southern liberals—many of whom, after years of struggle against intransigent forces in the segregated South, had finally begun to see the tide shift. Two southern liberals argued that the distinction between southern and northern segregation was both logical and necessary to sustain and advance desegregation in southern schools. Paul M. Rilling of the Southern Regional Council in an article in the *New Republic,* and the journalist Robert Sherrill writing in the *Nation,* believed, as Rilling put it, "the South *is* different." "To be sure, other regions shoot Panthers, stuff blacks into slums, flee integrated neighborhoods, demonstrate against employment ratios for blacks," Sherrill wrote. "Nevertheless, other sentiments do prevail in other regions and it is only these other sentiments in other regions—which the South calls hypocrisy—that have ever given the black man a chance in this country....If the South ever convinces other sections that 'you are just as guilty as we are because essentially you feel about the blacks as we do,' then the integration movement could very easily come to a halt."[51] The concern of these reformers was real. The struggle for school desegregation in the South had been an arduous, plodding fight, one that had not come and could not be sustained without committed support from liberal forces outside of the region. The fear was that Ribicoff's willingness to muddy the waters of school desegregation policy would not desegregate northern suburbs, but would merely give fuel to the segregationist countermovement in the South, a movement that many liberals rightly suspected received a sympathetic hearing at the highest levels of the Nixon White House.

The problem with this critique, however, was that it underestimated how far white middle-class suburbanites were willing to go to protect the racial and class makeup of their neighborhoods and schools. Sherrill and Rilling assumed that white racism really was a regional phenomenon, attributable to a certain set of mind specific to the South. Sherrill noted the existence of northern "callousness toward Negroes," yet only as a perfunctory rhetorical concession. The "perversities of the South," as he called them, remained the region's alone. Racism, according to Sherrill, had "infected" Congress only because of the South's traditional congressional power due to seniority provided by one-party rule; it had moved to other areas of the country primarily because of the "the migratory habits of Southerners."[52]

Another southern liberal, columnist Tom Wicker, wrote in the *New York Times* that the federal desegregation effort in the South was "the best possible beginning on a nearly insurmountable national problem." Southern school desegregation was "the symbol of the need, the banner of the intent." The Stennis amendment, according to Wicker, suggested that "there is no longer even an intent."[53] Liberals accused segregationists, along with sympathetic officials in the Nixon administration, of trying to confuse and fragment what Rilling called "the national consensus for desegregated education."[54] But, in fact, what the Stennis controversy suggested was that without the South as a "symbol" and a "banner," there was very little consensus about school desegregation at all.

This chapter has focused on how three influential Mississippi tropes have operated historically, but given that they live on in historical memory—and in doing so, shape our current understanding about the South and its relationship to the nation—some summary observations are in order. First, it is important to recognize that a metaphor like the closed society, and the concept of the exceptional South, was an important instrument for social and political reform in 1960s America. The image of the closed society helped solidify a liberal-moderate coalition that passed the 1964 Civil Rights Act and that was crucial in propelling the fight against Jim Crow segregation. No one who knows the history of the South should be entirely cynical about the accomplishments of the 1964 Civil Rights Act; it was critical in providing the legal tools for battling the entrenched forces of southern white supremacy.[55]

The closed society metaphor also reflected a tangible difference in how white racism operated in 1960s America. There were, to be sure, distinctive aspects to white Mississippians' racism—the fact that as late as 1964 only 6.7 percent of African Americans in Mississippi were registered to vote, or the way that law enforcement in the state, going all the way to the governor's office, showed a remarkable indifference throughout Freedom Summer to white extremist infiltration of local and state police forces.[56] Martin Luther King Jr. offered a point of comparison between the North and South, one that shows how tricky regional juxtapositions can be. "I have never in my life seen such hate," King told reporters after his 1966 march through the Marquette Park, Chicago Lawn, and Gage Park neighborhoods of Chicago. "Not in Mississippi or Alabama. This is a terrible thing." Comparing the violence in Mississippi to Chicago a few days later, however, King noted that southern brutality "came in many instances from the policemen themselves," whereas Chicago police were "doing a good job of seeking to restrain the violence."[57] However many bricks and bottles were thrown in Levittown or Cicero, very little in the urban and suburban North could compare to the Klan's reign of terror in Mississippi from 1963 to 1967.

Still, it is important to recognize the limits of the closed-society metaphor and the notion of southern exceptionalism that is implicit in it. Civil rights activists abandoned the notion of Mississippi as exceptional because it limited the kinds of reforms that national political leaders would pursue. They understood how easy it was to single out the South, to make racism merely a problem of Deep South states like Mississippi. As Howard Zinn wrote in the *Southern Mystique*, during the civil rights movement the South went through "the early stages of a kind of shock therapy." Yet it was important to remember, Zinn argued, that the rest of the nation was not the doctor administering the therapy, but rather the next patient in line.[58]

Today the memory of the closed society—of the exceptional racist South—is a key trope in a triumphal narrative of the civil rights movement. It is one of the most familiar stories in modern America, celebrated by all but the most unreconstructed segregationists: a color-blind, religiously oriented civil rights movement exposed the racist, un-American rednecks from the rural Deep South, shamed the rest of white America into living up to its own stated principles, and in doing so solved the American Dilemma. Whatever noble uses to which the closed-society metaphor may have been put in the past, today it is often the tool of this fundamentally conservative narrative, one that turns a complex history into a tidy morality play and that forecloses more profound and troubling lessons that Americans might draw from the history and memory of their nation in the civil rights era.[59]

It *is* troubling to think that the South's evil was just the nation's evil in concentrated form, or that white northern hypocrisy was an essential part of civil rights reform. Whether it was the student Left's trope of Mississippi as synecdoche or the southern Right's scapegoat metaphor, by the end of the 1960s both ends of the political spectrum had come to reject the liberal notion of the exceptional South. White racism was seen as a national phenomenon. For the Left that was the tragedy; for the Right it was their vindication. Yet in rejecting the framework of southern exceptionalism, the synecdoche and scapegoat tropes both suggest that in the civil rights era, regional distinctions among Americans were less important than were racial ones.

NOTES

1. Edward L. Ayers, "What We Talk about When We Talk about the South," in *All Over the Map: Rethinking American Regions*, ed. Ayers, Patricia Nelson Limerick, Stephen Nissenbaum, and Peter S. Onuf (Baltimore: Johns Hopkins University Press, 1996), 66.

2. Walker Percy, "The Fire This Time," *New York Review of Books,* July 1, 1965, 3–4.

3. James C. Cobb, *The Most Southern Place on Earth: The Mississippi Delta and the Roots of Regional Identity* (New York: Oxford University Press, 1992).

4. Robert Sherrill, *Gothic Politics in the Deep South* (New York: Ballantine, 1968), 260.

5. For more on Mississippi and southern distinctiveness, see Larry J. Griffin, "Southern Distinctiveness, Yet Again, or, Why America Still Needs the South," *Southern Cultures*, 6, no. 3 (Fall 2000): 47–72.

6. James W. Silver, *Mississippi: The Closed Society* (New York: Harcourt, Brace & World, 1964), 9. Also see James W. Silver, *Running Scared: Silver in Mississippi* (Jackson: University Press of Mississippi, 1984).

7. For an early example of the metaphor of the civil rights movement as the Second Reconstruction, see C. Vann Woodward, "The 'New Reconstruction' in the South: Desegregation in Historical Perspective," *Commentary*, June 1956, 501–8. For the formulation of the Oxford riot as the last battle of the Civil War, see Willie Morris, "At Ole Miss: Echoes of a Civil War's Last Battle," *Time*, Oct. 4, 1982.

8. Silver, *Running Scared*, 101; Calvin Trillin, "State Secrets," in *Voices in Our Blood: America's Best on the Civil Rights Movement*, ed. John Meacham (New York: Random House, 2001), 499–516; Stephen L. Taller to Mississippi Chamber of Commerce, Dec. 21, 1964, 99-29-0-44, Erle Johnston to Taller, Jan. 22, 1965, 99-29-0-45, Mississippi State Sovereignty Commission Files, Mississippi Department of Archives and History (hereinafter cited as MSSC). Also see J. Michael Butler, "The Mississippi State Sovereignty Commission and Beach Integration, 1959–1963," *Journal of Southern History*, 68, no. 1 (Feb. 2002): 146 n74.

9. Lee Barker to Hodding Carter, Jr., July 14, 1966, Correspondence Files, Carter (Hodding and Betty Werlein) Papers, Mitchell Memorial Library, Mississippi State University. An incomplete list of books published in the mid-1960s that dealt with the racial crisis in Mississippi alone includes the following: Hodding Carter III, *The South Strikes Back* (Garden City, N.Y.: Double Day, 1959); P. D. East, *The Magnolia Jungle: The Life, Times, and Education of a Southern Editor* (New York: Simon and Schuster, 1960); Frank Smith, *Congressman from Mississippi* (New York: Pantheon Books, 1964); Nicholas Von Hoffman, *Mississippi Notebook* (New York: D. White, 1964); Hodding Carter, Jr., *So the Heffners Left McComb* (Garden City, N.Y.: Doubleday, 1965); Len Holt, *The Summer that Didn't End* (New York: Morrow, 1965); Shirley Tucker, *Mississippi from Within* (New York: Arco, 1965); William McCord, *Mississippi: The Long Hot Summer* (New York: Norton, 1965); Robert Canzoneri, *I Do So Politely: A Voice from the South* (Boston: Houghton Mifflin, 1965); Russell Barrett, *Integration at Ole Miss* (Chicago: Quadrangle Books, 1965); Walter Lord, *The Past that Would Not Die* (New York: Harper & Row, 1965); Sally Belfrage, *Freedom Summer* (New York: Viking Press, 1965); Elizabeth Sutherland, ed., *Letters from Mississippi* (New York: McGraw-Hill, 1965); U.S. Commission on Civil Rights, *Voting in Mississippi: A Report* (Washington: GPO, 1965); *Mississippi Black Paper* (New York: Random

House, 1965); William Bradford Huie, *Three Lives for Mississippi* (New York: New American Library, 1968). Silver, *Running Scared*, 107.

10. William H. Chafe, *Civilities and Civil Rights: Greensboro, North Carolina and the Black Struggle for Freedom* (New York: Oxford University Press, 1980); Matthew D. Lassiter, *The Silent Majority: Suburban Politics in the Sunbelt South* (Princeton, N.J.: Princeton University Press, 2006), 44–118.

11. Ronnie Dugger, "Old Times There Are Not Forgotten," *Nation*, June 29, 1964, 659–60.

12. Louis Harlan, Review of *Mississippi: The Closed Society*, *Journal of American History*, 54, no. 3 (1967): 723–24; David Cohen, *Phil Ochs: A Bio-Bibliography* (Westport, Conn.: Greenwood Press, 1999), 30.

13. Gunnar Myrdal, *An American Dilemma: The Negro Problem and Modern Democracy* (New York: Harper and Brothers, 1944).

14. James W. Loewen, *Lies My Teacher Told Me: Everything Your American History Textbook Got Wrong* (New York: New Press, 1995), 230.

15. Clayborne Carson, *In Struggle: SNCC and the Black Awakening of the 1960s* (Cambridge, Mass.: Harvard University Press, 1981); Taylor Branch, *Pillar of Fire: America in the King Years, 1963–1965* (New York: Simon and Schuster, 1998); Gary Gerstle, *American Crucible: Race and Nation in the Twentieth Century* (Princeton: Princeton University Press, 2001).

16. Howard Zinn, *The Southern Mystique* (New York: Knopf, 1964), 10.

17. C. Vann Woodward, *The Strange Career of Jim Crow* (New York: Oxford University Press, 1955).

18. Zinn, *Southern Mystique*, 218.

19. Lillian Smith, "The South on the Couch," *Chicago Tribune*, Oct. 18, 1964, K4.

20. Charles A. Raines, Review of *The Southern Mystique*, *Library Journal*, 89, no. 18 (1964): 3970. For a more thoughtful critique, see C. Vann Woodward, "Southern Mythology," *Commentary*, May 1965, 60–63.

21. Mario Savio, "An End to History," in *The Berkeley Student Revolt: Facts and Interpretations*, ed. Seymour Martin Lipset and Sheldon S. Wolin (Garden City, N.Y.: Anchor Books), 216.

22. Jo Freeman, *At Berkeley in the Sixties: The Education of an Activist, 1961–1965* (Bloomington: Indiana University Press, 2004), 236.

23. Godfrey Hodgson, *America in Our Time: From World War II to Nixon—What Happened and Why* (New York: Doubleday, 1976), 292–99. Also see Robert Cohen and Reginald E. Zelnik, eds., *The Free Speech Movement: Reflections on Berkeley in the 1960s* (Berkeley: University of California Press, 2002), 83–102.

24. C. Vann Woodward, *The Origins of the New South, 1877–1913* (Baton Rouge: Louisiana State University Press, 1951), 321–49 (*The Nation* quoted on 324); *Williams v. Mississippi*, 170 U.S. 213 (1898).

25. John Egerton, *The Americanization of Dixie: The Southernization of America* (New York: Harper and Row, 1974); Dan T. Carter, *The Politics of Rage: George Wallace, the Origins of the New Conservatism, and the Transformation of American Politics* (Baton Rouge: Louisiana University Press, 1995); Carter, *From George Wallace to Newt Gingrich: Race in the Conservative Counterrevolution, 1963–1994*

(Baton Rouge: Louisiana University Press, 1996); Dewey Grantham, *The South in Modern America: A Region At Odds* (New York: Harper Perennial, 1995).

26. Earl Black and Merle Black, *The Rise of Southern Republicans* (Cambridge, Mass.: Harvard University Press, 2002), 205 (quotation), and more generally Earl Black and Merle Black, *Politics and Society in the South* (Cambridge, Mass.: Harvard University Press, 1987); Alexander Lamis, *The Two-Party South* (New York: Oxford University Press, 1988); David Lublin, *The Republican South: Democratization and Partisan Change* (Princeton: Princeton University Press, 2004).

27. Bruce J. Schulman, *From Cotton Belt to Sunbelt: Federal Policy, Economic Development, and the Transformation of the South, 1938–1980* (New York: Oxford University Press, 1991); also see James C. Cobb, *The Selling of the South: The Southern Crusade for Industrial Development, 1936–1990* (Urbana, Ill.: University of Illinois Press, 1993); Tony Badger, "Whatever Happened to Roosevelt's New Generation of Southerners?" in *The Roosevelt Years: New Essays on the United States, 1933–1945*, ed. Robert A. Garson and Stuart Kidd (Edinburg: Edinburg University Press, 1999), 122–38; Dale Krane and Stephen D. Shaffer, *Mississippi Government and Politics: Modernizers versus Traditionalists* (Lincoln, Nebr.: University of Nebraska Press, 1992), 114.

28. Lassiter, *Silent Majority*. Also see Kevin M. Kruse, *White Flight: Atlanta and the Making of Modern Conservatism* (Princeton: Princeton University Press, 2005).

29. James J. Kilpatrick, "In Defense of Mississippi," Folder 14b, Box 13, Owen Cooper Papers, Mississippi Department of Archives and History.

30. Medford Evans, *Civil Rights Myths and Communist Realities* (Conservative Society of America, June 1965), 8–9.

31. Zinn, *Southern Mystique*, 221.

32. Waring quoted in William D. Workman, *The Case for the South* (New York: Devin-Adair, 1960), 68; David R. Davies, *The Postwar Decline of American Newspapers, 1945–1965* (Westport, Conn.: Praeger, 2006), 73; Workman, *The Case for the South*, 62–84.

33. Rick Perlstein, *Nixonland: The Rise of a President and the Fracturing of America* (New York: Scribner, 2008), 106. For a more general discussion of press silence, see Arnold R. Hirsch, *Making the Second Ghetto: Race and Housing in Chicago, 1940–1960* (Cambridge: Cambridge University Press, 1983), 51–63; James N. Gregory, *The Southern Diaspora: How the Great Migrations of Black and White Southerners Transformed America* (Chapel Hill: University of North Carolina Press, 2005), 273–74, 415. For an example of a scholar using the weeklies, see Thomas Sugrue, *The Origins of the Urban Crisis: Race and Inequality in Postwar Detroit* (Princeton: Princeton University Press), 82, 223.

34. *Montgomery Advertiser*, March 11, 15, 1956. For more on Hall, see Daniel Webster Hollis, *An Alabama Newspaper Tradition: Grover C. Hall and the Hall Family* (Tuscaloosa, Ala.: University of Alabama Press, 1983).

35. *Montgomery Advertiser*, March 13–14, 1956.

36. *Montgomery Advertiser*, April 8, 10, 1956.

37. *Montgomery Advertiser*, March 6, 1956, 4A; March 7, 1956, 4A; March 18, 1956, 2B; March 20, 1956, 4A; March 21, 1956, 4A; March 24, 1956, 4A; March

28, 1956, 4A; April 3, 1956, 4A; April 13, 1956, 4A; April 17, 1956, 4A; April 29, 1956, 2B.

38. Andrews proposal cited in Robert Loevy, *To End All Segregation: The Politics of the Passage of the Civil Rights Act of 1964* (Lanham, Md.: University Press of America, 1990), 99–100.

39. "Bill To Redistribute Negro Population," Press Release, March 14, 1964, John C. Stennis Papers, Special Collections, Mississippi State University.

40. Neil R. McMillen, *The Citizens' Council: Organized Resistance to the Second Reconstruction, 1954–64* (Urbana, Ill.: University of Illinois Press, 1971, 1994), 182–83.

41. Kilpatrick, "In Defense of Mississippi."

42. *Congressional Record*, March 20, 1964, 5795; *Chicago Tribune*, March 21, 1964, 7.

43. Joseph Crespino, *In Search of Another Country: Mississippi and the Conservative Counterrevolution* (Princeton: Princeton University Press, 2007), 176–82, 198–204.

44. *New York Times* [hereinafter cited as *NYT*], Dec. 14, 1969, 40.

45. *Los Angeles Times*, Jan. 24, 1970, 1A.

46. For a fuller account of the Stennis amendment and its implications for federal school desegregation policy, see Joseph Crespino, "The Best Defense Is a Good Offense: The Stennis Amendment and the Fracturing of Liberal School Desegregation Policy," *Journal of Policy History*, 18, no. 3 (2006): 304–25.

47. Abraham Ribicoff, *America Can Make It!* (New York: Atheneum, 1972), 14–48.

48. *NYT*, Feb. 12, 1970, 36.

49. Quoted in *Congressional Record*, Senate, 91st Congress, 2nd Session, Vol. 116, Part 8, April 1, 1970, 10012-19; *Washington Post*, Feb. 13, 1970, A18.

50. *Washington Post*, Feb. 15, 1970, 49.

51. Robert G. Sherrill, "Ribicoff Rides the Tide," *Nation*, March 16, 1970, 295–96; Paul M. Rilling, "Desegregation: The South Is Different," *New Republic* (May 16, 1970), 17–19.

52. Sherrill, "Ribicoff Rides the Tide," 295.

53. *NYT*, Feb. 24, 1970, 42.

54. Rilling, "Desegregation," 17.

55. Gary Orfield, *The Reconstruction of Southern Education: The Schools and the 1964 Civil Rights Act* (New York: Wiley-Interscience, 1969).

56. Lawson, *In Pursuit of Power*, 297. Also see Crespino, *In Search of Another Country*.

57. Taylor Branch, *At Canaan's Edge: America in the King Years, 1965–68* (New York: Simon and Schuster, 2006), 511–12.

58. Zinn, *Southern Mystique*, 219.

59. On conservative memory of the civil rights movement, see Renee Christine Romano and Leigh Raiford, eds., *The Civil Rights Movement in American Memory* (Athens: University of Georgia Press, 2006). Also see Joseph Crespino, "The Civil Rights Movement, *C'est Nous*," *Reviews in American History*, 34, no. 4 (December 2006): 537–43.

5

BLACK AS FOLK

The Southern Civil Rights Movement and the Folk Music Revival

Grace Elizabeth Hale

Blacks and whites stand singing with their arms linked and crossed, ready for a charge or a blow. The blacks wear dark suits, crisp white button-down shirts, and pleated dresses—the middle-class clothes that civil rights activists use to tell the country that they are citizens. Their faces are serious, earnest even, and their voices are strong.

> Oh deep in my heart, I do believe,
> We shall overcome someday.[1]

In photographs and film footage of the now iconic Friday night finale at the 1963 Newport Folk Festival, the stage is crowded. Peter, Paul and Mary are there, at the height of their fame. Joan Baez is there, too, the beautiful star of the folk revival, in love with the music and Bob Dylan. Pete Seeger brings the gravitas earned through more than two decades of political and cultural work, from his start in the Popular Front–linked folk song revival of the 1930s and 1940s and his playing with Woody Guthrie in the Almanac Singers to the redbaiting of his popular postwar group the Weavers and their blacklisting as suspected communists in the 1950s. Well-practiced in joining his politics and his music, Seeger had been playing benefit concerts for the Student Nonviolent Coordinating Committee (SNCC) since the fall of 1962, and he brought Dylan and Theodore Bikel to sing with him at a voter-registration rally in Greenwood, Mississippi, a few weeks before the festival. But it is SNCC's Freedom Singers, the four field workers Bernice Johnson,

Cordell Reagon, Rutha Harris, and Charles Neblett, who bring the authentic-ity and the romance. They do not just sing on stages. They lead hot churches full of worried people in song. They sing on marches and picket lines, at sit-ins and voter-registration rallies, and in crowded jails in Selma and Albany and McComb. They are conduits of an "authentic" African-American rural culture that stretches back centuries in the South. They are the "real" folk. With them on the Newport stage, the other folk singers and the mostly white, northern, middle-class audience can evoke, at least temporarily, a simple world where black and white, the old and the new, the people left out of the present and the people alienated from it and looking to the past, can all come together to clasp hands and sing and conjure racial integration.[2]

Still, the performance, in every meaning of the term, was not simple then and is not still. A great deal of regional and racial history and myth played out upon that stage, a merging reenacted just as powerfully exactly one month later when Dylan and Baez and the Freedom Singers stood in front of the Lincoln Memorial and lent their voices as Mahalia Jackson led a quarter of a million demonstrators in "We Shall Overcome." In Newport and at the March on Washington, two streams of people came together to try to change history. For a moment there, the white children of plenty—the people the whole postwar world was supposed to be for—met and joined the people locked out of the American Dream by the color of their skin. One group wanted to get out, to express its alienation from the suburbs, the Ivy League expectations, the late-model cars and other markers of status, the whole mid-dle-class life completely laid out for them. And the other group wanted to get in, to achieve the good jobs and suburban neighborhoods and the possibility of upward mobility—the very security that the other group was fleeing. It was an odd coalition, shaky at best, full of irony and strongly dependent upon a mostly northern middle-class fantasy of black as folk, of rural southern blacks as crucial reservoirs of authenticity in a modernizing world.[3]

Many young white middle-class Americans across the nation, schooled by fifties childhoods full of rhythm and blues songs and the folk music sing-a-longs of camp and college, had grown up romanticizing African Ameri-cans as outsiders. In the increasingly popular folk music revival that some of these young people helped create, fans borrowed from and changed white beatniks' belief that urban blacks and jazz were the antithesis of the suburban masses and their middle-class consumer culture. For many northern, white, middle-class folk music fans, rural blacks still living in the South and recent southern black migrants to northern and western cities became living pieces of a past before the world came to be mass-produced, advertised, and sold. Southern blacks somehow existed apart from modern American life, not just politically and economically because of segregation but culturally as well. In this way of thinking, African Americans from the South were more "real," more "authentic," and even more moral than other Americans. This particular white fantasy stood in sharp contrast with a vision being crafted by many sociologists, journalists, and political officials of northern urban blacks as culturally damaged and deprived [for more on the cultural-deprivation thesis, see chapter 2 of this volume].[4]

In 1963 and 1964, especially, images of "authentic" rural southern blacks proved powerful tools in the fight for civil rights. Mississippi Freedom Democratic Party member and former sharecropper Fannie Lou Hamer, testifying on live television before the credentials committee at the 1964 Democratic National Convention in Atlantic City, made clear the kind of power that presentations of blacks as "folk" could command. SNCC, too, evoked this image in photographs, pamphlets, posters, and support rallies to raise money, educate white people, and recruit new volunteers. In particular, SNCC understood that the presentation of the songs of the southern civil rights movement as folk songs mobilized the idea of southern blacks as the folk. Celebrating the artistic value and moral integrity of rural southern black culture dramatized the injustice of political and economic exclusion. It also, inadvertently, helped focus white liberal attention on the struggles of African Americans in places like Selma and Greenwood, rather than Detroit or Philadelphia or Los Angeles (figure 5.1).[5]

FIGURE 5.1. At a civil rights boot camp in Canton, Ohio, student volunteers for the Mississippi Summer Project link arms and sing freedom songs as they prepare to head south in 1964. A coalition of civil rights groups recruited more than one thousand white college students, mainly from northern states, to help register black voters during Freedom Summer. The campaign was part of a successful effort to focus national media attention on racial injustice and segregationist violence in Mississippi, especially after Klansmen murdered three civil rights workers. © Steve Schapiro/CORBIS.

Music became a central part of the movement in the South because civil rights activists found that singing together connected black people, gave them courage, and aurally marked their claim to spaces that segregation denied them. Outside the movement and its local contexts, however, the sounds and pictures of folksinging protesters helped produce and circulate an alternative image of the South as a place where African Americans preserved a distinct and "authentic" rural culture. If the South was the place that racism flourished, it was also the place, paradoxically, where "real" black folk survived and black culture flourished. The idea of southern black people as the folk helped broaden support for the southern movement by attracting many folk music fans to the cause, but it also limited the ability of some northern middle-class whites to see African-American oppression elsewhere in the nation, in urban places where people did not sing. In the early 1960s, many folk fans sided with the "folk" in their battle with southern white racists but found "angry" northern blacks harder to love.[6]

By promoting an image of southern rural blacks as the folk, the folk music revival helped create a new white liberal vision of regional and racial difference, a new form of southern exceptionalism. Alienated and damaged, urban black culture outside the South, in this way of thinking, produced anger, riots, and criminals. Authentic and innocent, rural black culture inside the South produced the southern civil rights movement— nonviolent, interracial organizers joining their voices in song.

In the beginning, the protests were quiet. In 1955, in the empty buses of Montgomery, this silence spoke the message of resistance. Later, at lunch counters and on Trailways buses, the silent presence of black and white students sitting together announced the audacity of their challenge to the segregation that some whites called "the southern way of life." The young demonstrators remained quiet as people poured salt and ketchup and sugar on them. They gasped in pain but rarely spoke, even when their opponents beat them with fists and sticks and rocks and burned them with cigarette butts. In the beginning, their silence helped communicate the message of black respectability and even dignity. They remained quiet and nonviolent in public, even in the face of sadism. Better than the Americans who attacked them, nonviolent black demonstrators deserved their rights.

But at some point civil rights protestors began to sing as part of their protests. Sure, they were singing hymns, in Martin Luther King's words, "traditional songs which brought to mind the long history of the Negro's suffering," in the mass meetings held each week during the Montgomery Bus Boycott. Singing became a part of the civil rights movement because many early participants were devout Christians and because organizers held meetings in the only independent black institutions that existed in most places in the South, the churches, where people always sang when they gathered. The black choral tradition helped make both the spirituals and traditional Protestant hymns into a part of the movement.[7]

But music entered the movement from the Old Left-labor organizing tradition as well. At Highlander Folk School, a labor education center in Grundy County, Tennessee, musical director Zilphia Horton added group singing to Highlander's labor organizing programs in the 1930s. As union locals and, later, black community groups came to Highlander for workshops in the forties and fifties, Horton taught them songs that she had learned from previous visitors and asked them in return to teach her the songs they used in their own communities. She became a kind of living archive of protest music. After she died, white folksinger Guy Carawan took over the job.[8]

By the 1950s, Highlander was hosting citizenship-training classes such as the program Montgomery activist Rosa Parks attended and also running organizing workshops for college students every Easter. In March 1960, some of the students involved in the Nashville movement joined sit-in activists from around the South at Highlander. They asked Carawan to return with them to Nashville.[9]

In Nashville, Carawan joined the civil rights movement and began teaching the activists protest songs. A few weeks later, Ella Baker of the Southern Christian Leadership Conference (SCLC) invited Carawan to a meeting she was putting together in Raleigh, North Carolina. Held in April 1960 at Shaw University, the "Southwide Student Leadership Conference on Nonviolent Resistance to Segregation" became better known as the gathering where black and white student activists created SNCC. About two hundred students came together to share information from local sit-in movements. Carawan infused the spirit of the labor organizing tradition and the old left-wing folk song movement into the new organization by teaching the founders of SNCC the songs of Highlander.[10]

One of these songs was "We Shall Overcome." By 1963, most Americans would be able to recognize this most publicized of what became known as the Freedom Songs, the music of the civil rights movement. But in 1960 few people had heard "We Shall Overcome," even though the song had a long history. While out on strike in 1945–1946, some of the members of the Food and Tobacco Workers Association, a mostly African-American and female union in Charleston, South Carolina, attended a labor workshop at Highlander. One of them, Lucille Simmons, turned the old gospel song "I'll Overcome Someday," written by African-American composer Charles Albert Tindley in 1901, into a labor song, "We Will Overcome." Horton learned "We Will Overcome" from Simmons, added her own additional verses, and then taught the song to activists and musicians who visited the school. One of these people, an unidentified southern textile worker, then moved to New York City and taught the song to white labor activist Joe Glazer, who recorded it in 1950 for the CIO. Pete Seeger learned the song from Zilphia in 1946 or 1947, added some additional verses, and changed "will" to "shall." Around 1950, he taught his version of the song to a folk-singer who taught another folksinger who in turn taught Carawan. Cara-wan, too, changed some verses. When he went to work at Highlander in 1959, he brought the song back there. Horton had stopped playing it some time in the fifties, before she died in 1957. Carawan began to teach the song again to workshop participants. A young activist in the Montgomery Bus Boycott, Mary Ethel Dozier, added a new verse there. As police searched Highlander in 1959—they were always trying to shut it down—activists sat in the dark for an hour and a half and waited. After a while, someone began to hum "We Shall Overcome," and everyone joined in. Dozier sang, "We are not afraid, we are not afraid, we are not afraid today."[11]

At the Highlander meeting in March and the Raleigh meeting in April, a white folksinger taught the future leaders of SNCC a black union song that was a reworking of a black hymn. "We Shall Overcome," the most well-known song of the southern civil rights movement, literally grew out of the merging of the black church, the folk music revival, and the inter-racial labor organizing tradition.[12]

Around 1960, civil rights activists in the South began to sing every-where. But they did not just perform the old spirituals and hymns. They sang contemporary adaptations of old spirituals like "Keep Your Eyes on the Prize" and "We Shall Not Be Moved," songs that Carawan taught the students at the Raleigh conference. And they wrote their own lyrics to old songs. Freedom Singer Bernice Johnson Reagon remembered the moment in a meeting in Albany, Georgia, in 1962 when she "had the awareness that these songs were mine and I could use them for what I needed": SNCC activist "Charlie Jones looked at me and said, 'Bernice, sing a song.' And I started 'Over My Head I See Trouble in the Air.' By the time it got to where trouble was supposed to be, I didn't see trouble, so I put 'freedom' in there." In the Hinds County, Mississippi, jail for his participation in the freedom rides, James Farmer of CORE rewrote "Which Side Are You On?" a song originally written by Florence Reese during the 1932 coal strike in Harlan County, Kentucky. Other activists adapted songs made popular by Ray Charles and Harry Belafonte. They also wrote their own songs. The Nashville Quartet—James Bevel, Bernard Lafayette, Joseph Carter, and Sam Collier—was already adapting rhythm and blues and other popular song lyrics to movement use when they met Carawan in 1960.[13]

Civil rights activists sang all these songs in the jails as well. In the Nashville jail, protestors were segregated by race and gender. "The contact which became more real then was vocal," Candie Anderson remembered. "Never had I heard such singing." It became standard prison practice to sing to connect the separate cells and to pass the time. "When they lock you up in a Mississippi jail they separate the blacks and the whites. To vary the singing, a song contest was started between the two sides," SNCC field secretary Cordell Reagon remembered. In 1961, the forty days that

the Freedom Riders spent in the Mississippi State Penitentiary at Parchman Farm became a Highlander-style song swap as members of SNCC and
CORE taught each other their separate repertories.[14]

Across the South, civil rights protesters also sang as they marched,
marking their claims on their rights and on the landscapes of their cities
with their voices as well as their bodies, with sound. They sang to stop the
beatings. After the freedom rides, Cordell Reagon remembered a Parchman guard beating a demonstrator. "With blood streaming down his face,
he began to sing 'We Shall Overcome.' The guard turned red-faced and
walked away." They sang to withstand the violence. At a Nashville demonstration, students sang "We Shall Overcome" as they ran down a street
lined by a rock- and brick-throwing mob. "This was not a pretentious
display of nonviolence," Julius Lester, a SNCC member and musician
who wrote about the use of music in the movement, insisted. "The song
was simply their only recourse at a time when nothing else would have
helped." Activists made singing itself a form of direct action.[15]

Civil rights activists sang their way through the threats and the fear
and doubt. When Bob Moses started SNCC's first voter-registration project
in Mississippi, in Amite County in the southern part of the state, segregationists tried hard to drive him out. They arrested and jailed him, beat
him up, and murdered Herbert Lee, a local black man working with Moses.
He was not sure he could continue the struggle. But driving to the courthouse, he remembered a song, "Jacob's Ladder." "I sang it in my mind
again and again like a mantra. 'Every rung goes higher, higher. Every rung
goes higher, higher....' On the one hand, it was spiritual and on the other
hand it had a wider political meaning, and it was all connected in this act
of driving down to the courthouse." Singing helped Moses maintain the
courage to stay in the movement.[16]

In Albany, a small city in Southwest Georgia, singing helped transform
the student-led protests into a truly community-wide assault on racial segregation during 1961–1962. Charles Sherrod and Cordell Reagon, already
experienced field secretaries, opened the Albany SNCC office in October
1961. For the very first mass meeting, "the church was packed before eight
o'clock. People were everywhere, in the aisles, sitting and standing in the
choir stands, hanging over the railing of the balcony, sitting in trees outside the window," Sherrod recalled. "When the last speaker among the
students, Bertha Gober, had finished, there was nothing left to say. Tears
filled the eyes of hard, grown men who had seen with their own eyes mer-
ciless atrocities committed....And when we rose to sing 'We Shall Overcome,' nobody could imagine what kept the church on four corners."
New York Times folk music critic Robert Shelton heard about the music
in Albany and headed south in the summer of 1962 to see for himself.
SNCC field secretary Charles Jones told him, "there could have been no
Albany Movement without the music. We could not have communicated
with the masses of people without the music, and they could not have

communicated with us. They are not articulate. But through songs, they expressed years of suppressed hope, suffering, even joy and love."[17]

In Albany, the practice of singing freedom songs developed when the student-led protests met the old black choral tradition still thriving in Southwest Georgia. When Cordell Reagon arrived in Albany, members of the local NAACP youth chapter were already singing freedom songs. Some, like "This Little Light of Mine," people learned at church. Others, like "We Shall Overcome," they learned from television coverage of the civil rights movement. Reagon, who served as a song leader in the Nashville movement, taught Albany residents some of the songs that activists had adapted elsewhere. Many black Christians in Albany and the surrounding rural areas continued to sing the old religious songs in the old ways and taught them to organizers. Singing helped move the whole community into the movement. Citizens of all ages, not just college and high school students, sang for hours in mass meetings and then marched out to participate in demonstrations and voter-registration drives all over the city and nearby countryside. As Bernice Johnson Reagon remembered, "there was more singing than there was talking. Songs were the bed of everything."[18]

Somehow, class and generational differences among blacks, and the deep rural versus town divide, disappeared as peoples' voices came together in song. As black folksinger and SNCC member Julius Lester argued in 1964, freedom songs "crumble the class barriers within the Negro Community....The professor and the plumber, the society matron and the cleaning woman, the young college student and the unlettered old man stand beside each other united by a song and a dream. They march together and are jailed together." Reagon remembered her time in jail with a group of women who ranged from teenagers to eighty-year-old grandmothers. "I would start a song and everybody would join in. After the song, the differences among us would not be as great. Somehow, making a song required an expression of that which was common to us all....The music was like an instrument, like holding a tool in your hand." It turned out to be a tool, however, that black activists could not completely control.[19]

White people often have used their understanding of black musical abilities to mark black difference. Blacks can sing, dance, and play popular music better than whites, some whites have long believed, in a way of thinking that goes back to slave musicians who played at their masters' dances. The popularity of minstrelsy, from its antebellum beginnings to its 1890s revival, spread these ideas and lodged them in the very foundations of America's mass-consumer culture. Whites' celebration of blacks as talented entertainers has often obscured the important political foundations of the African-American musical tradition, including songs of hope and defiance, resistance to slavery and segregation, and communal solidarity. African Americans might be musically superior, the stereotype has long suggested, but natural talent just proved black inferiority in other pursuits that required practice and reason.[20]

When civil rights activists began to make singing not just the background of the movement but a form of direct action, they contradicted the claim, made visually in the sit-ins and the freedom rides with their middle-class clothes and their manners and their seriousness, that they were just like other Americans. Instead, they announced that they were different. A singing movement was not a movement of ordinary Americans. It was better, more authentic, and more moral (figure 5.2). It was a movement of people outside of modern America, where radio and records had taken the place of family pianos and neighborhood singing. It was, as the increasingly popular folk music revival taught its fans, a movement of the authentic, rural folk. Images of singing protesters connected the

FIGURE 5.2. July 7, 1963: Black and white demonstrators sing freedom songs as they await police buses after their arrest on trespassing charges at suburban Baltimore's Gwynn Oak Amusement Park, which resisted eight years of civil rights protests against its Jim Crow policies. Most of these activists are wearing suits or dresses to dramatize their middle-class respectability and, by implication, the injustice of segregation in public consumer spaces. The white male in denim overalls, however, is dressing "authentically" in what had become the unofficial uniform of the rural southern black folk. © Bettmann/CORBIS.

southern civil rights movement with the long history of white interest in black music.

At the end of the fifties, folk music conjured up visions of bohemia, of poor artists, intellectuals, and beatniks struggling in racially mixed enclaves like Greenwich Village in New York City and the North Beach section of San Francisco. Folk songs carried a glimmer, too, of forbidden politics, of communism and socialism and militant labor unions, of a singing Left driven underground by political persecution. This racially ambiguous, bohemian, vaguely leftist aura paradoxically became exactly what made folk music popular during the period from about 1958 to 1965, known as the folk music revival.

Still, the folk revival was a part of popular culture even as it also critiqued that culture. Listening to and making their own folk music, white middle-class teenagers and college students learned that romanticizing "the folk" was a form of rebellion against mid-century values and what people then called "mass culture." Modern America, folk music implied by providing a counterexample, was fake, plastic, slick, mass-produced, and new. Mainstream America was also racially segregated. Feelings were packaged and clear there. Passions were tidy and controlled. Folk music was the opposite of all these things. It could be gentle and pure or wild and raw, but it was always deep and real and full of feeling. It was something to be crazy about, something to love. It was the opposite of mainstream commercial music, with its racially defined genres and racially identified performers. To find folk music as a white teenager or young adult was to find a seemingly more pure, allegedly noncommercial version of the mid-fifties teenage rebellion of rock. A fan could listen to all four-plus hours of Harry Smith's *Folkways Anthology of American Folk Music* (1952) straight through, trying to tell the black musicians from the white, or go to a folk festival and see Mississippi John Hurt and others walk out of the past of the records and onto the stage to play. Fans could spend days trying to master every nuance of white Maybelle Carter's or black Elizabeth Cotton's guitar styles. Or they could sing along in Washington Square or in a neighbor's den or in a coffeehouse near a college. Mass culture asked people to make a purchase. But the folk revival insisted that people participate. And participating, joining with the rural folk, gave middle-class fans access to what they imagined as an alternative world. Sharing folk music, its fans claimed, created a kind of communal warmth and elation. The music, they insisted, simply made them "feel good," "a part of something."[21]

By 1963, the height of the folk music revival, fans and critics divided folk musicians into two categories—traditionalists playing old tunes or their own songs in some "recognizable as old" style—and revivalists such as Baez and Dylan, playing old songs and sometimes their own compositions in styles copied from the performances or records of the traditionalists. If a musician was of the folk—if she grew up in a mountain hollow or beside a cotton patch—then she was a traditionalist and whatever she played was folk music. If a musician grew up middle-class and college-educated, outside the Appalachian mountains or the rural South or West, then she had to learn to play exactly like the traditionalist musicians. Folk fans called these musicians revivalists. The categories were never fixed and rigid, but the belief that the difference existed only grew in importance. At stake were the musicians' and the music's authenticity, the very quality that distinguished folk from other commercial music. Traditionalists were the folk. Revivalists made themselves "authentic," in an always ambiguous and contradictory process, by copying the folk.

As folk music scholars have argued, the folk revival of the fifties and sixties transformed commercial music from the twenties and thirties—both the blues and the music that would later be called country—back into folk music, the authentic expression of the people, free from the taint of the market.[22] And this process had a profound effect on African Americans. Black musicians, whatever their places of birth and recording histories and varied playing styles, became, in the context of the revival, born-again folk. This happened to Leadbelly and Big Bill Broonzey and Odetta, to differing degrees, and it would happen to the young civil rights activists who performed freedom songs.

Because many northern whites imagined the South as the place the folk survived, it was not hard for the folk music revival to position singing activists as the folk, too. When the music critic Robert Shelton went to hear the singers in the Albany movement, he compared their music to the urban folk scene then flourishing in places like New York:

> The beatnik guitar-pickers of Greenwich Village are trying to say
> something in their music, but they don't know quite what it is that
> they want to say. The Negroes of the South know what they are
> singing about and what they want out of life. Because they know
> their music rings with more meaning and conviction. Because their
> music is not just a "kick," a hobby, a form of exhibitionism, or a "gig,"
> it is a different story of folk music than one encounters among the
> pampered, groping, earnestly searching young people one meets in the
> Greenwich Villages of the North.

Different meant better, more "real."[23]

It perhaps did not matter, then, that many folk fans' imagination of the folk was wrong, colored by more than a century of romance, by cake walks, coon songs, *Uncle Remus*, and Appalachian jugs, the Child ballads and "Alexander's Ragtime Band," slicked-up spirituals and summer camp singing, *Porgy and Bess* and college song swaps. It did not matter much that the politics of the folk revival were completely contradictory, coupling liberalism's sense of the individual's ability to make him or her very self with conservatism's belief in the essential otherness of the poor. Folksinging required a person to feel someone else's life, just for a moment, even if that life was more a product of one's own imagination than any life lived poor in Mississippi. Performing the songs, singing along with the feelings, meant feeling them, too. The mid-century folk music revival was flawed as both political analysis and social history, but it was a perfect exercise in empathy. And this, in the end, despite all the romanticism, pushed many northern white folk fans to support the southern civil rights movement.

Singing could be a form of direct action. Singing could also represent the movement in its most interracial moment, in the first half of the sixties. But singing also could provide a way to promote the movement by exploiting some whites' willingness to see southern blacks as the folk. Performing freedom songs as folk music in benefit concerts spread news of movement activities and raised money and volunteers. Freedom song concerts, however, also softened civil rights activists' indictment of American racism, paradoxically obscuring its harshest implications by invoking fantasies about the survival of the folk. And the image of singing activists helped locate both that racism and the fight against it in the South, pulling attention away from the problems in other places where civil rights demonstrators were more likely be portrayed as angry and alienated rather than as innocent rural folk.

Whites' folk romanticism, popular across a political spectrum ranging from liberals to leftists, was a rather mild form of racism in the context of mid-twentieth century America, but it was not equality. The folk revival reconstructed privilege based on love for difference rather than hatred of difference. It imagined southern blacks as superior, if living outside of modern time, rather than as inferior. It hit black people with sentimentality and primitivism—what Julius Lester called "too much love"—rather than fire hoses or bullets. Still, benign indifference or neutrality, not love, was the opposite of hate. Folk romanticism insisted that blacks play the role of the folk if they wanted white support. It insisted that African Americans were still objects, not subjects—containers of "authenticity" and "real" culture.

No one did more than Pete Seeger to fuse the folk music revival, the civil rights movement, and the idea of southern blacks as the folk. For Seeger and other singers with connections to the earlier Old Left folk song movement, songs about contemporary events and politics were folk songs because "the people" had always "created songs about things happening around them—hard times, the struggles of unions, peace and war." The freedom songs were authentic folk songs that linked the old singing traditions to the present struggles.[24]

Sometime in the first half of 1962, CORE attorney Len Holt wrote Jim Forman, executive secretary of SNCC: "We have sang the song 'We Shall

Overcome' so much that it seems that by the mere force of the song's tim-
bre the theme is coming true. What am I talking about? Simply this, Pete
is concerned enough to give SNCC a helping hand, a helping voice, and a
helping banjo." "There is a need," Holt believed, "for a bard of the Southern protest movement, . . . an entertainer whose life reflects the ideals they
are singing for or portraying. . . . I hope that the Pete Seeger tour will push
some SNCC person in that direction." This kind of cultural program, Holt
concluded, "could serve the same function for the movement as the Jubilee Singers did for Negro education."[25]

Beginning in the 1870s, the Jubilee Singers traveled across the United
States and Europe singing "authentic" Negro spirituals, polished to appeal
to audiences more accustomed to hearing classical music, in order to
raise money for Fisk University. The students at Fisk, an all-black college
in Nashville, Tennessee, had not grown up singing these songs. Most of
them were part of the South's upwardly aspiring black middle class, which
worked hard to distance itself from behaviors and forms of expression
linked to slavery. But the Jubilee Singers, and other groups inspired by
their success, sang right over any easy distinction between interpreting
a historical form of black expression and playing music that appealed to
rich white people by confirming their folk image of blacks. In fact, explorations of black folk culture throughout the twentieth century always
displayed this tension, whatever the politics of the revivalists or audiences. Pete Seeger's father and his stepmother's family, for example, told
sentimental stories about their maid Elizabeth "Libba" Cotton, much like
the mammy stories that had circulated since the Civil War among white
southerners. The difference was that the Seegers helped Cotton secure a
Folkways Records contract and appearances at folk festivals.[26]

Seeger, like the Jubilee Singers, performed in a folk tradition that he
had not grown up with but had self-consciously learned. The Jubilee Singers, however, were black. Schooled by the minstrel-song revival of the
late nineteenth century, most whites did not need much imagination to
see these college students as the literal embodiment of premodern folk.
Imagining Seeger as an authentic folk singer was more difficult, especially
for young folk fans without any sense of Seeger's Old Left past. In 1962,
however, when Holt wrote the letter to Forman, Seeger was popular and
SNCC was broke and in no position to turn away assistance. "If I Had A
Hammer," a song he had written, was a top hit for Peter, Paul and Mary.
And Seeger, who had played a benefit in Birmingham, Alabama, for Martin Luther King Jr. and the Montgomery Bus Boycott back in 1956, had a
deep interest in civil rights. As the press reported on the growing role of
music in the movement, Seeger could hardly contain his excitement. Here
at last was a successor to the labor union drives of the thirties, a movement that combined folk music and leftist politics at a grassroots level.
Seeger wanted to be a part of it. That fall, he played a series of benefits for

SNCC across the South at historically black colleges such as Morehouse in Atlanta.[27]

Seeger saw his concerts, whether they were SNCC benefits or not, as chances to educate folk music fans about the southern movement. "We'll tell your heroic story everywhere we possibly can," Seeger wrote Bob Moses and others who were in jail in Mississippi in May 1963. "We'll sing it, we'll speak it until the whole country knows about it. You guys are working for the freedom of our whole country." "We Shall Overcome" and other freedom songs became folk songs for people who heard Seeger perform them in concert or on records, simply because he was singing them. More than anyone else, Seeger made the music of the civil rights movement part of the folk music revival. And that, in turn, connected the civil rights movement, especially the young activists of SNCC, to a new group of potential supporters and volunteers: young white folk fans. But Seeger also understood the power of authenticity, of performances of folk music by the "folk" themselves. "Don't forget to make sure that the Freedom Singers or some group will be coming to the Newport Folk Festival the last week in July," he wrote Jim Forman.[28]

Sometime in late 1961 or early 1962, Highlander's Guy Carawan traveled to Albany and recorded a sound documentary of the local movement. *Freedom in the Air*, originally sold by SNCC to raise money for the Albany project, was later released on Folkways Records. Like Seeger, Carawan believed that the music of the black freedom movement had the power to turn folk music fans into civil rights supporters. He wrote to Forman, "I am convinced now after playing the Albany documentary for a number of good-sized audiences of people who are not in the South and are uninformed about what goes on there that it can really move and exhilarate them." Forman responded that SNCC had formed its own "group of Freedom Singers" in November 1962. The Seeger tour had not "raised that much money." Why not send out a group with a direct connection to the southern civil rights movement to perform freedom songs?[29]

Down in Albany, the same fall that Seeger toured the South, Forman encouraged Cordell Reagon to pull together a group of musicians to travel and perform freedom songs. SNCC leaders believed that these Freedom Singers could become a powerful fund-raising tool. Rutha Harris and Bernice Johnson were from the Albany area. Reagon had met the talented Charles Neblett in the Cairo (Ilinois) movement. Charles's younger brother Carver "Chico" Neblett and Bertha Gober sometimes joined them. In October, the Freedom Singers performed a few songs at a civil rights benefit in Chicago, "The Gospel Sing for Freedom," that failed to raise much money. Their formal debut occurred on November 11, 1962, when they played with Seeger at Morehouse College in Atlanta.[30]

Johnson, then just nineteen and not yet married to Cordell Reagon, met Pete Seeger at the home of SCLC's Andrew Young the day of the concert and talked to him about her interest in singing. By then, Johnson had been expelled from Albany State College for her civil rights activities and joined SNCC's full-time staff. Seeger told Johnson about the Almanac Singers, the group he, Woody Guthrie, and others had formed in the 1940s to sing folk and labor songs to raise support and funds for the union movement. Johnson envisioned the Freedom Singers touring the country performing the same function for the civil rights movement. Johnson later called Pete's wife, Toshi, and asked her to set up a tour for the Freedom Singers. Until the Seegers left the country on a world tour in August 1963, Toshi served as the Freedom Singers unpaid manager, giving SNCC the benefit of her Old Left connections and fund-raising knowledge and connecting the group with sympathetic activists and journalists across the country.[31]

From the perspective of SNCC leaders, Johnson, Reagon, Harris, and Neblett were authentic because they had worked and suffered in Albany and other SNCC projects—they had been expelled from school, arrested, beaten, and jailed. "The primary importance of this music," the Freedom Singers' earliest press materials argued, was "not the tune or the beat, but the words and the desperation with which they are sung." For the larger folk music world, however, the Freedom Singers were authentic not only because of their movement activities—rare was the press release that did not mention their arrests and time in jail—but also because of their song choices and their performance styles. As Robert Shelton wrote in the *New York Times*: "The unaccompanied voices, the rhythmic drive, and their sense of conviction put the Freedom Singers in the top level of American folk groups." "If folk music is an expression of the forces at work in the people," critic Ralph Gleason declared in the *San Francisco Chronicle*, "this group is as authentic an American folksinging group as ever walked the earth. They are real, they write their own material and above all, they can sing.... There is a 'mystique' about SNCC." The Freedom Singers were folksingers because they sang versions of old-time songs such as "Pick a Bale o' Cotton" as well as protest songs like "We Shall Not Be Moved" on their album *We Shall Overcome*, recorded to raise money for SNCC. They were folksingers because 1963 was the height of the folk music revival, and they sang a cappella. And they were folksingers because they were black. In the eyes of the white fans of the folk revival, the race and the politics of the Freedom Singers made them traditionalists—actual representatives of folk communities—even as most of them were in fact former college students, more like middle-class revivalists.[32]

Not surprisingly, the Freedom Singers raised a lot more money performing for mostly white audiences outside the South than Seeger had by singing for mostly black audiences inside the South. In their first tour, from February to June 1963, they played sets at the folk music club Mt. Auburn, in Cambridge, Massachusetts; Community Church in Boston;

Judson Memorial Church in New York City; a series of synagogues in Connecticut; and the Newark YMCA. They joined Pete Seeger onstage at his concert in Chicago. And they played colleges and universities, including West Virginia University, Swarthmore, Penn State, Oberlin College, Iowa State, and the University of Missouri. Over the next three years, with an ever-changing lineup of musicians, the Freedom Singers played across the North and West, from elite universities such as Yale and Columbia, to liberal colleges such as Reed and Smith, to big state universities like the University of Illinois and Ohio State. In the South, they played at black universities to recruit activists and at local civil rights projects to raise morale.[33]

Beginning in 1962, the Freedom Singers were an essential part of SNCC's effort to create a northern fund-raising network. Dinky Romilly and Betty Garmen, white staff members charged with coordinating the new SNCC offices in Chicago, New York, and elsewhere and with creating Friends of SNCC support groups outside the South, understood how the Freedom Singers might generate interest in and funds for the organization. While some college students would come to meetings to hear SNCC activists on speaking tours, groups like the Dartmouth Christian Union and the LA Friends of SNCC could tap the campus interest in folk music by hosting the Freedom Singers, and then the musicians could spread the word between songs. "Our real purpose is to carry the story of the movement to the North," Charles Neblett told a student newspaper in 1963. "Newspapers and UPI won't give the real story, and SNCC had to find another way to get it out." Concert announcements and reviews of the Freedom Singers records placed SNCC's name in college newspapers, music magazines, and national publications like the *New York Times*. In 1963, the Freedom Singers and other musicians helped raised about $93,000, one-third of SNCC's funds for the year.[34]

SNCC's promotional materials promoted the Freedom Singers as "the folk." Under a photo of a black man looking out a barred jailhouse-like window and striped by its shadows, the caption read: "The songs the Freedom Singers sing come from the country churches, the stockades, the prisons and the dusty roads of the South." "Freedom singers are the freedom movement, for everyone in the movement sings the freedom songs," a press release announced. "They sing them in the field; they sing them at rallies and conferences, and they sing them when they leave the South, bringing to others the spirit of freedom. All civil rights workers, all persons who work for justice are freedom singers." "The Freedom Singers have traveled widely across the country," other marketing materials declared, "raising the spirits of Americans everywhere, giving them a feeling of what it means to break the bonds of oppression." The letters, college newspaper articles, and even bad student poetry that host groups sent SNCC afterward suggested that audiences viewed the Freedom Singers as the authentic and righteous folk, coming to tell the outside world about the South and their fight against racism and injustice.[35]

At SNCC benefits and concerts, audiences often joined in the music. Singing along became a way to share the emotions of the struggle, to hear the sounds of the jail and the mass meeting, to feel the power of the picket and the march. Not everyone who heard them, of course, could drop everything and go south. But singing was a way to participate, to experience the movement and not just support it financially. The Freedom Singers, Bernice Johnson Reagon argued, made "people who were not on the scene feel the intensity of what was happening in the South." Somehow, the Freedom Singers' records never quite did it, and SNCC never made much money selling them. Only singing along in person took the audience there. All that was required was to feel the music, as voices filled the bodies of their makers and joined each other and filled other bodies. Deep in the heart, it was not an argument or an ideology. It was a feeling. It was the tap of the foot and the leap of faith. It was the song itself. All a person had to do was sing along.[36]

Singing was self-expression in unison. It produced emotions in both listeners and participants. It did not matter that the sources and the contours of the alienation that brought people there were different. Being denied a decent paying job or the right to vote was not the same thing as rejecting the vision of the good life promoted by the middle-class mainstream. But singing expressed each person's feelings simultaneously. For a moment, in the singing, these differences did not matter. Certainly the opponents of integration had no trouble seeing what these groups had in common. Someone sent the Atlanta office a copy of a SNCC fund-raising ad that ran in the *New York Times*. Across the text, in thick capital letters, he wrote "Nigger Lovers." In the corner of the ad, over the coupon with SNCC's address made for cutting out and sending in a contribution, he wrote "Beatnicks [*sic*]." The station manager of Bob Jones University, a conservative all-white religious institution in South Carolina, returned SNCC's "cheap trashy record entitled 'The Freedom Singers Sing Freedom Now!'" with its "obnoxious music" and accused Mercury Records of "crusading for a few beatniks." Beatniks, folk music fans, supporters of equal rights—what was the difference?[37]

The folk music revival taught white students—and folk fans were mostly white—to love blacks, especially rural southerners, as the "real" folk. These were the people who created the Negro spirituals and blues that Baez and Dylan sang. Odetta and Leadbelly were the folk in the flesh, never mind their actual histories. And so were the Freedom Singers, with their pure voices and their real politics. Folk music concerts and Freedom Singers benefits gave white northern and western audiences the South as they wanted to see it, a place of good and evil, black and white, where innocence fought against hatred and violence. Listening to the music, white audience members could connect with the "authenticity" of the folk and renew their own innocence. They were not responsible for the evil down there. They were on the side of morality and right.

Never mind the messy protests that CORE was sponsoring in suburban Boston and all over New York City in the early 1960s—activities that occurred even as the SNCC Freedom Singers held concerts in these same places. Never mind the local civil rights movement in Philadelphia. Folk music and the romance of the outsider pushed many young white northerners to care most about the fight in the South. In the Mississippi Summer Project of 1964, white college students arrived at training sessions with guitars strapped on their backs, learned to sing freedom songs, and came home from Mississippi wearing overalls. One even listed his ability to play "American Folk Guitar"—he had taken "extensive lessons from Rev. Gary Davis, a Negro blind singer from North Carolina"—as a skill that made him a desirable candidate for Freedom Summer. The volunteers, money, and media attention in turn helped create the political coalition that forced federal action in the region. Still, while SNCC was carrying out the most radical civil rights work in the South, the organization's exploitation of the romance of the folk to raise funds for those programs helped many white northern liberals ignore the organizing work under way right outside those concert halls. As one white summer volunteer wrote home, Mississippi "is so different from the North where there is the intense, bitter hatred which makes working in Harlem or Roxbury or Philadelphia so heartbreaking." Some Freedom Summer activists—Mario Savio, for example—returned home to organize against racism outside the South. Still, the image of southern blacks as the folk made it easier for many white volunteers to care more about the fight in the South than to work in the places where many of them lived and where black residents did not seem so innocent or sympathetic.[38]

The romance of southern blacks as the folk helped advance the African-American freedom struggle in the early sixties. It appealed to folksingers, folk revival fans, and college students in the North and West, and it generated positive press. Some civil rights activists, with varying degrees of self-consciousness, decided to exploit this romance—they could not have stopped it if they had wanted to—in their fight for equality. SNCC in particular used the Freedom Singers, folks in the flesh, to build a largely white and northern fund-raising base in 1963 and 1964. Romanticizing southern blacks as the folk, as people who possessed a valuable culture, just might, paradoxically, help end their economic, political, and social oppression. Dependent as it was on the idea of blacks as more "authentic" than other Americans, however, folk romanticism could not help generate equality. It had little to offer activists outside the South who did not sing.

Still, the most damaging effects of the romance of the outsider have come in the long years since the demise of SNCC. Seeing southern blacks as the folk strips away political ideology and strategy. The southern movement appears then as organic, as somehow natural, like blacks' fabled talent for singing. It is less political work, in much public memory, than the unstoppable expression of a people long oppressed. It is a concert that asks people simply to sing along.

NOTES

1. "We Shall Overcome," Guy and Candie Carawan, *Sing for Freedom: The Story of the Civil Rights Movement through its Songs* (Bethlehem, Penn.: Sing Out, 1990), a combined reprint of *We Shall Overcome* (1963) and *Freedom is a Constant Struggle* (1968); Folder 26, Freedom Songs, Student Nonviolent Coordinating Committee Records, Martin Luther King Center, Atlanta, Georgia [hereinafter SNCC Records]; *Voices of the Civil Rights Movement: Black American Freedom Songs, 1960–1966*, Smithsonian Folkways, 1980, 1997.

2. Robert Cantwell, *When We Were Good: The Folk Revival* (Cambridge, Mass.: Harvard University Press, 1996), 293–52, 354; David Hajdu, *Positively Fourth Street: The Life and Times of Joan Baez, Bob Dylan, Mimi Baez Farina, and Richard Farina* (New York: North Point Press, 2001), 164–68.

3. Bernice Johnson Reagon, "Songs of the Civil Rights Movement," (Ph.D. Dissertation, Howard University, 1975), 165–67; Taylor Branch, *Parting the Waters: America in the King Years, 1954–1963* (New York: Simon and Schuster, 1988), 877–81; *We Shall Overcome: Documentary of the March on Washington,* Folkways FH 5592.

4. Daryl Michael Scott, *Contempt and Pity: Social Policy and the Image of the Damaged Black Psyche, 1880–1996* (Chapel Hill: University of North Carolina Press, 1997).

5. Clayborne Carson, *In Struggle: SNCC and the Black Awakening of the 1960s* (Cambridge: Harvard University Press, 1981); James Forman, *The Making of Black Revolutionaries* (Seattle: University of Washington Press, 1997), reprint of 1972 edition.

6. Bernice Reagon, "The Song Culture of the Civil Rights Movement," liner notes to *Voices of the Civil Rights Movement.*

7. Martin Luther King, Jr., *Strive toward Freedom* (New York: Harper and Row, 1964), 53–89; Reagon, "Songs of the Civil Rights Movement," 94; Alfred Maund, "We Will All Stand Together," *Nation,* March 3, 1956.

8. "They Hear America Singing," *Time,* July 19, 1963.

9. Reagon, "Songs of the Civil Rights Movement," 81–82; Cantwell, *When We Were Good,* 289; Carawan, *Sing for Freedom*; John M. Glen, *Highlander: No Ordinary School* (Knoxville: University of Tennessee Press, 1996).

10. Carson, *In Struggle*; Forman, *Making of Black Revolutionaries*; "SNCC: Founding Statement," in *"Takin' It to the Streets": A Sixties Reader,* ed. Alexander

Bloom and Wini Breines (New York: Oxford University Press, 2003), 22; Mary King, *Freedom Song: A Personal Story of the Civil Rights Movement* (New York: Williams Morrow, 1987).

11. Reagon, "Songs of the Civil Rights Movement," 64–89; Robert Shelton, "Rights Song Has Own History of Integration," *New York Times,* July 23, 1963; Carawan, *Sing for Freedom,* 15, 238–39; Pete Seeger and Bob Reiser, *Everybody Says Freedom* (New York: Norton, 1989), 8, 37–41; Norm Cohen, *Folk Song America: A Twentieth Century Revival,* Smithsonian Collection of Recordings, 1990, 77; *We Shall Overcome,* PBS Home Video, 1990; Kerran L. Sanger, *When the Spirit Says Sing: The Role of the Freedom Songs in the Civil Rights Movement* (New York: Garland, 1995).

12. Carson, *In Struggle,* 25–27; Seeger, *Everybody Says Freedom,* 36, 8.

13. Reagon quoted in *No Easy Walk (1962–1966),* Episode 4 of *Eyes on the Prize,* PBS Video, 1987; James Farmer, *Lay Bare the Heart: An Autobiography of the Civil Rights Movement* (Westminster, Md.: Arbor House, 1985); Seeger, *Everybody Says Freedom,* 44–51, 64–65; Carawan, *Sing For Freedom,* 32–36, 45, 77; Bernice Reagon, "In Our Hands," *Sing Out!* January/February 1976, 2.

14. Clipping, "Out of Southern Jails: Freedom Singers Present Story," *Carltonian,* May 8, 1963, Freedom Singers File, Folder 6, Box 70, SNCC Records; Bob Moses letter reprinted in Forman, *Making of Black Revolutionaries,* 233.

15. Reagon, "Songs of the Civil Rights Movement," 83; Julius Lester, "Freedom Songs in the South," *Broadside* 39 (February 7, 1964).

16. Robert Shelton, "Singing for Freedom: Music in the Integration Movement," *Sing Out!* December 1961/January 1962; Seeger, *Everybody Says Freedom,* 244.

17. Charlotte Devree, "The Young Negro Rebels," *Harper's Magazine,* October 1961, 134–35; Howard Zinn, *SNCC: The New Abolitionists* (Boston: Beacon, 1964), 128–29; Shelton, "Singing for Freedom," 4–17.

18. Carawan, *Sing for Freedom,* 27–28; Reagon, "Songs of the Civil Rights Movement"; *No Easy Walk.*

19. Lester, "Freedom Songs in the South"; Reagon, "In Our Hands," 1.

20. On the compatibility of white racism and white love for black music, see Brian Ward, *Just My Soul Responding: Rhythm and Blues, Black Consciousness, and Race Relations* (Berkeley: University of California Press, 1998).

21. Jeff Todd Titon, "Reconstructing the Blues: Reflections on the 1960s Blues Revival," in *Transforming Tradition: Folk Music Revivals Examined,* ed. Neil V. Rosenberg (Urbana, Ill.: University of Illinois Press, 1993), 220–22; Cantwell, *When We Were Good*; Cohen, *Folk Song Revival*; Irwin Silber, Editorial, *Sing Out!* Sept. 1964.

22. Cantwell, *When We Were Good,* 189–238.

23. Shelton, "Singing for Freedom," 17.

24. Biographical Press Material, Seeger File, Folder 3, Box 20, SNCC Records.

25. Len Holt to Jim Forman, 1962, Seeger File, Folder 3, Box 20, SNCC Records.

26. W. E. B. DuBois, *The Souls of Black Folks* (1903, rpt., New York: Oxford University Press, 2007); Cohen, *Folk Song America*, 12–14; Ed Badeaux, "Please Don't Tell What Train I'm On," *Sing Out*, 14, no. 4 (September 1964), 6–12; Pete Seeger, *Rainbow Quest: Elizabeth Cotton*, 1966 television show, Shanachie Entertainment, 2005.

27. Miles College Seeger Concert Promotional Materials, Morehouse College Seeger Concert Promotional Materials, Seeger File, Folder 3, Box 20, SNCC Records; David King Dunaway, *How Can I Keep from Singing* (New York: McGraw-Hill, 1981), 219–24.

28. Pete Seeger to Chico, Bob [Moses], and Sam, May 31, 1963, Seeger to Jim Forman, May 31, 1963, Folder 3, Box 20, SNCC Records. Seeger's manager Harold Leventhal collected writer's royalties for three songs copyrighted to SNCC workers, and Seeger included SNCC freedom songs on his records in the mid-sixties, including *We Shall Overcome*, Columbia Records, 1963. See Freedom Singers, Folder 6, Box 70, SNCC Records.

29. Guy Carawan to Jim Forman, May 15, 1962, Jim Forman to Carawan, Nov. 1962, Folder 4, SNCC Records; Reagon, "Songs of the Civil Rights Movement"; Review of "Freedom in the Air" in *The Reporter*, December 7, 1963; SNCC News Release, Freedom Singers File, Folder 10, Box 130, SNCC Records.

30. Carson, *In Struggle*, 64; Reagon, "Songs of the Civil Rights Movement," 39–40.

31. Reagon, "In Our Hands"; Reagon, "Songs of the Civil Rights Movement"; Dunaway, *How Can I Keep from Singing*, 224–25; Toshi Seeger to Julian Bond, Feb. 4, 1963, Toshi Seeger File, Folder 4, Box 20, SNCC Records.

32. Press materials, Freedom Singers File, Folder 10, Box 130, SNCC Records; Robert Shelton, "Negro Songs Here Aid Rights Drive," *New York Times*, June 23, 1963; Ralph Gleason, "The Voice of Freedom," *San Francisco Chronicle*, April 25, 1965, clipping in Freedom Singers File, Folder 7, Fundraising-Freedom Singers File, Folder 8, Box 70, SNCC Records; Freedom Singers, *We Shall Overcome*, Mercury Records, 1962; Mercury Records File, Folder 5, Box 71, SNCC Records. The 1964 lineup was all men—James Peacock, Marshall Jones, Charles Neblett, and Emory Harris.

33. Freedom Singers File, Folder 10, Box 130, SNCC Records.

34. Neblett quoted in "Out of Southern Jails: Freedom Singers Present Story," *Carltonian*, May 8, 1963, Freedom Singers, Folder 6, Box 70, SNCC Records; Fundraising Folders, New York, Atlanta, and other offices' files, and Benefits, Folder 2, Box 121, SNCC Records; Forman, *Making of Black Revolutionaries*, 293, 307, 430, 449, 454. CORE also started a group, the CORE Freedom Singers; see CORE Papers, microfilm, Series II, Reel 11.

35. Freedom Singers File, Folder 6, Box 70, SNCC Records.

36. Reagon, "In Our Hands," 2, Fundraising-Mercury Records File, Folder 5, Box 71, SNCC Records.

37. Hate Mail, Folder 11, Box 15, Jim Ryerson (Station Manager, Radio Station WMUU, Bob Jones University) to Morrie Diamond (Mercury Records), Aug. 19, 1964, Mercury Records, Folder 5, Box 71, SNCC Records.

38. Kenneth Kipnis, Mississippi Summer Project Application Form, Mississippi Sovereignty Commission Papers Online, SCR ID # 2-166-1-8-1-1, http://www. mdah.state.ms.us/arlib/contents/er/sovcom/result/php; Elizabeth Sutherland Martinez, ed., *Letters from Mississippi: Personal Reports from Civil Rights Volunteers of the 1964 Freedom Summer* (Brookline, Mass.: Zephyr Press, 2002), 23–24, 58.

6

RED NECKS, WHITE SHEETS, AND BLUE STATES

The Persistence of Regionalism in the Politics of Hollywood

Allison Graham

"The poorest county in America isn't in Appalachia or the Deep South," Thomas Frank wrote in 2004. "It is on the Great Plains, a region of struggling ranchers and dying farm towns, and in the election of 2000, . . . George W. Bush carried it by a majority of 80 percent." In his popular 2004 analysis of this historical anomaly, *What's the Matter With Kansas?* Frank claimed that the economic practices responsible for stripping the Midwest of its once prosperous farms were helping to fuel a perverse, counterintuitive revolution. Instead of resisting the onslaught of agribusiness, descendants of the state's nineteenth-century populists and abolitionists were greeting it enthusiastically—inviting, in effect, the corporatization of the American Heartland. This was not just the "mystery of Kansas," he suggested. It was "the mystery of America," in which "the political geography of social class has been turned upside down."[1]

In Kansas, though, this political shift seemed "more staggering than elsewhere," so extreme that a particular rural boomtown in the western part of the state had already been cited by several anthropologists as typical of the "permanent breakdown" of middle-class, middle-American life at the beginning of the twenty-first century. In Garden City and its neighboring hamlet Holcomb, the majority Latino population was living in "rubbish-strewn" trailer parks and working for few to no benefits in "brooding slaughterhouses" that spewed "unearthly odors" into the prairie breeze. If, as Frank repeatedly pointed out, Kansas has long functioned as "a stand-in for the nation as a whole, the distilled essence of who we are," then the United States, like the now ironically named Garden

City, might very well be "a civilization in the early stages of irreversible decay."[2]

The same year that Frank published his study of Kansas, the production crew of the film *Capote* arrived near Garden City. Hoping that the story of Truman Capote's 1959 investigation of the recent Clutter family murder outside the town (that culminated in the 1966 publication of *In Cold Blood*) could be shot on location, the crew and director Bennett Miller quickly realized the futility of discovering vestiges of pastoral stillness in the American heartland and decamped far north to the Canadian province of Manitoba.

The irony of leaving the country in order to find "the country" (in both senses of the term) was not lost on the film's creators, but it is only one of several geographic ironies that pervade *Capote*'s conception, production, and cultural implications. Released in 2005, the film places two of the nation's most famous southern writers (Truman Capote and Harper Lee, author of *To Kill a Mockingbird*) at the center of a drama set on the brink of the modern civil rights movement, yet makes only passing reference to the writers' home—and none at all to the political crisis that would soon strike a fatal blow to the region's insularity. In doing so, *Capote* does more than simply invert the traditional role that white southern characters have played in American movies for well over half a century. It also turns its moral compass 180 degrees from the lush backlot of America's original crime scene to track the roots of national guilt into cinematically unexpected territory.

The film's examination of artistic ruthlessness and deception, in particular, manages to upend the moral position of one of American fiction's most trusted protagonists: the white southern child (or childlike adult) who observes and comments upon social inequality (Forrest Gump, Scout Finch in *To Kill a Mockingbird*, and Huck Finn, to name three prominent examples). Truman Capote was another of these children, providing his boyhood friend Harper Lee with her model for the character of Charles Harris "Dill" Baker, Scout Finch's summer neighbor during the 1930s.[3] If Lee would later be devastated by the moral discrepancy between Truman the boy and Truman the adult, Bennett Miller and screenwriter Dan Futterman would be intrigued. The dissembling sophistication of a childlike man, in fact, provided them with the narrative DNA for a new kind of southern story, one vastly different from its Hollywood ancestors.

By the late 1950s, a cinematic "southern strategy" had begun to emerge in American films in response to mounting racial pressures that could no longer be evaded in mass entertainment. White southern resistance to federal decisions about children's education provided Hollywood with a fairly safe narrative entry into the larger subject of racism. Often displaced in romances and westerns, the southern "problem" began to be framed as an issue of *schooling*. The theme of the reeducation of recalcitrant white

FIGURE 6.1. April 1967: Alabama natives Truman Capote and Harper Lee, author of *To Kill a Mockingbird*, walk through the streets of Holcomb, Kansas, during the filming of *In Cold Blood*, released later that year. © Steve Schapiro/CORBIS.

southerners would become a generic convention in films attempting to assure audiences that a solution to southern lawlessness was readily at hand—*if*, that is, white southerners were even teachable. "Teachability," in fact, operated as more than a "rural versus urban" or "ignorance versus sophistication" theme in socially conscious films about the South. Time and again, narrative suspense regarding the white southerner's capacity for moral reeducation amounted to tacit "proof" of inherent, regionally based differences among Americans. If, as I have argued before, Hollywood located intellect and virtue as functions of place, then racism could be effectively understood as a cultural aberration rather than a national deformity.[4]

The liberal vision of the late 1950s and early 1960s ensured that narratives about a backward region would themselves often look backward, to pasts scarred by traumatic experiences. Characters trapped in the emotional and social abyss of the Hollywood South—like those played by Marlon Brando in *Sayonara* (1957), Andy Griffith in *A Face in the Crowd* (1957), Paul Newman in *The Long, Hot Summer* (1958), Robert Mitchum in *Thunder Road* (1958), and Elvis Presley in *Wild in the Country* (1961)— were forced to choose between remaining "down there" in benighted ignorance or climbing *up*, toward enlightened tolerance, maturity, and, usually, higher social class. Some required professional help to unlock their swamp-submerged nightmares. In psychiatric treatment, Joanne Woodward's tortured housewife in *The Three Faces of Eve* (1957) finally remembered the terrifying rural tradition that had shattered her personality, and more than thirty years later, Nick Nolte's character in *The Prince of Tides* (1991) would flee his native South Carolina for New York, where, at a safe distance, he could excavate the memory of his rape by a group of rampaging escaped convicts.

In recent years, the posttraumatic southern syndrome (our cinematic PTSS, it might be said) has shown little sign of abating. *Monster's Ball* (2001), *40 Shades of Blue* (2005), *Junebug* (2005), *Transamerica* (2005), *The Skeleton Key* (2005), *All the King's Men* (2006), *Black Snake Moan* (2007), *Walk the Line* (2007), numerous adaptations of John Grisham novels, and the documentaries *Paradise Lost* (1996) and *Paradise Lost 2* (2000) have dutifully disinterred the bleached cadavers of families past for national appraisal: drunken, racist patriarchs; resentful or violent sons; confused, abused daughters. Even the "other" Capote film, *Infamous* (2006), situated Truman himself as a character from the past, already dead and remembered by a host of friends and enemies primarily as a twisted clown on the run from a gothic childhood.

Rather than amplify an implicit northern/southern schism built upon metaphoric tensions between progress and torpor, enlightenment and blindness, *Capote* locates a far different continental divide. "Two worlds exist in this country," Truman Capote (Philip Seymour Hoffman) tells an interviewer in the film, "the conservative, quiet" world and its violent, criminal underbelly. The convergence of these worlds in the Clutter farmhouse is the imagined scene that holds his fascination, and its description is the climax of his book, *In Cold Blood*.[5] The "two worlds" theme runs through *Capote* as well, in the visual juxtapositions of light Kansas and dark Manhattan, white Kansans and "half-breed" murder suspect Perry Smith, death row cells and New York cocktail parties.

In the temporal displacement of *Capote*, however, a more dramatic convergence of worlds occurs. Truman's captivation with the clash of "light" and "dark" America may drive the text he is writing, but the film he is *in* is driven by an awareness of a differently factionalized culture. Looking back at the end of the Eisenhower years, when conservatism in the heartland conjured images of family farms and locally owned stores, *Capote* cannot help but be nostalgic. After all, Thomas Frank noted in 2004, the Kansas of the 1960s "was much closer to Minnesota than it was to Alabama"—far more "blue" than "red." Emphasizing just how different the new, radically red Kansas was from its past persona, Frank dismissed racism as the key to the state's current political profile. "The one thing [Kansas] doesn't do," he claimed, "is racism." "Kansas," he emphasized, "is not Alabama in the sixties."[6]

Capote makes the same point early on. "This make you miss Alabama?" Harper Lee (Catherine Keener) asks Truman on their first drive through the plains on their way to Garden City. "Not even a little bit," he replies, and, indeed, this Kansas seems far removed from Lee's and Capote's home state. Alvin Dewey (Chris Cooper), the chief investigator in the Clutter case, could not be more different from a stereotypical Deep South lawman of the sixties. To one farmer's pronouncement that the Clutter family was most likely killed by "a whole bunch of Mexicans," Dewey calmly states his equal opportunity theory of criminality: whether the killers are "Eskimo" or any other group, he doesn't care.

Neither Kansas nor middle America seems morally benighted in *Capote*, as if Garden City, in the state once known as the Garden of the World, were in an Edenic time warp. Oddly, it is Alabama—a state never even seen in the film—whose peculiar moral blight lurks in the subtext and stalks the glamorous gatherings in Manhattan. At the beginning of the film, the shame of the nation is in final dress parade at Lippincott's editorial offices. As Harper and Truman, the two friends from Monroeville, Alabama, collect the grim details of a contemporary, real-life horror story from the heart of the country, the type is being set back in New York for a fictional horror story from the Deep South of thirty years earlier, a children's Halloween tale that together with its 1962 film adaptation would help to shape Americans' understanding of their nation's historic moral flaw.

At the moment just prior to the publication of *To Kill a Mockingbird*, however, Truman Capote has decided that a new kind of writing should be developed for exploring "big," "serious" issues. Leaving aside the argument that the "nonfiction novel" had seen print before Truman made grand statements that he was "blazing a trail" in American literature, the film places repeated emphasis on the idea—voiced by *New Yorker* editor William Shawn (Bob Balaban)—that *In Cold Blood* would "change the way people write." It is at this point in U.S. history, on the eve of the 1960s, that two approaches to the national narrative converge: temporally displaced, sentimental fiction and contemporary, subjective nonfiction. The recounting of this convergence in the film *Capote* is itself both a hybrid of these genres—a temporally displaced, semi-fictionalized tale of true crime—and an ironic comment upon the failure of both forms to explain adequately social outrage and political absurdity.

To Kill a Mockingbird and *In Cold Blood* bear some striking similarities, not the least of which are the rapidity with which they achieved status as bestsellers and American "classics," and the immediacy of their adaptation into prestigious black-and-white films. Both literary works place their stories of "two Americas" (black/white, middle class/working class) in rural settings, both involve criminal trials and the uneven or unjust application of the law, and both deal with racism and racial fantasy. Both tales display filial respect for upstanding white lawmen—Atticus Finch and Alvin Dewey—and both employ the theme of stunted growth to emphasize their concern with emotional and social paralysis (Perry Smith's unnaturally truncated legs, Tom Robinson's unusable arm, Boo Radley's inability to leave his father's house, even Dill's "puny" size). "It is no mistake," literary critic Eric Sundquist has argued, "that the white children in *To Kill a Mockingbird* never grow up. In Scout's retrospective narration, they remain ever poised for the hypothesis of desegregation."[7] But the children do grow up, we learn in 2005, and by the time the adult Scout and Dill write their stories, the hypothesis has become law and "the bill" that Atticus claimed was "all adding up" and that he hoped would not come due "in you children's time"[8] now awaits payment—largely because of the Supreme Court decision issued five years before they entered Kansas, in which Topeka, the state capital, was named as defendant.

Eric Sundquist describes Lee's novel as a work that "offers an anatomy of segregation at the moment of its legal destruction."[9] *Capote*, it might be said, balances equally ironic tensions. As the nation embarks on its infatuation with the nostalgic story of Jem, Scout, and Dill, embracing its redemptive vision of white America, the disintegration of that vision is already forming in the mounting stack of Truman's typed pages, and in the historical context of that writing in the early to mid-1960s (assassinations, racial explosions, war).

Journalism, Truman said in the 1950s, "always moves along on a horizontal plane, telling a story, while fiction—good fiction—moves vertically, taking you deeper and deeper into character and events. . . . By treating a real event with fictional techniques it's possible to make this kind of synthesis."[10] He could not have found a more literal canvas upon which to test his thesis. "Out there . . . the land is flat," Capote wrote in the first paragraph of *In Cold Blood*, "and the views are awesomely extensive."[11] Not so the world of southern Alabama. "*Down* there," views are awesomely circumscribed. It's as "lonesome" as Kansas turns out to be, but one's gaze is intruded upon, he observed in *Other Voices, Other Rooms*, by the "desolate miles of swamp and field and forest," by "hollows where tiger lilies bloom the size of a man's head," and where "luminous green logs . . . shine under the dark marsh water like drowned corpses."[12]

The Deep South is, clearly, "deep," and perhaps best explored through excavation—down into the red clay, black loam, or treacherous currents of the Mississsippi River that were continuing to sweep away countless murdered bodies—rather than through plowing, which might better suit the relatively less stratified social landscape of the Midwest. In the South, one can dig indefinitely into the hierarchies and complications of class and race that stretch more thinly across the Great Plains. "Nervous," Truman says in the film about his experiment in "deep" journalism, he nevertheless, like Dill, becomes a straddler of worlds, literary and regional.

After all, Dill is the only character in *To Kill a Mockingbird* who ever leaves Maycomb, disappearing in the fall and returning each summer full of outlandish lies. It is he, Scout's "pocket Merlin," who brings a sense of the outside world to the insulated Alabama town. In fact, Dill probably instigates the culture-shattering crisis of the story in the first place. On the first page of the novel, the grown Scout says that she always maintained that the white-trash Ewell family had "started it all," but Jem ("four years my senior," hence of clearer memory, perhaps) "said it all started long before that. He said it began the summer Dill came to us, when Dill first gave us the idea of making Boo Radley come out."[13]

In *Capote*, Bennett Miller chooses to visualize Truman's apparently lifelong ability to discern secrets hidden to others through a careful compositional scheme. "We stacked the head of the film with a bunch of large landscape shots," he explained the year of the film's release, images that extend "past when you would expect a cut." When the cut finally occurs, the peacefulness of this montage is shattered by a graphic scene in which Nancy Clutter's murdered body is found. The discovery is immediately followed by a now-disconcerting seventeen-second shot of the same vast farmland seen in the film's opening. "The look is very different from the wheatfields you saw earlier," Bennett noted. "Here there is tilled land after the harvest, rows of dirt and then barren trees that speak volumes. That landscape [in this context] says 'death and mortality.'"[14] Similar shots of exaggerated horizontal composition build upon this connotation.

The film's spatial tension, however, is not between the open prairie and the shadowed Deep South; it is between Kansas and New York City. Establishing shots of vertical buildings introduce sequences of constricted space—parties and events at which Truman transfixes tightly clustered groups of people by recounting stories about Kansas. At one such party Harper Lee stands on the periphery, diffidently acknowledging a man's congratulations on her about to-be-published novel ("A children's book, right? Or is is *about* children?"), while in an adjoining room Truman entertains a spellbound audience. "I lit the room as though I was going to emphasize everything equally," cinematographer Adam Kimmel has noted, "and then I created a small pool of clean, white light for Truman."[15] One story completed, another taking shape in the movement between rooms, genres, and regions—Kansas, the more "real" place, Truman told friends in a letter, providing the "facts" that are then spun into embellished narratives for New Yorkers.[16] Proving that Kansas can indeed be dug into, not just plowed, for realistic fiction, Truman later admits to Harper Lee that the imprisoned murderer Perry Smith is a "gold mine."

Truman identifies himself in Kansas as a New Yorker, yet in New York he identifies himself (in his first appearance in the film) as "a white man from the South." But it is Lee's role in the film as the "moral conscience" of Truman's project (according to director Bennett Miller) that positions the

South itself as the moral bedrock of the story—so much so that Truman's access to locals is accomplished solely because Detective Alvin Dewey's wife Marie was, like Truman, born in New Orleans and is an avid reader of fiction.[17] When at their first meeting Truman urges Marie to load up her red beans and rice with hot sauce, he solidifies their regional bond ("Alvin will hate this," she giggles), and, indeed, this "southern connection" becomes the key that unlocks the criminal secrets of the Midwest.

Grown into liberal adults of the 1960s, Dill (Truman)—the practically orphaned child of a wayward mother and negligent father—and Scout (Harper) march uninvited into an alien culture with courage and discipline. Not surprisingly, it is Dill who loses his bearings along the way; Scout, who absorbed conduct lessons from Atticus, stays on ethical course. Having safely distanced herself from her tale of small-town violence, and having constructed a fictional, romanticized version of her own family in *To Kill a Mockingbird*, Harper Lee has little trouble respecting the border between fiction and nonfiction.

Lacking the steady hand of idealized fatherly guidance, Truman ends up as one might expect Dill to: cornered in one of his own stories. Insisting upon the technical removal of himself from *In Cold Blood*, his narrator is able to be omniscient. *Capote* redresses this narratorial absence, or what screenwriter Dan Futterman calls the book's "central dishonesty," by inserting Truman into nearly every scene of the film, insisting upon the author's creation of the situation he's reporting on.[18] Early on, Truman's ability to create and control dialogue is self-assured and deft. But these performances are merely warm-ups for his more serious inventions. When he puts in motion a *legal* narrative by finding a "proper" lawyer who can make a feasible appeal for accused murderers Perry Smith and Dick Hickock, that story assumes its own momentum, fueling a cycle of new appeals and delaying the completion of his book. Outliving their narrative function, the killers cannot be written off the page. Unable to adapt the facts to his prescribed narrative, Truman the wunderkind finds himself artistically, morally, and physically paralyzed. While American history is being remade all around him by forces in which he seems to have little to no interest, the displaced southern "documentarian" so intent on creating a new way of extracting national significance from a small-town atrocity comes to the conclusion that he can change history only by inventing it, by falling back upon what he knows best: southern fiction.

A displaced northern documentarian seems to have come to the same conclusion in 2005. Charged with finding national significance in a southern urban atrocity, Spike Lee also would revert to what he knew best: Hollywood genre. Lee's Home Box Office documentary *When the Levees Broke* (2006), a four-hour epic released to public and critical acclaim on the first anniversary of Hurricane Katrina's landfall, signaled its allegiance to the dialectical formula of liberal films of the 1950s and 1960s in its opening montage juxtaposing "old" and "new" New Orleans. The generic "racial reversal" of civil rights films such as *In the Heat of the Night* (1967) and *Guess Who's Coming to Dinner?* (1968), in which defensive white male authority is supplanted by the assured new voice of black masculinity (i.e., Sidney Poitier, Hollywood's annointed prince of black respectability), cycles back into action when New Orleans mayor C. Ray Nagin intones the first line of the documentary. "We come to you with facts," he announces to a congressional committee in Washington, implicitly imbuing the subsequent narrative with the mantle of authenticity. So invested is Lee in burnishing and preserving Nagin's authority that, later in the film, he allows radio host Garland Robinette to credit the mayor's famous, expletive-ridden outburst on the night of September 1, 2005, with finally shaming the federal government into sending federal troops to New Orleans. This fallacious correlation stands uncorrected in the film as "proof" of Nagin's heroic status in the city's battle with the Federal Emergency Management Agency (FEMA), the Department of Homeland Security, and George W. Bush (whose 2000 presidential candidacy Nagin, a Democrat, had supported—a fact omitted from the film).

One of the most significant aspects of the production and reception of *When the Levees Broke* must be the sheer fact of HBO's swift allocation of funds and substantial airtime to Lee's project (eight hours in prime time during the period of August 21–29, 2006). In their rush to find superlatives to describe the film (which had itself been rushed into completion for the anniversary), reviewers sidestepped the topic of narrative authority: the issue of *who* speaks for *whom*—and why. Considering the desultory structure of the narrative, one could be forgiven for asking why HBO would bet its considerable resources on this particular filmmaker to chronicle this particular disaster. In 2005, New Yorker Spike Lee continued to be the most famous black director in the nation, a fact that could ensure a sizable audience for the documentary. But the striking absence of other cinematic interpreters on national television screens speaks volumes about Hollywood's understanding of race. Executive boardroom logic might hold that hiring Lee to tell the "Katrina story" (as if the sprawling catastrophe were a single coherent tale) would ensure fairness: he's African American, a high percentage of New Orleans victims were African American, so what would emerge from the investment would escape charges of white bias. Significant mainstream airspace, in other words, was available to one black voice, much as significant mainstream screen space had been available to one black actor in the 1960s.

Ever the student and practitioner of American genres, Lee delivered a product containing familiar characters and themes. As a result, a catastrophe in one of the most culturally and racially complex cities in the United States became a tone poem in black and white. Erased from the palette were not only thousands of Latinos (who had begun migrating to the city as early as two weeks after the storm, leading Mayor Nagin to complain one month later that New Orleans was in danger of being "overrun by Mexican workers"), but also Asians.[19] The absence of the latter is especially perplexing in a film that emphasizes social injustice, for the almost immediate return home of the East New Orleans Vietnamese community, in the face of the city's determination to block many residents' resettlement, earned national press attention as early as one week after the levees broke.[20]

The centuries-long exoticization of New Orleans has both aided and hindered the city's faltering recovery, providing tautological justification for bringing back a unique culture (it should be restored because it *should* be restored) and for abandoning it altogether (the "sinfulness" of the place, according to voices on the Christian right, ensured its destruction and legitimates its desolation).[21] "Do You Know What It Means To Miss New Orleans?" Louis Armstrong asks during the opening montage of *When the Levees Broke*, in that famous anthem of mystification, and Lee does little to dispel the notion of the city's essentially indescribable uniqueness.

Whether Lee would admit it or not, the power of the exoticism he endorses is largely dependent upon the familiar tropes of historical racism that support the narrative spine of his story (namely, images of unending oppression and poverty amid ameliorative musical innovation). Nostalgically stalled in the past, yet purporting to confront us with tough truths about the contemporary South, *When the Levees Broke* cannot resist the pull of myth. Lee's reversion to the siren song of the Old South is unfortunate, for the "new" New Orleans may well be the face of twenty-first-century America. The privatization of public services, the massive corporate exploitation of immigrant workers from the Southern Hemisphere, and the failure of democratic processes in the wake of local disaster are problems whose national and global implications can scarcely be comprehended through a lens trained on the black and white dynamics of a plantation-styled world.

Melodrama is not the only genre that locates contemporary social significance in the mists of post-Confederate narrative conventions. One of the most commercially successful films of 2006, Sacha Baron Cohen's mockumentary *Borat*, reached back to the 1960s for its comic inspiration. In deciding to launch his fictional alter ego Borat Sagdiyev, a fictitious Kazakhstani broadcast journalist in search of "the cultural learnings of America," on a picaresque road trip across the United States, Cohen invoked—and then skewed—the nation's mythic pioneer trek. When the trip from New York to California inexplicably veers south (and stays there for much of the film's eighty-six minutes), the British comedian unleashes his sharpest satire. For Borat, the detour is a sentimental journey; the Deep South is his old stomping ground from his days on *Da Ali G Show*, the

HBO series that ran from 2003 to 2004 and featured Cohen in his three most famous personae: the wannabe gangsta Ali G, Borat, and Bruno, a gay Austrian fashion reporter (who would also venture south from time to time to interview, for example, a white Baptist pastor in Little Rock crusading for the conversion of gays, and does so again in Cohen's 2009 film *Bruno*).

On HBO, Borat appeared in segments entitled "Borat's Guide to America," in which he interviewed unsuspecting people, usually white southerners, about race, religion, and American culture. At a plantation in South Carolina, he talked with a tour guide who was once former First Lady Barbara Bush's classmate at Ashley Hall, an exclusive girls' boarding school in Charleston. Refusing to respond to his sexual allusions, she finally grew exasperated at his references to slavery (especially when he asked a costumed white actor performing seventeenth-century carpentry if he were a slave for sale). In Jackson, Mississippi, Borat interviewed James Broadwater, a white evangelical Christian Republican running for Congress, who claimed that Jews most likely would go to hell when they died; while in the city Borat also paid a visit to a group of white male wine connoisseurs who called themselves the Jackson Brotherhood of Knights of the Vine, a name whose Klan connotations certainly would not have escaped Cohen.

The continuation of Borat's southern visits in the hit movie makes sense given his creator's academic interest in the region. Sacha Baron Cohen majored in history at the University of Cambridge and wrote his undergraduate thesis on the modern civil rights movement in the United States. "The Black-Jewish Alliance: A Case of Mistaking Identities," he has said, focused on "Jewish involvement in the civil rights movement in the sixties," especially "the Schwerner, Chaney, Goodman deaths [at the hands of white men in Mississippi], and how they were perceived and whether there really *was* a black-Jewish alliance [emphasis his]."[22] Cohen revives the sixties civil rights movement's "southern strategy" of using northern, often Jewish, college students to draw media attention to racist practices in barely disguised fashion. Posing as a naïve, anti-Semitic Slav, the Jewish satirist tempts arrrest and encounters social expulsion from South Carolina to Mississippi. (The actor would even stay in character when police questioned him and his crew, a tactic that frightened him once when appearing as Bruno at an Alabama-Mississippi football game for a segment of *Da Ali G Show*. The crowd chanted, "Faggot, faggot!" at him, convincing Cohen that "60,000 bigots" might actually like to kill him.[23] He later took his revenge by exposing the drunken racism of several white University of South Carolina fraternity brothers in *Borat*.)

While embarrassing and humiliating white men and women, Borat is oddly respectful of African Americans. Given the historical racism of Eastern Europe that Cohen instills in his alter ego, we might expect Borat's anti-Semitism, like that of Nazi sympathizers, to inform a larger racism. Cohen's liberal sixties script, however, limits the cinematic playing field to a black/Jewish alliance (Cohen's suggestive and complicated layering of race-friendly Borat upon the blackface of Ali G) and its white southern antagonists. In a scene in downtown Atlanta, Borat asks a group of black men how he can be more like them. But as George Saunders suggested in a parodic article in *The New Yorker*, perhaps a reshoot of the film should consider "a list of common racial slurs that Sacha could try out on the brothers, just to see what they do to him....That seems to be the ethos of the rest of the film,...so I sense a little inconsistency here."[24]

Saunders, however, is offering a twenty-first-century critique of a mid-twentieth century work of comedy. Remove most of the expletives and nudity, and *Borat* could take its place with the satirical songs of Tom Lehrer ("I Wanna Go Back to Dixie," for example, or "National Brotherhood Week," in which "Lena Horne and Sheriff Clark are dancing cheek to cheek"), the anti-segregation riffs of Lenny Bruce, and the weekly skits of television shows like *That Was the Week That Was* and *The Smothers Brothers Comedy Hour*—many of which found white southern hypocrites, and the "patriotic" linking of anticommunism to racism, to be easy targets. Borat himself plays upon, and even appears to vindicate, the postwar rhetorical campaign of segregationists against godless communism. There he stands with the Jackson wine-lovers: the former Eastern Bloc enemy, a hopeless primitive among indulgent Cold War victors whose way of life remains as firmly god-fearing and racially segregated as it was on the night of Medgar Evers's murder in 1963. Ironically, though, despite Borat's anti-Semitism, he himself embodies the Jewish/Communist "alliance" so mythicized and denounced by white southern politicians, returning (like the specters of Goodman and Schwerner) to stir up race trouble in the Deep South. He even finds love with a large, black Alabama prostitute. Like a hip "Mammy," she comforts and marries Borat, and they start a multiracial family back in the ex-USSR.

The sixties liberalism of *Borat* is complemented by its soundtrack, an homage to late sixties/early seventies films about the failure of the American Dream. Its "confused stranger in New York City" montage revises a similar one from the 1969 film *Midnight Cowboy*, with Borat standing in for baffled Texas hick Joe Buck. "Born to Be Wild," an anthem from another 1969 film, *Easy Rider*, accompanies Borat's and his cameraman's ice cream-truck flight from New York to the South (where, unlike Captain America and Billy the Kid, they only will be socially expelled, not murdered). Borat's customized imitation of Dirty Harry ("Go ahead, Jew, make my day") is yet another reminder that Cohen's America is suspended in forty-year-old amber; held up to the light, the gloss of contemporary knowingness fails to conceal old fissures between law and order, black and white, Jewish and Gentile, liberal and conservative, North and South.

As much as *Borat* reduces the South to the imaginary terrain of regional exotica (even the progress of the road trip makes no geographical sense), the film takes a sharp turn from the liberal scripts of sixties social-problem films. Doggedly following the scent of white patrician guilt that he picked up during his television days with Ali G (and that Cohen picked up in his student days in the early nineties), Borat stubbornly refuses to be sidetracked by rednecks, hicks, or hillbillies, riding herd instead on pastors from upscale Birmingham suburbs, wine collectors and GOP politicians from affluent areas of Jackson, "fine" diners at Alabama plantations, privileged matrons from Charleston, and aggrieved fraternity boys from South Carolina who believe that "minorities have all the power." This Kazakhstani's South isn't the bloody backwoods of *To Kill a Mockingbird*, *Deliverance* (1972), or *Mississippi Burning* (1988), but it is just as criminal. In the presence of a startlingly *un*-politically correct, decidedly backward foreigner, tongues loosen and the sanitized facade of plantation tourism and New South progressivism cracks unappealingly, exposing antebellum mildew and Cold War mold. No more slavery in the South? No, one of the Mississippi oenophiles informs Borat in the *Ali G* "wine tasting" segment. "It's a good thing for them, but...," one man trails off. "But not so much for you?" Borat completes the thought. "Right," his host confirms.

The choice of Cohen to play an effete, gay French stockcar driver in *Talladega Nights: The Ballad of Ricky Bobby* (2006) was, in this sense, culturally astute, for the character's villainy is a product of the intense antipathy of the film's working-class hero, Ricky Bobby (played by Will Ferrell), and his family to anything suggestive of education or "taste." *Talladega Nights* was clearly intended as a parody of post-9/11 "Americanness," with Will Ferrell barely disguising his character's resemblance to George W. Bush (whom Ferrell skewered in comic skits throughout Bush's presidency). After the election of 2004, NASCAR itself became media code for "red state, Republican, Christian America," and the southerness of the film's major characters is secondary to their "Americanness" (red, white, and blue overwhelm the set design). Not surprisingly, Cohen, in character as driving ace Jean Girard, was roundly booed at the Talladega Superspeedway during the production—the second time that he had been booed by a crowd in Alabama.[25] Ricky Bobby's giving an arrogant Frenchman a long victory kiss in front of thousands of NASCAR fans could not be mistaken for anything other than mockery of George Bush's (and red America's) blustering, empty machismo. In *Talladega Nights*, the South takes a hit for red America—the red America created by television news and comedy, that is. Although Hollywood typically finds conservative America far more humorous when it is south of the Mason-Dixon line, in this case Bush's own faux-southerness necessitated the regional specificity of the film.

If southern white privilege is Sacha Baron Cohen's target in *Borat*, situating a character like Jean Girard among the fine diners and wine tasters of the region would serve only to make pretentious or upwardly mobile southerners seem comfortably American in their failure to impress an arrogant Frenchman. Setting a character like Borat loose among this social stratum, however, ensures their moral debasement. But at what price? Cohen, his co-writers, and his director surely knew that if Borat were to savage poor southern whites with equal fervor, the results would be decidedly unfunny. Would the real-life counterparts of Jed Clampett, Flem Snopes, and Bob Ewell be struck speechless by a poor foreigner's inexperience with modern plumbing, his superstitions about Jews, and his familiarity with incest? Scatology, undisguised prejudice, and sexual aberration routinely have found cinematic welcome in the homes of the rural poor and ignorant (just as they do in Borat's home village). The manifest joke is on those who now banish indecency from the Big House but who have profited from its historical practice. The latent joke, however, is on those who are assumed—by Hollywood, by Cohen's fan base—to live in an unhypocritical world of lax sanitation, open bias, and everyday crudeness. Cohen may go after the "big guns" of the South, but he will not tamper with the political usefulness of regional class stereotypes. His film's humor depends upon it.

So, too, does the humor of *Forrest Gump* (1994), whose eponymous hero is, next to Scout Finch, probably the most adored southern "child" narrator in American film. But Forrest's naïvete, unlike Borat's, points accusing fingers at no one except a violent, incestuous white sharecropper. From the perspective of a white "idiot"[26] (as Winston Groom calls Forrest in his novel, and which should, but doesn't, lend irony to the film), racism is bafflingly silly—much like Atticus's explanation to Jem that the Klan was a laughable sham operating "way back around nineteen-twenty."[27] Unlike poor white southern characters from the liberal films of the 1950s and 1960s who found themselves forced to accept tolerance and civility or face imprisonment, social expulsion, or death, Forrest never needs to mature: he is morally pure from birth. To some degree, *Borat* employs a similar theme: as a throwback to the "black-Jewish alliance," Borat/Cohen is rewarded for his lack of racism with a happy marriage—something he could not achieve in the "U. S. and A." Borat leaves the South before overcoming his anti-Semitism, but in keeping with the cinematic function of southern "lessons," the childish foreigner need only demonstrate his seemingly innate acceptance of black Americans to find Hollywood acceptance.

Capote, on the other hand, refuses to insist upon the inherent innocence or ignorance of its childlike main character—and, further, refuses to redeem the chastened southern adult. The tiny, precocious Alabama boy goes north, but he isn't ridiculed for either his appearance or his lack of sophistication. Instead, he is celebrated for his wit and urbanity—so much so that he becomes an operative of *The New Yorker*. His comeuppance occurs *because* he has learned too well the lessons of northern liberalism. To some degree, Truman taught New Yorkers how to be "real" New Yorkers. As George Plimpton reminisced in 1998, "Truman was born in this tiny town of Monroeville, Alabama, total population 1,600 and rose to become this great social arbiter in New York," a "social lion" who "managed to mesmerize New York and give one of the most famous balls ever given" during his reign as the "most famous writer in the country."[28]

Deviations from other "southern" conventions complement this significant inversion of mainstream cinema's regional prescriptions. If the Hollywood South has only one season (summer), *Capote*'s Kansas exists in eternal winter. The open collars, fans, and mopped brows of sweltering southern courtrooms (like Atticus's in Maycomb) are replaced in Holcomb by buttoned-up brown and gray overcoats and impassive American Gothic faces. The unpopulated, "flaxen" wheatfields in *Capote*, according to cinematographer Adam Kimmel, are intended to signify Garden City's and Holcomb's "innocence,"[29] an unthinkable (if not parodic) rationale for the production design of a film set in the South of the late 1950s and early 1960s.

Even the climax of countless southern narratives—the obligatory lynch-mob scene—fails to escape revision in *Capote*. In *To Kill a Mockingbird*, Scout, accompanied by Jem and Dill, manages to disperse the vigilantes who have come to lynch Tom Robinson by embarrassing them, but the viewer does not see the event from Tom's point of view. Tom's voice from inside the jail is the only sign of his presence. In *Capote*, however, the visual shock of a jail cell installed in a corner of the sheriff's kitchen brings criminality and domesticity (Truman's "two Americas") into one shared space, and invites Truman's eventual movement from cultural and literal outsider to intimate fellow cellmate, sitting next to Perry on his death-row mattress. This time, though, Scout cannot call off a one-man lynch mob; she can't shame Truman the way she did the group's poorest member. For this time, the vigilante isn't a redneck with a rope; it's a New Yorker with a Bergdorf scarf.

If *To Kill a Mockingbird* and *Forrest Gump* use the coming-of-age formula as a device for talking about *national* maturity, *Capote* manages to invert even this genre's trajectory. Whatever "lessons" the southern white man may learn in Kansas are buried beneath the spectacle of Truman's degeneration from a childlike but self-possessed practitioner of his art to a drunken, pabulum-slurping man who can only stammer excuses to the effect of "it's not my fault."

In our current climate of knowingness about "purchased" news, fake journalism, and what satirist Stephen Colbert calls "truthiness," describing *Capote* as a critique of journalism would be a mistake. Not only do films categorized as such (like *All the President's Men*, *Broadcast News*, and *Good Night and Good Luck*) ultimately exonerate and even venerate American journalists, which *Capote* does not do, but they, like *When the Levees Broke*, also allow mainstream assumptions about narrative control, story selection, and journalistic "integrity" to remain unchallenged.

Capote suggests something different, something subtle but troubling to people even at the time its story took place. Borrowing the conventions of the southern narrative—rural locales, violence, trials, jails, racism, upstanding white lawmen, and, most important, the "innocent" white witness—the movie relocates regional and racial tension to the 80 percent (at the time) white Midwest and rethinks the role of liberalism and social class in the shaping of "national" stories. Truman Capote deceives, manipulates, and suffers, but he would not do so without the eager assistance of his editor, William Shawn (a composite created by screenwriter Dan Futterman of Shawn and Joseph Fox, the publisher of *The New Yorker*).[30] Nor would he do so without the knowledge that an adoring audience, maintained by Shawn's public relations skills, waits on tenterhooks for his gala readings, his episodic installments in the pages of the magazine, the publication of the "big book" itself, and the inevitable movie version.

The "on the road" pairing of Truman Capote and Harper Lee reworks the "buddy" formula of attracted opposites to offer a contrast between the "two worlds" of moral invention and amoral truth-telling, old-fashioned fiction and new-ish journalism. The "ever faithful historians," as they called themselves in a letter to Alvin Dewey in 1960, each contributed a compelling version of the national narrative.[31] But it is the fictional version, *To Kill a Mockingbird*, that so much of the population has embraced for its "authenticity" (of place, time, and voice). For tens of thousands of people—at least—the sense of "the real South" seems to saturate the book and the 1962 movie version (even though *To Kill a Mockingbird* was obviously filmed in California, despite the conviction of host Robert Osborne of Turner Classic Movies in 1999 that "you'd swear it was done *entirely* on location").

Adopting Lee's strategy of temporal displacement, *Capote* looks back at a watershed moment in national myth making without alluding to a single incident in the traumatic decade of the 1960s (except, of course, for the publication and filming of *To Kill a Mockingbird*). No television, radio, or newspaper tells us anything about the rest of the world. Indeed, the film's focus is not on a writer's *reacting* to the world but, rather, on a writer's *creating* a world. Here, a southern white man stands condemned of immorality by a character who is not only his best friend (Harper Lee) but also the "moral conscience" of the film, condemned *not* for being a southern white man but for making choices driven by the cultural demands of "bicoastal" liberal tastes.

By placing a southern white man at the center of an emerging way of representing national culture, a way that exploits what many *New Yorker* readers would surely consider the exotica of "flyover" America for publishing and film profit, *Capote* reverses the old formula of class-based southern guilt. For once, a privileged white son of the Deep South—not a cracker, redneck, or hillbilly (not Bob Ewell, in other words)—is held accountable for ethical transgressions. And these transgressions are motivated by the culture industry deep in the heart of political "blueness"—hardly a new or surprising idea, but one that Hollywood and Madison Avenue had long evaded through 2005.

Catpote's postscript tells us that although Truman became the most famous writer in the United States after the publication of *In Cold Blood*, he never wrote another book (a point challenged by fans of *Music for Chameleons*, a 1980 collection of nonfiction and fiction short works).[32] Those who remember, or search for, further biographical information are confronted by the spectacle of a man who publicly displayed his artistic paralysis on national television, to the point of giving warning in the 1970s of his eventual suicide. How odd that Truman Capote and Harper Lee, the two comrades who offered vastly different "classic" tales of American violence and injustice, had nothing left to say by the mid-1960s.

Truman Capote died in 1984 at the height of the Reagan era, a cultural moment he helped to create. The blurring of fiction and nonfiction in national politics and the Hollywoodization of journalism coincided with the decline of prosperous working-class America across the Midwest in the 1980s and the cynically motivated revitalization of a romanticized notion of patriotic white Americans (for whom it was supposedly "morning again" in 1984). The white southern man of the 1950s and 1960s may have faced punishment for his "inherent" racism and criminality, but by 2005 his presence was primarily an allusion to old regional allegories. Having lived through a decade of mounting demands for social integration in their own backyards, Truman Capote and Harper Lee were several steps ahead of Hollywood, prowling a new frontier of imminent national *dis*integration. Regionalism would offer them no insight here.

That the motivation for the slaughter of the Clutter family might have been as banal and unnuanced as that of the criminals in Hannah Arendt's *Eichmann in Jerusalem* was not a thesis that Truman was intellectually prepared to accept.[33] His psychological reading of Perry Smith's behavior was culturally astute and readily embraced by a readership drilled in the nostrums of psychoanalysis. Psychological interpretation also offered an avenue into the synthesis of fiction and nonfiction for which Truman was searching—the flatness of "scientific" observation and analysis combined with the depth of narrative reconstructions of complexes and associations.

Just as the legal discourse within *To Kill a Mockingbird* functioned as a way of persuading readers in 1960 that a way out of racist practices now existed (that had not in the 1930s), *In Cold Blood*'s psychiatric discourse offered an escape route from the escalating violence of the 1960s, a different way of understanding the "causes" of random social brutality. *Capote* looks back at a time when artists struggled with answers to racism and social violence, and believed their ideas somehow mattered. In this, it is surely nostalgic. But the film (like *In Cold Blood*) leaves open to question just how the Clutter murders were committed, and by whom, exactly. (So much in the book is suspect, and in the film we must not only trust Truman's point of view of Perry's "confession" but also keep in mind Perry's sister's admission that her brother is himself capable of great deceptions). Because *Capote* weaves possible psychological explanations into the script without giving them narrative priority, the central question in the film is how and why Truman's involvement in the case led to his self-destruction (rather than the how and why of the crime itself).

Scanning the pages of the *New York Times* early in the film, Truman alights upon the buried story of the Clutter murders. Biographical material attests to Truman's avid desire to take on a nonfictional subject and the fact that he had been waiting for the "right one" to appear. Swooping into remote Kansas to scavenge for good material, Truman was in no small way an avatar of the plundering corporate raiders of later years—with one difference: remorse, self-castigation, and slow suicide are not characteristics of the CEOs who created the "tragic land," as Thomas Frank calls it, of contemporary Kansas.[34]

A question that haunts discussions of *Capote* is why neither Truman nor Harper Lee ever produced substantial work after their Kansas experience. Truman had insisted that his story take place "out there," beyond the reach of urban news and culture in an imagined center of all-Americanness (Lee's biographer, in fact, describes the highway the two writers took into Garden City as the "Road to Nowhere").[35] Looking at his conviction from the film's 2005 point of view, we might well wonder where such a place would exist now, or what Truman's narrative experiment would even mean in an era of fabricated journalism and fake news. But the study undertaken by two Deep Southerners of a region vastly different from theirs crystallized a number of other temporally dependent ironies. The presumption of white southerners attempting to dissect midwestern social violence while the white South was entering the most dramatic phase of its own resistance to social justice was ironic enough. Forty-five years later, with white southern theatre majors—not rednecks or crackers—burning down black *and* white churches in rural Alabama just to be "stupid," and middle-class white Kansans describing themselves as the most politically "victimized" demographic group in the country, the political geography of social class *and* regionalism did indeed appear to have been turned upside down.[36] By the time *Capote* was nearing completion in 2004, neither the South nor the Midwest "meant" what it did in 1960. Nevertheless, U.S. Army spokespersons that year blamed the torture at Abu Ghraib on "recycled hillbillies"[37] and national journalists laid responsibility for George W. Bush's reelection at the trailer steps of NASCAR devotees.

The cultural plundering of the South started many decades ago, abetted by well-intentioned writers like Harper Lee. As if foreseeing the overproduction and eventual depletion of "authentic" southern characters, towns, and tourist sites, Truman Capote rushed to a "gold mine" that extended far beyond Perry Smith's brutalized psyche—a barely known, sparsely populated landscape of seeming authenticity. *Capote*'s central irony is the complicity of two southerners in the literary reconstruction and exoticization of yet another region. Now fully explored and exploited, the Midwest can take its place with the South as a nostalgically rendered set of signifiers. With the accelerating erasure of regionalism in the face of all-American corporate sprawl, Truman's spatial metaphors for literary genres now seem quaint. The economic strip-mining of the nation has flattened the landscape in more than one way. The digging already done, perhaps "horizontal" journalism is the only appropriate genre left with which to tell the "national story"; and even journalism, in yet another irony, has "synthesized" fiction in ways that Truman, with his cutting wit, probably *could* have imagined.

Eric Sundquist believes that *To Kill a Mockingbird* chronicles the nightmare of America's own growing up.[38] But in the time separating the novel's publication in 1960 and our contemporary reading of the book, the United States entered what seems to be its moral and economic senescence. *Capote* locates the moment of decline in the denouement of southern resonance—in the recognition of national, not simply regional, political culpability. In the last shot of the film, flying back to New York from the hangings in Kansas, Truman holds on his lap Perry Smith's sketch of him. On top of that he has placed a black-and-white photograph of Perry as a child. The criminal dimensions of his artistry are finally unavoidable, and it is a murderer's rendering of Truman's face that will stare back at him for the next nineteen years. Little wonder that he is struck speechless, and that he essentially will remain so for the rest of his life.

"Can it be," film historian David Thomson asked in 2005, "that it's not so much that the movies died as that history has already passed them by?"[39] *Capote* ironically demonstrates this possibility, locating an inconvenient contemporary fact simultaneously in the time of its cultural denial (2005) and in the period of its emergence (the 1960s). Hollywood's insistence that America's "innocence" was lost during the violent decade of the sixties has undeniable political power, and its dependence upon a regional understanding of this national trauma may perhaps have even greater cultural power. Cinematically speaking, the South is America's past, its Oedipal nightmare, its site of criminal revelation. Not coincidentally, some of the most successful screenwriters of the 1960s (like Stirling Silliphant, who wrote *In the Heat of the Night*, the first movie of the civil rights era to be set in the contemporary South) acknowledged the importance of personal psychoanalysis in their work. The story of the "discovery" and "defeat" of racism has become a national genre, told again and again to convince ourselves that the ordeal is over, and that it wasn't "our" fault. Like the hero of *Good Will Hunting* (1997), Americans can repeat to themselves that it was the fault of others—bad white men of little education and even lesser means—a strategy emphatically rejected in *Capote*. This genre, whether labeled the "southern film" or the "civil rights film," locates the origin of national sin "down there," in a region that, try as we might, cannot be emotionally severed from the heady aspirations of cultural consciousness.

The South of the cinematic imagination may bear little resemblance to a geographical area of the same name, but our familiarity with its "story," and our internalization of its narrative requirements, ensure that region will always trump nation in the "blame game." Thomas Frank may assert that the new mystery of America is that the political geography of social class has been turned upside down, but cultural logic tells us something different: that what was "down there" is far more mysterious, far more dangerous, and far more difficult to dislodge from the depths of the national imagination.

NOTES

1. Thomas Frank, *What's the Matter With Kansas? How Conservatives Won the Heart of America* (New York: Metropolitan Books, 2004), 1, 76, 104.

2. Frank, *What's the Matter*, 76, 53–55, 29, 59.

3. Harper Lee, *To Kill a Mockingbird* (New York: Warner Books, 1982; original 1960).

4. Allison Graham, *Framing the South: Hollywood, Television, and Race during the Civil Rights Struggle* (Baltimore: Johns Hopkins University Press, 2001).

5. Truman Capote, *In Cold Blood: A True Account of a Multiple Murder and its Consequences* (New York: Vintage, 1994; original 1965).

6. Frank, *What's the Matter*, 89, 179.

7. Eric J. Sundquist, "Blues for Atticus Finch," in *The South as an American Problem*, ed. Larry J. Griffin and Don H. Doyle (Athens: University of Georgia Press, 1995), 206.

8. Lee, *To Kill a Mockingbird*, 221.

9. Sundquist, "Blues for Atticus Finch," 183–84.

10. Gerald Clarke, *Capote: A Biography* (New York: Carroll and Graf, 1988), 357.

11. Capote, *In Cold Blood*, 3.

12. Truman Capote, *Other Voices, Other Rooms* (New York: Vintage, 1994; original 1948), 3.

13. Lee, *To Kill a Mockingbird*, 8, 3.

14. "Film of the Moment: Capote," *IFP: The Source for Independent Filmmakers*, http://www.ifp.org/, October 25, 2005, 3.

15. Author interview with Adam Kimmel, January 27, 2006.

16. Clarke, *Capote*, 336.

17. Thomas Mallon, "Big Bird," *The New Yorker*, May 29, 2006, 79.

18. Jay Stone, "Actor Finds His Voice as Writer of *Capote*," *Ottawa Citizen*, December 28, 2005, C8.

19. Roberto Lovato, "Rebuilding the Big Easy," *Salon*, October 19, 2005, http://dir.salon.com/story/news/feature/2005/10/19/latino_new_orleans/index.html. Also see "Immigrants Rush to New Orleans as Builders Fight for Workers," October 11, 2005, http://www.workpermit.com/news/2005_10_11/us/new_orleans.htm; Miriam Jordan, "New Orleans Suit Over H-2B Guest Workers," August 2006, http://www.workingimmigrants.com/2006/08/new_orleans_suit_over_h2b_gues.html. The latter documents a corporate application to the U.S. Labor Dept. for immigrant workers filed five weeks after the storm that falsely claimed that no hurricane evacuees would apply for work in post-Katrina New Orleans. Such claims ignited and exacerbated tensions between African Americans and Latinos in the aftermath of the disaster.

20. "All Things Considered," broadcast on National Public Radio (http://www.npr.org/), began its coverage of the Vietnamese community Honeysuckle Lane on September 3, 2005, and followed the neighborhood's rebuilding efforts for the next year. Also see Christine Hauser, "Sustaining Close Ties, Vietnamese Toil To Rebuild," *New York Times*, October 10, 2005.

21. Pentecostal televangelist John Hagee, for example, said in a 2006 NPR interview that "Hurricane Katrina was, in fact, the judgment of God against the city of New Orleans"; see Media Matters for America, "County Fair" Blog Posting, February 28, 2008, http://mediamatters.org/items/200802280018. Two days after Katrina struck the Gulf Coast, the director of Repent America (a Philadelphia-based evangelical organization), Michael Marcavage, said that "this act of God destroyed a wicked city"; see Repent America, "Hurricane Katrina Destroys New Orleans Days before 'Southern Decadence,'" August 31, 2005, http://repentamerica.com/pr_hurricanekatrina.html.

22. Sacha Baron Cohen interview with Robert Siegel, "All Things Considered," National Public Radio, July 23, 2004, http://www.npr.org/templates/story/story.php?storyId=3613548.

23. Sacha Baron Cohen interview with Terry Gross, "Fresh Air," National Public Radio, January 4, 2007, http://www.npr.org/templates/story/story.php?storyId=6723074.

24. George Saunders, "'Borat': The Memo," *The New Yorker*, December 4, 2006, 57.

25. Cohen interview with Terry Gross.

26. Winston Groom, *Forrest Gump* (New York: Pocket Books, 1994).

27. Lee, *To Kill a Mockingbird*, 147.

28. Tanya Stanciu and Amy Nickell, "Trumpeting Truman: A Conversation with George Plimpton about Truman Capote," *Gadfly,* June 1998, http://gadflyonline.com/archive-plimpton.html.

29. Kimmel interview.

30. Meghan O'Rourke, "Philip Seymour Hoffman," *Slate,* January 31, 2006, http://www.slate.com/id/2135151/.

31. Gerald Clarke, ed., *Too Brief a Treat: The Letters of Truman Capote* (New York: Vintage, 2004), 276.

32. Truman Capote, *Music for Chameleons* (New York: Random House, 1980).

33. Hannah Arendt, *Eichmann in Jerusalem: A Report on the Banality of Evil* (New York: Viking, 1963).

34. Frank, *What's the Matter,* 239.

35. Charles J. Shields, *Mockingbird: A Portrait of Harper Lee* (New York: Henry Holt, 2006), 135.

36. In March 2006, two students at Birmingham-Southern College and one student at the University of Alabama at Birmingham confessed to setting nine Baptist churches on fire, thereby unleashing what the state's attorney general called "a reign of terror that had gripped rural Alabama and riveted the attention of the nation"; see Doug Lederman, "3 Students Charged in Ala. Church Fires," *Inside Higher Ed,* March 9, 2006, http://insidehighered.com/news/2006/03/09/arson.

37. Seymour M. Hersh, "The Gray Zone," *The New Yorker,* May 24, 2004, 41.

38. Sundquist, "Blues for Atticus Finch," 185.

39. David Thomson, *The Whole Equation: A History of Hollywood* (New York: Knopf, 2005), 370.

Part III

BORDER CROSSINGS

7

A NATION IN MOTION

**Norfolk, the Pentagon, and the
Nationalization of the Metropolitan South,
1941–1953**

James T. Sparrow

In 1952, in the midst of the Korean War, C. Vann Woodward opened his landmark essay, "The Irony of Southern History," with a troubled observation: "In a time when nationalism sweeps everything else before it, as it does at present, the regional historian is likely to be oppressed by a sense of his unimportance." Toward the end of the decade, Woodward continued to bemoan the homogenizing trend of nationalization, ruing that "the time is coming, if indeed it has not already arrived, when the Southerner will begin to ask himself whether there is really any longer very much point in calling himself a Southerner." The "Bulldozer Revolution," that "advance agent of the metropolis," was razing the very landscape that had made the South a Place, in the fully capitalized sense of the word.[1]

Bulldozers were the most visible emblem of the forces remaking the South at mid-century, but they represented much more than material or even economic transformation. The total social experience of war mobilization, not simply defense spending per se, made the changes that came to the South between Pearl Harbor and the end of the Korean War transformative rather than evolutionary. War brought ordinary Americans into more intimate contact with the national state than had ever been the case, even during the palmiest days of New Deal reform, when states and localities made use of federalism to interpose themselves between Washington and the grassroots. Federal power during wartime steadily encroached on local communities and the elites who ruled them, although most southern communities were able to sustain the rudiments of home rule and stave off social upheaval for some time.[2] As a result, the relationship of regional identity and race relations to national sovereignty was forever altered by the response to global war that overtook the United States in the middle decades of the twentieth century.

This essay examines that transformation through case studies of Norfolk and the Pentagon, two metropolitan sites in Virginia that epitomized southern dynamism while also serving as headquarters for a vast new military establishment that bestrode the free world. Both places were exceptional, and so they generally have not been incorporated into the established narratives of the New South. Yet in their particularly intense patterns of militarization and modernization, these two Virginia landscapes highlight many of the key social processes and political openings that gradually worked to nationalize the region in the postwar period. Before turning to these case studies, it is necessary to place them within a larger context of national reconfiguration.

NATIONAL CIRCULATIONS AND REGIONAL RECONFIGURATION

Just two decades before Woodward's lament, scholars and federal policymakers had stressed the vast gulf that appeared to separate the South from the rest of the nation. According to this "regionalist" school of thought, led by University of North Carolina sociologist Howard Odum, the underdeveloped South had diverged fatefully from the rest of the nation. Despite being blessed by "superabundant" natural resources, the former states of the Confederacy had cultivated "a landscape of dilemmas" marked by the extravagant waste of both natural and human resources, and by enduring "folkways" that seemed to root southern distinctiveness in the very soil. The regionalists believed that only comprehensive planning on the magnitude of the Tennessee Valley Authority (TVA)—which sought to reorient nearly every facet of southern life toward a more modern, democratic pattern—could return the South to the nation, making it a region among regions rather than a section apart.[3]

New Deal policymakers agreed that national planning could modernize the poorest parts of the South through the TVA and other development projects. Throughout the 1930s and 1940s, policymakers targeted the problem of southern underdevelopment through an array of federal policies, including crop subsidies, land conservation, rural electrification, wage and hour standards, and military base location. All these measures and more lavished federal largesse on the region, reflecting the concerns of liberal reformers as well as conservative southern Democrats in Congress. "The South is the Nation's Number One Economic Problem," announced President Franklin D. Roosevelt in 1938, who shared their fears that southern "backwardness" threatened national recovery from the Depression.[4]

In the end it was the eventualities of war, rather than the grand plans of the regionalists or the sly designs of southern Democrats, that tipped the South toward convergence with the other regions of the United States. In the decades following Pearl Harbor, the South shifted from being the poorest, most economically stagnant corner of the nation to the most dynamic part of the booming Sunbelt.[5] The southern economy took off during World War II, especially in metropolitan centers such as Norfolk, Atlanta, Birmingham, Dallas, and Houston. Although the North and West enjoyed higher absolute levels of federal investment, the South's relative position within the national political economy nonetheless changed dramatically, as its share of total federal investment went up by a third over its prewar portion, and the kinds of investments it received proved formative for its nascent industries. Because it lagged so far behind the other regions, its rates of industrial expansion, military encampment, and growth of sheer federal government presence outstripped those of the North and the West.[6]

As a consequence, southern incomes rose much more rapidly than did those outside the region, shooting up from a dismal 50 to 60 percent of national per capita levels during the 1930s to somewhere between 60 and 80 percent by 1950, then to upwards of 90 percent by 1980. During the 1940s alone, the proportion of southern workers employed as skilled operators, craftsmen, salespersons, clerical workers, managers, and professionals increased at a rate markedly higher than in the rest of the United States. This is not to say that the growth was evenly distributed across the region—far from it. The long-term transformation was concentrated in the burgeoning metropolitan areas of the South, whose populations expanded five times more rapidly than their competitors in the more heavily urbanized North and West. The leap in southern urbanization was especially dramatic for large metropolitan areas: nine of the nineteen largest cities in the nation that grew most rapidly during the 1940s were located in the South. But gains were not restricted to the largest cities. Half of all southern cities with populations of 10,000 or more increased in population by at least 25 percent during the decade. By 1950 the South was still less urbanized than the West and North, but its burgeoning urban centers now represented roughly half of all U.S. cities that had expanded during the decade.[7]

Historical narratives of this period often focus on the flood tide of southern exodus known as the Great Migration, and with good reason. Roughly a quarter of the southern labor force left home during the war. As James Gregory has demonstrated in his magisterial study of the black and white migrations from the South during the twentieth century, the exodus (which really took off during World War II and continued for decades thereafter) reworked the nation, the South, and the relation between the two.[8] As dramatic as southern migration was in these years, it was not an isolated phenomenon. Approximately one-fifth of the entire national population—somewhere between 25 and 31 million people—moved to new counties between 1940 and 1945, and roughly half of that migration was interstate.[9] Migrants from the Northeast and Midwest were just as much a part of this great national mix-up as were southerners. Indeed, nearly as many migrants to the West Coast—the prime wartime destination—came from the north-central states of the Midwest as from the South.[10] If the South stood apart from the other regions, it was due to its somewhat *lower* rate of out-migration: between April 1940 and September 1943, the South's population dropped by 3.4 percent, while those of the Northeast and the Midwest shrank by 5.7 and 4.3 percent, respectively. These differentials reflected the deferral of the South's large rural workforce from the draft, and the greater tendency of southerners to migrate to cities within the region, rather than to other regions.[11]

Migration meant more than just travel. In *Edwards v. California* (1941), the Supreme Court affirmed the constitutional right to free movement, ruling that the "poor laws of Elizabethan England" no longer applied to men like Fred Edwards, who had broken California law when he helped his brother-in-law Frank Duncan cross state lines to relocate from Texas in 1939 and subsequently receive public assistance. Because the most visible migrants to California during both the Depression and World War II were "Okies," the case held great resonance for southerners, announcing their right to escape desperate circumstances at home and realize the national dimensions of their citizenship. It held significance for the national interest, as well. An amicus curiae brief by Congressman John Tolan of California, the chairman of the Select Committee on National Defense Migration, claimed that without the right to move at will, defense migration would produce "2 [million] Stateless people in this country. Is that good for the morale of this country?...What strikes at civilian morale strikes at national defense." Justice Robert H. Jackson concurred with the majority opinion, noting that Duncan "owes a duty to render military service" not limited by his impoverishment. "Rich or penniless, Duncan's citizenship under the Constitution pledges his strength to the defense of California as a part of the United States, and his right to migrate to any part of the land he must defend is something she must respect under the same instrument." The duties of impending war had transformed a Depression-era debate about the rights of paupers, highlighting the national nature of citizenship and clarifying the right to migration so necessary to the war economy.[12]

While the metamorphosis brought on by mobilization for World War II and the Cold War was especially dramatic in the South, its convulsions wracked the entire nation. All of the great regions of the United States— the West and the North, as well as the South—were remade by three intertwining processes unleashed during World War II: migration, metropolitanization, and militarization. The nationalizing influences of these three great historical pulses can be seen with special vividness in the communities hosting the military headquarters of the Navy and the Army, whose decisions did so much to shape this "reconnaissance of regions."[13]

NORFOLK: THE TIDEWATER LEVIATHAN

In the 1940s, the military bases and shipyards in Hampton Roads stood on hallowed southern ground, yet they also served as signposts of regional reconfiguration. On the north side of the James River sat Newport News, Hampton and Elizabeth City, and Warwick. Facing them on the south side was Norfolk, the oldest city and urban heart of the metropolis, where one hundred vessels docked at a naval operating base that commanded the defense of the Atlantic during the submarine war with Germany. It occupied a site that had been settled since the earliest days of the Tidewater, when the foundations of southern society were established. Its venerable navy yard predated the U.S. Navy itself, yet its modern works produced forty-two warships over the course of World War II and employed a peak workforce of forty thousand (nearly seven times larger than before the war).[14] Nearby were South Norfolk and Portsmouth, which housed thousands of new arrivals. To the east lay the Army's Camp Pendleton, surrounded by Princess Anne and Virginia Beach. By the end of the war, each of these was a large city by southern standards, and Hampton Roads stood apart as the largest military center in the world.[15] Local lives became further enmeshed in national and global developments in 1948, with the permanent headquartering of the Navy's Atlantic Command in Norfolk. Four years later, the North Atlantic Treaty Organization (NATO) also chose Norfolk for its Allied Command, Atlantic, which directed the world's first international navy. By mid-century, Hampton Roads had more in common with San Diego, the Navy's West Coast headquarters, than with nearby Richmond. It had become a leviathan on the Tidewater.

A flood of migrants made their way to Hampton Roads as a consequence of the military buildup. Over the course of World War II alone, 1.7 million servicemen passed through the area on their way overseas (and back), many of them black southerners enjoying a newfound freedom to travel and the prestige that came with a military uniform (figure 7.1). On the streets of Norfolk, they crossed paths with tens of thousands of civilians from across the nation, each of whom brought particular regional perspectives to bear on life in this boomtown. Between 1940 and 1944, the Hampton Roads population nearly doubled to 312,643 residents, with 80 percent of new migrants coming from outside of Virginia and 33 percent from outside the South. As with most migrants to war production areas, the vast majority (83 percent) were urbanites. Consequently,

Hampton Roads received one of the first federal designations as a "congested war area." Truly, the people of Norfolk found themselves "going among strangers," as the historian Pete Daniel has characterized the experience of World War II in the South.[16]

With this tremendous population growth came significant federal aid—and increased involvement in local affairs. By 1943, a profusion of civilian and military agencies, from the Public Building Administration to the Quartermasters' Corps, worked with city officials in Norfolk, Portsmouth, and Newport News to spend over $13 million in federal funds, matched by more than $10 million from local coffers, to extend water works and sewer lines; build roads, schools, parks, and hospitals; and support other

FIGURE 7.1. November 7, 1943: Black and white enlisted soldiers on the deck of the USS *Mohawk* arrive in Hampton Roads for rest and rehabilitation following fifty flight missions in North Africa. These are a few of the 1.7 million servicemen who moved through the bases and ports of Hampton Roads during World War II, making the area a military clearinghouse for soldiers of diverse backgrounds from all parts of the country. The metropolitan region of Norfolk/Hampton Roads continued to boom during the Cold War, especially after its selection as the location of the Navy's Atlantic Command. © The Mariners' Museum/CORBIS.

vital infrastructure. Housing dominated public investment in the area, with $127 million spent on public housing, mostly from federal funds, and $110 million spent on private residences, mostly from private loans backed by federal guarantees. As in other war-boom communities such as Detroit, the pattern of development concentrated poorly constructed public units, to which African Americans were largely confined, in crowded central city areas (where the population increased by 50 percent), while more expensive private units, to which whites were almost exclusively entitled, sprang up on the outskirts, pushing up suburban population levels by 100 percent. The federal government fostered this "decentralized urbanism" through policies that segmented real estate markets by class and race, literally underwriting property values with social privilege. Thus, federal-local cooperation during the war laid the groundwork for the postwar urban crisis, ultimately hollowing out the vitality of central cities by means of federally subsidized suburban growth, and in the process reinscribing hierarchies of racial difference onto the metropolitan landscape.[17]

Perhaps it is not surprising, then, that Norfolk became the site of the nation's first federally funded urban renewal project after the war. As the host of "Project Number One" of the Housing Act of 1949, Norfolk received federal authorization to clear forty-seven blocks that had deteriorated to slum status during the war, to be replaced by the Tidewater Park and Young Park developments. The city's bid for urban renewal funds doubtless had been bolstered by its early establishment of the Norfolk Redevelopment and Housing Authority (NRHA) and by the creation of the Norfolk Port Authority in 1948. City authorities had learned systematically to attune policies and priorities to attract as many federal dollars as could be had.[18]

Housing was not the only realm in which national solutions were needed for local problems. No public problem was more intimately local than that of vice, and yet Norfolk's reputation in that area became a national scandal during the war. In 1942, a glossy exposé titled "Norfolk Night" appeared in *Collier's*, voyeuristically illustrated with scenes from local bars and bawdy houses. Sensational coverage in other national magazines followed, the most lurid of which was "Norfolk—Our Worst War Town," published by *American Mercury* in 1943.[19] In response, city leaders sought to shift the blame by claiming that social problems were in fact national—and certainly not local—in scope. In an appearance before Congress, Col. Charles Borland, the city manager of Norfolk, insisted that the federal government should take even further responsibility for funding local affairs, including the operation of detention quarters for prostitutes. "This great influx in population has been brought about by the war," Borland explained, "and the city of Norfolk is unable to cope with all the problems it is faced with." Subsequent testimony sought to establish the precise proportions of venereal disease "imported" into various Hampton Roads communities from outside the area.[20] As historians Beth Bailey and David Farber have shown for Hawaii, another place overwhelmed by the national military buildup, venereal disease and prostitution provided one of the most dramatic demonstrations of the inability of local communities to provide for the public welfare in wartime. In Norfolk, as in Hawaii, locals turned to the military to provide solutions that otherwise would have been rejected as unwarranted incursions of distant authority.[21]

The most vivid challenge to regional traditions came in the area of race relations, which altered dramatically in southern cities, while the countryside languished under the yoke of rules long set by planters and other local elites. This was not so much a regional development as it was a national urban one. In the North and Midwest, clashes over employment, housing, transportation, and public amenities crested in 1943 in tandem with migration of African Americans out of the South. Urban turf wars over the "the second ghetto" and white dispersion to northern suburbs both began in earnest during this period, sparking race riots in Detroit, Harlem, and in scores of smaller cities as well. Similarly explosive conflicts emerged in war plants where black employees made even modest gains, prompting white "hate strikes" that shut down production and sometimes brought bloodshed.[22]

The turmoil that the war unleashed in the South was caused not only by the rawness of racial tensions but also by the fact that community leaders now had to answer to war agencies whose polices were set in Washington. In this sense, the war mobilization by its very nature politicized everyday life, raising awareness of "the national" and "the local" in the process. Official propaganda touting liberal war aims only exacerbated this effect, emboldening the black press, civil rights groups, and ordinary African Americans to push wherever possible for the "Double V": victory over racism at home as a necessary complement to the war against Nazi racial supremacy overseas. Consequently, the freedoms fostered by migration, city living, and employment assumed a more heightened political significance than in peacetime, directly demonstrating as they did what it meant to evade or challenge the tyranny of local customs. As both the defenders and the challengers of Jim Crow knew, the federal government was the source of these new developments.

Perhaps the most menacing example of federal intervention was also the most toothless: the Fair Employment Practices Commission (FEPC), created by President Roosevelt to head off the March on Washington organized by black labor leader A. Philip Randolph in 1941, but never provided with enforcement powers or a sufficient budget. Despite these liabilities, the FEPC proved to be a powerful catalyst of change that would destabilize local race relations in Hampton Roads and elsewhere in the metropolitan South. The black communities of Hampton Roads were able to make impressive claims of citizenship during these years, bolstered by the assertiveness of black railroad unions, the prominence of black workers in waterfront jobs, and by a larger than usual share of new migrants. Nearly 30,000 African Americans held defense jobs in the Hampton Roads area during World War II. As they found themselves systematically shunted to the lowest rungs of the war economy, many turned to the FEPC.[23]

The politicized process of filing discrimination charges helped forge a shared consciousness, activism, and tenacity that had been lacking in earlier years. In 1942, Timothy Hill provided an example of this new resolve when he wrote directly to Paul McNutt, the head of the War Manpower Commission, to complain about a supervisor who had thwarted his inquiries about promotion and advancement in the Paint Department of the Newport News Shipbuilding and Drydock Company. The supervisor had told Hill that he sought "too much money for a colored man." He expected to be drafted for his insolence "any-day." ("I am not the only one doing that way," he added.) Hill pressed his case despite the hostility and threats he encountered, and the FEPC launched a full investigation that ultimately required the company's vice president to answer to the federal government.[24] Scores of similar complaints about stymied training and promotions flowed into the FEPC's Washington office when black workers' grievances were ignored by an internal commission at the naval air station.[25]

Such complaints could not be dismissed at the federal level, even if they were evaded by industry. The "battle for production" had become too central to both the ideology and the economics of the national war mobilization. Consequently, this kind of bold challenge to Jim Crow cropped up in all of the metropolitan war centers, but most strikingly in the South. A black worker in the Houston shipyards who had been denied training and promotion to the position of mechanic echoed the sentiments of his Norfolk brethren when he wrote to the FEPC in March of 1943: "We who have qualified to fill some important jobs in war plants would like to send fighting material...to our men in Service as fast as we can [but] they will not allow us because we are colored."[26] War work allowed African Americans to assert a direct connection between their efforts and the fighting on the front lines, and to suggest a treasonable obstruction in the racial discrimination of their employers. In the urban centers of the North and West, where party competition amplified the leverage available to black unionists and community organizers, a kindred, if more powerful, civil rights movement began to take root.[27]

The largely symbolic nature of the FEPC's authority may seem severely proscribed by today's standards. Yet it was taken very seriously by those most affected by its limitations. When the FEPC appeared in danger of expiring in 1943, African Americans in Norfolk raised money to campaign for a permanent agency.[28] After the war, the battle for a permanent FEPC would remain a central concern of civil rights organizations—especially outside the South, where many fair employment councils were in fact created.[29] The inclusion of African Americans on local war boards similarly provided a public voice, a vote, and a legitimacy whose memory could not be erased when the war ended. In Norfolk, this role appears to have inspired an upsurge in civic activity and a gutsy voter registration drive.[30]

Heightened expectations and politicized racial consciousness were not the only results of the politics of fair employment. A fireman on the Norfolk Southern Railway helped permanently alter national labor law in 1944, when the Supreme Court ruled favorably on his case, *Tunstall v. Brotherhood of Locomotive Firemen and Enginemen*.[31] Like many railway unions whose racial policies had been highlighted by well-publicized FEPC hearings, the Brotherhood had signed an exclusive contract with the Norfolk Southern Railway. This resulted in Tunstall's replacement by a white employee, despite his three decades of accumulated seniority. With assistance from the Norfolk chapter of the NAACP, Tunstall appealed to the Supreme Court, which consolidated his case with the companion litigation *Steele v. Louisville & N.R. Co.*, involving a nearly identical claim brought by a black Alabama fireman. In his concurring opinion, Justice Frank Murphy pointed out that although the Brotherhood was a private organization, the U.S. Congress had conferred on it powers of representation in the Railway Labor Act of 1934. In what must have been news to the white brotherhoods, whose restrictive practices had not troubled labor law for a decade, Murphy observed: "A sound democracy cannot allow such discrimination to go unchallenged. Racism is far too virulent today to permit the slightest refusal, in the light of a Constitution that abhors it, to expose and condemn it wherever it appears in the course of a statutory interpretation."[32]

Over time, the rulings in *Tunstall* and *Steele* would dilute the power of white brotherhoods to exclude black workers, linking a union's right to represent workers to the fairness of its practices. In a postwar political economy that channeled many of the most valuable public goods (such as health care) through private channels, this right to membership, though limited, was crucial.[33] The Supreme Court ruling in these labor discrimination cases was of a piece with its verdict in *Smith v. Allwright* (1944), which also prohibited racial exclusion from a voluntary association granted the power of representation: the Democratic Party. Although southern Democrats would spend two decades working around this decision, it provided one more instance of federal power eroding home rule—and one more crack in the Solid South.[34]

THE PENTAGON: A WORLD'S FAIR GONE TO WAR

On September 11, 1941, the U.S. Army broke ground on a new headquarters that could accommodate its burgeoning office staff, then scattered among seventeen different buildings in the District of Columbia. Built on land that had seceded not once but twice, and made of sand and gravel dredged from that great sectional boundary, the Potomac River, the Pentagon was to become the "nerve center" of the nation's first large standing army—and of all the military branches when it became the headquarters of the National Military Establishment (subsequently renamed the Department of Defense) from 1947 onward. From the earliest days of its opening in the spring of 1942, the Pentagon functioned as the nexus of a militarized national political economy and culture whose global ambitions in World War II and the Cold War would rework the sectional dynamics that had defined American life since the Civil War.

The new home of the War Department was located on some of the most sacred soil of sectionalism. It stood adjacent to the Arlington National Cemetery in northern Virginia, within sight of the Lee Mansion. The Pentagon represented a very different order of regional reconstruction than had been envisioned by the Federals who had overrun the plantation of Robert E. Lee's in-laws more than eighty years earlier in their war against the "Slave Power." During World War II, U.S. Army officials heatedly rejected the notion that "social experiments" such as integration could be entertained at a moment of such peril. The leaders of the armed forces admitted only one overriding goal: to win the war as quickly as possible. And yet, after almost four years of "total warfare" from 1941 to 1945, followed by constant preparation for the possibility of World War III, and then the "limited war" waged in Korea from 1950 to 1953, experiments and expedients such as troop integration would be among the least of the changes inaugurated by the new military establishment.

The Pentagon was located in, but was not really of, the South. It seemed to have dropped down out of the sky from some world of the future. Not long after all five rings of the world's largest office building had been completed, the reporter Sidney Shalett brought readers of the *New York Times* on a tour. "There's a tang of nostalgia," he wrote of the complex. "You have been here before." Trying to place the memory, Shalett looked out across the Potomac to see a familiar vista suddenly transformed. Viewed from the Pentagon, the dome of the Jefferson Memorial and the obelisk of the Washington Monument reminded him of the alien trademarks of the 1939 New York World's Fair, the Trylon and the Perisphere. The Pentagon, Shalett declared, "is the World's Fair Gone to War."[35]

The Pentagon as a landscape was a harbinger of the decentralized urbanism that the defense economy would help foster in northern Virginia, and in so many metropolitan areas around the nation. Viewed from the air—the only vantage point from which the entire building could be seen—the swirling feeder roads and sprawling parking lots made apparent that the Pentagon existed within its own infrastructural ecosystem (figure 7.2). Early accounts of the opening of the "Army's Giant 'Five-by-Five'" invariably included layered diagrams of its five concentric rings, whose massive

FIGURE 7.2. An aerial view of the Pentagon, "the nerve center of the U.S. Army," taken on January 11, 1945. Located in the suburbs of northern Virginia, the Pentagon became a primary symbol of the militarization of the southern landscape and the decentralized urbanism promoted by federal defense spending during and after World War II. © Bettmann/CORBIS.

scale and segmented space anticipated the horizontal flow of postwar shopping malls. (The Pentagon opened with its own dedicated shopping concourse).[36]

Journalistic reports of the Pentagon's wonders emphasized the building's "efficiency" despite its gigantism. Although the complex was large enough to swallow the Pyramid of Cheops, Chicago's Merchandise Mart, or five Capitol buildings, offices with functional identifiers such as "5C535" were never more than a six- or seven-minute walk away, thanks to the building's pentagonal design. Receiving over thirty thousand workers through its doors each day during World War II, fed by a bus station comparable in size to New York's Pennsylvania Station, serviced by the largest private switchboard on earth, surrounded by thirty miles of new highways and fifty acres of parking lots, and commanding its own D.C. zip code (despite its Virginia location), the Pentagon constituted more than a city within a building; it represented a new way of ordering public space.[37]

If the Pentagon seemed a world unto itself, it also sent lines of command out into the wider world. By the spring of 1945, it was already clear that this encampment was in truth a global one. *Fortune* referred to the Pentagon's inhabitants as "agents for the armies and air forces scattered from Fort Knox to the Rhine, from the Presidio to the Philippines." To highlight the nation's odyssey from sectional conflict to global war, the article reminded readers that "here on the bank of the Potomac where Lee once maneuvered centers American twentieth-century might."[38] Following the example of their nineteenth-century predecessors charged with Indian removal from the continental interior, the military brass installed in the Pentagon by the late 1940s directed troops toward the new twentieth-century global frontier that separated the "free world" from communist territory.[39]

Much like the Navy's headquarters in Hampton Roads, the Army's pentagonal HQ in Arlington transformed its surrounding community by channeling the concentrated clout of a total war mobilization into a social topography previously organized around more local patterns. This was true even for Washington, D.C., which until Pearl Harbor remained a sleepy, provincial southern town. Because it housed the war agencies, the Washington metropolitan area expanded at a staggering pace during World War II. In the District of Columbia, the population more than doubled from 1940 to 1943. Arlington County grew by 50 percent during the same period. By 1950, the District had become the center of a world-class metropolis, filled with migrants from around the country and around the world.[40] A pattern of metropolitan consolidation and population dispersion to outlying suburbs played out along roughly the same lines as in Hampton Roads, and for the same reasons.

The landscape surrounding the Pentagon changed dramatically in a few short years. Before World War II, a ragged assortment of brickyards, refineries, meat-rendering facilities, pawnshops, gas stations, and squatters' shacks known as "Hell's Bottom" had populated the marshy plain where the Pentagon now stood. "Only woods and stream" had marked the land outside the incorporated boundaries of nearby Alexandria, one of Virginia's oldest cities. "The most drastic change in the old rural Virginia setting," reported *National Geographic* in 1953, "is the rise of great apartment cities, especially along the routes of the new arterial highways." Vast complexes of apartments appeared almost overnight astride the brand-new Shirley Highway, the first limited-access highway in the state, which ran south and west from the very parking lots of the Pentagon. The contrast between Old Town Alexandria, with its stately brick homes on the compact grid of the eighteenth-century mercantile city, and the curving suburban streets lined with one-story apartment buildings interspersed by lawns, demonstrated the spatial reorientation that the war-fueled metropolis had undergone.

"More space and lower rents lure Washingtonians to Arlington," explained *National Geographic*, as did the fresh air, sunlit lawns, recreational facilities, and basement "hobby shops" offered in modern subdivisions with names evocative of the Old South, such as "Colonial Village" and "Lee Gardens." A new $15 million shopping center in Arlington County contained an anchor department store and eighteen smaller establishments, as well as parking spaces for two thousand automobiles. By the early 1950s, Arlington residents lived a modern suburban existence that would have seemed positively futuristic even to the thousands who had crowded into group apartments and hot beds only a few years earlier during the wartime housing crunch. The curvilinear landscape of the postwar metropolis covered every last acre of the land where Union troops had once encamped on their way to occupy and reconstruct the South.[41]

Arlington County's decentralized urbanism shared the same liabilities that marked the other war-boom metropolises across the nation. Residential development stratified postwar communities according to spatial boundaries of class and race. Yet bureaucratic momentum could also work in the opposite direction under the right conditions, eroding rather than reinforcing local hierarchies of difference, especially when they stood in the way of national priorities. Such was the case with racial segregation within the Pentagon building.

Although the land surrounding the Pentagon remained safely ensconced in all the prerogatives of Jim Crow, the state of Virginia had ceded to the U.S. government the grounds on which the building stood. According to the same executive order that had created the FEPC in 1941, the federal government was prohibited from discriminating against its employees on the basis of race, creed, color, or national origin. The Army viewed this civilian regulation with indifference. It unapologetically adhered to racial segregation in its personnel policies, as it had for decades. However, the Department of War was a civilian, cabinet-level agency, and therein lay the rub. Consequently, when President Roosevelt conducted his inspection of the Pentagon site just prior to its opening in the spring of 1942, he pointedly noted the wasteful construction of duplicate bathrooms, only to be told that Virginia's segregation laws required separate facilities. Roosevelt soon made his disapproval known. Subsequently, the rooms' signage was left indeterminate regarding their racial designation and the bathrooms were effectively desegregated.[42]

A little more than a week after Roosevelt's visit, when War Department employees began working in the Pentagon building, the question of segregation erupted into violence. Black employees of the Ordnance Department refused to eat in a separate "Negro" cafeteria room, prompting a white guard to strike one of the men viciously. The guard, and the private contractor who employed him, asserted that Virginia law applied to the cafeteria until the construction of the building was complete. The Ordnance employees refused to back down, despite the intimidation. Tellingly, the most active participants in this spontaneous protest were recent migrants from distant places outside the South: Jimmy Harold (who was struck by the guard) had moved from Detroit six months earlier. His co-worker Henry Bennett had recently arrived from Indiana State Teachers College in Terre Haute. Ruth Bush, a transplanted New Yorker, had initially helped set the scene by confronting another guard blocking her entrance to the main lunchroom with bitter and powerful words: "This is America, not Germany. I am an American; I'll die for America, therefore I have every right that any other American has. Just think, I have brothers in the war now, fighting."[43]

When Bush and the others presented their case, the War Department's civilian aide for Negro affairs, Judge William H. Hastie, intervened forcefully and brought the matter to the attention of Secretary of War Henry Stimson, who ordered an investigation. But the Army immediately sought to bury the altercation with a rigged investigation by the Inspector General. The defense contractor continued to insist on his legal duty to observe Virginia segregation law. Fortunately for the black Ordnance employees, General Brehon Somervell, commanding officer in charge of the Pentagon construction project, exercised the discretion accorded him as a military authority in wartime. He ordered "the discontinuance of any enforced segregation" inside the Pentagon, and there the matter stood for the duration of the war (and afterward). Similar complaints by black workers prompted other public facilities in the vicinity to desegregate. By 1946, the "lone stronghold of Jim Crowism on federal property" in the immediate area was Washington National Airport.[44]

At the same time that the Pentagon reworked its immediate environs, it also remade individual men, inducting them from all corners of the nation and subjecting them to basic training and extended tours of duty. Military service placed GIs in the same boat for the duration, forcing them to accommodate one another or confirm for themselves their differences. The racial attitudes and practices the men brought with them from their hometowns assumed a new cast within a military bureaucracy that placed uniformity and order above personal attitudes or local traditions. The power of bureaucracy over regional folkways can be seen in the progress of military desegregation in the early 1950s, a surprisingly sudden development given the Army's rigid adherence to Jim Crow a few years earlier.

Through military service, a generation of young men encountered a cross-section of the nation's population, produced through the social engineering of selective service classification, screening procedures, testing, training, and assignment to a unit whose relationship to the local communities from which its men were drawn was far more tenuous than in earlier conflicts. At basic training, as green enlistees experienced their indoctrination to military culture, they also had to adjust to the outlooks and expectations of men from other parts of the country, and to the distant communities in which they were based. One white soldier, apparently unfamiliar with southern mores, wrote in shock at the end of his War Department morale questionnaire that "there are [sic] too much Jim Crowism in the Army....The Negro are [sic] not given a fair chance....The white officers are more hard [sic] on Negro [than] white." Another white soldier observed: "I think the Negro soldier should be allowed to converse with the WAC [Women's Army Corps] on this post, because after all they are supposed to be fighting for a Democracy." For many young men new to the South, it seemed that the whole "Army think[s] slow, talks slow, and acts slow just like a lazy Southerner." Others noted tensions between men from the East and West coasts. In many cases, the World War II military experience helped reinforce negative regional stereotypes.[45]

The most severe clashes of regional identity occurred when black soldiers from the North encountered white southerners in military camps, bases, and local southern towns. As the thousands of letters written to Judge Hastie and his successor, Truman Gibson, attested, the southern noncommissioned officers in charge of training camps were quick to uphold Jim Crow customs. One correspondent wrote of "this hell hole," Camp Livingston, Louisiana: "Brother, if you are colored, you don't stand a chance down here." He then catalogued a wide range of abuses visited upon black troops by white officers, including being excluded from everything from United Service Organization Camp Shows, to special training, to watching in outrage as "even the German prisoners of war have more freedom and opportunities than us." The author was driven to distraction reflecting on how skilled and educated soldiers were "led like lambs to the slaughter to die for a democracy that doesn't exist down here."[46] Over the course of the war, this "Hitlerism at home," as the proponents of the Double V termed it, sparked concerted opposition among black troops, boosted enrollment in the NAACP, and prompted numerous violent outbreaks in camps throughout the South.[47] Many of the bitterest fights involved black soldiers in uniform (especially officers) whose presence on streets off base failed to elicit salutes, or whose efforts to eat in local restaurants were refused with icy stares and worse.[48] These encounters educated and steeled a cohort of men who returned home and assumed leading roles in the early civil rights movement. As veterans, they held a moral authority that made their protests difficult to ignore or discount.[49] White southerners devoted to segregation took note. The roving journalist John Gunther wrote during his 1944 tour of the fifty states that "almost every victim of lynching since the war has been a veteran."[50]

While universal military service certainly heightened racial tension and militancy among soldiers of all races, it also helped to erode stereotypes and ultimately laid the foundation for one of the first (and arguably the most thorough) desegregation efforts, of the U.S. Army. Civil rights activism of the sort provided by A. Philip Randolph and the NAACP helped pave the way, prompting President Harry Truman's 1948 executive order requiring the desegregation of the military. But during the next two years the Army dragged its feet while the Navy and Air Force pursued only modest steps toward eliminating segregation. With the coming of the Korean War, the Army's stance changed unexpectedly as a result of happenstance, military policy, bureaucratic momentum, and a well-timed investigation by Thurgood Marshall of the NAACP Legal Defense Fund.[51] The resulting abandonment of segregated troop formation, which the Army nearly completed by the end of the Korean War in 1953, demonstrated that even the most rigidly structured institutions and communities could discard or circumscribe tradition when subjected to the right pressures.

Surprisingly, one of the Army's first major steps toward desegregation took place in South Carolina, on the watch of two of the period's most committed segregationists: Governor Strom Thurmond, who had challenged Truman in 1948 under the Dixiecrat banner, and Thurmond's successor, the southern power broker James F. Byrnes. Fort Jackson, located just outside of the capital city of Columbia, had firmly resisted even the mildest gestures toward integration pursued by the Army brass during and immediately after World War II. By the summer of 1950, when the United States suddenly entered into war against North Korea, Fort Jackson was on the verge of shutting down, its segregated facilities in place but largely vacant. This contingency—in tandem with the abandonment of racial quotas in the Army's Korean War draft, and a policy made by Pentagon brass that assigned nearly all southern draftees to induction at Fort Jackson—created logistical circumstances that favored quiet desegregation of the Army units assembled there. The inductees were simply too numerous (37,160 had arrived by November), the proportion of black soldiers too great (26 percent, reflecting African-American need as well as determination to serve), and the existing staff too limited to handle the double burden of sustaining Jim Crow. The commander in charge, Brigadier General Frank McConnell, moved expeditiously to ensure that efficiency of processing, rather than traditions of segregated troop assignment, would prevail.[52]

Responses to the "open secret" at Fort Jackson were surprisingly mild, given South Carolina's storied role in sustaining the racial order of the South. Thurmond's grip on state politics allowed him to avoid locking horns with the Army by simply ignoring it, with no political repercussions. Byrnes, upon assuming the governorship, admitted to President Eisenhower that "the exclusive Federal jurisdiction, both civil and criminal, over Federal installations...is generally recognized. It can be disputed by no one." Local reactions were generally muted or cautiously positive. Congressman John Riley acknowledged that states' rights ended at the boundary of federal property. Others local leaders, eager to court the Army's favor so as not to kill the golden goose of military spending in the area, made no protest.[53]

As the Korean conflict took its initial, volatile course between the summers of 1950 and 1951, a similar combination of logistics, pragmatism, bureaucratic inertia, and official Army policy brought about the gradual abandonment of Jim Crow. The long tradition of segregated troop assignments began to erode with the manpower crunch and general disarray caused by the North Korean and Chinese counteroffensive in late 1950. The timing of this transition was also likely influenced by the NAACP's overseas investigation of high court-martial rates for black troops during the conflict. By the end of the Korean War, the U.S. Army was effectively a desegregated institution.

Social scientists confirmed the normative effects of bureaucracy and established policy with "Project Clear," a study of the impact of desegregation on morale and combat efficiency. Their research revealed to Army policymakers that the experience of serving alongside soldiers of another race (especially in combat) provided a powerful counterweight to preexisting racial attitudes, lessening opposition to desegregation over time.[54] Regardless of their outlook, nearly all soldiers went along with military policy once it was implemented. Even white soldiers who frankly admitted to prejudice acknowledged that serving alongside black soldiers had changed their perspectives, at least in practical terms. As one white infantryman told the Project Clear interviewers, "back in the states, I don't like 'em as good as I do over here. Over here, everybody's here to do a job. Back in the states you don't see them as much. Over here you might sit down and shoot the shit with one of them for three or four hours." A captain back in the States admitted that, as a white Tennessean, prejudice came naturally to him, but after serving with a black college professor in Germany he realized "that man gave me an education in race relations."[55]

CONCLUSION

In the short run, the boisterous growth of the Army and the Navy during the 1940s and early 1950s posed a modest challenge to southern sovereignty and white supremacy because both branches of the armed forces were devoted to their own traditions, including a rigid adherence to racial segregation. Nonetheless, the changes unleashed by militarization were momentous in the long term. Metropolitanization, and the migration that drove it, generated greater immediate upheaval, although its segmented pattern of settlement ultimately dampened the raw social energies that had threatened to break out in 1943 at the peak of mobilization.

What amplified the transformative potential of all these changes, and laid the groundwork for a new regional dynamic in which southerners led lives much more similar to those of their fellow Americans in other regions, was the growing salience of national citizenship in a polity where the federal government in times of crisis could brook little or no resistance to its priorities. Until the civil rights showdown of the late 1950s and 1960s, southern communities found many ways to evade such confrontations. Yet there was a logic to nationalization that the New South could not ultimately escape. Both guns and butter were available for most of the Cold War, at least in the military-favored South. But states' rights could not stand in the path of the warfare state, nor could local communities court the economic abundance of the Sunbelt and expect to remain unchanged in their social relations. The South was finally becoming a region among regions, rather than a section apart. It took more than defense dollars and bulldozers on the old plantation to bring this shift about, although both were critical; it required all the force of a nation in motion.

NOTES

This essay is dedicated to the memory of Jack Thomas, whose vision regarding all things regional—and everything else, for that matter—was an inspiration and model. I owe special thanks to the following people for their willingness to provide constructive criticism on earlier drafts of this essay: Thomas Jessen Adams, Jane Dailey, Douglas Flamming, William Leuchtenburg, William Novak, and of course Matthew Lassiter and Joseph Crespino, whose generosity and insight have been exceptional.

1. C. Vann Woodward, "The Irony of Southern History" and "The Search for Southern Identity," in *The Burden of Southern History* (Baton Rouge: Louisiana State University Press, 1960), quotations from the 3rd ed. (1990), 3, 6–7, 189.

2. Cf. Roger Lotchin, *Fortress California, 1910–1961: From Warfare to Welfare* (New York: Oxford University Press, 1992).

3. Howard Odum, *Southern Regions of the United States* (Chapel Hill: University of North Carolina Press, 1936), 61; Odum, *The Way of the South: Toward the Regional Balance of America* (New York: MacMillan, 1947); Robert L. Dorman, *The Revolt of the Provinces: The Regionalist Movement in America, 1920–1945* (Chapel Hill: University of North Carolina Press, 1993), 181–93.

4. Bruce J. Schulman, *From Cotton Belt to Sunbelt: Federal Policy, Economic Development, and the Transformation of the South, 1938–1980* (New York: Oxford University Press, 1991), 3–87; U.S. National Emergency Council, *Report on Economic Conditions of the South* (Washington: GPO, 1938).

5. Schulman, *Cotton Belt to Sunbelt*; Numan V. Bartley, *The New South, 1945–1980* (Baton Rouge: Louisiana State University Press, 1995); Gavin Wright, *Old South, New South: Revolutions in the Southern Economy since the Civil War* (Baton Rouge: Louisiana State University Press, 1996); Dewey Grantham, *The South in Modern America: A Region at Odds* (New York: HarperCollins, 1994); Philip Scranton, ed., *The Second Wave: Southern Industrialization from the 1940s to the*

1970s (Athens: University of Georgia Press, 2001); Pete Daniel, *Lost Revolutions: The South in the 1950s* (Chapel Hill: University of North Carolina Press, 2000); Pete Daniel, "Going Among Strangers: Southern Reactions to World War II," *Journal of American History*, 77, no. 3 (December 1990): 886–911.

6. David L. Carlton, "The American South and the U.S. Defense Economy: A Historical View," in *The South, the Nation, and the World: Perspectives on Southern Economic Development*, ed. Carlton and Peter Coclanis (Charlottesville: University of Virginia Press, 2003), 151–62; Gregory Hooks, "Guns and Butter, North and South: The Federal Contribution to Manufacturing Growth, 1940–1990," in Scranton, *Second Wave*, 255–85.

7. Lorin Thompson, "Urbanization, Occupational Shift and Economic Progress," in *The Urban South*, ed. Rupert B. Vance and Nicholas J. Demerath (Chapel Hill: University of North Carolina Press, 1954), 44; Wright, *Old South, New South*, 239–69; Albert G. Ballert, "The Rises and Declines of American Urban Centers during the 1940s," *Land Economics*, 28, no. 3 (August 1952): 203–11.

8. James N. Gregory, *The Southern Diaspora: How the Great Migrations of Black and White Southerners Transformed America* (Chapel Hill: University of North Carolina Press, 2005).

9. "27 Million U.S. Citizens Change Homes in War," *Chicago Tribune*, September 2, 1945, 3; Susan B. Carter, ed., *Historical Statistics of the United States: Earliest Times to the Present* (New York: Cambridge University Press, 2006), Series Ac424–25.

10. Henry Shryock, *Population Mobility within the United States* (Chicago: Community and Family Study Center, University of Chicago, 1964), 235.

11. Rudolph Heberle, *The Impact of the War on Population Redistribution in the South* (Nashville: Vanderbilt University Press, 1945), 14–15.

12. *Edwards v. California*, 314 U.S. 160 (1941); U.S. Congress, House of Representatives, *Hearings before the Select Committee Investigating National Defense Migration* (Washington: GPO, 1942), Part 26, 10214, 10227–231; Charles D. Chamberlain, *Victory at Home: Manpower and Race in the American South during World War II* (Athens: University of Georgia Press, 2003).

13. D. W. Meing, *Global America, 1915–2000* (New Haven: Yale University Press, 2004), 159–67.

14. Edmund S. Morgan, *American Slavery, American Freedom: The Ordeal of Colonial Virginia* (New York: Norton, 1975); Thomas C. Parramore, *Norfolk: The First Four Centuries* (Charlottesville: University Press of Virginia, 1994).

15. U.S. Congress, House Committee on Naval Affairs, *Investigation of Congested Areas, Part I: Hampton Roads, Virginia, Area, March 24–27, 1943* (Washington: GPO, 1943), 82, 111–12 (turnover extrapolated from an 8-month rate, but in line with other shipyards during World War II); Parramore, *Norfolk*, 335, 339.

16. U.S. Committee for Congested Production Areas, *Final Report* (Washington: GPO, 1944), 6; *Observations on the Sample Censuses in Ten Congested*

Production Areas (Washington: GPO, 1944), 3, 5, 8–9; Daniel, "Going among Strangers."

17. The term "decentralized urbanism" is from Greg Hise, "Home Building and Industrial Decentralization in Los Angeles: The Roots of the Postwar Urban Region," *Journal of Urban History,* 19, no. 2 (February 1993): 95–125. Also see Kenneth T. Jackson, *Crabgrass Frontier: The Suburbanization of the United States* (New York: Oxford University Press, 1985); Thomas J. Sugrue, *The Origins of the Urban Crisis: Race and Inequality in Postwar Detroit* (Princeton: Princeton University Press, 1996); David M. P. Freund, *Colored Property: State Policy and White Racial Politics in Suburban America* (Chicago: University of Chicago Press, 2007). On Hampton Roads, consult *Investigation of Congested Areas*, 138, 203, 311, 350–57; Parramore, *Norfolk*, 338, 340–41; Annie Lash Jester, Martha Woodruff Hiden, Kemper Kellogg, and William Stauffer, *History of the City of Newport News, 1941–1945* (Richmond: Baughman Co., 1948), 70–77.

18. Thomas W. Hanchett, "Roots of the 'Renaissance': Federal Incentives to Urban Planning, 1941 to 1948," *Journal of the American Planning Association,* 60 (1994): 197–208; Forrest R. White, *Pride and Prejudice: School Desegregation and Urban Renewal in Norfolk, 1950–1959* (Westport: Praeger, 1992); Parramore, *Norfolk*, 352–57.

19. Parramore, *Norfolk*, 331–4.

20. *Investigation of Congested Areas*, 5, 308.

21. Beth Bailey and David Farber, *The First Strange Place: The Alchemy of Race and Sex in World War II Hawaii* (New York: Free Press, 1992), 95–132.

22. Gregory, *Southern Diaspora*, 16; Sugrue, *Origins of the Urban Crisis*; Dominic J. Capeci, *Layered Violence: The Detroit Rioters of 1943* (Jackson: University of Mississippi Press, 1991); Capeci, *The Harlem Riot of 1943* (Philadelphia: Temple University Press, 1977).

23. Earl Lewis, *In Their Own Interests: Race, Class, and Power in Twentieth-Century Norfolk, Virginia* (Berkeley: University of California Press, 1991), 167–98.

24. Case in Folder "N," Reel 26, Microfilm Record of Selected Documents of Records of the Committee on Fair Employment Practice [hereinafter FEPC Records].

25. Lewis, *In Their Own Interests*, 182–83.

26. Freddie Barrett Letter, March 6, 1943, in Houston Shipbuilding Case Folder, Reel 25, FEPC Records.

27. Martha Biondi, *To Stand and Fight: The Struggle for Civil Rights in Postwar New York City* (Cambridge: Harvard University Press, 2003); Gregory, *Southern Diaspora*; Merle Reed, *Seedtime for the Modern Civil Rights Movement: The President's Committee on Fair Employment Practice, 1941–1946* (Baton Rouge: Louisiana State University Press, 1991).

28. Lewis, *In Their Own Interests*, 176; Eric Arnesen, *Brotherhoods of Color: Black Railroad Workers and the Struggle for Equality* (Cambridge: Harvard University Press, 2001), 181–202.

29. Biondi, *To Stand and Fight*; Reed, *Seedtime*.

BORDER CROSSINGS

30. Lewis, *In Their Own Interests*, 167–98. Also see Biondi, *To Stand and Fight*; Arnesen, *Brotherhoods of Color*, 181–229.

31. *Tunstall v. Brotherhood of Locomotive Firemen and Enginemen*, 323 U.S. 210 (1944).

32. *Steele v. Louisville & N.R. Co.*, 323 U.S. 192 (1944).

33. Arnesen, *Brotherhoods of Color*, 234; Jennifer Klein, *For All These Rights: Business, Labor, and the Shaping of America's Public-Private Welfare State* (Princeton: Princeton University Press, 2003).

34. *Smith v. Allwright*, 21 U.S. 649 (1944).

35. Sidney Shalett, "Mammoth Cave, Washington, DC," *New York Times*, June 27, 1943; C. B. Overman, "I Run the World's Biggest Building," *American Magazine*, January 1951, 129. Also see Steve Vogel, *The Pentagon, A History: The Untold Story of the Wartime Race to Build the Pentagon—And to Restore It Sixty Years Later* (New York: Random House, 2007).

36. "The Army's Giant 'Five-by-Five,'" *Popular Mechanics*, March 1943, 8–9; Shalett, "Mammoth Cave"; Alden P. Armagnac, "Nerve Center of the Fighting Forces," *Popular Science Monthly*, February, 1943, 49–53.

37. Henry F. Pringle, "My Thirty Days in the Pentagon," *Saturday Evening Post*, October 16, 1943, 27, 58, 61; Armagnac, "Nerve Center."

38. "The Pentagon: U.S. Army Headquarters Become the Powerhouse of the Nation," *Fortune*, April 1945, 122–23.

39. Hanson Baldwin, "U.S. 'Frontier' Is Issue: The Rhine or the Pyrenees Is Debated Among Pentagon Building Groups," *New York Times*, October 10, 1948.

40. David Brinkley, *Washington Goes to War* (New York: Knopf, 1988), 105–6; Carl Abbott, "Dimensions of Regional Change in Washington, D.C.," *American Historical Review*, 95, no. 5 (December 1990): 1367–93; *County and City Data Books*, University of Virginia, Geospatial and Statistical Data Center, http://fisher.lib.virginia.edu/collections/stats/ccdb/data, retrieved August 17, 2007.

41. Albert W. Atwood, "Across the Potomac from Washington: Growing Pains Afflict Arlington County and Alexandria as the Nation's Capital Overflows into Near-by Virginia," *National Geographic*, January 1953, 1–33.

42. Vogel, *Pentagon*, 200, 217.

43. Vogel, *Pentagon*, 222–25.

44. "Pentagon Battle Revealed," *Chicago Defender*, June 22, 1946, 13; Vogel, *Pentagon*, 222–29.

45. [American Soldier] Free Comment I & E Questionnaires, Formerly Security-Classified Microfilm Copy of Records Relating to the Morale of Personnel (1941–45), Frame 347, Reel 10, Frame 76, Reel 41, Frame 176, Reel 19, Frame 92, Reel 19, 1942–1946, Special Staff, Information and Education Division, War Department General and Special Staffs, RG 165, National Archives II, College Park; Morton Sosna, "The GI's South and the North-South Dialogue during World War II," in *Developing Dixie: Modernization in a Traditional Society*, ed. Winifred Moore, Joseph Tripp and Lyon Tyler (Westport: Greenwood Press, 1988), 311–26.

46. Pvt. James Pritchell to the Asst. Civilian Aide to the Secretary of War, January 12, 1944, Camp Livingston, LA Folder, Box 186, General Subject File 1940–1947, Records of the Civilian Aide to the Secretary of War, RG 107, National Archives II, College Park.

47. Richard Dalfiume, *Desegregation of the U.S. Armed Forces: Fighting on Two Fronts, 1939–1953* (Columbia: University of Missouri Press, 1969), 64–81.

48. Bailey and Farber, *First Strange Place*; Lizabeth Cohen, *A Consumers' Republic: The Politics of Mass Consumption in Postwar America* (New York: Knopf, 2003), 90–96; Robin D. G. Kelley, *Race Rebels: Culture, Politics, and the Black Working Class* (New York: Free Press, 1996), 17–75.

49. John Dittmer, *Local People: The Struggle for Civil Rights in Mississippi* (Urbana: University of Illinois Press, 1994); Charles M. Payne, *I've Got the Light of Freedom: The Organizing Tradition and the Mississippi Freedom Struggle* (Berkeley: University of California Press, 1995); Steven F. Lawson, *Black Ballots: Voting Rights in the South, 1944–1969* (New York: Columbia University Press, 1976).

50. John Gunther, *Inside U.S.A.* (New York: Harper & Bros., 1947), 687.

51. Dalfiume, *Desegregation of the U.S. Armed Forces*, 201–19.

52. Andrew H. Myers, *Black, White and Olive Drab: Racial Integration at Fort Jackson, South Carolina, and the Civil Rights Movement* (Charlottesville: University of Virginia Press, 2006), 74–91.

53. Myers, *Black, White and Olive Drab*, 86–91 (Byrnes quoted on 86).

54. Original report reprinted in Leo Bogart, ed., *Project Clear: Social Research and the Desegregation of the United States Army* (New Brunswick: Transaction, 1992). Also see Gary Gerstle, *American Crucible: Race and Nation in the Twentieth Century* (Princeton: Princeton University Press, 2001).

55. Bogart, *Project Clear*, 96, 183.

8

THE COLD WAR AT THE GRASSROOTS

Militarization and Modernization in South Carolina

Kari Frederickson

Lenwood Melton, age seventy-seven, has lived in the village of Graniteville, South Carolina, his entire life. Nestled in Horse Creek Valley, Graniteville was built in the 1840s to house employees of the Graniteville Company, the South's second oldest textile mill. Melton hails from a family of mill workers. He spent his early years in company housing; later, his father built the family a home up on Breezy Hill, just beyond the mill village. Like his father, brother, and sister before him, Lenwood went to work for the Graniteville Company as a teenager. In the 1950s, his wife, Edith—herself the daughter of millworkers—took a job as a secretary working for the operations office of the new Savannah River Plant (SRP). Located ten miles from Graniteville, the Savannah River Plant was a massive facility constructed in the early 1950s and dedicated to producing materials for the hydrogen bomb. With the aid of Edith's income, the family moved into the comfortable brick ranch house that they continue to occupy today. Sitting on his front porch, Lenwood Melton could pitch a rock and hit any number of homes owned by former textile employees who made their homes in this middle-class enclave after casting their lots with the new Cold War enterprise.[1]

With the construction of the Savannah River Plant, Melton and his neighbors found themselves suddenly thrust into the vortex of the Cold War. In early 1950, following the revelation that the Soviet Union had exploded an atomic device, the U.S. Atomic Energy Commission (AEC) recommended the creation of the hydrogen bomb, a thermonuclear weapon whose destructive powers were projected to be hundreds of times greater than that of the bombs dropped on Hiroshima and Nagasaki. The arms race had begun. To create this new "super" bomb, the nation needed a facility to produce tritium and plutonium. The AEC chose the Du Pont Corporation of Wilmington, Delaware, to direct the new atomic project.[2] AEC and Du Pont officials spent four months investigating some 114 potential sites.[3] On November 28, 1950, they announced the selection of a South Carolina location that bordered the Savannah River along the state's western border with Georgia, near the town of Aiken and about twenty miles from the city of Augusta. A massive undertaking, the plant site ultimately occupied about 250,000 acres of land in Aiken, Barnwell, and Allendale counties. The $2 billion plant was the largest construction project to date in the United States, on par with the construction of the Panama Canal. When operations commenced in October 1952, the Savannah River Plant represented the jewel in the crown of the nation's expanding nuclear arsenal.[4]

The promises, opportunities, and problems that accompanied the creation of the Savannah River Plant and other defense-related installations are part of the larger story of what scholars call the region's "second wave" of industrialization.[5] Beginning in the New Deal years, and escalating during World War II, an emerging generation of southern business and political leaders adopted a new and lucrative relationship with the federal government. Partly casting aside old antipathies, these apostles of development came to view federal aid as "the engine of economic growth."[6] Federal dollars provided the means by which the South could escape its economic colonialism to the North and acquire the development capital that the region sorely lacked. The campaign to win federal contracts and defense installations, as well as to attract industry generally, became a broad-based effort in which local and state political leaders, industrial development commissions, chambers of commerce, and newspapers joined together to "sell the South."[7]

The Cold War accelerated and intensified the militarization of the southern economy. Private industry competed for defense contracts, and states aggressively pursued funds for infrastructure improvement. Although the impact of federal projects in the South during the New Deal and wartime eras was impressive and unprecedented, the region as a whole did not receive its share of federal spending compared to other sections of the country. The southern states more than made up for this disparity during the Cold War period. Although Southern California emerged as the largest beneficiary in terms of total defense dollars received, in terms of its dependence on the defense establishment for both employment and income, the South surpassed the national average.[8] By the early 1970s, the southern states were providing the Pentagon with 52 percent of its ships, 46 percent of its airframes, 42 percent of its petroleum products, and 27 percent of its ammunition. From Tenneco's Newport News shipbuilding plant in

Hampton Roads, Virginia, to General Dynamics and LTV Corporation in Texas, the military and the federal government created a new high-tech industrial workforce whose cultural tastes, spending habits, and political allegiances changed the face of the South.[9]

Modernization of society and culture accompanied the militarization of the southern economy. The Savannah River Plant employed thousands of highly skilled and educated scientists and engineers who almost overnight created a vibrant middle class in a part of South Carolina where almost none before had existed. Scores of suburban subdivisions and national retail outlets served the housing and lifestyle needs of these new white-collar residents and offered new opportunities to longtime residents, thus helping to break down the intense localism that had characterized the surrounding area. Longtime residents of this critical Cold War defense area eagerly anticipated the economic windfall expected to accompany the arrival of the new defense installation. For many residents of the mill villages in Horse Creek Valley, the Savannah River Plant was an economic godsend, making it possible for many of them to enter the middle class and giving them new opportunities to participate in the region's expanding mass consumer culture. Most native South Carolinians as well as newcomers proudly embraced their new roles in the nation's Cold War weapons program.

Altogether, this burgeoning middle class, the influx of national retail establishments and a flourishing consumer culture, and mass suburbanization introduced a larger culture heralding efficiency, consumption, technological innovation, and progress—all components of a vaguely defined notion of "modernity"—that threatened to displace the region's older rural culture. The creation of the Savannah River Plant decisively reordered the area's traditional rural landscape, not only through the institution of newly built structures such as suburban tract housing but also by blurring traditional geographic boundaries and by introducing a new understanding of land and space defined by Cold War imperatives. The emergence of the modern military state literally imprinted itself upon the southern landscape. In a region where the relationship between town and country had once been relatively fluid, planners of the military-industrial complex introduced modern concepts of boundaries and land use that rendered the environment subordinate to technology and security.

This section of the South was no stranger to change. During the nineteenth century, Aiken County was at the forefront of technological innovation, both regionally and nationally. The city of Aiken was established in 1835 as a way station along the Charleston to Hamburg railroad, the first in America to provide regular passenger and freight service with steam-powered locomotives.[10] In 1833, the South's first textile mill was constructed in the tiny village of Vaucluse, located in Horse Creek Valley in Edgefield District.[11] William Gregg purchased the factory in 1843, and two years later he developed the more successful Graniteville Company and nearby village, which became the model for the mill building explosion later in the century.[12]

The tri-county region out of which the Savannah River Site would be carved was already undergoing economic and demographic changes when AEC officials arrived in the early 1950s. During the previous decade, the declining cotton economy of large landowners and sharecroppers had begun to give way to a more diversified agricultural mix.[13] The rural areas of Aiken County had lost population since 1940, with sharecroppers in particular leaving in droves. Scores of vacant farm houses bore testimony to the area's decline.[14] This small human tributary joined the larger rushing torrent of 4 million migrants—a quarter of the region's rural population—who left the South during the war years.[15] Home to some of the South's oldest textile mills and mill villages, Horse Creek Valley was representative of this transition during the 1940s and early 1950s.

Whereas depopulation characterized the countryside and mill villages, Aiken retained much of its nineteenth-century charm. Though the city lay only a few miles outside the Valley and numerous rural hamlets, the residents of the farms, the mill villages, and Aiken itself lived in different worlds. Aiken boasted a population of only 7,000 on the eve of the Savannah River Plant's construction and had gained fame as a winter retreat for wealthy horse owners from the North.[16] Mrs. Lulie Hitchcock of Long Island came to Aiken in the 1870s, after she discovered that its temperate climate and sandy soil were ideal for raising and training thoroughbreds. She soon convinced many of her wealthy friends in the horsey set—northerners who owned some of the nation's leading racing stables—to make Aiken their winter home. These "Winter Colonists," as they became known, built sprawling mansions that they called "cottages," with names such as Rosehill, Whitehall, and Joye Cottage.[17] The cottages lined the city's beautifully landscaped 150-foot-wide boulevards, which were divided by lovely parks, lush with towering magnolias and filled with dogwoods, camellias, and azaleas. Aiken proudly adopted the slogan "The City of Parkways." Most of these broad avenues were still unpaved in 1950, out of consideration for the sensitivity of horses' hooves.[18]

When not extolling its parkways, Aiken promoted itself as the "Sports Center of the South." Colorful brochures and promotion pieces heralded the region's luxurious accommodations, cultural attainments, and recreational opportunities. Polo players from around the world began arriving in Aiken shortly after the first recorded game in 1882; for the next half century, the city was known as the "Newport of South Carolina." By the early 1940s, Aiken boasted seventeen polo fields but only two movie theaters.[19] Even the town's baseball team was nicknamed the "Tourists."[20] Aiken's pre-1950 promotional materials likened the local sporting culture to that of European nobility. The city boasted of flat racing ("the sport of kings"), drag hunts ("colorful replicas of the old type of fox hunting, accompanied by all the thrills and ceremonies so well known in England and other European countries"), steeplechase, and horse shows. Many Kentucky Derby winners began their careers at the annual Aiken trials on the beautifully laid out Mile Track.[21] Visitors could go horseback riding along the hundreds of miles of bridle paths in Hitchcock Woods, hunt in the many nearby fields, or fish in one of the nearly 1,000 ponds and lakes in Aiken County. The area boasted numerous fine turn-of-the-century era hotels that had been host to such luminaries as Winston Churchill and John Jacob Astor, as well as an assortment of dukes, duchesses, barons, countesses, and ambassadors.[22]

In his scathing 1973 account, novelist Pat Conroy observed that "Aiken is a town of categories"—one either belonged to the Winter Colony, Old Aiken, or the Valley.[23] Old Aiken, the longtime residents of the town who could trace their ancestors back several generations, found their economic salvation in the Winter Colony. They were the year-round merchants and professionals who made their living off of the northern visitors. With the arrival of the Winter Colonists, Conroy observed, Aiken developed a "social schizophrenia: The Old Aikenite seems inferior to the Winter Colony, but, by God, he feels superior to every other bastard that comes to town."[24] At the bottom of the social ladder in Aiken County were the mill folks from the Valley. Only a mile or two separated the Valley from the city, but mill village residents lived in an entirely different social and economic world. Although Aiken's merchants considered themselves a class apart from the mill workers, they nevertheless welcomed mill dollars. Few mill workers from the Valley, however, could afford the prices at Aiken's small, locally owned shops.[25] Esther Melton, born and raised in Graniteville, recalled that in 1946 it cost her two months' salary to purchase a dress from Julia's, a pricey dress shop in downtown Aiken. Melton and her family and friends preferred the larger, more affordable chain department stores, such as J.B. White's, Belk's, and JC Penny, located in Augusta some ten miles away.[26] Residents of Aiken County's rural communities likewise shopped across the state line in Augusta.[27] In 1946, seeking to capitalize on postwar prosperity, Aiken's merchants conspired to lure working-class consumers from the Horse River Valley and the countryside through a campaign to "Shop Aiken First." The merchants staged the Aiken Cotton Festival, which became an annual five-day event. Despite the success of the festival, most Valley and rural shoppers continued to travel to Augusta.

The lure of federal dollars, especially in the postwar era, seduced many southern boosters obsessed with economic development and threatened the identity—if not the livelihood—of cities such as Aiken. South Carolina's political leaders aggressively pursued federal projects as part of their long-term growth strategy to modernize the state. Elected in 1946, Governor Strom Thurmond (from neighboring Edgefield County) was among the scores of former GIs who returned to the South determined to transform the region and its leadership. "We need a progressive outlook, a progressive program, a progressive leadership," Thurmond declared during the course of his gubernatorial campaign. "We must face the future with confidence and with enthusiasm."[28] For Thurmond and other like-minded southern politicians, this progressive future depended on development funded by both private investment and federal dollars.[29]

The Savannah River Plant was the latest in a string of federal projects that state lawmakers had successfully courted. Six years prior to its arrival, leaders in South Carolina and Georgia cooperated in securing federal money to build the Clarks Hill Project, a series of eleven dams created along the Savannah River to improve navigation, promote flood control, and provide power and recreation to a bi-state region. The electric power produced by the Clarks Hill Project proved instrumental to the creation of the SRP.[30] By all indications, politics played no role in the AEC's decision to place the new plant in South Carolina; rather, geography and population density were central considerations.[31] The ideal site required, among other factors, "low population density, proximity to a fairly large urban center,...and an adequate supply of water of specified purity."[32]

The arrival of the Savannah River Plant transformed the surrounding region demographically, geographically, and economically. As Pat Conroy noted, the rule of Aiken's Winter Colonists eroded when "some eggheaded son of a bitch, who probably didn't know a pastern from a coronet, split the atom. The world and Aiken would never be the same."[33] Between 1950 and 1952, more than 30,000 temporary construction workers and 6,000 permanent employees and their families—nearly 180,000 persons in all—flooded into the area.[34] Even though the SRP was crucial to the national security state's expanding nuclear arsenal, and although the Korean War had presented the specter of a constant state of war readiness, the Truman administration rejected the garrison state model. Washington policymakers chose not to impose excessive government and military controls on critical resources and opted instead to rely on existing cities, such as Aiken, and private enterprise to absorb the new residents. Almost overnight, Aiken's function and economic orientation changed, from an upscale tourist town with rudimentary connections to rural communities into a modern space whose built environment and residents alike were reconfigured by the actions of AEC and Du Pont. Federal and corporate officials transformed Aiken and other surrounding small towns such as Williston and Barnwell into "dormitory suburbs" to house the new workforce.[35] The Savannah River Plant, and not Aiken itself, became the region's new center.

The Winter Colonists adjusted their lives to the new arrivals. One winter resident noted that the wealthy in Aiken considered "inheritance taxes...a hell of a lot worse nuisance than this hydrogen bomb."[36] Many owners of Aiken's capacious homes took in temporary workers. "Sandhurst," built in 1900 for W. H. Sands of New York, was a sprawling eleven-acre estate that included a three-car garage, carriage house, servants' apartments, caretaker house, groom cottage, two stables, and tennis courts. In the early 1950s, it housed eighty-six construction workers.[37] Thousands of other construction personnel lived in temporary trailer courts on the city's perimeter and in military-style barracks in small villages. To accommodate those workers who had brought their families, Du Pont contracted for the installation of four thousand trailer units in Aiken, Augusta, Williston, and Barnwell. The trailers were each suitable for a family of four; however, 15 percent of trailer families had between five and seven members, contributing to overcrowded living conditions. Du Pont hired a Philadelphia company to create four massive trailer park "cities" throughout the region, housing some twenty thousand people. Aerial photographs of these temporary cities show row upon row of trailers, with as many as a thousand units in a single "city." In contrast to the variety and idiosyncrasy of rural architecture, the barracks and especially the trailer parks imposed a stifling monotony upon the landscape, based upon a model of military efficiency only rarely disturbed by vegetation. Du Pont also built permanent housing, much of which was a failure. The AEC wanted to diffuse the impact on any single community, so planners spread the houses around, often in tiny villages with no amenities or services.[38]

The construction, safety, and security requirements of the Savannah River Plant had an immediate and dramatic impact on the local landscape, both inside and outside the plant boundaries.[39] The pursuit of federal dollars encouraged South Carolina leaders to adopt a more expansive and benign definition of "federal intervention," even as the economic salvation promised by outside investment complicated other traditional political boundaries. Although winning projects for South Carolina held the greatest political benefit for South Carolina's elected officials, geographic realities, such as flood control, often dictated that states work together to secure federal aid. Through such combined efforts, the area surrounding the Savannah River basin acquired a regional identity tied to modernization and development and adopted the name "The Central Savannah River Area," designating a metropolitan region that included parts of both South Carolina and Georgia. The new name, created by C. C. McCollum of Wrens, South Carolina, was chosen from among 2,500 entries in a contest sponsored by the *Augusta Chronicle*.[40] The militarization of the southern economy cemented this development-oriented geography and landscape, which blurred traditional boundaries and began to break down the intense localism of traditional communities.

The commandeering of this vast rural space for military needs meant that the Savannah River Plant, and by extension the Cold War, quite literally imprinted itself upon the landscape. Even a cursory look at a map of the area reveals that the SRP dwarfs any other geographical feature and is itself represented as a part of the landscape. Yet the plant site typically is rendered a pale neutral color, usually light gray or white, a stark visual representation of a vast, secret space.

The Savannah River Plant likewise reconfigured understandings of place and space, most starkly evident in comparisons of how residents of the pre-plant region and AEC/Du Pont officials referred to the land. In the official construction history of the SRP, Du Pont describes the shape of the site—the borders—as "nearly octagonal," revealing the desire of plant creators to superimpose a definable shape over the irregular borders of the plant, which in many instances follow specific terrain requirements.[41] The need for precision, for measurement, was antithetical to rural under-standings of space, which often privileged natural markers over geometric shapes as boundaries.

The people who actually lived within the pre-plant boundaries viewed this space differently. The AEC displaced roughly 8,000 residents to make way for the plant. The largest community was the town of Ellenton (figure 8.1). Although the AEC referred to the 250,000 acres that would constitute plant property as "sufficiently isolated," and to nearby towns and hamlets as "islands of uncontrolled population," the communities within the pre-plant boundaries were, in fact, interconnected. Residents of Dunbarton and Myers Mill used buses and the railroad for regular visits to Ellenton for entertainment.[42] The AEC's terminology also implied that the country-side and towns were distinctly separate places and that residents' experi-ences were limited to the towns themselves, when, in fact, they regarded the countryside as part of their community. They hunted in the woods, fished in the rivers and streams, and swam in the lakes, ponds, and creeks. Natives experienced the land in a personal, almost visceral way. But the new Cold War enterprise did not value local knowledge of the land. One contemporary journalist covering the creation of the plant noted that "the man who commands a knowledge of the valley's history and of its terrain and waters is sure to stand in well with his neighbors. To know indisput-ably where Mister Walker lived before he lived where he lives now, to be able to guide a skiff around a submerged stump in the swamp—these have been immeasurable assets."[43] But within three years, Cold War necessities rendered an enormous swath of South Carolina countryside secret, inac-cessible, and unknowable to the people who had once lived, worked, and played there.

In nearby Aiken, the impact of the plant on the landscape was almost as dramatic. Most of the permanent operations staff—managers, scien-tists, engineers, and technicians—chose to live in and around Aiken. By 1953, the city's permanent population had tripled. Private develop-ers created twenty-seven new subdivisions. The area surrounding the

FIGURE 8.1. Downtown Ellenton, South Carolina, c. 1950. Ellenton was one of several small towns and villages slated for destruction to make way for the Savannah River Plant. The town's vernacular architecture was typical of small rural communities in the South and contrasted with the architectural homogeneity of suburban residences and commercial chains that came to signify Aiken's post-1950 growth. Courtesy of the U.S. Department of Energy.

Savannah River Plant, which at the close of World War II was categorized as underdeveloped and primarily rural, now reflected a Cold War suburban identity as an important outpost on the frontier of nuclear science, as well as an integral component of the national defense state.

Developers of the new subdivisions marketed homes directly to plant employees, promoting the efficiency and convenience of the suburbs. One advertisement touted the "really large, complete modern home[s]...ideally located only...minutes from the new Savannah River Plant."[44] Most of these middle-class houses were ranch style and about 1,200 square feet. The subdivisions themselves were typical of 1950s suburbs across the nation in their layout, with large, elongated blocks and curving streets. Developers built these neighborhoods hastily, with little regard for geography. Residential construction often took place in low areas with known histories of drainage problems. Crosland Park, Aiken's largest subdivision, was cursed with chronic sewage overflow.[45] Built on a 200-acre tract north of the city, Crosland Park consisted of 542 homes; the majority rented at $75 a month to plant employees and the remaining units sold for just under $10,000.[46] Researchers from the University of North Carolina studying the area's rapid urbanization observed that the sewage problem in Crosland Park and in other subdivisions reflected a lack of planning and a disregard for the terrain. This particular suburban sewage problem, the researchers noted, was exacerbated by Aiken County's rolling sandy pine hills, which gave "rise to certain dangers of contamination of wells from sewage disposed of by means of open pit privies, cesspools, or septic tanks."[47]

These new subdivisions differed greatly from the rural landscape, as well as the surrounding area's existing towns and textile mill villages. Graniteville exhibited the layout and geographic logic of most mill villages. Built to harness the power of the swift-moving Horse Creek, the mill dominated its landscape, with rows of small company-owned homes ascending the valley walls but still oriented toward the center of production. Residents of the villages of Graniteville, Langley, Bath, and Vaucluse regarded (and still do regard) themselves as residents of "the Valley." The newer subdivisions built to accommodate the influx of plant employees possessed no such orientation and engendered no such connection with local geography.

The names of the new housing developments—Crosland Park, Forest Heights, Kilkenny Acres, Richmond Hills, Dartmoore Woods—conjure up geographical elements that, in most instances, never existed or were destroyed to make way for the subdivisions. By contrast Graniteville's neighborhoods bore names that resonated with a sense of time and place. Local history contends that the neighborhood of "Shakerag" earned its name during the influenza pandemic of 1918. During the outbreak, caregivers to the sick would hold rags over their mouths to protect themselves from the virus and could frequently be seen shaking these rags outside, apparently to rid them of the germs.[48] "Battle Row" designated a street in Graniteville whose residents were particularly quarrelsome; "Rock Town" was a semicircle of homes so-named because they were built of granite and sandstone; and "New Town" connoted those houses located up Breezy Hill, away from the Valley, so-called because they were newer than the village's existing homes.[49] The Cold War housing boom of the 1950s severed connections with the land itself and brought about the loss of a traditional sense of place and history.

Firmly ensconced in Aiken's sprawling suburbs, the Du Pont employees created a middle class almost overnight. A number of children of the Valley also entered this emerging middle class. E. C. Thomas, who returned to work at the Graniteville Company following his service in World War II, recalled that local textiles could not compete with the wages offered at the atomic plant.[50] Although he chose to remain at the mill, other Valley natives such as Owen Clary and Ronnie Bryant cast their lots with the Savannah River Plant. The son of a carpenter and a self-described "bad ass Valley boy," Clary worked summers in the corduroy division of Gregg manufacturing. His future might have been in textiles had the SRP not come along while he was in high school. After receiving a history degree from Furman University, Clary taught history at the Coast Guard Academy and eventually took a job as an industrial engineer with the SRP. His college education and white-collar employment allowed him to purchase a home in the Kalmia Hill subdivision located halfway between Graniteville and Aiken, a lovely middle-class neighborhood with winding streets and towering magnolias.[51]

Ronnie Bryant made the switch from textiles to the bomb plant because, as he recalled, "it looked like there was no future in the Graniteville Company. All the good jobs were taken, or people were in line for the good jobs, so you had to look elsewhere for opportunity." Bryant left for a position working in the lab at the Savannah River Plant, a job he landed because he had taken high school chemistry. It was a smart financial move, as his take-home pay immediately increased by almost 50 percent.[52] Bryant remained at the plant for the rest of his career, a move that placed him firmly within the Valley's emerging middle class. Bryant eventually purchased a brick ranch home on Laurel Drive. Not exactly part of a planned neighborhood, Laurel Drive parallels the old trolley line connecting Graniteville and the city of Aiken. Like the old trolley line before it, Laurel Drive became something of a middle-class residential spur that physically connected the old money of Aiken to the working-class areas of the Valley.

Although the Savannah River Plant did not hire African Americans in nearly the numbers of their white counterparts, black residents of the region likewise benefited economically from the new opportunities provided by Cold War development. Shepherd Archie, for example, began working as a janitor at the SRP. After eleven months, he was transferred to the transportation department. Eventually he worked his way up to a supervisory role "over all the heavy equipment in roads and grounds." Archie recalled that blacks' "lives changed tremendous from poor to middle class. They got a better life out of that, by this plant coming....Now most of them own homes, nice homes and all, so they benefit."[53] It is likely that black employees of the plant were the target customers for a new subdivision marketed to black residents in the 1950s. The Harlem Heights subdivision, located one-and-a-half miles from the city limits of Aiken, offered potential buyers city water and "nice wide streets." The advertisement urged black home buyers "not [to] confuse this [subdivision] with the low, poorly located home sites generally offered to the colored people....This is for the discriminating home seeker who wishes to give his family the best, rear their children under the very best of conditions and frankly, don't you think you owe that to them?"[54]

Although Aiken merchants welcomed the spending power of the new white middle class, the social acceptance of the newcomers—"Du Ponters," as they were called—was slow to materialize. To Old Aiken, those restaurateurs, merchants, realtors, and lawyers who made their living off the Winter Colonists, the Du Ponters were Aiken's "new Negroes," according to Pat Conroy—"technological Negroes to be sure, but Negroes, nevertheless," segregated in their suburban enclaves on the city's perimeter and shunned from the established social networks.[55]

Shut out of the social scene of the Winter Colony and Old Aiken, the Du Ponters created alternative civic institutions such as a community theater group and the United Way. The wives of Du Pont employees organized the Town and Country Club, a social and cultural organization, after receiving the so-called Aiken Freeze, the frosty reception given to outsiders.[56] Employees of the plant were instrumental in organizing the area's first historical society, with the plant's official historian listed as its first secretary. Savannah River Plant supervisors and employees worked very hard to relate their work to the surrounding community. Farmers of Aiken County flocked to a public program on radioisotopes and their applicability to agricultural research.[57] The YWCA sponsored a popular lecture series on subjects ranging from the nature of matter to nuclear reactors. More than six hundred school teachers attended an all-day seminar on the incorporation of atomic energy into the curriculum. Du Pont employees also founded local chapters of their professional associations and made them relevant to the community. For example, the Savannah River Subsection of the American Chemical Society contributed $125 for science books for the local high school and counseled students on careers in chemistry and atomic energy.[58] Arthur Tackman, assistant manager of the Savannah River Plant, was named Aiken County "Citizen of the Year" in 1953, after only two years of residence. He served as campaign chairman of the American Red Cross–Community Chest, coordinator of committees of the Cotton Festival, and a leader of the local Boy Scouts.[59]

Newly developed subdivisions housing Du Pont employees quickly organized civic associations that lobbied city hall for improved services. Savannah River Plant employees provided volunteer labor to build a public swimming pool in Williston, and they organized and staffed various suburban fire departments. Buzz Rich, an Aiken attorney whose family arrived in the early 1950s and whose mother worked at the plant, later recalled: "All those guys [Du Ponters] had a lot of energy, . . . all that brain power, coming into that small southern town. They had time on their hands, in the evenings and weekends. . . . They got involved and started all of these activities." Owen Clary, who worked at the plant before heading up a local food bank, remarked that many of the Du Pont employees were civic-minded. "They were generous with their time and always volunteered for fundraising activities."[60] By 1955, only five years after the AEC decided to build the plant, Du Pont employees were either leading or participating in all of the major community institutions in Aiken.

The local newspaper heralded the new retail establishments that accompanied economic development and population growth in the 1950s as "tribute[s] to the progressive spirit of Aiken."[61] Accompanying the new suburbs were shopping centers, chain department stores (such as J.B. White, Sears, and JC Penny), chain drug stores, numerous supermarkets, a drive-in movie theater, an expanded McCrory's, and scores of restaurants.[62] The arrival of expanded commerce also attracted mill folks from the Valley. Working-class residents were more inclined to patronize these establishments than small shops and stores, thus drawing them closer to Aiken and making it less necessary to travel to Augusta. Sylvia Bryant recalled that "once White's was built, we started shopping [in Aiken]."[63]

City planners facilitated this retail expansion by remaking the built environment in service to automobile consumers from the suburbs and surrounding towns. In November 1951, Aiken rezoned eight downtown blocks from residential to business to allow for commercial growth.[64] Two years later, the city council voted to narrow several of Aiken's beloved boulevard green spaces, in order to widen the streets and create more parking.[65] This decision to sacrifice aesthetics for commerce drew harsh criticism from longtime residents of the City of Parkways, led by fixtures of Old Aiken such as the headmaster of the prep school and Eulalie Salley, the city's best-known realtor to the Winter Colonists.[66] In 1956, city leaders made another concession to retailers when they moved to amend Sunday blue laws. In a scathing editorial, the *Aiken Standard and Review* lambasted the city council for "plac[ing] the almighty dollar above Almighty God."[67] One local resident lamented the changes economic prosperity and expansion had brought to Aiken. In "A Tale of Two Cities," Thomas H. Williamson contrasted old and new Aiken:

> Two cities are growing
> In the boundaries of one,
> One city of sadness
> And the other of fun
>
> One the old city
> The other one new,
> One where serenity
> Reigns the year thru.
>
> One where the hustle
> And bustle remain,
> And we have little choice
> Betwixt pleasure and pain.[68]

By the early 1960s, the social character and built environment of Aiken County had changed significantly. The number of professional and technical workers had tripled in the course of a decade. In 1950, the vast majority of the population was employed in agriculture and textiles; by 1960, the number of men and women employed in nonagricultural industries represented 93 percent of the workforce. Aiken County's clerical workforce doubled, as women moved from textiles to office work at the Savannah River Plant. "Engineers Technical" appeared as a local employment category for the first time in the 1960 census.[69] With a burgeoning middle class and a massive high-tech facility that reordered the community's economic and social life, modernity had overtaken the region. With these profound changes, the "progress" that Governor Thurmond sought had finally arrived.

After the arrival of the Cold War, the city of Aiken changed its marketing strategy. No longer merely an enclave for elite tourists, Aiken had transformed itself into a dynamic and progressive example of the modern New South. Festival programs and other promotional materials highlighted Aiken's progressive government and its modern conveniences, its "fine, up-to-date shops" and "multiple shopping units adjacent to the city proper." Aiken adopted a new city seal in the mid-1950s; it is divided into quadrants depicting golfers, a thoroughbred, an antebellum mansion, and the atomic energy symbol with the word *progress* stamped across it.[70] Furthermore, Aiken's boosters began promoting the area as a place to live, not just to visit. The arrival of the bomb plant encouraged further industrial development, and by the end of the decade, Owens-Corning Fiberglass Corporation and electronics maker Pyle National had built plants in Aiken County.[71] By 1960, the city's brochures no longer heralded Aiken as the "Sport Center of the South." Its new slogan was "Charm and Progress," illustrating the attempts of city boosters to meld tradition and modernity. On the cover of promotional brochures, a photograph of a modern brick ranch home replaced the polo player with jodhpurs and whip, as boosters promoted the middle-class suburban lifestyle rather than celebrations of elite recreation. Instead of colorful descriptions of upscale sports, marketing literature included data on housing costs, public schools, health care, and churches.[72] Aiken's recreational offerings and focus on the wealthy and on nature, while still plentiful, became secondary to the emphasis on "progress," community, and technology.

The Du Pont Corporation encouraged this connection between the Savannah River Plant and the achievement of the "good life." In fact, few corporations in the postwar era better represented the American Cold War promise of economic prosperity through mass consumption than Du Pont. Eager to rid itself of the "Merchants of Death" stigma from its unseemly profits earned in World War I, Du Pont began investing heavily in the research and development of consumer-related goods such as nylon, cellophane, and Freon. By 1952, Du Pont offered more than 116 products in a wide range of industries. The corporation created a patriotic self-image that did not rely on military commitment but instead on its production of consumer goods. The *Savannah River News*, the plant's employee newsletter, promoted this perception of Du Pont—and, by extension, the Cold War—as the provider of better living through the freedom of mass consumption. Employees—both newcomers to the region and longtime residents—embraced this new consumption-based American identity as the traditional rural and textile production-based identity faded into the past.

The company newsletter frequently published articles and photographs of employees enjoying their newfound prosperity as part of the area's new middle class. The newsletter proudly pointed out that "many SRP employees have long known the joys that come with home ownership," the ultimate symbol of the American Dream in the postwar period. Another marker of the "good life" was the durable consumer good. In a 1955 article, a reporter for the *Savannah River News* asked a group of employees, "what outmoded possession do you next plan to replace?" Margaret Scott, who worked in Communications at the plant, answered that "my next dream come true will be to trade in my old washer for a new automatic washer and dryer combination. I plan to do this through our convenient payroll plan for buying Savings Bonds."[73]

In 1960, ten years after the Atomic Energy Commission made the decision that changed Aiken forever, the city celebrated its 125th anniversary. In a commemorative brochure, Ken Kilbourne of the Chamber of Commerce composed a descriptive narrative of the hypothetical Aiken in the year 2000. Like most time-traveling flights of fancy, scientists play a key role in this Aiken of the future. By 2000, local scientists had transformed Aiken into a model city that, in Kilbourne's vision, embodied the perfect mix of technology and mass consumption. Declaring the natural environment dangerous, scientists had rendered it irrelevant by creating a protective shell over Aiken, allowing them to exert maximum control over the environment. The result, the scientists argued, would be "less physical fatigue, [fewer] colds, miseries" that threatened human existence. The same scientists who had launched the nuclear project that had suddenly thrust Aiken into the center of an unstable, chaotic world would in the future bring security, control, and certainty. In Kilbourne's fantasy, Aiken would be entirely rezoned; gone were the beautiful boulevards and nineteenth-century homes that lined the streets of the central city. The suburb would become king, with the central city given up completely to shopping. Despite the fifty-year presence of the Du Pont middle class, social divisions would persist into the year 2000. In the city of the future, the mayor's office would be shared by one representative of the shopkeepers (representing Old Aiken) and one representative of the "suburban interests."[74]

Kilbourne's prognostications were just one man's fanciful dreams of the future; still, one is struck by how completely transformed is his "future

Aiken." The Winter Colony, which had once provided the livelihood of so many, as well as defined the city's character, plays no role. From his perspective, though, a mere ten years after the AEC's fateful pronouncement, such a development may not have been such a stretch. By 1960, the exigencies of the Cold War and the arrival of a multinational corporation with a clearly defined culture had set in motion dramatic changes that threatened to erase what had been distinctive about Aiken. Such was also the case in other southern communities in which Cold War militarization took hold. Most residents of these communities now deemed "critical defense areas" embraced the opportunity to partake in a middle-class lifestyle and welcomed the benefits that their new militarized economy would bring. Yet they remained mindful of the costs. Like those promoting Aiken's "charm and progress," most southerners eagerly grasped the promise of the future while hoping to retain the best of the past.

NOTES

1. Lenwood Melton, interview with author, May 2, 2003, Graniteville, South Carolina.

2. For general histories of Du Pont, see Leonard Mosley, *Blood Relations: The Rise and Fall of the du Ponts of Delaware* (New York: Atheneum, 1980); Max Dorian, *The du Ponts: From Gunpowder to Nylon* (Boston: Little, Brown, 1961); Gerard Colgy Zilg, *Du Pont: Behind the Nylon Curtain* (Englewood Cliffs, N.J.: Prentice-Hall, 1974); "The Wizards of Wilmington," *Time*, April 16, 1951, 98.

3. Daniel Lang, "Camellias and Bombs," *New Yorker* 27 (July 7, 1951), 42.

4. United States Atomic Energy Commission, Press Release, November 28, 1950, in Atomic Plant—Miscellaneous File, Burnet R. Maybank Papers, Special Collections, Marlene and Nathan Addlestone Library, College of Charleston, Charleston, South Carolina; U.S. Department of Energy, *Facts and Data on the U.S. Atomic Energy Commission's Savannah River Plant in South Carolina* (n.d.), 3–5; U.S. Department of Energy, *The Savannah River Plant* (Washington: GPO, 1980), 9; *Aiken Standard and Review*, November 29, 1950.

5. Bruce J. Schulman, *From Cotton Belt to Sunbelt: Federal Policy, Economic Development, and the Transformation of the South, 1938–1980* (New York: Oxford University Press, 1991); James C. Cobb, *The Selling of the South: The Southern Crusade for Industrial Development, 1936–1990*, second edition (Urbana: University of Illinois Press, 1993); Philip Scranton, ed., *The Second Wave: Southern Industrialization from the 1940s to the 1970s* (Athens: University of Georgia Press, 2001); William Faherty, *Florida's Space Coast: The Impact of NASA on the Sunshine State* (Gainesville: University Press of Florida, 2002); Christopher Scribner, *Renewing Birmingham: Federal Funding and the Promise of Change, 1929–1979* (Athens: University of Georgia Press, 2002); David R. Goldfield, *Cotton Fields and Skyscrapers: Southern City and Region, 1607–1980* (Baton Rouge: Louisiana State

University Press, 1982); Goldfield, *Region, Race, and Cities: Interpreting the Urban South* (Baton Rouge: Louisiana State University Press, 1997).

6. Anthony J. Badger, "Albert Gore and the Politics of the Modern South," paper presented at the Organization of American Historians annual meeting, April 4, 2003, cited with permission of author; Schulman, *Cotton Belt to Sunbelt*, 128.

7. Dewey W. Grantham, *The South in Modern America: A Region at Odds* (New York: HarperCollins, 1995), 265, 270; the phrase is from Cobb, *Selling of the South*. Also see Goldfield, *Cotton Fields and Skyscrapers*, 190; Goldfield, *Region, Race, and Cities*, 253.

8. Jordan A. Schwarz, *The New Dealers: Power Politics in the Age of Roosevelt* (New York: Knopf, 1993), 319–20; Schulman, *Cotton Belt to Sunbelt*, 140, 149. For Southern California and defense-related growth, see Gerald D. Nash, *The American West Transformed: The Impact of the Second World War* (Bloomington: Indiana University Press, 1985); Lisa McGirr, *Suburban Warriors: The Origins of the New American Right* (Princeton: Princeton University Press, 2001), chap. 1. In their study of the rise of the "gunbelt," authors Ann Markusen et al. note that as defense-related activity grew during the post-World War II era, "interregional per capita incomes have converged, with spectacular gains by the southern states." See Ann Markusen et al., *The Rise of the Gunbelt: The Military Remapping of Industrial America* (New York: Oxford University Press, 1991), 21. David L. Carlton takes a somewhat different position regarding the impact of defense spending. Although he acknowledges that, since the end of World War II, the South has received an increasingly greater proportion of its income from defense spending, the actual "mix" of spending has not benefited the region as much as other parts of the country. In particular, he argues, the South has lagged behind other regions in its receipt of prime contracts. See Carlton, "The American South and the U.S. Defense Economy," in *The South, the Nation, and the World*, ed. Carlton and Peter Coclanis (Charlottesville: University of Virginia Press, 2003), 152–53.

9. Schulman, *Cotton Belt to Sunbelt*, 136; Markusen, *Rise of the Gunbelt*; "Southern Militarism," *Southern Exposure* (Spring 1973), 61.

10. *South Carolina: The WPA Guide to the Palmetto State* (1941), reprint (Columbia: University of South Carolina Press, 1988), 160; Louis Cassels, *Coontail Lagoon: A Celebration of Life* (Philadelphia: Westminster Press, 1974), 47.

11. The village of Vaucluse was part of Edgefield District until 1871, when it became part of newly created Aiken County; Michael E. Staugger, *The Formation of Counties in South Carolina* (Columbia: South Carolina Department of Archives and History, 1998), 14, 16.

12. Broadus Mitchell, *William Gregg: Factory Master of the Old South* (1928), reprint (New York: Octagon Books, 1966), 11–14, 33–75.

13. E. I. du Pont de Nemours and Company, "Savannah River Plant Construction History," Volume I: Administration (January 1957), 35–36; F. Chapin, Jr., et al., *In the Shadow of a Defense Plant: A Study of Urbanization in Rural South Carolina: A Final Report of the Savannah Urbanization Study*

(Chapel Hill: Institute for Research in Social Science, University of North Carolina, June 1954), 14.

14. Bureau of the Census, *United States Census of Agriculture, 1940*, Vol. 1, Part 3: *Statistics for Counties* (Washington: GPO, 1942), 442; Bureau of the Census, *United States Census of Agriculture: 1950*, Vol. 1, Part 16: *Counties and State Economic Areas: North and South Carolina* (Washington: GPO, 1952), 456; Chapin, *In the Shadow of a Defense Plant*, 5–10, 16; Mary Beth Reed et al., *Savannah River Site at Fifty* (Washington: GPO, 2002), 112–13 (quotation in note), 155.

15. Pete Daniel, "Going Among Strangers: Southern Reactions to World War II," *Journal of American History,* 77 (December 1990), 886.

16. "The Atom," *Time,* December 11, 1950, 22.

17. Dorothy MacDowell, *An Aiken Scrapbook: A Picture Narrative of Aiken and Aiken County, South Carolina* (Aiken, S.C.: self-published, 1982).

18. Lang, "Camellias and Bombs," 40.

19. *South Carolina: The WPA Guide to the Palmetto State*, 159.

20. See, for example, *Aiken Standard and Review,* June 16, 1952, 5.

21. Lang, "Camellias and Bombs," 40.

22. Register, Willcox Hotel, Aiken County Historical Museum, Aiken, South Carolina.

23. Pat Conroy, "Horses Don't Eat Moonpies," in *Faces of South Carolina: Essays on South Carolina in Transition*, ed. Franklin Ashley (Columbia, S.C.: self-published, 1974), 47.

24. Conroy, "Horses Don't Eat Moonpies," 49.

25. Sylvia Bryant, telephone interview with author, November 6, 2006.

26. Esther Melton, interview with author, Graniteville, South Carolina, May 3, 2002; Esther Melton, telephone interview with author, November 6, 2006.

27. T. Browder and Richard Brooks, *Memories of Home: Reminiscences of Ellenton* (1996), 63–64, Savannah River Archaeological Research Program, South Carolina Institute of Archaeology and Anthropology, University of South Carolina, Columbia, South Carolina.

28. Walter Edgar, *A History of South Carolina* (Columbia: University of South Carolina Press, 1999), 517.

29. Kari Frederickson, *The Dixiecrat Revolt and the End of the Solid South, 1932–1968* (Chapel Hill: University of North Carolina Press, 2001), 171.

30. Edgar, *History of South Carolina*, 503; Reed, *Savannah River Site*, 97–103, 136–37.

31. Lang, "Camellias and Bombs," 42.

32. Chapin, *In the Shadow of a Defense Plant*, 1; Jobie Turner, *Aiken for Armageddon, 1950–1955*, Master's thesis, University of Georgia, 1998, 20–22. Also see C. H. Topping, "Plant 124 Site Survey," Engineering Department, E. I. du Pont de Nemours and Company, November 27, 1950, Box H-10-1, Series 43, Records of the Atomic Energy Commission, RG 326, National Archives and Records Administration, Southeastern Regional Archive, Morrow, Georgia.

33. Conroy, "Horses Don't Eat Moonpies," 47.

34. Chapin, *In the Shadow of a Defense Plant*, 30–32.

35. Monica Schach-Spana, *Reactor Control and Environmental Management: A Cultural Account of Agency in the U.S. Nuclear Weapons Complex*, Ph.D. dissertation, Johns Hopkins University, 1998, 154.

36. Lang, "Camellias and Bombs," 46.

37. Caption, Winter Colony Exhibit, Aiken County Historical Museum, Aiken, South Carolina.

38. Chapin, *In the Shadow of a Defense Plant*, 187.

39. My concept of "landscape" echoes that of Mart A. Stewart, "as land shaped by human hands and...created...in accordance with both aesthetic and social values or in order to organize or facilitate certain kinds of modes of production." I would add that landscapes represent cultural values, in this case, the primacy of efficiency. See Mart A. Stewart, "Southern Environmental History," in *A Companion to the American South*, ed. John B. Boles (Malden, Mass.: Blackwell, 2002), 414–15.

40. Reed, *Savannah River Site*, 109.

41. E. I. du Pont de Nemours and Company, "Savannah River Plant Construction History," 10.

42. Browder and Brooks, *Memories of Home*, 63, 64.

43. George McMillan, "H-Bomb's First Victims," *The Reporter*, March 6, 1951, 17.

44. *Aiken Standard and Review*, February 22, 1952.

45. Minutes, Aiken City Council, April 27, May 11, 1953.

46. Reed, *Savannah River Site*, 229.

47. Chapin, *In the Shadow of a Defense Plant*, 4, 194.

48. Esther Melton, telephone interview with author, September 20, 2003.

49. Otis Melton, telephone interview with author, November 4, 2006.

50. E. C. Thomas, interview with author, May 2, 2003, Graniteville, South Carolina.

51. Owen Clary, telephone interview with author, October 26, 2005.

52. Ronnie Bryant, interview with author, May 2, 2003, Graniteville, South Carolina.

53. Quoted in Reed, *Savannah River Site*, 294–95. Also see Deborah Holland, *Steward of World Peace, Keeper of Fair Play: The American Hydrogen Bomb and Civil Rights, 1945–1954*, Ph.D. dissertation, Northwestern University, 2002, 105, 120–21.

54. *Aiken Standard and Review*, January 23, 1953, 12.

55. Conroy, "Horses Don't Eat Moonpies," 50.

56. *Aiken Standard and Review*, June 18, 1952, 8; Jean Orth, interview with author, Aiken, South Carolina, August 11, 2005; Carolina Wells, interview with author, Aiken, South Carolina, August 11, 2005.

57. *Aiken Standard and Review*, March 11, 1954, 2.

58. *Aiken Standard and Review*, March 13, 1956, 2; March 20, 1956, 3.

59. *Aiken Standard and Review*, January 15, 1954, 1.

60. Owen Clary, telephone interview with author, October 26, 2005.

61. *Aiken Standard and Review*, February 18, 1952, 1.

62. *Aiken Standard and Review*, June 20, 1952, 4.

63. Melton Interview; Clary interview; Juanita Thomas, interview with author, May 2, 2003, Graniteville, South Carolina; Lenwood Melton, interview with author, Graniteville, South Carolina, May 2, 2003.

64. *Aiken Standard and Review*, November 30, 1951, 1.

65. *Aiken Standard and Review*, April 15, 1952, 1.

66. *Aiken Standard and Review*, February 2, 1951, 1.

67. *Aiken Standard and Review*, June 6, 1956, 6.

68. *Aiken Standard and Review*, January 20, 1954, 4.

69. Reed, *Savannah River Site*, 244–45, 246 (quotation).

70. "Aiken's Answer to Town Problems: Citizen, Chamber of Commerce, City Hall Teamwork," *The American City,* September 1956, 188.

71. Brochure, "Aiken, South Carolina," c. 1960s, Brochure File, Subject Files, Aiken Chamber of Commerce, Aiken, South Carolina.

72. Aiken Chamber of Commerce, "Charm and Progress" Brochure, c. 1960, Brochure File, Subject Files, Aiken Chamber of Commerce, Aiken, South Carolina.

73. *Savannah River News*, April 15, 1955, 3.

74. Aiken Chamber of Commerce, "Commemorating the 125th Anniversary of the City of Aiken," 1960, Aiken County History File, Historical Files, Aiken Chamber of Commerce, Aiken, South Carolina.

9

AFRICAN-AMERICAN SUBURBANIZATION AND REGIONALISM IN THE MODERN SOUTH

Andrew Wiese

Among the more striking developments in recent southern history has been the size and speed of African-American migration to the suburbs. Between 1960 and 2000, the number of southern black suburbanites grew by 5.5 million, a figure similar in size to the mid-century exodus of African Americans from the region. By 2000, 47 percent of African Americans in the metropolitan South lived in suburbs (compared with just 25 percent in 1960), and the region as a whole accounted for nearly 60 percent of black suburban growth in the United States.[1] By the end of the century, hundreds of thousands of black families had made comfortable homes in southern suburbia, a territory long assumed to be the province and privilege of whites.

Driven by thousands of individual success stories, African-American suburbanization appeared to be a fitting epilogue to a regional history marked by racial oppression. The suburban boom represented the fruits of civil rights mobilization and the unprecedented social and spatial freedoms that it offered to a growing black middle class. It signaled, too, the convergence of southern urban history with metropolitan trends nationwide. But the story of black suburbanization in the modern South was also more complicated, and these complications reveal both a more crooked path toward racial progress and a more subtle set of shifts between region and nation at the turn of the twenty-first century.

Among the areas of greatest national conformity, African-American suburbanization in the late twentieth century tended to extend rather than erode historic patterns of spatialized racial inequality in the metropolitan

United States. Through the 1990s, African-American suburbanites had lower median incomes, lower rates of home ownership, and less housing price appreciation than white suburbanites. Blacks living in the suburbs were also more likely to pay higher taxes and receive lesser quality services than white peers. Racial segregation, while declining at the century's end, still underpinned tenacious inequality among the suburbs where most whites and most African Americans lived. These differences, founded on racial discrimination against the places where African Americans resided, remained perhaps the most important basis for racial inequity in the early twenty-first century.

At the same time, developments since the 1990s heralded the potential for change in these basic patterns. Like rapidly growing metropolitan areas nationwide, many southern suburbs attracted a deluge of new migrants. In the South, especially, a significant proportion were African Americans, part of a growing return migration of blacks to the region. This group exercised a range of new housing options, from affluent black subdivisions to new melting-pot suburbs. Large numbers of immigrants and their children, too, put down roots in booming metropolitan areas of the New South. Drawn by new jobs to rapidly growing communities, the larger share of these newcomers upset historic racial patterns in the South and across the metropolitan United States. The result was not only greater residential integration than at any time in a century but also the establishment of diverse, multiracial communities in economically vibrant suburban areas. While the return migration of middle-class African Americans highlighted the endurance of regional variation, these trends illustrated more broadly that southern suburbs were in step with, and often at the leading edge of, trends in black suburbanization nationwide.

The contemporary convergence of suburban patterns across the United States stands in contrast to the mid-twentieth century, when black suburbanization in the South was one of many features that set the region apart. Unlike the well-known model of northern "second ghetto" formation, many southern cities followed a predominantly suburban strategy of black community building after World War II. In the urban North and West, African-American communities grew overwhelmingly through concentrated racial transition in existing neighborhoods, a process shaped by the mass migration of southern African Americans, federally subsidized urban renewal at the urban core, and defensive white homeownership on the periphery.[2] In contrast, for fifteen years after World War II, African-American communities in the urban South grew mainly through the construction of new housing, much of it on the urban periphery. White and black civic leaders across the urban South cooperated to create informally sanctioned "Negro expansion areas" on the suburban fringe. Preserving segregation and mitigating local violence, on the one hand, they facilitated, on the other hand, greater African-American access to suburban homes and amenities than in any other part of the country. Racial transition played a role, to be sure, but during the 1940s and 1950s it took a back seat to new construction and negotiated community expansion.[3] Thus, in the mid-century South, distinctive patterns of economic, racial, and political life were accompanied by a discrete pattern of race-structured city building and suburbanization.

By the end of the 1950s, however, politically sanctioned "Negro expansion" had run its course. With the acceleration of downtown-oriented highway and urban renewal programs in the South, the collapse of the Jim Crow system, and civil rights insurgency across the nation, patterns of southern and non-southern black community growth converged. During the 1960s, 1970s, and 1980s, black communities in the urban South grew largely through racial transition in existing neighborhoods, whether in the city or across its borders. Excluded from most suburbs, displaced from existing communities throughout the city, and re-concentrated within expanding black sectors of the city and inner suburbs, African Americans experienced intensified housing segregation, even as Jim Crow began to fall away in public accommodations and the law. By 1970, nineteen of the twenty most residentially segregated cities in the United States were in the South, and several dozen southern metropolitan areas exhibited levels of housing segregation that rivaled hypersegregated metropolitan archetypes such as Chicago and Detroit.[4]

By century's end, however, even as national trends predominated, southern suburbanization retained several distinctive features. Reversing patterns of the 1960s and 1970s, southern metropolitan areas generated comparatively low—and falling—levels of residential segregation. Supported by a return migration of middle-class black households from other parts of the United States—a majority of whom moved straight to the suburbs—southern suburbia attracted a larger share of metropolitan-area blacks than suburbs in other regions. Southern states became home to a disproportionate share of the nation's affluent black suburbs, and the region led the way in housing starts designed specifically for upscale black homebuyers. More than in any other part of the country, black southerners were at home in the suburbs.[5] By the start of the new century, black suburbanization in the South offered evidence both for the declining significance of region in the nation's metropolitan history and for ongoing—though shifting—instances of regional peculiarity.

Tracing African-American suburbanization in Atlanta since World War II, this essay illustrates both national similarities and persisting regional differences in this ongoing migration. Atlanta offers both strengths and weaknesses as an exemplar. After World War II, no southern city built as many new homes for African Americans, and nowhere else did African Americans play as great a role in the process. Indeed, Atlanta served as a New South model for "Negro housing" efforts throughout the South.

A half-century later, the city was not just a regional leader but a national one as well, boasting the nation's second-largest black suburban population—more than 900,000 people in 2000—and comprising 13 percent of black suburbanites in the South. Atlanta was home to the region's largest black businesses, and it reveled in its longstanding reputation as a "mecca" for "enterprising blacks."[6] Moreover, Atlanta was one of the most economically vibrant metropolitan areas in the country, growing at three times the national average during the 1990s. In these ways, Atlanta's postwar history was distinctive, but not unrecognizably so. In the sprawling shape of its suburbs, in the patterns of their settlement, and in the processes through which Atlantans of every color produced residential space, Atlanta was on the cutting edge of trends that characterized, first, the region and, increasingly, the nation as a whole.

As early as the late 1940s, federal officials, national home builders, and a variety of social scientists recognized that there were important differences in black community building between southern and non-southern cities.[7] In the metropolitan North, African-American residential areas grew largely through racial transition in formerly white neighborhoods. In the urban South, however, black communities grew mainly through the construction of new housing for a decade and a half after World War II.[8] As the sociologists Karl and Alma Taeuber explained in 1965, "the newer, smaller Southern city is still growing and annexing territory. The housing stock as a whole in these cities is fairly new, so there is only a small supply of old housing to be filtered down.... Consequently, the best housing available to Negroes in these cities is housing newly built specifically for Negroes."[9] In the 1950s, builders completed some 220,000 units of housing for African Americans in the metropolitan South, compared to just over 100,000 in the North (most of which were public housing projects). These new homes constituted 57 percent of the housing gained by southern black communities during the decade, compared to just 17 percent in the North (exact figures are not available for the much smaller African-American population in the West).[10]

Among the most profound differences between black suburbanization in the South and other parts of the country was the process of planning and political negotiation that underlay the southern variety. In southern cities such as Memphis, Orlando, Houston, and New Orleans, white and black civic leaders collaborated to ease the postwar housing crisis by building new black communities at the edge of town.[11] For white elites, the object was less about providing better housing than about preserving racial segregation and avoiding the turmoil that resulted when African Americans moved into white neighborhoods. By contrast, African Americans sought primarily to build better black neighborhoods. Their willingness to compromise over segregation reflected a tradition of racial advancement rooted in cohesive black communities and a deep ambivalence toward residential integration, not to mention a pragmatic appraisal of what was possible in the postwar South. For the black contractors, real estate brokers, and civic leaders who advocated "Negro expansion," overcoming segregation did not necessarily imply integration. Rather, it meant surmounting the inferior conditions and second-class citizenship that discrimination imposed. In housing, they wanted equality—by which they meant new housing, expanded home ownership, and a residential landscape common to middle-class suburbs nationwide—and they believed they could achieve it on a racially separate basis.[12]

The compromise that was separate suburbanization reflected not only differences in the aims of black and white communities but also their unequal power. White insistence on racial segregation, reinforced by the threat of violence, remained a rigid constraint on African-American planning. Nonetheless, black civic leaders viewed separate community building as a means of racial improvement, as well as an immediate remedy for the appalling conditions in which most blacks lived in the urban South.[13] Given this reality, they made it their first priority to expand and improve the supply of available housing. Just as well, some perceived the construction of up-to-date neighborhoods as an assertion of equality and, thus, a direct challenge to white supremacy in which separation was a badge of inequality. As Atlanta housing activist Robert Thompson put it, the construction of even small numbers of "luxury" homes was important, "if for no other reason than to assist in changing the white man's image of the Negro relative to the Negro's desire to live decently in suburbia."[14] Through the 1950s, southern black community leaders acknowledged no contradiction in building self-contained African-American communities at the same time as they attacked segregated schools and public accommodations. Ironically, their compromise on segregation facilitated the construction of the finest African-American residential neighborhoods in the United States, and it opened greater opportunities for black southerners to buy homes in new suburban neighborhoods than existed in any other region of the country.

Several distinguishing features of southern urban history facilitated the process of "Negro expansion" in the metropolitan South. First, compared to larger cities in the North, the urban South exhibited low population densities and more dispersed settlement across metropolitan areas. Second, the black population of most southern cities grew more slowly than those in the northern and western cities that were targets of African-American migration. The African-American population of the six largest non-southern metropolitan areas grew by 2.6 million between 1940 and 1960, an increase of 167 percent. By contrast, the eight largest southern metropolitan areas, which included comparatively fast-growing Washington, D.C., Atlanta, Houston, and Miami, gained just 835,000 black residents, an increase of 76 percent.[15] Finally, since African Americans had owned land and lived on the fringes of southern cities for more than a century, their demands for housing were easier to accommodate than in either the North or West, where they were widely perceived as interlopers. In short, southern metropolitan areas not only contained more available land on which to build but also much of it already belonged to African Americans, and black populations were growing slowly enough that new construction could accommodate the lion's share of home-seekers.[16]

In Atlanta and other southern cities, postwar suburbanization built on a long history of black settlement in the suburban fringe, a process illustrated by events on Atlanta's west side. Anchored by Atlanta University, the west side had long been attractive to upwardly mobile families. During the 1920s, an entrepreneur named Heman Perry cashed in on this allure by opening the Washington Park subdivision just west of the campus. To increase the area's appeal, Perry deeded land to the city for a public park and for Atlanta's first black public high school. A decade later, developer W. A. Fountain laid out the Fountain Heights subdivision on nearby Ashby Street, and during World War II, contractor Walter Aiken built a 250-home subdivision just south of Fountain Heights. During the war, Aiken and other black investors purchased more undeveloped suburban land to the west as outlets for future expansion.[17]

The ability of southern cities to annex suburban land after World War II also proved essential to the process of "Negro expansion." Unlike most large metropolitan areas in the North, where independent suburbs ringed the city and blocked its expansion, many southern cities grew geographically through mid-century by annexing their suburban fringe. During the 1940s and 1950s, cities as diverse as Tampa, Dallas, Memphis, Charlotte, Oklahoma City, and Atlanta annexed suburban areas double or triple their size.[18] Annexation gave control over outlying land to central city authorities who hoped to minimize racial transition in older white neighborhoods by drawing African-American housing demand away from them. As a result, much of postwar residential expansion in the urban South— "suburbanization" in other parts of the country—took place inside the newly drawn limits of a central city.

In Atlanta, the key moment in the postwar housing struggle came in 1946, when twenty-five black civic leaders met to "discuss and work out plans for developing more housing for Negroes."[19] The gathering was a who's who of the black financial and real estate communities in Atlanta. At the suggestion of Walter Aiken, the city's leading black builder, the group established subcommittees to "investigate further the possibilities of getting out-let areas for Negro expansion" and to create a private corporation to buy and develop land.[20] Aiken and his allies recognized that solving the housing shortage would require concerted effort among blacks as well as support from white leaders, so that "both groups fully understand that Negro citizens may live and build additional houses without intimidation and fear."[21]

Calling itself the Atlanta Housing Council (AHC), the group published a report in May 1947, outlining plans for six suburban areas that represented "the most logical and appropriate areas for the expansion of Negro housing."[22] Like "Negro expansion areas" in other southern cities, each was adjacent to a "present Negro area" in the outer rim of the city.[23] The areas were convenient to employment centers and existing black institutions, and each was sufficiently isolated from whites to minimize resistance. Several of the proposed sites were secluded by railroad tracks, roadways, or industrial strips. Where they were not, the report proposed surrounding them with "green-belts or strip parks," a suggestion that would be followed in many future developments (figure 9.1).[24]

Among white officials, responses to the report were cautious but supportive. The Chamber of Commerce requested clarification of boundaries and characteristics of affected neighborhoods. Officials from the surrounding counties, where the expansion areas were located, "consented to cooperate" in providing services to existing African-American sections. The local office of the Federal Housing Administration lent advice and support, and the Atlanta press praised the group's "realistic and practical approach" to the problems facing blacks and whites in the city.[25] For its part, the City Planning Commission adopted the concept of "Negro expansion" in its 1952 "Up Ahead" metropolitan plan.[26] Lacking force in law, the AHC proposal nonetheless became the de facto master plan for black community building in Atlanta for the next dozen years.

Essential to white acceptance of the plan were several related, but uncoordinated, actions on the part of African Americans themselves. Most important was the continued "infiltration" of African Americans into white neighborhoods. As black families moved, racial friction mounted. Mob gatherings, house bombings, and other incidents raised the specter of a race riot such as the city had suffered in 1906 and a number of northern cities experienced during and after World War II.[27] As important as the threat of violence was blacks' access to the ballot. Following a 1946 Supreme Court decision invalidating Georgia's white primary, Atlanta blacks launched a massive voter registration drive that tripled the number of registered black voters. Although African Americans remained unequal citizens throughout the long tenure of Mayor William Hartsfield (1937–1941, 1943–1962), by the late 1940s they were key members of the electoral coalition that kept him in office. Their relationship with the racially pragmatic mayor won them modest concessions in city services and support for efforts to help themselves, including the campaign to build what banker L. D. Milton called "sound, orderly and well-conceived housing developments for Negroes."[28]

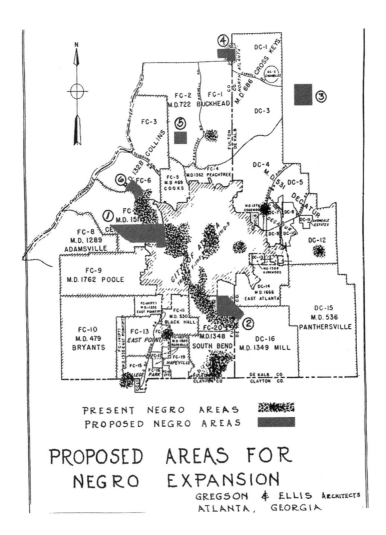

FIGURE 9.1. Across the South, politically negotiated community expansion and new home building characterized a distinctive pattern of black suburbanization during the 1940s and 1950s. The Atlanta Housing Council, made up of black civic and business leaders, published this proposal for separate but equal suburban developments in 1947. "Proposed Areas for Negro Expansion," Atlanta Housing Council, 1947, courtesy of the Atlanta Urban League Papers, Robert W. Woodruff Library of the Atlanta University Center, Box 242, Folder 1.

Finally, black Atlantans gained leverage in the housing effort because the concentration of African-American real estate and financial institutions in the city allowed them to take initiative without waiting for whites to act. By 1955, Atlanta's black lenders had invested more than $14 million in first-mortgage loans for black home buyers, paving the way for larger white institutions to underwrite a growing program of housing construction.[29] Against this backdrop, black civic leaders took concrete steps to build new housing in the suburban areas outlined in the 1947 proposal. Walter Aiken was already at work on two subdivisions inside the west side "expansion area number one" at the time of the report. Within months, the Housing Council launched additional plans to find and develop land on the west and south sides, an effort they expanded to five of the six areas by 1950.[30]

To the south of the city, black housing leaders focused on building modestly priced apartments to meet the needs of families with moderate incomes. The AHC recruited Morris Abram, a leader in the city's racially progressive Jewish community, to build a 450-unit apartment project in South Atlanta on land that had belonged to the A.M.E. Church. Completed in 1950, the Highpoint Apartments modeled various features of suburban landscape planning, with one- and two-story brick-clad buildings set back from winding streets in a parklike setting.[31] Most important, the development opened the door to modern housing for black Atlantans who wanted to live outside the urban core but who could not afford to buy a home.

On the west side, the coalition focused on building single-family homes for the growing black middle class. By the mid-1950s, the AHC had initiated more than a dozen subdivisions, an effort that would continue through the early 1960s. In the area where Heman Perry had pioneered comprehensive neighborhood planning for African-American expansion in the 1920s, black Atlantans built what would become, for a time, the premier black residential district in the country. By 1952, when the city annexed the six suburban expansion areas, African-American developers and white allies had initiated new construction in five of the areas proposed in 1947, and by the end of the decade, they had produced 12,000 new homes, approximately half of them single-family houses. Altogether, two-thirds of the additional housing units gained by black Atlantans during the 1950s were brand-new.[32]

By the end of the 1950s, however, politically sanctioned "Negro expansion" had run its course in Atlanta and other southern cities. Vacant land for the construction of new housing became increasingly scarce as white suburbs hemmed in postwar expansion areas and raised political obstacles to further expansion. Moreover, federally funded highway and renewal projects reached their peak, displacing tens of thousands of black households and overwhelming the effort to re-house them through new construction. At the same time, white migration to suburbs reduced demand for in-town neighborhoods and opened opportunities for African Americans to move into older white areas. Over the next two decades, developers continued to build new subdivisions for African Americans, authorities erected public housing in outlying areas, and apartment construction accelerated near the core, but new dwellings would not play as large a role in the growth of the African-American housing stock as they had in the 1950s.

Just as they did outside the South, the majority of new black home-seekers settled in existing city and inner-suburban neighborhoods that were being vacated by whites. This process, which Arnold Hirsch famously labeled "second ghetto" formation, followed similar patterns across the United States and resulted from the same set of implicit compromises.[33] In Atlanta and elsewhere, downtown institutions, businesses, and politicians opted to expand the central business district at the expense of working- and lower-middle-class neighborhoods—white as well as black. Meanwhile, African-American civic leaders, who had cooperated with these same elites to build better black housing in the 1950s, lost influence. In rhetoric and reality, the focus of their efforts shifted from "expansion" to "relocation."[34]

Nationwide, block-by-block racial transition, accelerated by urban demolition, left deep scars in the urban fabric and body politic, and this process contributed to the lasting stratification of metropolitan areas on the basis of race. In many white neighborhoods, the appearance of black families ignited violence or panic selling. "Blockbusters" in the real estate industry, who manipulated racial fear for profits, often hastened the transition. Complicating matters, white financial institutions generally refused to write mortgages in changing neighborhoods, forcing black homebuyers to turn to predatory lenders. Mom-and-pop stores followed their customers to newer locations, draining investment from local retail districts, and changing neighborhoods attracted absentee owners who maximized profits by cutting maintenance and crowding their properties. In city and suburban areas alike, municipalities regularly cut back services and loosened land-use restrictions as neighborhoods changed racial status. Thus, all across the country, transitional neighborhoods were likely to convey social and economic disadvantages to their new residents, reinforcing racial inequality across metropolitan space, even as African Americans, for the time being, gained improved housing and facilities.[35]

In Atlanta, this process remade the metropolitan area after 1960, bringing the city's urban geography into growing conformity with patterns nationwide. Like many southern cities, Atlanta had spent federal monies for public housing and urban renewal since the 1930s and 1940s, but it was not until the late 1950s that redevelopment activities reached their peak. The full onset of urban renewal in Atlanta fundamentally altered the equation between black community growth and new housing on the suburban fringe. In contrast to the 3,400 black households uprooted by redevelopment projects during the 1950s, the city's 1959 urban renewal plan projected the displacement of 9,100 black families in its first five years alone (a fivefold annual increase). Adjusting for population growth, officials estimated that the city would need an additional 17,000 housing units for African Americans by 1964, just shy of the 18,000 units (12,000 new and 6,000 transferred from whites) that the city had added through intensive effort during the whole of the previous decade.[36]

To complicate matters, outlying land for the construction of new housing became increasingly scarce. As the Atlanta Citizens Advisory Committee for Urban Renewal concluded in 1960, "it is practically impossible at this time to locate vacant land for low- or middle-income Negro housing that will meet the requirements of government agencies and not meet violent objections on racial grounds."[37] Without access to "suitable vacant land," the committee concluded, racial transition would be the only way to meet the shortfall in African-American housing—an option that promised, in their words, "racial strife and the disruption of existing communities."[38]

Four years later, Robert Thompson, an Atlanta Urban League official who had played a key role in the postwar "Negro expansion" effort, affirmed the Advisory Committee's predictions. Surveying "minority housing" across the metropolitan area in 1964, Thompson listed more than a dozen city neighborhoods that had recently changed or were currently changing from white to African American. On the west side, in particular, whites were in full retreat from a sector stretching several miles west from the campus of Atlanta University. By 1970, a mostly black region reaching to the margins of Fulton County had supplanted the former patchwork of white and black communities.[39]

Meanwhile, as in other metropolitan areas, pressures for socioeconomic change followed hard on the heels of racial transition. In response to the demand for housing among African Americans displaced from urban renewal sites, developers built cheap apartments at high density throughout newly black areas. Thompson's survey revealed twenty-nine new apartment complexes ranging from three units to three hundred units constructed for African Americans after 1960. Most were located on the city's west side, the area envisioned by black civic leaders in the 1940s as a district of single-family homes for the black middle class.[40] "With one or two exceptions," Thompson concluded, "these units exhibit little or no imagination in design, and they have been crowded on relatively small tracts of land....Unless the better housing code is enforced quickly and serious attention given to planning nonwhite neighborhoods,...there will be created bigger and worse slums than those now being torn down."[41] Thompson's plea fell on deaf ears, but his fears of socioeconomic decline proved well-founded.

By 1980, the twin processes of African-American residential expansion and white suburban flight had produced a great arc of black residential neighborhoods encompassing the west, south, and southeast sides of the city.[42] In south and southeast Atlanta, especially, black home-seekers pushed across the city limits into the inner suburbs of southern DeKalb and Fulton counties, creating a new ring of predominantly African-American suburbs. In the Panthersville, Candler-McAfee, and Gresham Park areas southeast of the city in DeKalb County, for instance, African-American populations ballooned from fewer than 4,000 to more than 39,000 during the 1970s. By 1980, blacks constituted 85 percent of the population in the three neighborhoods, and thousands of other African-American families were replacing whites in the adjoining communities. Featuring tidy sub-divisions of brick ranch homes, rolling lots, and abundant shade trees, these new neighborhoods marked a step into the suburban middle class for thousands of families.[43] At the same time, accelerated racial transition and ongoing discrimination portended a set of challenges that dogged these and similar communities across the country.

Among the most significant of these challenges was the disinvestment of black communities by major lending institutions. In 1988, the *Atlanta Journal and Constitution* documented pervasive racial redlining across the metropolitan area. At that time, white middle-class areas of metro Atlanta received five times as many conventional mortgage loans as African-American neighborhoods of the same social standing, and affluent blacks were more likely to be refused loans than were working-class whites. In Gresham Park, banks and savings and loans provided just 4 percent of loans, forcing African-American residents to borrow the rest from shady "subprime" lenders. Across the city, private lenders were systematically concentrating housing capital in white communities, transferring wealth from black depositors in some parts of the metro area to white home buyers in the rest. Despite policy changes sparked by the original study, updated analysis in 1996 showed only minor improvements. Consistent with national findings on mortgage discrimination, the study found that white areas of the metropolis were still receiving four times the mortgage investment of comparable black neighborhoods, including those in the close-in suburbs.[44]

Over time, the effects of race- and place-based discrimination were obvious in many inner suburbs of southern DeKalb County. In the Candler-McAfee, Gresham Park, and Panthersville areas—neighborhoods that represented the leading edge of black suburbanization in the 1970s and 1980s—racial turnover preceded a slow socioeconomic transition from middle-class pio-neers to a growing working-class population. By century's end, middle-class black families were leaving the public schools, and disinvestment was evi-dent in the landscape.[45] The retail strip along Candler Boulevard presented a gritty sweep of discount clothing, furniture, and auto parts outlets, liquor stores, fast-food restaurants, and small hair and nail care salons (figure 9.2). National chains were scarce. Vacancies were high, and repair spotty. Perhaps the most palpable sign of disinvestment was the paucity of commercial banking facilities and the dominating presence of pawn shops. In the housing stock, too, evidence of capital flight was clear. Proudly maintained ranch homes stood opposite properties in various states of disrepair, from broken screen doors and unkempt lawns to burn-scars and boarded windows. Taken as a whole, the neighborhoods betrayed clear signs of racial stratification similar to inner suburbs across the United States where African-American families had moved in large numbers after 1960.[46]

FIGURE 9.2. The Candler-McAfee area of southern DeKalb County was among the most important targets of black middle-class suburbanization outside Atlanta during the 1970s. Like many inner-ring suburbs across the country where African Americans moved after 1960, the area experienced racial resegregation, disinvestment, and socioeconomic decline over time, changes which were reflected in its commercial corridor. Photograph by Andrew Wiese, 2006.

Atlanta's new suburban pattern, typified by the migration of middle-class families to racially changing inner-ring suburbs, signaled the city's full convergence with prevailing patterns of black suburbanization nationwide by 1990. Across the United States, hundreds of thousands of upwardly mobile African Americans pursued better housing, schools, and opportunities in inner suburbs during the 1970s and 1980s. In Los Angeles, for example, 40,000 African Americans resettled in nearby Inglewood and Compton during the 1970s. More than 30,000 moved across Cleveland's eastern limits to the suburbs of East Cleveland, Cleveland Heights, and Warrensville Heights, followed by another 35,000 to these and other inner suburbs during the 1980s. Adjacent to Newark, the inner suburbs of Essex County, New Jersey, such as East Orange and Irvington, attracted 84,000 new black residents during these two decades, and east of Washington, D.C., Prince George's County, Maryland, mushroomed by 278,000 over the same period.[47] Despite residents' immediate gains in housing and services, social scientists indicated that the same processes that had beset changing city neighborhoods were following them to the suburbs. Redlining, retail flight, service cutbacks, and declining public schools hampered black economic progress in many of these and other inner suburbs. "Black suburbanization as it is now occurring," concluded the geographer Harold Rose in 1976, "represents the spatial extension of the ghettoization process with all that implies regarding the quality of life dimensions for its residents."[48]

By the 1990s, evidence from Atlanta and around the United States suggested that the nation's suburbs remained largely separate and unequal. Despite the growing access of black homeowners to newer, more economically dynamic suburban areas, three-quarters of black suburbanites in 1990 lived in older, inner-ring suburbs—like Candler-McAfee—that exhibited various fiscal shortcomings such as high taxes, mediocre services, low-performing schools, and anemic property appreciation.[49] Furthermore, the tendency of whites to avoid integrated neighborhoods, and many African Americans' disposition to eschew untested white communities, meant that the majority of black suburbanites lived in racially identifiable, if not segregated, neighborhoods. In Atlanta and Washington, D.C., which were home to one in six African-American suburbanites nationwide in 2000, the average black suburbanite lived in a majority-black neighborhood.[50] Meanwhile, research continued to show a correlation between race and spatial disadvantage.[51] Rather than upsetting the familiar division of metropolitan areas into racially stratified white and black spaces, the suburban explosion of the post-civil rights era expanded it over a greater area. These factors—material distinctions that conveyed disparate advantages and disadvantages to residents on the basis of race—remained among the most salient features of suburban life through the end of the twentieth century without respect to region.[52]

Even as black suburbanization through the 1990s tended to minimize differences among the regions, new trends unfolding during the decade and since indicate that the relationship between region and nation remains in flux. First, southern metropolitan areas were ground zero for an escalating return migration of well-educated African Americans to the region. Drawn by robust job prospects, growing black political and economic power, and longstanding cultural ties, these migrants enhanced the economic status of black communities, and especially black suburbs, across the South.[53] As a result, contemporary southern cities were home to a disproportionate share of the nation's affluent black suburbs and a greater share of new housing starts aimed at black homebuyers—factors that reinforced regional particularities that were decades in the making. At the same time, robust economic growth in many southern metropolitan areas attracted migrants from all over the world. Joining African-American newcomers in brand-new suburban neighborhoods across the South, these recent arrivals unsettled historic patterns of race and residence, complicated the region's traditional white-black racial order, and pushed levels of racial segregation to historic lows. In this last respect, fast-growing southern cities such as Orlando, Jacksonville, Charlotte, Houston, and Dallas, as well as Atlanta, looked increasingly like other dynamic and diversifying metropolitan areas across the country. Thus, by the first decade of the twenty-first century, black suburbanization in the South offered evidence for both the convergence and continuing differentiation of region and nation.

In metropolitan Atlanta, which attracted 459,000 black newcomers during the 1990s, African-American return migration swelled the city's large black middle class and provided an effective market for new housing built with them in mind. The focal point for this trend was southern DeKalb County, which gained 131,000 African Americans during the decade. New housing in DeKalb ran the gamut from two-bedroom townhomes in well-landscaped compounds to brick-encrusted mansions in amenity-rich gated communities (figure 9.3). Interspersed among these lush landscapes of African-American economic mobility were influential black megachurches, such as the 22,000 member New Birth Missionary Church in Lithonia, and new "upscale" shopping malls, such as the Gallery at South DeKalb, which advertised itself as "catering primarily to the upscale African-American customer." For some social commentators, DeKalb County had become the "promised land" of the black middle class.[54] Represented in Congress and the county executive's office by black officials, and home to thousands of black executives and entrepreneurs, DeKalb offered upwardly mobile families the possibility of enjoying both the cultural comfort of a black community and the economic advantages of upper-middle-class suburbia.

FIGURE 9.3. Upscale subdivisions such as Eagle's Ridge in southern DeKalb County, marketed as a "beautiful swim and tennis community," attracted tens of thousands of middle-class black homebuyers in the 1990s and early 2000s. Fueled in part by the return migration of well-educated African Americans to the South, affluent black subdivisions such as this one reflected both continuing regional variation and nationwide efforts by many black families to balance economic and social goals by moving to predominantly black suburbs. Photograph by Andrew Wiese, 2006.

Amid the forested hills and the new subdivisions cloaked in greenery, it was easy to overlook that new neighborhoods such as Brook Glen, Lithonia, Browns Mill, and Stone Mountain, which marked the peak of black suburban achievement in the twenty-first century, were scarcely fifteen minutes down the county road from declining inner suburbs such as Candler-McAfee. Like middle-class African Americans across the country, these suburbanites lived much closer to the working class than did their white peers. Residents of south DeKalb County, rich and poor, shared the same school district, the same churches, and many of the same commercial facilities, and together they contributed to a tax base with less aggregate resources than residents of the mostly white counties north of Atlanta. By 2007, 64 percent of children in the DeKalb County schools, which were 75 percent black, were eligible for free or reduced-price lunches, a benefit tied to lower-income status that is often linked to significant challenges in student achievement.[55] As urban analyst Myron Orfield points out, however, "school demographics are a powerful prophecy for communities.... When the perceived quality of a school declines, it can set in motion a cycle of middle class flight and disinvestment."[56] In the context of persistent racially stratified suburbanization in Atlanta and elsewhere, such trends cast doubt on the capacity of these new suburbs to meet the economic goals of many residents over the long run. If south DeKalb was the "promised land" for the black middle class, this status remained troublingly precarious.

Reinforcing this impression, Atlanta, like many U.S. metropolitan areas, showed clear patterns of racially polarized growth at the end of the twentieth century. In the words of the Brookings Institution, metropolitan Atlanta faced a "stark divide" between job growth, investment, and population expansion to the north and black suburban settlement to the south.[57] In 1998, three-quarters of African Americans lived in the region's two central counties, Fulton and DeKalb, and the great majority lived in mostly black neighborhoods in the southern half of these counties. Suburban DeKalb County, which boasted a narrow black majority in 2000, was especially divided by race. Just 20 percent of residents north of Interstate 20 were black, while African Americans made up 80 percent of those living south of the highway. Meanwhile, the fastest-growing counties in the metropolitan area—Cobb, Gwinnett, and Cherokee—lay to the north of the city, and all had populations less than 10 percent black in 1990. Even with large numbers of recent black migrants, they ranged from 2.5 to 19 percent black in 2000. During the 1990s, the vast majority of new jobs and new investments opened in the northern suburbs of the city; likewise, 70 percent of metropolitan population growth in the 1990s took place north of the city center.[58] By contrast, Atlanta's southern suburbs, especially those areas where the largest number of African-American families lived, showed little or no net gain in jobs or investment. This was especially striking given the settlement of tens of thousands of affluent black families in the region during these same years. Growing black migration to Atlanta's northern suburbs after the mid-1990s began to erode this pattern, but the principal features of polarized growth since the 1960s remained intact.

In these respects, Atlanta's recent history reflected common trends across metropolitan America, in which the best African-American neighborhoods were often located farther and farther from the places where the largest part of regional job growth, investment, and white population expansion were taking place. In metropolitan areas as diverse as Chicago, Denver, Dallas, San Diego, and Washington, D.C., the greatest number of minority suburbanites were settling in the opposite direction from the suburbs with the highest rates of job growth and investment. Moreover, the suburbs where most African-American families lived displayed significant fiscal challenges that hindered the economic prospects of their residents. Patterns of uneven metropolitan growth—including a "spatial mismatch" between suburban job centers and areas of minority suburbanization, and close links between race and spatial disadvantage—were common across the country.[59]

In a recent departure from these persisting trends, however, many southern metropolitan areas began to see the largest proportion of black suburbanites settle in predominantly white (and often economically dynamic) suburbs, a trend that produced rising levels of residential integration across the region by 2000. By contrast with 1970, when southern metropolitan areas led the nation in residential segregation, at the turn of the century only Miami, among all of the larger southern cities, made the top-ten list. Bolstered by rapid migration and the growth of sprawling new suburbs, cities such as Tampa, Orlando, Dallas, Fort Worth, Richmond, Charlotte, and others registered indices of dissimilarity (the most common statistical measure of residential segregation) less than 55, which was a sixty-year low.[60] By the early 2000s, African-American families were moving to places that would have seemed unlikely even fifteen years earlier—fast-growing but predominantly white southern suburbs, such as Winter Garden and Oviedo, Florida, near Orlando; DeSoto County, Mississippi, south of Memphis; and high-tech employment hubs such as Loudon County, Virginia, near Washington.[61] In Atlanta, too, booming Cobb and Gwinnett counties on the city's flourishing north side witnessed significant black migration after the late 1990s. Between 2000 and 2007, the two counties gained as many as 131,000 African-American residents, including 86,000 in Gwinnett, which abutted the upscale black communities near Stone Mountain in southern DeKalb County.[62] In many such places, new migrants played a key role in this growth. As one resident of Charlotte explained, black newcomers were "not privy to what old or established patterns or regions were about."[63] They settled in the best neighborhoods that they could afford, balancing convenience to jobs, schools, and amenities, much like their nonblack peers.

Further complicating this picture, many high-growth southern suburbs were also magnets for newcomers from around the globe. In Gwinnett County, for instance, one-quarter of the population was Latino or Asian American by 2007. Twenty-eight percent reported speaking a foreign language at home, and with African Americans comprising 23 percent, "minorities" stood poised to become the county majority by 2010. Unlike many of the suburbs where African Americans had moved since the civil rights era, Gwinnett County boasted a robust fiscal profile and job opportunities for workers across the economic spectrum. It was home to the largest shopping mall in the Southeast, a new minor league baseball team, and dozens of high-tech businesses. Even so, it remains unclear whether the new multiracial communities in places like Gwinnett and Cobb counties will ultimately transcend older patterns of race and space or reproduce them in some new alignment of racialized inequality. Even as rates of home ownership and education rose in both counties after 2000, "minority" families accounted for almost all of population growth, and in Cobb County the number of whites actually declined.[64] Whatever the outcome, in the short term these trends demonstrated a departure from the concentration of black suburbanites in areas with significant economic disadvantages, holding out the hope that historical links between race and space may at last have begun to come undone.

By the end of the twentieth century, many of the most obvious symbols of southern exceptionalism had steadily eroded. At the same time, several longstanding regional attributes that had been overshadowed by the negative images of a racially distinctive South remained alive in the new century. As the historian Charles Payne notes, southern black communities historically had cultivated a greater "civic capacity" to meet collective needs.[65] In the 1950s, just as in the 1990s, this capacity for self-help underlay the dramatic expansion of new and better black neighborhoods in southern suburbia. Likewise, African Americans' deep cultural roots in the South provided the foundation for the boomerang migration of talented blacks—a southern "brain gain" that swelled the region's black middle class and encouraged the growth of affluent African-American suburbs as well as growing integration in some of the South's most dynamic suburban areas.[66]

Even in these ways, however, it is worth pointing out that southern metropolitan areas proved to be national exemplars rather than regional outliers. Just as African-American families pioneered new territory in the suburban South, their numbers also grew in predominantly white suburban areas outside the South, from the sprawling exurbs of St. Louis and Indianapolis to Pittsburgh's traditionally exclusive northern rim.[67] Furthermore, during the building boom of the 1990s and early 2000s, developers outside of Chicago, Detroit, and Los Angeles constructed high-end homes with the black middle class in mind.[68] What was distinctive about these trends in places like Atlanta, Dallas, or Orlando was more a matter of scale than of kind. In the new century, rapidly growing southern cities looked increasingly like the model for trends in fast-growing metropolitan areas across the country.

As African Americans entered the new century, an unprecedented number did so as suburbanites. Their efforts to make homes and rear children, to build institutions as well as equity, posed a continuing challenge to the legacy of spatial disadvantage embedded in the metropolitan landscape. Given trends in Atlanta and other booming cities, there was more reason to be optimistic in 2009 than at any time in the last fifty years that the long chain binding race, space, and disadvantage might be broken.

As growing numbers of African Americans look south for a better life, it is all but certain that the region will be at the cutting edge of whatever this new history will bring.

NOTES

1. Andrew Wiese, *Places of Their Own: African-American Suburbanization in the Twentieth Century* (Chicago: University of Chicago Press, 2004), 256; William Frey, "Black Migration to the South Reaches Record Highs in 1990s," *Population Today,* February 1998, 1–3; Frey, "Migration to the South Brings U.S. Blacks Full Circle," *Population Today,* May/June, 2001, 625.

2. Arnold R. Hirsch, *Making the Second Ghetto: Race and Housing in Chicago, 1940–1960* (New York: Cambridge University Press, 1983); Thomas J. Sugrue, *Origins of the Urban Crisis: Race and Inequality in Postwar Detroit* (Princeton: Princeton University Press, 1996).

3. Wiese, *Places of Their Own,* 164–208.

4. Thomas Hanchett, *Sorting Out the New South City: Race, Class, and Urban Development in Charlotte, 1875–1975* (Chapel Hill: University of North Carolina Press, 1998), 261.

5. Frey, "Black Migration to the South"; Frey, "Migration to the South Brings U.S. Blacks Full Circle," 625; Ernest Holsendolph, "Blacks' Income Gains Not All of the Story," *Atlanta Journal-Constitution,* September 22, 2002, P6; Reynolds Farley and William Frey, "Changes in the Segregation of Whites from Blacks During the 1980s," *American Sociological Review,* 59 (February 1994), 23–45; Jennifer LaFleur, "Black Wealth Blossoms in Suburbs," *Dallas Morning News,* June 25, 2005; Alex Marshall, "The Quiet Integration of Suburbia," *Virginian-Pilot,* July 25, 2003, A1.

6. See, for example, Phyllis Garland, "Atlanta: Black Mecca of the South," *Ebony,* 26 (August 1971), 152–57. "Enterprising blacks" in Charles Whitaker, "Is Atlanta the New Black Mecca?" *Ebony,* 57 (March 2002), 148.

7. "Negro Housing: New Vistas Opened for South by Private Industry," *Christian Science Monitor,* October 18, 1948, 1 [sect. 2]; Donald Wyatt, "Better Homes for Negro Families in the South," *Social Forces,* 28 (March 1950), 297–303; Albert L. Thompson, "Negro Mortgagees and Builders in the South," *Insured Mortgage Portfolio,* 18 (3rd Quarter, 1953), 9–11; "What Builders are Doing about Minority Housing," *House and Home,* 6 (April 1955), 146–47.

8. Wiese, *Places of Their Own,* 164–208.

9. Karl and Alma Taeuber, *Negroes in Cities: Residential Segregation and Neighborhood Change* (Chicago: Aldine, 1965), 193.

10. In the West, "non-whites" gained 100,000 new homes during the 1950s, but the proportion available to African Americans is unknown because of the large number of Asian Americans and Native Americans included in the category. On the West Coast alone, 381,000 Asian Americans made up 27 percent of

"non-whites" in 1960. U.S. Census of Housing: 1960, Vol. IV, *Components of Inventory Change*, Pt. 1A (Washington: GPO, 1962), 64, 86, 108, 130; U.S. Census of Population: 1960, Vol. I, *States and Small Areas*, Pt. 1, U.S. Summary (Washington: GPO, 1963), lviii.

11. Wiese, *Places of Their Own*, 164–208; Nathan Glazer and Davis McEntire, eds., *Studies in Housing and Minority Groups* (Berkeley: University of California Press, 1960); Ronald Bayor, *Race and the Shaping of Twentieth-Century Atlanta* (Chapel Hill: University of North Carolina Press, 1996), 53–92; Christopher Silver and John Moeser, *The Separate City: Black Communities in the Urban South, 1940–1968* (Lexington: University of Kentucky Press, 1995), 125–62; William H. Wilson, *Hamilton Park: A Planned Black Community in Dallas* (Baltimore: Johns Hopkins University Press, 1998); Raymond A. Mohl, "Making the Second Ghetto in Metropolitan Miami, 1940–1960," *Journal of Urban History*, 21 (March 1995), 398–99.

12. Wiese, *Places of Their Own*, 165–74.

13. Booker T. McGraw, "Wartime Employment, Migration, and Housing of Negroes in the U.S.," *Midwest Journal*, 1 (Summer 1949).

14. Robert A. Thompson, Memorandum to Phillip Hammer, "Atlanta Urban Renewal Survey," June 25, 1957, Box 243, Atlanta Urban League Papers, Robert Woodruff Library, Atlanta University, Atlanta, Georgia [hereinafter AUL Papers].

15. The six non-southern metropolitan areas were New York, Chicago, Philadelphia, Detroit, Los Angeles, and Cleveland. The southern cities were Baltimore, Birmingham, New Orleans, Memphis, Atlanta, Houston, Dallas, and Miami. U.S. Census of Population: 1940, *Census Tracts* (Washington: GPO, 1943), Table 1; Census of Population and Housing: 1960, *Census Tracts*, Table P-1.

16. Taeuber and Taeuber, *Negroes in Cities*, 124–25.

17. Wiese, *Places of Their Own*, 175–78; Mildred Warner et al., "Community Building: The History of Atlanta University Neighborhoods" (Atlanta, 1978), 9; Timothy Crimmins, "Bungalow Suburbs: East and West," *Atlanta Historical Journal*, 26 (Summer-Fall 1982), 83–94; "Walter H. Aiken," Biographical Sheet, Box 7, Long-Rucker-Aiken Papers, Atlanta History Center, Atlanta, Georgia.

18. Kenneth Jackson, *Crabgrass Frontier: The Suburbanization of the United States* (New York: Oxford University Press, 1985), 144–46; Clarence Ridling and Orin Nolting, eds., *The Municipal Year Book*, Editions 1948–1960 (Chicago: International City Managers Association, 1948–1960).

19. Walter Aiken, "Report on the Committee on Housing for Negroes," February 15, 1949, Box 254, AUL Papers.

20. Temporary Coordinating Committee on Housing [TCCH], "Minutes," December 4, 1946, Box 254, AUL Papers.

21. TCCH, "The Community Housing Corporation", n.d. [1948], Box 252, AUL Papers.

22. Atlanta Housing Council [AHC], "Proposed Areas for Expansions of Negro Housing in Atlanta, Georgia," May 1947, Box 244, AUL Papers.

23. See Mohl, "Making the Second Ghetto," 398–99; Wilson, *Hamilton Park*, 33–66; Silver and Moeser, *Separate City*, 125–62.

24. AHC, "Proposed Areas for Expansions of Negro Housing."

25. Minutes, Meeting between AHC and Officials from Fulton and DeKalb Counties, May 14, 1948, Box 254, AUL Papers; Silver and Moeser, *Separate City*, 136–44.

26. Bayor, *Race*, 29–32, 59–60.

27. Walter H. Aiken, Joint Committee on Housing, *Study and Investigation, Hearings before the Joint Committee on Housing, 80th Congress, Proceedings at Atlanta, Georgia*, October 29, 1947 (Washington: GPO, 1948), 1254–56; Bayor, *Race*, 59; Kevin Kruse, *White Flight: Atlanta and the Making of Modern Conservatism* (Princeton: Princeton University Press, 2005), 42–77.

28. Bayor, *Race*, 15–52; Hylan Lewis and Robert Thompson with Carl Coleman, "Housing for Negroes in Atlanta and Birmingham: Report Prepared for the Commission on Race and Housing," draft, 1956, in the possession of Robert A. Thompson; L. D. Milton to AHC, June 13, 1947, Box 238, AUL Papers.

29. Robert Thompson, Hylan Lewis, and Davis McEntire, "Atlanta and Birmingham: A Comparative Study of Negro Housing," in *Studies in Housing and Minority Groups*, 41, 45–46; Thompson, "Negro Mortgagees and Builders in the South," 9–11.

30. Thompson et al, "Atlanta and Birmingham."

31. "Fulton Commissioners Approve Plan for Negro Housing," *Atlanta Daily World*, February 9, 1950; "South's Smartest Apartments," *Atlanta Daily World*, June 1, 1950.

32. Robert A. Thompson, "A Report of the Housing Activities of the Atlanta Urban League," June 18, 1951, Box 244, AUL Papers; Thompson et al., "Atlanta and Birmingham," 26; Citizens Advisory Committee for Urban Renewal, "The Story of Negro Housing in Atlanta," (ca. 1960), 4, Box 3, Atlanta Bureau of Planning Papers, Atlanta History Center, Atlanta, Georgia.

33. Hirsch, *Making the Second Ghetto*; Mohl, "Making the Second Ghetto," 395–427.

34. Robert A. Thompson, Correspondence, Box 249, File 14, DeKalb Urban Renewal, AUL Papers.

35. Hirsch, *Making the Second Ghetto*; Sugrue, *Origins of the Urban Crisis*, 181–258; Kruse, *White Flight*, 234–66; Wiese, *Places of Their Own*, 243–54.

36. Citizens Advisory Committee for Urban Renewal, "The Story of Negro Housing in Atlanta," 2, 4–5.

37. Ibid., 3.

38. Ibid., 4.

39. Ibid.

40. Robert A. Thompson, "Some Observations About Minority Housing in Atlanta, Georgia," May, 1964, Box 252, File 30, AUL Papers.

41. Ibid., 9.

42. See Kruse, *White Flight*.

43. U.S. Census of Population and Housing: 1970, *Census Tracts*; U.S. Census of Population and Housing: 1980, *Census Tracts*.

44. Bill Dedman, "The Color of Money," *Atlanta Journal-Constitution*, May 1–4, 1988; Elvin Wyly and Steven Holloway, " 'The Color of Money' Revisited: Racial Lending Patterns in Atlanta's Neighborhoods," *Housing Policy Debate*, 10 (1999), 555–600. On national trends, see Stephen Ross and John Yinger, *The Color of Credit: Mortgage Discrimination, Research Methodology, and Fair Lending* (Cambridge, Mass.: MIT Press, 2003).

45. Free or reduced price lunch eligibility ranged from 79 to 94 percent in DeKalb elementary schools, http://www.greatschools.net/schools.page?district=55&state=GA, accessed July 24, 2008.

46. John Logan and Mark Schneider, "Racial Segregation and Racial Change in American Suburbs, 1970–1980," *American Journal of Sociology*, 89 (January 1984), 875–76; Harold M. Rose, *Black Suburbanization: Access to Improved Quality of Life or Maintenance of the Status Quo?* (Cambridge: Ballinger Press, 1976), 250–63; Wiese, *Places of Their Own*, 212–17, 243–54.

47. *Wiese, Places of Their Own*, 212–17, 243–54; Census of Population: 1980, Vol. 1, *Characteristics of the Population*, Chapter B, General Population Characteristics, Parts 6, 12, 22, 37 (Washington: GPO, 1982); U.S. Census Bureau, "American FactFinder," 1990 Summary Tape File 1 (STF 1); http://factfinder.census.gov, (accessed January 3, 2009).

48. Rose, *Black Suburbanization*, 262–63. Also see Harold X. Connolly, "Black Movement to the Suburbs," *Urban Affairs Quarterly* (September 1973), 28; Karl Taeuber, "Racial Segregation, the Persisting Dilemma," *Annals of the American Academy of Political and Social Science*, 422 (November 1975), 90.

49. Thomas J. Phelan and Mark Schneider, "Race, Ethnicity and Class in American Suburbs," *Urban Affairs Review*, 31 (May 1996), 659–71; Mark Schneider and Thomas J. Phelan, "Black Suburbanization in the 1980s," *Demography*, 30 (May 1993), 269–79.

50. John R. Logan, "The New Ethnic Enclaves in America's Suburbs" (Albany: Lewis Mumford Center, 2001).

51. Logan and Schneider, "Racial Segregation and Racial Change," 875–76; David Harris, "All Suburbs are Not Created Equal: A New Look at Racial Differences in Suburban Location" (University of Michigan, Population Studies Center, Research Report No. 99–440, 1999), 13; John Logan, "Separate and Unequal: The Neighborhood Gap for Blacks and Hispanics in Metropolitan America" (Albany: Lewis Mumford Center, 2002).

52. George Galster, "Black Suburbanization: Has it Changed the Relative Location of the Races?" *Urban Affairs Quarterly*, 26 (June 1991), 621–28; Logan, "New Ethnic Enclaves."

53. William H. Frey, "The New Great Migration: Black Americans' Return to the South" (Brookings Institution, May 2004); William Frey, "Diversity Spreads Out: Metropolitan Shifts in Hispanic, Asian, and Black Populations since 2000" (Brookings Institution, March 2006), 7.

54. Kirk Kicklighter, "Many Middle-Class Blacks Prefer Own Communities," *Atlanta Journal and Constitution*, May 6, 2001, A16; Ellen Barry, "Atlanta Suburbs Bloom for Blacks," *Los Angeles Times*, February 27, 2004, A1; DeKalb County Visitor's Bureau, www.dcvb.org/shopping/htm, accessed October 15, 2006.

55. DeKalb County Schools information based on Georgia Department of Education statistics, www.greatschools.net/cgi-bin/ga/district_profile/55, accessed January 3, 2009.

56. *Atlanta Metro Patterns: A Regional Agenda for Community and Stability* (Metropolitan Area Research Corporation, October 2003), 10.

57. *Moving Beyond Sprawl: The Challenge for Metropolitan Atlanta* (Washington: Brookings Institution, 2001), 5.

58. Ibid., 8; U.S. Census Bureau, *Census 2000 Redistricting Data* (Public Law 94–171), Summary File, Matrices PL1 and PL2.

59. Myron Orfield, *American Metropolitics: The New Suburban Reality* (Washington: Brookings Institution Press, 2002); also see maps at the Metropolitan Area Research Corporation, "The Struggle to Grow Equitably," http://www.metroresearch.org/projects/sge.asp, accessed July 24, 2008.

60. Logan, "New Ethnic Enclaves."

61. Audra Burch, "Orlando is Destination of Choice for Many Blacks Heading South," *Knight Ridder Tribune News Service*, December 24, 2002, 1; Michael Laris, "Diverse Faces Give Loudoun A New Look," *Washington Post*, August 14, 2005, T3; Jerome Wright, "We're All Looking for the Good Life," *Memphis Commercial Appeal*, August 27, 2006, V4.

62. U.S. Census Bureau, "American FactFinder," Cobb County and Gwinnett County, Ga., Census 2000, and U.S. Census, Population Estimates Program, General Demographic Characteristics, July 2007, http://factfinder.census.gov, accessed January 2, 2009.

63. Celeste Smith, "Adding Diversity to the Suburbs," *Charlotte Observer*, October 19, 2008, http://www.charlotteobserver.com/276/story/260158.html.

64. Mary Lou Pickel, "Gwinnett's Minorities Surge toward Majority," *Atlanta Journal-Constitution*, August 7, 2008, http://www.ajc.com/gwinnett/content/metro/gwinnett/stories/2008/08/07/census_0807.html; U.S. Census Bureau, "American FactFinder," Gwinnett County, Georgia.

65. Charles Payne, "Comment," End of Southern History? Conference, Atlanta, Georgia, March 2006.

66. Myerson, "Black Mecca," 52.

67. Jake Wagman, "Blacks Join Trek to Far Suburbs," *St. Louis Post-Dispatch*, August 17, 2005, A1; "Anti-Racism Coalition Turns 10 Years Old," *Pittsburgh Post-Gazette*, September 14, 2006, N1; Amos Brown, "Indy Area's Black Population Reaches 250,000," *Indianapolis Recorder*, August 12, 2005, A3.

68. Wiese, *Places of Their Own*, 255–57.

10

LATIN AMERICAN IMMIGRATION AND THE NEW MULTIETHNIC SOUTH

Mary E. Odem

On April 10, 2006, Atlanta witnessed one of the largest demonstrations for social justice in the South since the civil rights era. Fifty thousand people, the vast majority Latino, walked a three-mile loop from the Plaza Fiesta shopping center in suburban DeKalb County and then listened to speeches by Latino, African-American, and white politicians and local activists (figure 10.1). Marchers in Atlanta were part of coordinated nationwide demonstrations that brought millions of immigrants and their supporters to the streets to call on the U.S. Congress to offer legal status and citizenship to undocumented immigrants and to protest a House of Representatives bill that would speed up deportations, build a wall at the Mexican border, and criminalize illegal immigrants.

Protesters in Atlanta had an additional goal: to challenge State Senate Bill 529, the Georgia Security and Immigration Compliance Act. Introduced by Republican lawmaker Chip Rogers, from the predominantly white suburban county of Cherokee, Bill 529 represented one of the most far-reaching and punitive efforts in the nation to address undocumented immigration. The Georgia legislature soon passed the act, which denied unauthorized immigrants access to public benefits and employment and enlisted state and local police in the enforcement of federal immigration laws.[1]

The rally in Atlanta was the largest but by no means the only demonstration for immigrants' rights in the South. Thousands of protesters marched in cities across the region, including Columbia, South Carolina; Charlotte, North Carolina; Jackson, Mississippi; and Birmingham, Alabama. Latino construction workers, janitors, gardeners, cooks, nannies, salespeople, and

FIGURE 10.1. April 10, 2006: Mariela Caceres holds a sign during an Atlanta march for immigrant rights that drew about fifty thousand participants. The protest, a major landmark in the rise of the multiethnic New South, took place in suburban DeKalb County at the Plaza Fiesta Mall, also known as "La Capital Latina de Georgia." On the same day in more than one hundred other cities, hundreds of thousands of immigrants and their supporters took to the streets for a national day of action billed as a "campaign for immigrants' dignity." © AP Images/ John Bazemore.

students joined the demonstrations and waved American flags along with the flags of Mexico, Guatemala, and El Salvador. Some participants carried signs with images of the Virgin of Guadalupe, the patroness of Mexico. Others held banners that read: "WE ARE NOT CRIMINALS. WE ARE HARD WORKERS," "THE U.S.A. IS MADE OF IMMIGRANTS," and "CIVIL RIGHTS FOR IMMIGRANTS." In Jackson, demonstrators sang "We Shall Overcome" in Spanish, evoking comparisons to marches led by Martin Luther King Jr. in the mid-1960s.[2]

The 2006 marches in defense of immigrants' rights illustrate the dramatic demographic transformations that have occurred in the U.S. South since the 1980s. For most of its history (after the expulsion and quarantine of indigenous peoples), the South was largely a biracial society. African Americans and whites constituted the vast majority of inhabitants in southern states, with the exceptions of Texas and Florida, and the black-white divide profoundly shaped the politics, social structure, and social geography of the region. The South's ethnic-racial landscape began to change rapidly in the late 1980s and 1990s, as a booming economy attracted a large number of immigrants, most from Asian, Latin American, and African countries, while relief agencies also resettled Southeast Asian refugees in the region. With the dramatic growth of its foreign-born population over the next quarter-century, the South became a major new immigration destination in the United States, home to millions of people originally from Latin America, Asia, and Africa.[3]

This essay examines the migration and settlement patterns of the largest group of foreign-born newcomers in the U.S. South—those from Latin America. Globalization and economic restructuring, in both the United States and Latin American nations, have led to mass migration to the South by peoples from Mexico, Guatemala, El Salvador, Colombia, Venezuela, Brazil, and numerous other countries in Central and South America. Towns, cities, and suburbs throughout the Southeast now feature Mexican *panaderías, tiendas,* and restaurants; Colombian bakeries; Spanish-language newspapers and radio programs; nightclubs featuring a variety of Latin music forms; and December processions in honor of Our Lady of Guadalupe. Apartment complexes and mobile home parks in the region are home to immigrants from Maya villages in the Guatemalan highlands; urban neighborhoods in Mexico City, Lima, and San Salvador; and rural towns throughout Mexico and Central America, among other places of origin.[4]

The rapid growth of immigrant populations in southern cities and states is part of a larger shift in the geography of immigration in the United States. In the second half of the twentieth century, six states received the vast majority of the nation's immigrants: California, Texas, Florida, New York, New Jersey, and Illinois. During the 1990s, however, the percentage of the nation's immigrants living in these states declined significantly for the first time, while many other states in the Southeast, Midwest, and interior West experienced unprecedented levels of new immigration. Significant numbers of the foreign-born have headed to nontraditional destinations—to Nevada, Minnesota, Nebraska, and Colorado, as well as Georgia, Tennessee, and the Carolinas. The geographic dispersal of immigrants nationwide has been accompanied by a shift in settlement patterns within metropolitan regions, as immigrants are increasingly bypassing the inner city and moving directly to the suburbs. This trend is happening throughout the country, but it is most pronounced in new metropolitan gateways such as Atlanta, Washington, D.C., and Las Vegas.[5]

The South's emergence as a new destination for Latin American immigrants has brought significant changes in the ethnic and racial dynamics of workplaces, neighborhoods, and local and state politics. This essay examines the developments that have taken place in ten southern states— Georgia, North Carolina, South Carolina, Virginia, Tennessee, Alabama, Mississippi, Arkansas, Louisiana, and Kentucky—that contained only small Latino populations prior to the 1980s, mostly Puerto Ricans or Cubans who had fled their country's revolution. This analysis of the South's new immigration gateways eliminates Texas and Florida, since each state has a longer and different history of Latin American immigration. Beginning in the 1980s in Georgia and North Carolina, and in the 1990s for the other southern states (except Louisiana), the Latino population skyrocketed, driven largely by mass immigration from Mexico, Central America, and South America.

LATINO IMMIGRATION TO THE SOUTH

Historically, the Southeast did not attract immigrants in large numbers (except for Texas and Florida) because of the region's slower pace of industrial development and the presence of a large number of poor blacks and whites who provided a steady pool of low-wage labor. During the great wave of immigration to the United States between 1890 and 1920, small groups of immigrant workers from Europe and China settled in the region, but the vast majority headed to urban areas in the Northeast, Midwest, and West to become part of the industrial workforce, or to areas of expanding commercial agriculture in the Southwest to work as farm laborers.[6]

Immigration to the United States declined sharply in the late 1920s and 1930s as a result of worldwide economic depression and the country's first comprehensive immigration restriction law, the Johnson-Reed Immigration Act of 1924, which established a national origins quota system with a hierarchical ranking of desirable national and racial groups. The act dramatically reduced the number of immigrants from southern and eastern Europe and excluded Asian immigrants altogether on the grounds that they were "racially ineligible for citizenship." Immigrants from Mexico and other nations in the Western Hemisphere were not subject to quota restrictions, in large part because powerful agricultural interests in Texas and California demanded a steady supply of cheap labor. During the 1920s, Mexican immigrants worked primarily in agriculture, but they also filled constructions jobs throughout the West and industrial jobs in Midwestern cities. While not subject to quota restrictions, Mexican immigration was deeply affected by the system of enforcement put in place by the Johnson-Reed Act. Through visa requirements and border control policies, the law subjected the informal migration between northern Mexico and the U.S. Southwest to legal regulation and categorized thousands of Mexican immigrants who participated in this migration as "illegal aliens." During the 1920s, an annual average of 62,000 legal and an estimated 100,000 undocumented immigrants from Mexico entered the country.[7]

The illegal status of many Mexican immigrants did not prevent the widespread use of their labor by Southwestern agribusiness, but it did place them in a more vulnerable and precarious situation in the U.S. During the Great Depression, Mexicans became convenient scapegoats for rising unemployment, and by the end of the 1930s more than 400,000 Mexicans had been deported or left the country. During and after World War II, growers in the Southwest once again recruited Mexican agricultural workers in large numbers through the *bracero* program, a contract labor system under which nearly 4 million Mexicans were imported to the United States on a temporary basis between 1948 and 1964.[8]

Civil rights activism in the 1960s led to a major reform of U.S. immigration policy, including the end of the *bracero* program and the passage of the Hart-Cellar Immigration Act of 1965, a landmark that repealed key discriminatory aspects of the 1924 Johnson-Reed Act. The 1965 law (and subsequent 1976 amendments) eliminated altogether the system of national origin quotas and substituted a system of numerical limits that applied equally to all countries. Further, the new law raised significantly the annual limit of immigrant admissions and placed a much stronger emphasis on family unification as a basis for admission. As a result, immigration to the United States grew rapidly in the years following 1965. Along with the increase in volume, the national origins of the foreign-born changed significantly, as countries of Asia, Latin America, and the Caribbean came to dominate the flow of immigrants to the United States.[9]

The Hart-Cellar Act removed the most blatant form of racial exclusion from U.S. immigration policy, but it also instituted new forms of restriction, particularly in regard to Mexican and Latin American immigrants. Under the Act, numerical quotas were imposed for the first time on immigration from Mexico and other Western Hemisphere countries. Given the extensive economic reliance on Mexican laborers, one might have expected the U.S. to increase substantially the number of legal residents permitted from Mexico. However, the 1965 law and subsequent amendments reduced that number, and thus inevitably produced increasing levels of illegal immigration. The initial quota of 20,000 per country was a fraction of the annual migration permitted from Mexico in the early 1960s, which included 200,000 agricultural workers under the *bracero* program and 35,000 regular admissions for permanent residency. Over the next two decades, undocumented immigrants came to dominate the flow of Mexican migrants to the U.S. Between 1965 and 1986, 1.3 million legal Mexican immigrants entered the country compared to an estimated 28 million undocumented immigrants.[10]

In the two decades following the passage of the 1965 immigration act, Mexican immigrants continued to head for traditional destinations in California, Illinois, Texas, and Florida. It was not until the late 1980s and 1990s that Mexicans and other Latin Americans began to arrive in massive numbers in nontraditional destinations of the Southeast and Midwest, as economic globalization and neoliberal policies restructured the economies of both Latin American countries and the United States. Mexico, under pressure by the World Bank, the International Monetary Fund, and the U.S. government, embarked on a program of neoliberal economic reforms in the 1980s that opened the country to full participation in the global market economy. Under President Carlos Salinas de Gortari, the Mexican government dismantled trade barriers, lowered tariffs, phased out subsidies, eliminated restrictions on foreign business ownership, and privatized state enterprises. President Salinas sought to institutionalize these reforms in the North American Free Trade Agreement (NAFTA), signed by the United States, Mexico, and Canada in 1994.[11]

NAFTA furthered the economic integration of Mexico and the United States and fostered transportation and communication networks between the two countries. The treaty's free market policies, however, displaced Mexican workers and farmers in record numbers through the downsizing of government bureaucracies and state enterprises, combined with land consolidation and capital-intensive production in rural areas. Mexican manufacturing suffered from the ending of tariff protections, while the flood of cheap American food products into the country damaged the agricultural sector. Economic pressures mounted in 1994 with the devaluation of the Mexican peso, which resulted in lowered wages and increased unemployment. The subsequent economic crisis sharpened the need for income and credit throughout Mexico, in middle-class as well as poor and working-class households, and encouraged out-migration not only from traditional sending states but also from new parts of the country. Additionally, large numbers of rural Mexicans drawn to *maquiladora* factories on the border lost their jobs and crossed into the United States after American corporations shifted production to even-lower-wage sites in Asia.[12]

In Central America, globalization and economic restructuring combined with political violence and social unrest to increase international migration during the 1980s and 1990s. U.S., and to a lesser extent European, investment supported the expansion of agricultural exports and industrial development in Central American nations, particularly Guatemala and El Salvador, which created new job opportunities but also prompted out-migration through the widespread displacement of small farmers and indigenous peoples. During the 1980s, El Salvador and Guatemala were torn by civil wars as right-wing governments launched campaigns of violent repression against labor unions, peasants, activist organizations, and indigenous communities. With the support of U.S. military aid and training, the armed forces of both countries carried out assassinations of suspected militants and large-scale massacres in regions thought to support guerrilla forces. At the height of the violence, thousands of Salvadorans and Guatemalans fled their home countries, many heading for the United States. Deteriorating economic conditions in the aftermath of war combined with economic restructuring to create high levels of unemployment and underemployment, which resulted in large-scale migration from Central America.[13]

As the volume of out-migration from Mexico and Central America increased, changes in U.S. immigration policy, especially the passage of the Immigration Reform and Control Act (IRCA) of 1986, contributed to a major shift in the destinations of Mexican and Central American migrants, from traditional southwestern magnets such as California and Texas to new locations in the Southeast and Midwest. IRCA's key features included stronger border controls, new sanctions on employers who hired undocumented laborers, and a path to legalization for immigrants who could demonstrate that they had resided and worked in the United States for at least five years. Under IRCA, approximately 3 million previously undocumented immigrants gained permanent legal residence. Of these, 2.3 million were Mexicans; the remaining 700,000 included immigrants from El Salvador, Guatemala, the Philippines, Colombia, Haiti, and several other nations.[14] Free to move about the country, increasing numbers of newly legalized immigrants left the crowded job and housing markets in California and the Southwest to pursue better opportunities elsewhere.

The new border controls under IRCA also reshaped the geography and nature of Latin American immigration. Increased border enforcement diverted migrants from traditional crossing points in California (San Diego) and Texas (El Paso) to more remote desert regions in Arizona and New Mexico. Instead of stemming the flow of illegal immigration, the new border policies actually encouraged undocumented workers to stay for longer periods in the United States or to make the move permanent in order to avoid the more costly and dangerous border crossings.[15] The heightened efforts to militarize the U.S.-Mexico border in the 1990s and after 9/11 (the erection of fences and walls, use of high tech surveillance on land and air, and doubling of the Border Patrol Force) has also failed to prevent the entry of undocumented migrants. In 1995, approximately five million undocumented migrants lived in the U.S. By 2005 the number had jumped to eleven million.[16]

The Southeast emerged as a strong magnet for immigrants, both legal and unauthorized, in the 1990s because of the availability of plentiful jobs for unskilled and semi-skilled workers. While global competition caused plant closings and layoffs in the steel, textile, and apparel industries in the South, other domestic and foreign corporations have been drawn to the region because of the relatively low taxes, cheap nonunion labor, and significant government subsidies provided to attract investment.[17] Poultry, pork, and seafood processing plants have opened throughout the rural South and hired substantial numbers of Latino workers. The poultry-processing industry in particular has flourished in the region; by the last decade of the twentieth century nearly half of all poultry processing in the country was concentrated in Georgia, Alabama, Arkansas, and North Carolina. Southern cities such as Atlanta, Birmingham, Greensboro, and Charlotte have become important locations for commercial banking and financial industries, high-tech research and manufacturing, and biomedical research. Many of the nation's largest corporations are headquartered in the Southeast, including Wal-Mart, Home Depot, Bank of America, and Federal Express. Rapid population growth has accompanied business expansion in southern cities and suburbs, creating high demand in the residential construction and service industries and consequently a need for low-wage labor.[18]

Faced with a tight labor market, southern employers in construction, food-processing, and agricultural industries actively recruited Latino workers, initially from Texas and California, and later directly from Mexico and Central America. By the late 1990s, a transnational process of chain migration facilitated employer recruitment efforts. As immigrants encouraged family members and acquaintances from their home towns to join them in southern towns and cities, migration streams developed that channeled further migration to those locations.[19] The region's Latino population expanded exponentially during the 1990s, with growth rates of between 300 and 400 percent for North Carolina, Arkansas, and Georgia; between 200 and 300 percent for Tennessee, South Carolina, and Alabama; and between 100 and 200 percent for Virginia, Mississippi, and Kentucky. In comparison, the Hispanic population at the national level grew from 22.4 million in 1990 to 35.3 million in 2000, a rate of 58 percent.[20]

By 2006, the Latino population in the ten southern states examined here had increased to more than 2.5 million, ranging from 46,348 in Mississippi to 696,146 in Georgia. Latino migrants have settled in a variety of localities throughout the Southeast—small towns and the rural countryside as well as major metropolitan areas, including a substantial presence in the inner-ring suburbs, with the South's highest Latino concentration found in the sprawling Atlanta region (467,418 residents in 2006). Latinos also have clustered in North Carolina's urban and suburban areas along the Interstate-85 corridor: 133,959 in Raleigh-Durham-Chapel Hill, 126,608 in Charlotte, and 114,120 in Greensboro-Winston-Salem (2006 data). Smaller but still substantial numbers of Latinos have settled in other southern metropolises, including Birmingham; Greenville, South Carolina; and Nashville, Tennessee.[21]

CHANGING RACIAL DYNAMICS

The rise of a new multiethnic South raises the critical issue of what mass Latin American immigration means for political culture and race relations in the region. How will the large and growing Latino population affect the black-white racial divide that has shaped southern politics, society, and culture for generations? According to historian David Goldfield, the pattern of southern and eastern European immigration to the South in the early twentieth century was "the suppression of ethnic identity in favor of racial solidarity." "The relatively low numbers of immigrants and the abiding racial divide promised an ethnic meltdown to a degree much greater than in larger northern cities," he observes. "What would happen if a substantially larger ethnic presence emerged in the South?"[22] Given the relatively short duration of significant Latino settlement in the South, scholars only recently have begun to address this question. While much research remains to be done, existing studies indicate that Latinos in the South are not following the previous path of suppressed ethnic identity. Instead, a new multiethnic dynamic is replacing the biracial divide that has characterized southern society and politics for so long.[23]

Any discussion of the impact of Latino immigration on race must consider that Latinos in the South are a diverse group in terms of nationality, race/ethnicity, class, and legal status. The largest national group by far is Mexican, but there are significant numbers of Guatemalans, Salvadorans, Hondurans, Puerto Ricans, Dominicans, Colombians, and Venezuelans. The Latino population is further divided along lines of race and ethnicity and includes whites of European descent, *mestizos* (mixed race, usually of Spanish and Indian descent), Afro-Caribbeans, and indigenous peoples from Guatemala and Mexico.[24]

Latino immigrants in the South are diverse in socioeconomic status as well. There is a sizable group of Latino professionals in the region, many of whom serve the growing immigrant population as lawyers, accountants, dentists, and doctors. Other Latinos work as independent entrepreneurs, particularly in the urban and suburban South, where immigrants have opened bakeries, restaurants, contracting and landscaping companies, clothing and jewelry shops, cleaning and child-care businesses, and taxi companies. South Americans are more likely to have higher educational and occupational levels than Mexicans and Central Americans, although each group is making noticeable advances in the professional and business arenas. By far the largest number of Latino immigrants in the South work as laborers in agriculture, food processing, manufacturing, service, and construction—low-wage jobs previously occupied by poor whites or African Americans. In agricultural production, Mexicans and Central Americans now comprise 80 percent of migrant farm workers in Georgia and 90 percent in North Carolina. In metropolitan Atlanta, more than 60 percent of Latino workers in 2000 were employed either in the construction industry or the service sector.[25]

Differences in legal status also characterize Latino immigrants in the South; the population includes naturalized citizens, legal residents, temporary workers, and undocumented immigrants. As in the rest of the country, a significant portion of Latino immigrants in the South are undocumented. A report by the Urban Institute estimated that in 2000, between 40 and 49 percent of all immigrants in the states of North Carolina, Georgia, and Arkansas were undocumented, and between 30 and 39 percent in South Carolina, Mississippi, Alabama, and Tennessee.[26] The increase in unauthorized immigration in the South reflects national trends. As of 2005, 11 million undocumented immigrants resided in the United States, and they constituted fully one-third of all immigrants in the country. Of the undocumented, 78 percent are from Mexico or other Latin American nations.[27]

The differences in legal status, nationality, ethnicity, and class suggest that Latinos will influence the region's racial landscape in multiple and complex ways. Several recent studies have examined how Latino immigration is transforming the racial and ethnic dynamics of southern workplaces and neighborhoods.[28] Racial/ethnic relations have been especially tense in the low-wage economy, where the presence of Latino workers has generated fears of job displacement and wage cuts on the part of native-born workers, both black and white. Policy experts disagree sharply about the impact of new immigrant workers on the American economy, with some arguing that they drive down the wages of native-born workers and others contending that they fill jobs that no one else wants. In the South, the expansion of urban and rural economies during the steady growth of recent decades no doubt created many new jobs that the native-born labor force could not fill. At the same time, as in the previous era of high immigration during the late 1800s and early 1900s, U.S. employers have used the ready supply of immigrant labor to speed up production, suppress wages, fragment the labor force, and undermine worker protests. As in other regions of high immigration, the hiring of large numbers of Latino laborers, both documented and undocumented, by southern employers has created conflicts between immigrants and native-born black and white workers at the lower end of the wage scale.[29]

The widespread use of immigrant labor in the South and elsewhere in the United States should be seen as part of the neoliberal reorganization of the economy and labor market. In the highly competitive global economy, U.S corporations have cut labor costs by creating a more "flexible" workforce through strategies of part-time work, outsourcing, subcontracting, and the recruitment of foreign-born workers. For workers in the United States, "flexibility" has meant the erosion of benefits, job security, safe working conditions, and collective bargaining rights. To achieve labor market flexibility and control, the meat- and poultry-processing industries have increasingly relied on recruiting immigrant workers and using labor contractors to hire large portions of their workforce. Poultry corporations began large-scale hiring of immigrant workers (both legal and undocumented) during a period of rapid expansion between 1980 and 2000, when American consumption of chicken doubled. Native-born and foreign-born workers alike have suffered from the harsh conditions in meat and poultry plants, including production speed-ups, disregard for health and safety standards, and pervasive violation of minimum wage laws.[30]

Sociologist Angela Steusse has examined the impact of economic restructuring on race relations and collective organizing in the poultry industry in rural Mississippi, where immigrants from Mexico, Guatemala, and South America now work alongside African Americans as low-wage laborers. The steady recruitment of foreign-born labor and the use of labor contractors, which has enabled poultry plants to evade government regulations, have put downward pressure on wages and working conditions and heightened tensions between African-American and Latino immigrant workers. African Americans have tended to blame immigrants for the deteriorating work conditions in the plants, while immigrants have interpreted the resistance of black workers (production slowdowns and long breaks) as evidence of laziness or lack of education. The ethnic and racial divisions have hampered the efforts of local labor activists to organize poultry workers in defense of their rights.[31]

The arrival of large numbers of Latino immigrant workers also has altered the racial dynamics in the carpet industry of northwest Georgia. A center of textile production for most of the twentieth century, Dalton, Georgia, and the surrounding southern Appalachian region has become a global center for the mass production of wall-to-wall carpeting. Until the 1970s, the textile industry relied primarily on the labor of low-income whites. Even after the civil rights revolution of the 1960s, a system of corporate paternalism preserved mill jobs for white workers and excluded blacks at the price of a strict anti-union workplace.[32]

In the 1980s and 1990s, however, carpet industrialists broke with paternalism and white privilege in the workplace by recruiting and hiring Mexican laborers on a mass scale. The influx of immigrants solved employers' problems of high turnover and labor shortages and weakened the ability of native workers to negotiate for better wages and conditions. Not surprisingly, the arrival of Mexicans in southern Appalachia has created tensions with native whites, who perceive immigrants as a source of competition and displacement. Newly formed anti-immigrant organizations and established hate groups like the Ku Klux Klan have grown in size and influence in the South since the 1990s as a result of mounting white resentment toward Latino immigrants.[33]

The incorporation of Latino immigrants into the southern workforce has generated not only conflict but also new forms of racial and ethnic collaboration. Labor organizers, civic leaders, and social justice activists have sought to mediate racial conflicts and forge new multiethnic coalitions. In North Carolina, black and Latino advocacy organizations came together in 1999 to form the African-American/Latino Alliance in an effort to find common ground in their struggles for economic justice in the poultry, agriculture, and construction sectors. African-American labor leaders also have worked with Latino advocates in the Mississippi Immigrant Rights Alliance (MIRA) and the Mississippi Poultry Workers' Center to organize poultry workers from different backgrounds and strengthen their voice in the industry. MIRA, a statewide coalition of immigrant, labor, and civil rights advocates, works with progressive elected officials to promote fair treatment of immigrants in Mississippi. Similar coalitions have been formed in other southern states, such as the Tennessee Immigrant and Refugee Rights Coalition.[34]

Established civil rights groups in the South also have turned their attention to the discrimination and exploitation of immigrants. The Southern Poverty Law Center (SPLC) of Montgomery, Alabama, a biracial civil rights organization founded in 1971, has documented and protested the harsh, discriminatory treatment of Latino workers by employers and nativist groups in the South. In 2004, the SPLC created the Immigrant Justice Project and published the exposé *Close to Slavery*, which details widespread abuses of immigrant labor in the federal H-2 programs that supply "guest workers" for the agricultural, forestry, and other industries. A number of African-American civil rights activists and labor leaders have publicly supported Latino-led initiatives for immigrant rights, such as the campaign for drivers' licenses for undocumented immigrants in Georgia, a collaboration organized by the Southern Regional Council, and the mass marches in defense of immigrants that took place across the South and throughout the nation in April 2006.[35]

LATINO SETTLEMENT IN METROPOLITAN ATLANTA

Latin American immigration is transforming racial relations and boundaries in southern neighborhoods as well as in workplaces and social justice organizations. A few scholars have begun to examine the impact of Latino immigration on racial residential patterns in southern metropolitan areas. A closer look at patterns of Latino settlement in Atlanta reveals some of the broader changes taking place in the urban and suburban South. In keeping with the national trend, immigrants to the urban South have been bypassing the inner city and moving directly to suburban locations. This development marks a significant departure from the historical pattern of immigrant settlement in central city neighborhoods.[36] Deindustrialization, economic neglect and decline of inner cities, and the growth of suburbs as employment as well as residential centers have all contributed to the shift toward suburban settlement. By 2000, more immigrants in metropolitan areas lived in suburbs than in central cities, and the rates of immigration growth for suburbs exceeded those for cities as well. Immigrant suburban settlement is part of a nationwide phenomenon but is particularly pronounced in metropolitan areas in the South and elsewhere that experienced dramatic growth in the post-World War II period. In metropolitan Atlanta, for example, nearly 96 percent of foreign-born residents lived in suburban locations in 2000.[37]

Latino settlement in Atlanta's suburbs has been shaped by the region's history of racial segregation and inequality, and at the same time is transforming historical patterns. In metropolitan Atlanta, there has been a long-standing divide in the city and suburban region between predominantly white neighborhoods in the north and predominantly African-American neighborhoods in the south. Inequalities in economic opportunity correspond with the geographic racial divide, as the metropolitan region's high rates of growth during the 1980s and 1990s occurred primarily in the mostly white suburbs north of the urban core. The growth of Atlanta's substantial black middle class, along with African-American suburbs south and east of the city, have mitigated, but by no means erased, the sharp north-south divide between prosperity and poverty (for more on African-American suburbs in Atlanta, see chapter 9 of this volume).[38]

Drawn by affordable housing and the proximity of jobs, the largest numbers of Latino immigrants have settled in predominantly white suburban areas north of the city in DeKalb, Cobb, and Gwinnett counties (figure 10.2). For the most part, they have moved into the aging inner-ring neighborhoods first developed in the post-World War II period to accommodate middle- and working-class white families. A main attraction for immigrants is the high degree of affordable housing, especially multifamily apartment complexes and modest single-family homes built in the 1960s and 1970s.

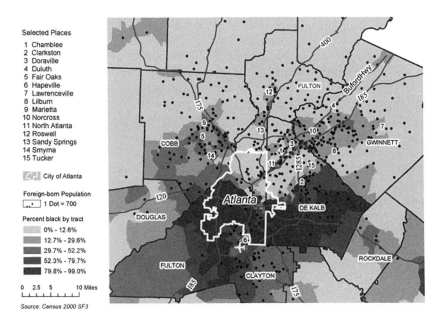

FIGURE 10.2. Distribution of African-American Population and Foreign-Born Population in the Atlanta Metropolitan Area, 2000.

There is little foreign-born presence in the neighborhoods with the highest concentrations of African-American residents, located in or near Atlanta's urban core, which are also the areas with the highest rates of poverty and slow-to-stagnant economic growth. However, small clusters of Latino immigrants have settled in suburban areas with significant African-American populations located south and east of the city in Clayton and DeKalb counties. Furthermore, the African-American as well as Latino populations are growing in north DeKalb, Cobb, and Gwinnett. Since 1990, a steady stream of African Americans has ventured into suburban areas north of the city.[39] With the growth of outer-ring suburbs in the 1980s and 1990s, affluent and middle-income white residents have continued to move farther outward to new subdivisions with larger homes and more racially homogenous demographics.[40]

The Chamblee-Doraville section of DeKalb County—the site of the 2006 immigrant rights march—was one of the first places in the metropolitan region to attract a large number of immigrants. Until the 1970s, the area was home mostly to white blue-collar workers. The national economic slowdown of that decade resulted in factory closings, layoffs, and the departure of many white residents from the area. The major thoroughfares, Peachtree Industrial Boulevard and Buford Highway, were strewn with empty commercial and industrial properties and sparsely populated apartment buildings. As rental vacancies climbed, apartment managers began marketing to immigrants, initially Southeast Asian refugees and later Chinese, Koreans, and Latin Americans. By 1990, Chamblee-Doraville had become the most ethnically diverse area in Georgia.[41]

In the 1990s, Latino and Asian immigrant settlements expanded from DeKalb to the neighboring counties of Cobb and Gwinnett. Largely white, middle class, and politically conservative, these suburban counties had grown rapidly in the 1960s and 1970s as a result of white flight from the city of Atlanta following the desegregation of its public schools, parks, and neighborhoods. Explosive economic and population growth continued in the 1980s and 1990s, as Cobb and Gwinnett became major job hubs for the metropolitan region and attracted large numbers of white middle-class migrants from outside the South.[42] Economic growth also attracted an increasing number of immigrants and ethnic minorities to Cobb and Gwinnett, in order to meet the high labor demand in the construction and service industries. As in DeKalb, Latino immigrants have settled primarily in older suburbs with tracts of small single-family homes and a supply of multifamily rental units.[43]

With the rise of suburban immigrant populations, new clusters of ethnic-owned businesses and commercial activity have emerged in the Latino and Asian enclaves of metropolitan Atlanta. In some cases, immigrants have helped to revive areas that faced economic and population decline. On the busy six-lane Buford Highway that runs through Chamblee and Doraville, immigrant entrepreneurs and consumers have converted numerous aging strip malls to large ethnic and multiethnic shopping centers, with names such as Chinatown Square (1988), Asian Square Mall (1993), and Plaza Fiesta (2000). A five-block section of Jimmy Carter Boulevard in Gwinnett County has become another hub of ethnic commerce. The four-lane highway contains a number of shopping plazas with Latino and Asian restaurants, shops, video stores, clinics, and real estate, accounting, and law offices.[44]

Formerly all-white suburbs in Atlanta are now home to increasingly diverse racial and ethnic populations that include Latinos, Asians, African Americans, and whites. The future of these multiethnic suburbs in the South depends to a large extent on the educational, economic, and political opportunities available to the new immigrant groups. The school districts in Atlanta's northern suburbs have struggled to accommodate the rapid and massive increase of foreign-born students with the establishment of ESOL programs (English for Speakers of Other Languages) and international welcome centers that provide orientation and language placement for newly arrived students. As of 2005, the Cobb, Gwinnett, and DeKalb school districts included foreign-born students from more than 170 different countries who spoke more than eighty different languages. Spanish-speaking students from Mexico and other Latin American countries form the largest language group, and the difficulties they face are particularly great. The dropout rate for Latino students in Georgia is among the highest in the country owing, in part, to the large number of recent immigrants among Latino youth in state.[45]

The growth of Latino political power will be instrumental in confronting the challenges facing Latino communities in the South. Latino political influence in metropolitan Atlanta has grown steadily and has begun to make an impact on state politics. In 2002, three Latino legislators from suburban Atlanta were elected to the Georgia state legislature. Representing a district in eastern Fulton County, Democrat Sam Zamarippa, a Mexican American, became the first Latino in the Georgia State Senate. Voters in Gwinnett County elected Democrat Pedro Marin, a native of Puerto Rico, and Republican David Casas, a high school teacher of Cuban ancestry, to the State House of Representatives. Strong advocates for Latino immigrants, Zamarippa and Marin promptly pushed for measures to allow undocumented immigrants access to driver's licenses and in-state tuition at public universities. Ultimately their efforts were unsuccessful as they faced stiff public and political opposition and became favored targets of anti-immigrant and hate groups, but their presence in the legislature marked the emergence of a new voice in southern politics.[46]

ANTI-IMMIGRANT POLITICS

The rise of anti-immigrant sentiment and policies in recent years threatens the possibilities for successful immigrant incorporation into southern society. The politics of backlash was not evident during the initial acceleration of Latino immigration to the Southeast in the 1980s and 1990s, before this population reached a critical mass. At the time, local authorities and the media paid only scant attention to the Latino newcomers, more often than not depicting them as hard workers who helped the local economy in various ways. By contrast, in historic immigration states such as California, the 1990s were marked by an intense anti-immigrant backlash that gave rise to measures such as Proposition 187, which sought to deny free public education and other benefits to undocumented children. During the early twenty-first century, however, anti-immigrant rhetoric and exclusionary policies rose sharply in new immigrant destinations owing to declining economic conditions and the heightened national preoccupation with terrorism and "illegal immigration" following the attacks of September 11, 2001.[47]

Public outcry about "illegals" stealing jobs, burdening taxpayers, and increasing crime rates led state and local officials across the Southeast to pass laws and ordinances limiting unauthorized immigrants' access to transportation, housing, employment, social services, and higher edu-cation. Southern locales were by no means alone in passing legislation targeting unauthorized immigration, as these regional trends took shape as part of a national wave of anti-immigrant backlash that proved most intense in areas with very high rates of recent migration, from metro-politan Phoenix to the Long Island suburbs. And although politicians and many U.S. citizens make a sharp distinction between "legal" and "illegal" immigrants, the reality is that the two groups are so intertwined (e.g., undocumented parents with American-born children) that laws affecting one category necessarily affect the other.[48]

Among the first pieces of exclusionary legislation were anti-congregating ordinances directed at Latino day laborers. In new immigration gateways throughout the nation, local residents and merchants have complained that day laborers, the mostly Latino workers who congregate in urban and suburban areas waiting to be hired for hourly wages, scare off customers and threaten the peace and security of the neighborhoods where they gather. In the late 1990s, a number of municipalities in Atlanta's northern suburbs passed anti-congregating laws that made it a crime for workers to "assemble on private property for the purpose of soliciting work as a day laborer without the permission of the property owner." Local authorities sometimes worked in collaboration with federal immigration officials to deport undocumented day laborers. In 1999, at the request of the police chief of the suburban city of Marietta (in Cobb County), undercover agents from the Immigration and Naturalization Service (INS) posed as contrac-tors and arrested sixty-two undocumented workers at a popular day-laborer recruitment spot.[49]

State officials in the South also have restricted immigrants' use of auto-mobiles and public roads by denying driver's licenses to unauthorized immigrants, a trend that has spread throughout the nation since 2001. The South's low-density suburban development patterns, dispersed job locations, and limited public transportation systems make residents espe-cially dependent on automobiles. Latino immigrants frequently use buses and taxi services, but they also depend heavily on privately owned auto-mobiles to get to work, go shopping, visit health facilities, and take chil-dren to school. In line with the national pattern, most southern states have prohibited unauthorized immigrants from obtaining driver's licenses by requiring proof of legal residence or valid Social Security cards as iden-tification. Tens of thousands of immigrants have been arrested, fined, and sometimes jailed for driving without a valid license.[50]

Until 2004, North Carolina stood as a notable exception to the stan-dard laws restricting undocumented immigrants from obtaining driver's licenses. State law had accepted the Individual Taxpayer Identification Number (ITIN) and a driver's license or voter registration card from another country as sufficient documentation to secure a North Carolina license. Following the terrorist attacks in 2001, the federal government criticized a number of states, including North Carolina, for making it too easy for undocumented immigrants to obtain driver's licenses. In response, the North Carolina Department of Motor Vehicles reduced the types of items it would accept for proof of identification, and then the state assembly passed legislation in 2006 to prohibit the use of the ITIN to obtain a license. Now applicants must show proof of a valid visa or Social Security number.[51]

At the neighborhood level, suburban localities throughout the country have used housing and zoning ordinances to discourage the settlement of Latino immigrants in certain areas. These zoning codes are intended to discourage multifamily housing and therefore maintain low-density neighborhoods characterized by detached single-family homes set on large lots. The diverse household arrangements of Latino immigrants have disrupted this suburban ideal. Immigrants often share apartments or houses with relatives and acquaintances to save on housing costs. Sometimes groups of young men, frequently from the same hometown, live together in rented apartments or houses to save money; many of them are supporting parents, siblings, wives, and children in their native countries. Some immigrant families (husband, wife, and children) who own or rent homes take in boarders, typically relatives or friends, to cover housing payments.[52]

Large immigrant households have upset established suburban residents and led to many complaints to local authorities about overcrowding. In response, in a number of places across the nation, local governments have pursued stricter enforcement of existing housing codes and revised or passed new ordinances to tighten regulation of immigrant households. Housing officials in Atlanta's northern suburbs in Cobb, Gwinnett, and Fulton counties stepped up enforcement of occupancy limits in response to an increasing number of complaints about overcrowding by immigrants. "We're a nice, clean city, and we just want to stay that way," explained the mayor of Lilburn, a suburb in Gwinnett County, in defense of an anti-"overcrowding" zoning ordinance passed in 2001.[53] In Fulton County, the suburban city of Roswell amended its housing ordinance and redefined "family" in an effort to shut down "illegal boardinghouses in single-family neighborhoods." The city council approved a new housing code in 2006 that allows no more than three unrelated people to reside in one single-family home; the law also altered the previous definition of family so that cousins no longer count as relatives.[54] Cobb County's board of commissioners created a new housing policy in 2005 that requires fifty square feet of sleeping space per person; penalties for violating the law range from a fine of $100 to $1000 and up to sixty days in jail. An enforcement officer reported that "ninety-five percent of the complaints I get are white folks complaining about Hispanic folks."[55]

Cherokee County, located in the outer-ring suburbs north of Atlanta, went even further in 2006 with passage of an ordinance that penalized property owners who rented or leased housing to unauthorized immigrants, modeled on similar policies in Hazelton, Pennsylvania, and Escondido, California.[56] Civil rights and immigrant advocates, including the American Civil Liberties Union and the Mexican-American Legal Defense and Educational Fund, quickly challenged the Cherokee ordinance, alleging that it would be enforced in a "discriminatory and disproportionate manner against legal immigrants and other persons of color" and would encourage "racial and ethnic profiling." The courts eventually found such laws to be unconstitutional, but the legal outcome has not dampened racial and ethnic tensions in suburban neighborhoods (figure 10.3).[57]

FIGURE 10.3. The rapid growth of the Latino population in Georgia, as in other new gateways across the nation, has sparked a potent political backlash against undocumented immigrants. Tensions are often highest in older suburbs such as Marietta, located in Cobb County to the north of Atlanta, where anti-immigration protesters rallied one week after the historic immigrant rights march of April 2006. © AP Images/Ric Field.

Southern anxieties about immigration have also generated renewed interest in "English-only" laws. Most southern states, along with numerous other states throughout the country, passed laws in the late 1980s that made English their official language. The legislative changes grew out of the political organizing of U.S. ENGLISH, Inc., a national organization formed in 1983 with the aim of "preserving the unifying role of the English language in the United States."[58] In the early twenty-first century, southern lawmakers once again took up the issue, this time in reaction to the increasing cultural and national diversity spreading throughout the region. Legislators in Georgia introduced bills in 2008 that would "strengthen" the state's English-only law, and the South Carolina state senate passed a bill in 2008 that would require all official documents, including the written exam for obtaining a driver's license, to appear in English only. Senator Glenn McConnell (R-Charleston) reported that the purpose of the bill was "to preserve the common thread of our culture."[59]

Much of the legislation targeting unauthorized immigrants has been passed by state and local governments since 2006, in the wake of rancorous discussions in the U.S. Congress and the national news media over the problem of illegal immigration. The failure to enact immigration reform at the federal level strengthened the efforts of state and local lawmakers to take action against unauthorized immigrants, and a record number of immigration bills came before state legislatures in 2006. Across the nation, eighty-four bills became law (more than double the number in 2005) out of 570 total pieces of legislation.[60]

The state of Georgia took the most aggressive and sweeping action to control illegal immigration of any state in the nation with the 2006 passage of the Georgia Security and Immigration Compliance Act (SB 529). Senate Bill 529 requires contractors and subcontractors doing business with the state to ensure that all of their workers have legal authorization to work; denies tax-supported benefits, including health care, to adults who cannot prove their legal residency; prohibits employers from claiming as a state tax deduction wages paid to undocumented workers; requires police to check the legal status of anyone who is arrested for a felony or for driving under the influence of alcohol, and to report any undocumented immigrants to immigration authorities; and authorizes the state to work with the federal government to train Georgia law enforcement officers to enforce immigration laws. The law reflects a compromise between politicians seeking aggressive action to end illegal immigration and business groups seeking to maintain an available pool of low-wage immigrant labor. After consulting with business lobbyists, Republican sponsor Chip Rogers crafted the bill so that companies would not be held responsible if an employee used false documents or if a subcontractor hired illegal workers without the knowledge of the employer.[61]

While it is too soon to know the full social and economic impact of the Georgia Security and Immigration Compliance Act, it is clear that the measure has created a climate of uncertainty and fear among Latino immigrants in the state. Realtors, car dealers, and retailers in immigrant neighborhoods have reported a noticeable decline in Latino customers, which they attribute to the sense of economic and social vulnerability that immigrants now feel. The parks and shopping plazas that had been social and recreational gathering places for Latinos in Atlanta have been noticeably less populated since the legislation went into effect. Police involvement in the enforcement of immigration law, as authorized by SB 529, has made Latino immigrants even more apprehensive and less willing to notify law enforcement when they are victims of or witnesses to crime.[62] The full consequences of Senate Bill 529 in Georgia warrant close attention, for the measure has already become a model for legislators in other states who are developing their own immigration policies.

Perhaps most threatening in the new legislation is the provision authorizing local law enforcement to participate with federal immigration officials in the enforcement of immigration law. Georgia is not alone in pursuing this dramatic shift in the role and purpose of state and local police. The U.S. Immigration and Customs Enforcement (ICE) is encouraging state and local law enforcement personnel to assist federal immigration enforcement in a program called 287(g). Congress authorized 287(g) in 1996, but state and local authorities really began to get on board after the terrorist attack in 2001. Six years later, thirty-four law enforcement agencies in fifteen states throughout the country were participating in 287(g).[63] In the South, sheriff's offices and police agencies in four North Carolina counties are currently cooperating with ICE, along with law enforcement agencies in Saluda and York counties in South Carolina, and in Hall, Whitfield, and Cobb counties in Georgia. The participation of local and state police in immigrant surveillance, raids, and deportations has alarmed immigrants and undermined their trust in law enforcement.[64]

The legal crackdown on immigrants may slow but will not halt the growth of the Latino population in the South. Even in the current economic recession, key industries in the region continue to depend on Latinos' labor. The South has become a multiethnic, multiracial region with diverse Latino communities in both metropolitan and rural areas. After two decades of growth these communities include many U.S.-born as well as foreign-born members, and many citizens and legal residents, as well as undocumented immigrants. Unlike the suppressed ethnicity of immigrant groups in the early twentieth-century South, Latinos today have created a notable ethnic presence in southern neighborhoods, schools, workplaces, and commercial centers, and they are an emerging voice in southern politics. Their political potential was clearly demonstrated in the

2006 marches for immigrants' rights when tens of thousands of Latinos filled the streets in peaceful protests reminiscent of the Civil Rights era. The exclusionary policies they protested have made the lives of Latino southerners more insecure, but have not dampened their struggle to make a place for themselves in the contemporary South.

NOTES

1. Eunice Moscoso, "House OKs Stiff Immigration Bill," *Atlanta Journal-Constitution*, December, 17, 2005, 1A; Carlos Campos, "Bill on Illegals Gets First Test," *Atlanta Journal-Constitution*, February 28, 2005, B5; Jim Tharpe, "Center Stage in Illegals Debate," *Atlanta Journal-Constitution*, February 19, 2006, A5.

2. Teresa Borden, "Immigration Rallies Fill Nation's Streets," *Atlanta Journal-Constitution*, April 11, 2006, A1; "Tens of Thousands Join Immigration Rally," The Associated Press, April 10, 2006, http://www.msnbc.msn.com/id/12250356/.

3. David Goldfield, "Unmelting the Ethnic South: Changing Boundaries of Race and Ethnicity in the Modern South," in *The American South in the Twentieth Century*, ed. Craig S. Pascoe, Karen Trahan Leathem, and Andy Ambrose (Athens: University of Georgia Press, 2005), 19–38; Raymond A. Mohl, "Globalization, Latinization, and the *Nuevo* New South," *Journal of American Ethnic History*, 22 (Summer 2003): 31–66; Mary Odem and Elaine Lacy, eds., *Latino Immigration and the Transformation of the U.S. South* (Athens: University of Georgia Press, 2009).

4. Arthur D. Murphy, Colleen Blanchard and Jennifer A. Hill, eds., *Latino Workers in the Contemporary South* (Athens: University of Georgia Press, 2001); Heather Smith and Owen Furuseth, eds., *Latinos in the New South: Transformations of Place* (Hampshire, England: Ashgate, 2006); Odem and Lacy, *Latino Immigration and the Transformation of the U.S. South*; Mary E. Odem, "Unsettled in the Suburbs: Latino Immigration and Ethnic Diversity in Metro Atlanta," in *Twenty-First Century Gateways: Immigrant Incorporation in Suburban America*, ed. Audrey Singer, Caroline Brettell, and Susan Hardwick (Washington: Brookings Institution Press, 2008), 105–36.

5. Audrey Singer, "The Rise of New Immigrant Gateways" (Washington: Brookings Institution, 2004); Singer, *Twenty-First Century Gateways*; Víctor Zúñiga and Rubén Hernández-León, eds., *New Destinations: Mexican Immigration in the United States* (New York: Russell Sage Foundation, 2005).

6. Goldfield, "Unmelting the Ethnic South"; Roger Daniels, *Guarding the Golden Door: American Immigration Policy and Immigrants since 1882* (New York: Hill and Wang, 2004).

7. Mae M. Ngai, *Impossible Subjects: Illegal Aliens and the Making of Modern America* (Princeton: Princeton University Press, 2004); Aristede R. Zolberg, *A Nation by Design: Immigration Policy in the Fashioning of America* (Cambridge, Mass.: Harvard University Press, 2006).

8. Ngai, *Impossible Subjects;* Zolberg, *Nation by Design;* Mary E. Odem, "Subaltern Immigrants: Undocumented Workers and National Belonging in the United States," *Interventions*, 10, no. 3 (2008): 359–80.

9. Daniels, *Guarding the Golden Door;* Zolberg, *Nation by Design.*

10. Zolberg, *Nation by Design;* Ngai, *Impossible Subjects;* Douglas S. Massey, Jorge Durand, and Nolan J. Malone, *Beyond Smoke and Mirrors: Mexican Immigration in an Era of Economic Integration* (New York: Russell Sage Foundation, 2002).

11. Douglas S. Massey and Kristin Espinoza, "What's Driving Mexico-U.S. Migration? A Theoretical, Empirical and Political Analysis," *American Journal of Sociology*, 102 (1997): 939–99; Massey et al., *Beyond Smoke and Mirrors*, 47–49, 73–83.

12. Massey, et al., *Beyond Smoke and Mirrors;* Mohl, "Globalization, Latinization, and the *Nuevo* New South."

13. Nora Hamilton and Norma Stoltz Chinchilla, *Seeking Community in a Global City: Guatemalans and Salvadorans in Los Angeles* (Philadelphia: Temple University Press, 2001), 17–35; Saskia Sassen, "Why Migration?" *Report on the Americas* 26:1 (July 1992): 14–19.

14. Massey, et al., *Beyond Smoke and Mirrors;* Jorge Durand, Douglas S. Massey, and Emilio A. Parrado, "The New Era of Mexican Migration to the United States," *Journal of American History,* 86 (September 1999): 518–36; Mohl, "Globalization, Latinization, and the *Nuevo* New South."

15. Douglas S. Massey, "March of Folly: U.S. Immigration Policy after NAFTA," *American Studies,* 41 (Summer/Fall 2000): 183–209.

16. Massey, et al., *Beyond Smoke and Mirrors;* Jeffery S. Passel, "Size and Characteristics of the Unauthorized Population in the U.S." (Washington, DC: Pew Hispanic Center, 2006). See http://pewhispanic.org/reports/report.php?ReportID=61.

17. James C. Cobb, *The Selling of the South: The Southern Crusade for Industrial Development* (Baton Rouge: Louisiana State University Press, 1982); Cobb, "The Sunbelt South: Industrialization in Regional, National, and International Perspective," in *Searching for the Sunbelt: Historical Perspectives on a Region,* ed. Raymond A. Mohl (Knoxville: University of Tennessee Press, 1990), 25–46.

18. Mohl, "Globalization, Latinization and the *Nuevo* New South"; Alfred E. Eckes, "The South and Economic Globalization, 1950 to the Future," in *Globalization and the American South,* ed. James C. Cobb and William Stueck (Athens: University of Georgia Press, 2005), 36–65; Odem, "Unsettled in the Suburbs."

19. Murphy, *Latino Workers in the Contemporary South;* Douglas S. Massey, "The Social and Economic Origins of Migration," *Annals of the American Academy of Political Science,* 510 (1990): 10–71; Massey and Espinoza, "What's Driving Mexico-U.S. Migration?"

20. U.S. Census Bureau, 1990, 2000; Rakesh Kochhar, Roberto Suro, and Sonya Tafoya, "The New Latino South: The Context and Consequences of Rapid Population Growth" (Washington, D.C.: Pew Hispanic Center, 2005); Mohl, "Globalization, Latinization, and the *Nuevo* New South."

21. U.S. Census Bureau, 2006 American Community Survey.

22. Goldfield, "Unmelting the Ethnic South," 26.

23. Barbara Ellen Smith, "Across Races and Nations: Social Justice Organizing in the Transnational South," in *Latinos in the New South*, 235–56; Steusse, "Race, Migration and Labor Control"; Rubén Hernández-León and Víctor Zúñiga, "Appalachia Meets Aztlan: Mexican Immigration and Intergroup Relations in Dalton, Georgia," in *New Destinations: Mexican Immigration in the United States*, ed. Zúñiga and Hernández-León (New York: Russell Sage Foundation, 2005), 244–74; Odem, "Unsettled in the Suburbs."

24. U.S. Census Bureau, 2006 American Community Survey; Odem and Lacy, *Latino Immigrants and the Transformation of the U.S. South*, xviv–xx.

25. Odem, "Unsettled in the Suburbs"; James H. Johnson, Jr., and John D. Kasarda, "Hispanic Newcomers to North Carolina: Demographic Characteristics and Economic Impact," in *Latino Immigrants and the Transformation of the South*, 70–90; Kochhar, "The New Latino South."

26. Jeffrey S. Passel, Randolph Capps, and Michael E. Fix, "Undocumented Immigrants: Facts and Figures" (Washington, D.C.: The Urban Institute, 2004), www.urban.org/url.cfm?ID=1000587; Jeffrey S. Passel, "Unauthorized Migrants: Numbers and Characteristics" (Washington, D.C.: Pew Hispanic Center, 2005), http://pewhispanic.org/files/reports/46.pdf.

27. Passel, "Size and Characteristics of the Unauthorized Population in the U.S." org/reports/report.php?ReportID=61.

28. Smith, "Across Races and Nations," 235–56; Steusse, "Race, Migration and Labor Control"; Hernández-León and Zúñiga, "Appalachia Meets Aztlan"; Odem, "Unsettled in the Suburbs."

29. Mohl, "Globalization, Latinization, and the *Nuevo* New South"; Hernández-León and Zúñiga, "Appalachia Meets Aztlan"; Steusse, "Race, Migration and Labor Control"; Charlie LeDuff, "At a Slaughterhouse Some Things Never Die," *New York Times*, June 16, 2000.

30. Eric Schlosser, *Fast Food Nation: The Dark Side of the All-American Meal* (Boston: Houghton Mifflin, 2001); Donald D. Stull, Michael J. Broadway, and David Griffith, eds., *Any Way You Cut It: Meat Processing and Small-town America* (Lawrence, Kans.: University of Kansas Press, 1995); Steve Striffler, *Chicken: The Dangerous Transformation of America's Favorite Food* (New Haven, Conn.: Yale University Press, 2005).

31. Steusse, "Race, Migration and Labor Control."

32. Randall L. Patton, *Carpet Capital: The Rise of a New South Industry* (Athens: University of Georgia Press, 1999); Douglas Flamming, *Creating the Modern South: Millhands and Managers in Dalton, Georgia, 1884–1984* (Chapel Hill: University of North Carolina Press, 1992); Joseph A. McDonald and Donald A. Clelland, "Textile Workers and Union Sentiment," *Social Forces* 63, No. 2 (1984): 502–21.

33. Hernández-León and Zúñiga, "Appalachia Meets Aztlan."

34. Elizabeth Martinez, "Black and Brown Workers Alliance Born in North Carolina," *Z Magazine*, March 2000, http://www.zmag.org/zmag/

viewArticle/13401; Steusse, "Race, Migration and Labor Control"; Smith, "Across Races and Nations."

35. Mary Bauer, *Close to Slavery: Guestworker Programs in the United States* (Montgomery, Ala.: Southern Poverty Law Center, 2007), http://www.splcenter. org/pdf/static/SPLCguestworker.pdf; Bob Moser, "The Battle of 'Georgiafornia,'" *Intelligence Report,* Winter 2004: 40–50; Ellen Griffith Spears, "Civil Rights, Immigration, and the Prospects for Social Justice Collaboration," in *The American South in a Global World,* ed. James L. Peacock, Harry L. Watson, and Carrie R. Matthews (Chapel Hill: University of North Carolina Press, 2005), 235–46.

36. Douglas Massey, "Ethnic Residential Segregation: A Theoretical Synthesis and Empirical Review," *Sociology and Social Research,* 69 (1985): 315–50; Richard Alba et al., "Immigrant Groups and Suburbs: A Reexamination of Suburbanization and Spatial Assimilation," *American Sociological Review,* 64 (1999): 446–60; John R. Logan, Richard D. Alba, and Wenquan Zhang, "Immigrant Enclaves and Ethnic Communities in New York and Los Angeles," *American Sociological Review,* 67 (2002): 299–322.

37. Singer, "Rise of New Immigrant Gateways"; Alba, "Immigrant Groups and Suburbs"; Logan, "Immigrant Enclaves"; Odem, "Unsettled in the Suburbs."

38. Brookings Institution Center on Urban and Metropolitan Policy, "Moving Beyond Sprawl: The Challenge for Metropolitan Atlanta" (Washington: Brookings Institution, 2000); Matthew D. Lassiter, *The Silent Majority: Suburban Politics in the Sunbelt South* (Princeton: Princeton University Press, 2006); Andrew Wiese, "African-American Suburbanization and Regionalism in the Modern South" (chapter 9 of this volume).

39. Wiese, "African-American Suburbanization and Regionalism in the Modern South"; Odem, "Unsettled in the Suburbs."

40. Odem, "Unsettled in the Suburbs"; Heather A. Smith and Owen J. Furuseth, "The 'Nuevo South': Latino Place Making and Community Building in the Middle-Ring Suburbs of Charlotte," in *Twenty-First Century Gateways,* 281–307.

41. Judith Waldrop, "The Newest Southerners," *American Demographics,* 15 (1993): 38–43; Charles Rutheiser, *Imagineering Atlanta: The Politics of Place in the City of Dreams* (New York: Verso, 1996), 88–93; Audrey Singer and Jill H. Wilson, "From 'There' to 'Here': Refugee Resettlement in Metropolitan America" (Washington: Brookings Institution, 2006).

42. Kevin M. Kruse, *White Flight: Atlanta and the Making of Modern Conservatism* (Princeton, Princeton University Press, 2005); Lassiter, *Silent Majority*; Brookings Institution, "Moving Beyond Sprawl."

43. Odem, "Unsettled in the Suburbs"; Smith and Furuseth, "The 'Nuevo South.'"

44. Susan M. Walcott, "Overlapping Ethnicities and Negotiated Spaces: Atlanta's Buford Highway," *Journal of Cultural Geography,* 20, no. 1 (Fall/Winter 2002): 51–76; Waldrop, "Newest Southerners"; Odem, "Unsettled in the Suburbs"; Smith and Furuseth, "The 'Nuevo South.'"

45. "Newcomer Center to Help Foreign Students Adjust," *Gwinnett Daily Post*, July 18, 2006; DeKalb County School System, "DeKalb English Language Learners (ELLs) Studies Program," http://www.dekalb.k12.ga.us/support/ell/.

46. "Georgia's New Latino Senator Ready to Help," *AP Online*, February 2, 2003, http://www.encyclopedia.com/doc/1P1-71458893.html; "Biographical Sketch," State Representative Pedro Marin, http://marinstatehouse.com/about.

47. Elaine Lacy and Mary Odem, "Popular Attitudes and Public Policies: Southern Responses to Latino Immigration," in *Latino Immigrants and the Transformation of the U.S. South*, 143–63.

48. Roberto Lovato, "Juan Crow in Georgia," *Nation*, May 26, 2008.

49. Odem, "Unsettled in the Suburbs"; *Atlanta Journal Constitution*, April 17, 1997, May 3, 1998; *Mundo Hispanico*, December 2000.

50. Odem, "Unsettled in the Suburbs"; Eunice Moscoso, "Driver's Licenses for Illegals to End," *Atlanta Journal-Constitution*, May 5, 2005, 1A; Greg Anrig, Jr., and Tova Andrea Wang, eds., *Immigration's New Frontiers: Experiences from the New Gateway States* (New York: Century Foundation Press, 2006).

51. Paula D. McClain, "North Carolina's Response to Latino Immigrants and Immigration," in *Immigration's New Frontiers*, 7–32.

52. Ivan Light, *Deflecting Immigration: Networks, Markets, and Regulation in Los Angeles* (New York: Russell Sage Foundation, 2006); Odem, "Unsettled in the Suburbs"; Anrig and Wang, *Immigration's New Frontiers*.

53. Andrea Jones, "Occupancy Limits Growing as an Issue," *Atlanta Journal-Constitution*, July 22, 2001, Gwinnett Extra, 1.

54. Paul Kaplan, "Law Tackles Boarding Houses," *Atlanta Journal-Constitution*, July 13, 2006, Northside Section, 3JH.

55. Richard Whitt, "How Many People Live Here?" *Atlanta Journal-Constitution*, June 20, 2005, 1A; Whitt, "Cobb Fines Owner over Full House," *Atlanta Journal-Constitution*, July 22, 2005, 1D.

56. Christopher Quinn, "Cherokee OKs Illegals Law," *Atlanta Journal-Constitution*, December 6, 2006, A1; Forsyth County North Carolina Illegal Immigration Relief Act Ordinance, http://spofga.org/build/2006/sept/southern_party_of_nc.php.

57. Mary Lou Pickel, "Illegal Immigrant Rental Law Put On Hold," *Atlanta Journal-Constitution*, January 6, 2007, B1.

58. U.S. ENGLISH, Inc., "Making English the Official Language," http://www.us-english.org/inc/.

59. The South Carolina Senate Republican Caucus, "Senate Passes English-Only Bill," http://scsenategop.com/senate-passes-english-only-bill.htm.

60. National Conference of State Legislatures, "2006 State Legislation Related to Immigration: Enacted and Vetoed," October 31, 2006, http://www.ncsl.org/programs/immig/6ImmigEnactedLegis3.htm.

61. Eunice Moscoso, "House OKs Stiff Immigration Bill," *Atlanta Journal-Constitution*, December, 17, 2005, A1; Carlos Campos, "Bills Plentiful, Unity Lacking on Immigrant Issue," *Atlanta Journal-Constitution*, January 30, 2006, A1;

Jim Tharpe, Carlos Campos, and Mary Lou Pickel, "Senate Bill Reveals Rift on Illegals," *Atlanta Journal-Constitution*, February 26, 2006, A1.

62. Linda Carolina Pérez, "Aplican Leyes Perforadas," *Mundo Hispánico*, July 26, 2007; Mary Lou Pickel, "Last Stop for Immigrants," *Atlanta Journal-Constitution*, July 30, 2007.

63. Daniel C. Vock, "With Feds Stuck, States Take on Immigration," Stateline.org, December 13, 2007, http://www.stateline.org/live/details/story?contentId=264483.

64. Elizabeth DeOrnellas, "Localizing Efforts to Process Illegals," *Daily Tarheel.com*, October 31, 2007, http://media.www.dailytarheel.com/media/storage/paper885/news/2007/10/31/StateNational/Localizing.Efforts.To.Process.Illegals-3068108.shtml.

Part IV

POLITICAL REALIGNMENT

11

INTO THE POLITICAL THICKET

Reapportionment and the Rise of
Suburban Power

Douglas Smith

In retirement, former Chief Justice Earl Warren acknowledged that most people considered *Brown v. Board of Education* (1954) the most important decision handed down by the Supreme Court during his tenure. Warren, however, disagreed. Instead, he unequivocally gave that designation to *Baker v. Carr* (1962), *Reynolds v. Sims* (1964), and the series of companion cases that established the principle of "one person, one vote" in all congressional and state legislative elections. Prior to these decisions, widespread malapportionment across the United States ensured the overrepresentation of rural and small-town areas while diluting the votes of metropolitan residents. In addressing this imbalance, according to Warren, the Court's decisions ushered in a revolution that changed the face of representative democracy in the United States.[1]

If the importance of Supreme Court rulings can be measured by the backlash they produced, then the reapportionment decisions of the 1960s were as pivotal as Warren suggested. In fact, *Baker* and *Reynolds* proved so controversial at the time that opponents launched a campaign to call what would have been the first Constitutional Convention in American history since the founding convention of the 1780s. Financed by many of the largest corporations in the United States, the effort played out in relative obscurity, overshadowed by more tumultuous events that dominated headlines in the 1960s. But by the end of the decade, thirty-three states, just one short of the two-thirds requirement, had petitioned for a convention to annul the decisions.

While opponents of reapportionment failed in their effort to overturn the "one person, one vote" standard, and while almost every state in the nation was forced to reapportion at least one branch of its legislature, the subsequent transformation of political power did not pan out quite as anticipated. First, the Court consciously chose to leave for another day the second half of what the *New York Times* referred to as the "twin evils of malapportionment and gerrymandering." Over time, of course, both political parties employed increasingly insidious methods of gerrymandering while adhering to the Court's mandate to draw districts that contained an equal number of people. Second, by the time of the Supreme Court's decisions in the 1960s, a new demographic reality confronted those who had fought hardest for reapportionment: the United States was becoming a suburban nation. Throughout the late 1940s and 1950s, as urban populations swelled across the United States, municipal officials and members of civic organizations such as the League of Women Voters (LWV) spearheaded efforts to reapportion state legislatures and congressional districts. In particular, urban interests chafed at their inability to wrestle away resources for education, housing, slum clearance, and transportation from the iron grip of rural and small-town politicians who dominated state legislative chambers far out of proportion to the populations of their districts. And while reapportionment did force state legislatures to take urban needs more seriously, it turned out that suburbanites, most of whom were white, often discovered that they had more in common with rural and small-town residents than with their disproportionately nonwhite urban neighbors.[2]

The most important reapportionment cases originated in the South. *Baker v. Carr* (1962)—in which the Supreme Court recognized for the first time that the federal courts had jurisdiction in apportionment disputes—came out of Tennessee. In *Gray v. Sanders* (1963), the Court struck down Georgia's infamous county unit system in an opinion in which William O. Douglas first wrote the phrase "one person, one vote." In *Wesberry v. Sanders* (1964), which also originated in Georgia, the Court ruled that all congressional districts must be drawn along the lines of equal population. Most controversially, the Supreme Court ruled in *Reynolds v. Sims* (1964), a case filed by litigants in Birmingham and Mobile, Alabama, that *both* houses of a bicameral legislature must be apportioned according to population.[3]

Without a doubt, malapportionment served as a vital component in the exercise of political power and the maintenance of white supremacy in the South. In every state in the region, rural and small-town voters—especially in the Black Belt—enjoyed far more representation than their numbers would have dictated. Urban residents struggled to have their concerns addressed in their state capitals. Tennessee, Alabama, and Georgia were quite typical of the region—20 to 25 percent of each state's voters were in a position to elect a majority of both branches of the legislature. In Florida, 12 percent of the citizenry commanded a majority in both houses. By contrast, Virginia appeared almost egalitarian: 37 percent of the Old Dominion's electorate was required to elect a majority of the General Assembly. When combined with the disfranchisement of most of the region's black citizens, minority control by rural areas assumed even starker proportions.[4]

Such malapportionment had devastating consequences. In August 1956, for example, the Virginia General Assembly met in special session to craft a response to the *Brown* decision. The key vote in the state's turn to massive resistance—defined primarily by the decision to close public schools rather than allow even a token amount of integration—narrowly passed the state senate, 21–17. The seventeen legislators who voted to comply with *Brown* represented more constituents than did the twenty-one who voted in favor of the school-closing laws—a point that, at the very least, challenges the notion of a Solid South and, more significantly, raises questions about the extent to which a rigged system of rural control determined the course of massive resistance.[5]

Writing about his first campaign for elected office, former President Jimmy Carter referred to *Baker v. Carr* as a "turning point" that shook "the foundation of the ancient political order." One day after the Supreme Court's decision in *Baker*, Atlanta attorney Morris Abram filed yet another suit in his nearly three-decade-long campaign to overturn Georgia's county unit system. The next day, a coalition of attorneys from urban areas across Georgia challenged the apportionment of the state legislature. According to Carter, "political leaders on both sides of the issue were obsessed with the subject." Opponents of reapportionment, in particular, recognized the racial implications of the pending lawsuits. Whether at work, church, or at Lions Club meetings, Carter's neighbors expressed a pervasive fear as to what it would mean for them once Atlanta—and especially the city's black voters—received a fair share of representation. Without a doubt, according to Carter, race constituted their central concern.[6]

The Supreme Court, on the other hand, never considered race a major issue while crafting its reapportionment decisions. In every reapportionment opinion, the Court spoke in terms of the rights of individual voters, never in terms of group rights and never in terms of racial discrimination. In fact, according to one Warren biographer, the Chief Justice made certain that the issues presented in the reapportionment cases were "sufficiently remote from racial discrimination" before moving forward with his majority opinion. In particular, Warren expressed some initial discomfort when Francis Beytagh, one of his law clerks, suggested *Reynolds v. Sims* as the vehicle through which the Court should announce the "one person, one vote" standard. At the time, the justices had heard oral arguments in reapportionment cases from six states—Alabama, Colorado,

Delaware, Maryland, New York, and Virginia—and the Chief Justice could have selected any of the cases as the lead opinion. Beytagh felt that the Alabama case addressed the issues in the most straightforward manner, but Warren, obviously aware of the intense animosity that the Court's desegregation decisions had generated in the South, wanted to make certain that it would not appear that the Court was intent on punishing the region. After a careful consideration of the issues, Warren concluded that "there was no valid reason to be concerned" and ultimately saw no reason to discuss the matter with any other justices, including Alabama native Hugo Black. Apparently no member of the Court ever objected to Warren's decision to accept Beytagh's recommendation.[7]

That the Court crafted its decisions in the reapportionment cases without any direct discussion of racial discrimination, at the precise time that civil rights moved to the forefront of the nation's conscience, does not suggest that the justices were unaware of the ways in which malapportionment remained intertwined with white supremacy.[8] But the Court's omission does suggest that the constitutional issues involved in the reapportionment debates of the post–World War II era went beyond matters of racial discrimination in the American South. When Earl Warren called the reapportionment decisions the most important of his tenure, he was not thinking in terms of racial justice but, rather, in terms of the rights of all individuals to have an equal voice in public affairs. Southern legislatures persistently violated the rights of urban dwellers, white and black, but so too did the legislatures of almost every other state in the nation. In this regard, southern reapportionment struggles must not be seen in a uniquely, or even primarily, regional context, but rather as part of a larger national debate that accelerated in the years after World War II (figure 11.1). Furthermore, viewing malapportionment through the lens of regional difference misses the more crucial role that reapportionment played in the postwar emergence of a suburban-based politics that must be understood in terms of competing rural, urban, and suburban interests on a national level.

Earl Warren knew better than anyone else that the South had no monopoly when it came to diluting the strength of urban voters. In fact, Warren himself had supported the continued malapportionment of his native California while serving as governor in the 1940s and 1950s, a fact that his critics raised repeatedly in the 1960s.[9] The malapportionment of the California legislature began in the 1920s when the state's voters passed a referendum that established a "federal plan"—apportioning the state assembly on a population basis and the state senate according to geography. Furthermore, California's system mandated that no county could have more than one senator and that no state senator could represent more than three counties. Consequently, by 1960 malapportionment in California was as severe as in any state in the nation; 11 percent of the

HERBLOCK'S EDITORIAL CARTOON

"If You Don't Like This Situation, You Can Cast Your Twentieth Of A Vote Against It"

FIGURE 11.1. A Herblock cartoon from the *Washington Post*, October 13, 1961, dramatizes the nationwide problem of rural domination through the malapportionment of state legislatures. Supporters of reapportionment viewed the conflict as a showdown between urban and rural interests, not simply as a racial or regional matter, but the most significant beneficiaries of the Supreme Court's "one person, one vote" rulings proved to be the fast-growing populations of America's suburbs. © Herb Block Foundation.

state's residents were able to elect a majority of the state senate. Nearly 6.4 million residents of Los Angeles County had one representative in the state senate, as did the 14,294 residents of three sparsely populated rural counties on the eastern slope of the Sierra. A voter in the eastern Sierra, therefore, enjoyed the electoral might of 446 residents of Los Angeles County.[10]

The disparity worsened throughout the twentieth century, but opponents of California's federal plan failed in 1948, 1960, and again in 1962 to pass ballot initiatives that would have assigned more representation in the state senate to the larger urban areas, especially Los Angeles. Residents of rural and small-town California shared a great deal with their counterparts elsewhere in the United States. In particular, they looked upon minority control of state government as the best guarantee that their lives would not come to be dominated politically, financially, or morally by city dwellers and their expansive dependence on government to provide a host of social services.[11]

Furthermore, urban-based business interests across the country, especially in the Sunbelt, supported malapportionment and rural political domination as a means of keeping taxes low, regulations to a minimum, and labor unions politically weak. In Los Angeles, for example, the Chamber of Commerce fought hard against the initial referendum in the 1920s—which was clearly aimed specifically at curbing the power of Los Angeles—but had determined by the 1940s that the rural-dominated state senate better protected its interests than a more equitably apportioned legislature. Furthermore, many urban-based businesses had extensive holdings in rural areas. As one observer of California politics noted at the height of the reapportionment debate of the 1960s, the farmers and businessmen were not only friends but "often the same person." The agribusiness, railroad, oil, liquor, and racing industries especially fit this description. Consequently, each time California voters went to the polls to consider revising the state's federal plan, business and industrial groups, including many of those based in Los Angeles, warned that reapportionment would benefit organized labor and urban political machines. During the 1948 campaign over Proposition 13, the state Chamber of Commerce declared, "this proposal is backed by Organized Labor, whose purpose is to gain control of our State Legislature. Don't let THEM get away with it. Keep the American form of government." Apparently the chamber felt no need, at the start of the Cold War, to explain further the danger posed by "THEM." Nor did the chamber recognize the irony in advocating a form of government as "American" that, in fact, left control of the state senate in the hands of a small minority.[12]

The experience in California mirrored, albeit in an exaggerated manner, what took place throughout the United States. As urban areas grew in size throughout the first half of the twentieth century, malapportionment worsened as rural and small-town residents joined with urban business interests to dilute the effective electoral power of increasingly nonwhite urban populations. The consequences of malapportionment, however, were not always as obvious as in the case of Virginia's embrace of massive resistance. For instance, Al Toffler of New York City wrote Mrs. Alexander Guyol, the director of public relations for the League of Women Voters of the United States, and asked for help as he considered writing an article on malapportionment. In particular, he asked if the league could provide "concrete illustrations of the harm that rural over-representation in the states causes." Toffler went on to explain that he had ample statistical evidence that "rural districts ARE over-represented," but he lacked evidence of the ways in which "these rural majorities refused to help the cities deal with their urgent problems." He added: "preferably these cases should show how legislative unconcern for urban problems either led to some kind of crisis, or aggravated existing crises."[13]

Had Toffler been familiar with the Commission on Intergovernmental Relations, he would have had no need to request help from Guyol. Appointed by President Eisenhower in 1955, the commission looked closely at the consequences of malapportionment. Not only did the commission single out the failure of state governments to provide adequate funds for slum clearance, urban renewal, low-income housing, and metropolitan transportation projects, but the commission noted that this failure left urban officials no choice but to turn to the federal government for aid.[14]

No organization spent more time than the League of Women Voters trying to focus the public's attention on the need for reapportionment. Although the national office of the league did not make reapportionment a priority until the mid-1960s, LWV chapters in more than two dozen states had actively studied the issue, highlighted the problems, and lobbied for change beginning in the late 1940s and accelerating throughout the 1950s. State leagues were especially active in Washington, Wisconsin, Maryland, Minnesota, Illinois, Oklahoma, Georgia, and Tennessee.[15]

As *Baker v. Carr* awaited a ruling in the Supreme Court, *The Oak Ridger* of Oak Ridge, Tennessee, reported on the activities of the local chapter of the LWV. Proclaiming "Housewife Agrees, It Has Lots To Do With the Price of Eggs," the newspaper went on to explain that every time Mrs. Murray Rosenthal "buys groceries and puts out three cents for every dollar she spends on eggs, milk, bread and sugar, she is adding to the kitty of funds used for state aid to education." These funds, of course, were controlled by rural and small-town legislators who made sure that the cities never received a fair return on their contribution to state coffers.[16]

Joining forces with municipal officials, labor groups, civic organizations, and some urban business interests, state leagues made modest headway in a few states. Most notably, the LWV led a successful campaign to establish a federal system of apportionment in Illinois in 1954 (in the 1950s reformers recognized that one branch of a state legislature based on population marked an improvement over the status quo and thus considered a federal system a positive step). In 1958, members of the Minnesota League of Women Voters supported litigation that led to a groundbreaking ruling in which a federal district court accepted jurisdiction in an apportionment case. That same year, the Oklahoma LWV helped elect J. Howard Edmondson governor. The thirty-three-year-old Edmondson made reapportionment a central plank of his campaign, and he won by the largest margin in state history.[17]

While Edmondson campaigned to reapportion the Oklahoma legislature, John F. Kennedy began to prepare for his bid for the nation's highest office. Fully aware that urban voters would constitute an important share of the electorate in 1960, Kennedy penned an article in the *New York Times Magazine* in which he condemned urban blight and decay as a clear consequence of urban underrepresentation. Borrowing language from muckraker Lincoln Steffens, Kennedy referred to malapportionment as "the shame of the states" and cited a litany of consequences: "overcrowded and hazardous schools, undermanned with underpaid teachers, ... slum housing, congested traffic, juvenile delinquency, overcrowded health and penal institutions and inadequate parking." Furthermore, he cited the malapportionment of districts for the U.S. House of Representatives to explain why Congress recently had failed to pass important housing, education, and labor legislation. Recognizing that equitable apportionment was no "panacea for the city's ills," Kennedy concluded that "one hundred million citizens—constituting a majority of the nation—will not forever accept this modern day 'taxation without representation.'" Such inequality, he reasoned, had consigned urban and suburban residents to second-class citizenship.[18]

Kennedy recognized that identifying the problem was far easier than finding a solution. As he noted, and as J. Howard Edmondson discovered after his election as Oklahoma's governor, defiant legislatures across the country simply refused to reapportion, despite dramatic population shifts from rural to metropolitan areas during the middle decades of the twentieth century. Such defiance flew in the face of state constitutional mandates to reapportion every ten years (and in a few cases, every five years), and yet state courts repeatedly deferred to the legislatures and opted not to get involved. Meanwhile, the federal courts heeded Felix Frankfurter's admonition, enunciated in 1946 in *Colegrove v. Green*, to avoid the "political thicket." Consequently, no meaningful reapportionment took place in Oregon for fifty years. In Alabama and Tennessee, no reapportionment at all occurred for sixty years. Unable to make any headway with the Oklahoma legislature, Edmondson ultimately filed an *amicus* brief in *Baker v. Carr* on behalf of the 70 percent of Oklahoma residents who were underrepresented.[19]

In 1959, after the state legislature again refused to consider reapportionment, representatives of Tennessee's largest cities filed suit in *Baker
v. Carr*. Officials in Memphis had refused to support a reapportionment
suit several years earlier. By 1959, however, the city was feeling a financial
pinch as a result of a decline in its allocation of state funds ever since the
death of Boss Crump in 1954. Nashville and its mayor, Ben West, also had
avoided the earlier round of litigation, partially out of fear of retaliation
by the rural-dominated legislature. By 1959, West had ceased to disguise
his animosity for the Tennessee legislature. Certainly he did himself and
his constituents no favors when, as president of the American Municipal
Association, he highlighted the problems of malapportionment in a series
of speeches with charts showing how the pigs and cows in rural Moore
County were much better represented than the people of Nashville and
Davidson County. The Nashville city council readily voted to provide substantial financial support for the litigation.[20]

A three-judge federal court acknowledged the obvious inequality in
Tennessee's apportionment scheme but refused to accept jurisdiction
under the "political thicket" doctrine. By the time *Baker v. Carr* reached
the U.S. Supreme Court, the city attorneys of Los Angeles, Dallas, Portland
(Oregon), Minneapolis, and other municipalities had joined the case, providing further evidence that the suit reflected not so much southern distinctiveness as a common burden experienced in similar terms by urban
residents throughout the nation.[21]

Initially argued in April 1961, *Baker v. Carr* was held over for reargu-
ment in October. In March 1962, a 6–2 majority on the Court decided that
the time had come to enter the "political thicket" and ruled that Tennessee's system of apportionment violated the equal protection clause of the
Fourteenth Amendment. The final vote, however, gave little indication of
the deep division among the justices. At the end of each term, William
Brennan and his clerks prepared detailed histories of the most important
cases decided that year. Brennan's history of *Baker* makes clear that the
case nearly came down 5–4, and that the majority almost broke apart
altogether.[22]

In *Baker*, the Court declined to set a standard that states had to meet
under the equal protection clause, instead limiting its ruling to the question of jurisdiction. In short, *Baker* opened the doors of the federal courts
to adjudicate apportionment disputes but went no further. Five votes did
not exist for anything more; the question of standards would have to wait
for another day. As Justice Brennan prepared to read publicly the majority
opinion, Chief Justice Warren passed him a handwritten note on which
he had scribbled, "It is a great day for the country."[23]

During oral arguments, it became clear that some of the justices were
troubled by the question of remedies and enforcement. Felix Frankfurter,
whose impassioned sixty-page dissent marked his final major opinion on

the Court (he had a stroke a week after the decision was announced and retired that summer), had long held that the federal judiciary could not fix the problem and thus ought to stay out of the fight. Frankfurter went so far as to suggest to Solicitor General Archibald Cox that enforcing school desegregation orders might turn out to be a "simpler" task than enforcing reapportionment decrees. Only a few years removed from massive white resistance to *Brown v. Board of Education*, Frankfurter no doubt worried about the reaction of individuals such as the speaker of the Pennsylvania House, who warned that if the Supreme Court claimed authority to force legislative reapportionment, "the only possible way to do it would be for the President to declare martial law, send in troops, hold guns at the legislators' heads and force them by sheer might."[24]

Despite such dire predictions, reaction to *Baker* turned out to be surprisingly mild. President Kennedy expressed unqualified support for the Court's ruling, unlike President Eisenhower in the wake of *Brown*. The Court's decision not to impose a specific standard diffused a more negative reaction (at least for the time being). Furthermore, a majority of the nation's population had much to gain from the outcome. Not surprisingly, then, most leading newspapers throughout the country supported the ruling. The *Dayton* (Ohio) *Daily News*, for example, opined that the Court had "issued an urban emancipation proclamation."[25]

Baker v. Carr did, indeed, open the floodgates as litigants in more than three dozen states filed reapportionment suits in federal district courts in the immediate aftermath of the Supreme Court's ruling. In Alabama, however, a group of six young lawyers had anticipated the Court's ruling in *Baker* and already filed suit in August 1961. Like Tennessee, the Alabama legislature had not reapportioned since 1901. By 1960, the 634,864 residents of Birmingham and Jefferson County had a single state senator and seven state representatives (one for every 90,695 residents), while the 15,417 residents of Lowndes County (most of whom were black and unable to vote) had their own state senator and two representatives in the lower house.[26]

Unlike the attorneys in *Baker*, who were supported by the relatively deep pockets of the urban establishment in Memphis and Nashville, the attorneys in Alabama who filed what ultimately became known as *Reynolds v. Sims* acted on their own and on a shoestring budget. Charles Morgan and George Peach Taylor, both in their early-to-mid thirties, initiated the proceedings on behalf of fourteen plaintiffs and residents of Jefferson County, all affiliated with the Young Men's Business Club, a relatively progressive alternative to the Chamber of Commerce. Morgan and Taylor listed themselves as plaintiffs to ensure that if the others dropped out, at least they would remain; indeed, several plaintiffs did disassociate themselves from the case after receiving pressure from employers. In November 1961, as the federal court awaited a ruling in *Baker*, Morgan and Taylor were joined by Jerome "Buddy" Cooper, a labor lawyer in Birmingham who provided financial support for the litigants. The following spring, David Vann and Robert Vance intervened on behalf of a group of Jefferson County voters who had supported John F. Kennedy in 1960, and John McConnell joined the case on behalf of residents of Mobile, the second most underrepresented area of the state.[27]

After the Supreme Court's decision in *Baker*, a three-judge federal district court in Montgomery, headed by Frank Johnson, gave the Alabama legislature a final chance to reapportion itself. When the legislature failed to pass an acceptable plan, the district court ordered a temporary reapportionment that in no way approached population equality, but which was designed to break the stranglehold of rural domination while causing a minimum of disruption. The district court reasoned that a newly elected legislature, while far from proportionately representative, would mark an improvement; furthermore the district court maintained jurisdiction and promised to act if the legislature did not.[28]

The district court's decision divided the plaintiffs' attorneys. Morgan, Taylor, and Cooper recognized that the ruling did not go as far as they had hoped, but they wanted badly to support Frank Johnson (who had been under intense pressure since a 1956 ruling that overturned Montgomery's segregated transportation system, a decision that paved the way for subsequent attacks on other aspects of segregation).[29] The trio emphasized that the district court's action marked the first time that a federal court in the United States had ordered an apportionment plan into effect, and that the court promised to maintain jurisdiction. Vann, Vance, and McConnell wanted to appeal the order but ultimately lacked the funds to do so. Meanwhile, Probate Judges B. A. Reynolds and Frank Pearce felt the district court had exceeded its authority. Backed by state officials (although not Attorney General Richmond Flowers) and anonymous donors with financial resources, Reynolds and Pearce appealed to the Supreme Court, thus assuming the costs of continuing the litigation.[30]

By the time the Supreme Court heard oral arguments in *Reynolds v. Sims* in November 1963, apportionment cases from fifteen states had made their way to the Court, as had *Wesberry v. Sanders*, a congressional reapportionment case from Georgia. Ultimately, the Court heard arguments in *Wesberry* and in six of the challenges to state legislatures—the Alabama case plus disputes from Virginia, Maryland, Delaware, New York, and Colorado. The facts presented by each case differed to some degree, but all raised the question as to what standard was required by the equal protection clause. During oral arguments, Charles Morgan asked only that the Supreme Court affirm the decision of the district court, but he acknowledged that population was "the one standard that is measurable in each instance, leaving less room for doubt and less room for question." Of the Alabama attorneys, only John McConnell argued that the equal protection clause required no less than that both houses of a state legislature be apportioned on an equitable population basis.[31]

McConnell's argument exceeded that put forward by the federal government, represented by Solicitor General Archibald Cox. While many other Justice Department officials supported an explicit embrace of a "one person, one vote" standard, Cox proved more ambivalent about the state cases than he had in *Baker*. In evaluating the apportionment schemes in all the cases before the Court, Cox argued that "the starting point for legislative apportionment be 'per capita equality of representation.'" But the solicitor general refused to insist that both houses of a state legislature be apportioned on a population basis. "When one house of a bicameral legislature is apportioned substantively according to population," announced the federal government's brief, "the Fourteenth Amendment may leave considerable room in the other house for recognition of conflicting objectives." The solicitor general, in other words, refused to rule out a federal system of apportionment at the state level.[32]

While legal scholars have always emphasized the importance of *Baker* in constitutional terms, the reaction to the Court's decisions of June 15, 1964, suggests that the sweeping nature of the *Reynolds* decision and its companion cases had a greater impact on the nation's political system. In announcing that the equal protection clause of the Fourteenth Amendment required that all legislative bodies be apportioned according to the principle of "one person, one vote," Chief Justice Warren wrote that "the right to vote freely for the candidate of one's choice is of the essence of a democratic society, and any restrictions on that right strike at the heart of representative government. And the right of suffrage can be denied by a debasement or dilution of the weight of a citizen's vote just as effectively as by wholly prohibiting the free exercise of the franchise." Furthermore, added Warren in his opinion's most frequently quoted line, "legislators represent people not trees or acres. Legislators are elected by voters, not farms or cities or economic interests."[33]

Having established the "one person, one vote" standard in the Alabama case, the Court proceeded to overturn apportionment schemes in Maryland, Virginia, Delaware, New York, and Colorado. While eight members of the Court voted to overturn Alabama's system of apportionment (only John Marshall Harlan dissented in all of the cases), Justices Potter Stewart and Tom Clark did so by applying a rationality test. Neither Stewart nor Clark accepted the much broader interpretation of the equal protection clause announced by the Court's six-member controlling majority.[34]

The Court's ruling in the Colorado case proved much more contentious. In 1962, not 1901, voters in every county in Colorado had passed a referendum that provided for a federal system. Furthermore, the voters rejected a separate ballot measure that specifically called for the apportionment of both houses on a population basis. Stewart and Clark argued passionately in favor of Colorado's plan. The six-person majority, again led by the Chief Justice, recognized the differences between the situations in Colorado and Alabama but concluded nevertheless that "an individual's constitutionally protected right to cast an equally weighted vote cannot be denied even by a vote of a majority of a State's electorate if the apportionment scheme adopted by the voters fails to measure up to the requirements of the Equal Protection Clause." Employing language that echoed that found in the *Brown* decision, Warren added: "A citizen's constitutional rights can hardly be infringed simply because a majority of the people chooses that it be." A week later the Court cited its decision in *Reynolds* to overturn apportionment schemes in nine additional states— Florida, Ohio, Illinois, Michigan, Idaho, Connecticut, Iowa, Oklahoma, and Washington. No region in the country was spared.[35]

The Court's rulings stunned observers. Anthony Lewis of the *New York Times* slipped a note to Archibald Cox as the Court announced its decisions and asked, "How does it feel to be present at the second American Constitutional Convention?" Cox replied, "It feels awful." Cox had enthusiastically supported a challenge to the "invidious discrimination" that pervaded Alabama's apportionment scheme, but he had never expected a ruling that unequivocally rejected a federal system at the state level. The following day, the *New York Times* remarked that the Court's rejection of the federal analogy was "the farthest reaching" decision "since *Marbury v. Madison* established the power of judicial review in 1803." A *Times* editorial added that "when the history of the Court under Chief Justice Warren is written, these decisions may outweigh even the school integration decision of 1954 in importance."[36]

Reynolds v. Sims produced a backlash unlike anything contemplated in the aftermath of *Baker v. Carr*. Members of Congress introduced more than one hundred bills and resolutions aimed at overturning or modifying the Court's ruling. Senator Everett Dirksen of Illinois, the Republican Minority Leader, soon emerged as the leader of congressional opponents to the Court's rulings (figure 11.2). Dirksen first supported a campaign to pass a constitutional amendment to remove apportionment disputes from the jurisdiction of the federal courts. When that proposal failed to generate much support, Dirksen offered a constitutional amendment that explicitly would have allowed a federal system at the state level. While obtaining a majority of votes in the Senate, Dirksen was never able to muster the necessary two-thirds. Illinois' senior senator, Democrat Paul Douglas, led the forces opposed to the Dirksen Amendment. That two representatives of the same midwestern state stood on opposites sides of the issue comes as no surprise. Dirksen came from Pekin, a small town outside Peoria, while Douglas hailed from Chicago. The two men defined, in their own lives as well as their politics, the deep divide between urban and small-town America.[37]

"My Dear Chaps, Have You No Refinement, No Finesse?"

FIGURE 11.2. A Herblock cartoon from the *Washington Post*, June 24, 1965, equates the practices of southern vigilantes who used violence to deny equal voting rights to African Americans with Illinois Senator Everett Dirksen's effort to amend the constitution to prevent court-ordered reapportionment. © Herb Block Foundation.

Unsuccessful in Congress, Dirksen and his forces took their campaign to the states and attempted to exploit a little-known and still never-used clause in Article V of the U.S. Constitution that allows two-thirds of the states to call a convention for the purpose of amending the Constitution. To this end, Dirksen hired Whitaker & Baxter, a California public relations firm that cut its teeth in state politics in the 1930s working against Upton Sinclair during his EPIC (End Poverty in California) campaign. In the late 1940s, Whitaker & Baxter made the jump into national politics when the American Medical Association hired the firm to defeat Harry Truman's program for national health insurance.[38]

Whitaker & Baxter proved a logical ally in Dirksen's campaign. The firm successfully had led opponents of reapportionment in California to victory each time an effort to reapportion the state senate appeared on the ballot—in 1948, 1960, and 1962. Given Whitaker & Baxter's track record, it came as no surprise when members of the California legislature turned to the firm for advice in the immediate wake of the *Reynolds* decision. Beginning in the late summer of 1964, Whitaker & Baxter oversaw efforts in California to garner support for a federal constitutional amendment. Led by generous contributions from Standard Oil of California and Pacific Gas & Electric, a range of industrial, agricultural, manufacturing, and petroleum companies provided financial support.[39]

In September 1965, soon after his second failure to garner two-thirds support in the U.S. Senate for an amendment, Everett Dirksen turned to Whitaker & Baxter to spearhead a national effort for his campaign. Although Dirksen waited until January 1966 to announce the formation of the Committee for the Government of the People (CGOP), he had spent months in consultation with Whitaker & Baxter laying the groundwork and lining up financial resources for a viable campaign. Clem Whitaker, Jr., who had taken over the firm from his father and stepmother in 1958, moved to Washington to guide the effort personally, meeting with Dirksen in his Senate office nightly to plot strategy.[40]

While supported generally by the American Farm Bureau Federation, the United States Chamber of Commerce, and the National Association of Manufacturers, among others, Whitaker & Baxter concentrated its efforts between September 1965 and January 1966 on procuring significant donations from major American corporations. Ultimately, CGOP raised hundreds of thousands of dollars, and perhaps more than 1 million, led by $30,000 each from DuPont, Standard Oil of Indiana, and General Electric. Proctor & Gamble followed with $25,000, and the Ford Motor Company added $20,000. After the official announcement of the formation of the Committee for the Government of the People, Whitaker & Baxter churned out almost daily press releases, announcing the support of various members of Congress or groups of prominent state officials.[41]

In April 1966, Everett Dirksen failed for the third and final time to push a constitutional amendment through the U.S. Senate. But rather than give up the campaign, Dirksen and his supporters intensified their efforts at the state level to gain passage of petitions calling for a constitutional convention. Whitaker & Baxter monitored the progress in every state, drafted a suggested document to ensure that all states worded their petitions in the same form, and contacted favorable interests in states where passage remained a viable possibility. By mid-1967, thirty-two states had petitioned Congress for a convention. In the spring of 1968, Whitaker & Baxter secured the necessary votes in the Alaska legislature, but Governor Walter J. Hickel, who had promised during the previous legislative session to remain neutral, prevailed upon key senators to withdraw support.[42]

Despite the potentially historic significance of the campaign to call a convention, it received relatively modest attention until May 1969, when Iowa became the thirty-third state to support a petition. With the movement just one state short of the required two-thirds, a congressional committee took notice and set out to determine how such a convention would be convened. Pundits and legal scholars debated whether such a convention could be limited to the issue of apportionment or if, in fact, the entire U.S. Constitution would be up for discussion. Ultimately, however, supporters of the Supreme Court's reapportionment decisions—led by the League of Women Voters, the AFL-CIO, the American Civil Liberties Union, the U.S. Conference of Mayors, and the American League of Cities—prevailed. Everett Dirksen, whose leadership of pro-convention forces proved irreplaceable, died from cancer in September 1969. In November, the Wisconsin assembly denied pro-convention forces a thirty-fourth petition.[43]

Time proved the ally of those who supported the Court's reapportionment decisions. By 1968, legislative action and court orders had reapportioned at least one branch of the legislature, and usually both, in forty-nine out of the fifty states. As legal scholar Robert Dixon wrote at the time, "in the space of five years, reapportionment virtually remade the political map of America." And despite the most dire predictions, reapportionment proceeded with relative ease—perhaps not a surprise given that the decisions did affirm the individual rights of a majority of citizens.[44]

Had Everett Dirksen lived, he would have discovered that the political consequences of reapportionment did not turn out as he had expected. Throughout the 1940s and 1950s, supporters of reapportionment commonly understood the issue in terms of urban underrepresentation and rural/small-town overrepresentation. Opponents of reapportionment feared that big-city political machines would come to dominate state legislatures. But by the 1960s, the United States was becoming a suburban nation, a development largely ignored by the key players who litigated the reapportionment battles. Few observers at the time, in fact, were as quick to recognize the importance of the link between demographic change and reapportionment as was journalist Karl Meyer. Writing in the *New Statesman* in the immediate aftermath of *Baker*, Meyer noted that "time has given a fresh twist to the problem. It is not the starving urban masses who are cheated by electoral devices in the states. By and large, the chief injustice is to suburbia, where, if only half a dinner is eaten, it is for reasons of dieting."[45]

The facts bore out Meyer's observations. As the 1960 census revealed, the vast majority of major American cities had lost population during the previous decade. Among the few cities that gained residents, virtually all of them were in the Sunbelt. In Atlanta, Houston, Dallas, San Diego, and Los Angeles, under-inhabited lands within city boundaries and relatively easy annexation laws allowed for the continued growth of city populations. Meanwhile suburban populations in every major metropolitan area grew by extraordinary margins. In New York, the suburbs exploded by 75 percent, in Los Angeles by 83 percent, in Chicago by 71 percent, and in Detroit by nearly 80 percent.[46]

The importance of such demographic change was not lost on William Boyd, an employee of the National Municipal League who had supported reapportionment as ardently as anyone in the nation. In the wake of the *Reynolds* decision, as opponents of reapportionment denounced the Court and warned of big-city domination, Boyd examined the results of the 1960 census. In a report entitled "Suburbia Takes Over," Boyd explained that "the suburbs and, in the long run, only the suburbs will gain in the upheaval resulting from reapportionment....Rather than being dominated by the big cities, as is commonly supposed, the new legislatures will see suburban representation increase the most in number." "The suburbs," Boyd concluded, "own the future."[47]

From the moment Earl Warren announced the Court's "one person, one vote" standard, political operatives, pundits, and journalists tried to figure out which party would benefit. According to *Newsweek*, Democrats appeared poised to make gains in about twenty states, especially in those where rural-based Republicans had been able to maintain control of both branches of the state legislature. Meanwhile, Republicans expected to see immediate gains in six southern states plus five more outside the region. But, as *U.S. News & World Report* opined, "suburban populations have been found generally to be more 'conservative' and more likely to vote Republican than city populations." Not coincidentally, while the GOP denounced the *Reynolds* decision in its 1964 platform, before long the Republican National Committee recognized the possibility of significant gains in all regions of the country. It turned out that a lot of potential Republican voters resided in the suburbs.[48]

The political rise of the suburbs meant, of course, that cities throughout the United States never attained the help they so desperately needed. Tom Osborn, a Nashville lawyer involved in the *Baker* litigation from the beginning, remarked as urban centers broke out in violence in the mid-1960s that the reapportionment decisions came too late to adequately address urban needs. Earl Warren concurred with Osborn's analysis. "Our cities are in crisis," the Chief Justice told an interviewer, "and are in great danger of disruption to a point that threatens the entire fabric of our society." Warren went on to explain that the worst of the urban ills might have been avoided if urban residents had enjoyed adequate representation at the time that central city populations swelled—between World Wars I and II. Even by the time of the *Colegrove* "political thicket" decision in 1946, Warren suggested, it may have been too late to bring about the change necessary to have avoided the worst of the urban crisis.[49]

Ironically, reapportionment freed suburbanites across the country from urban control just as effectively as it ended rural and small-town domination. Prior to reapportionment, urban and suburban populations were often lumped together into legislative districts. As long as suburbanites remained outnumbered by urban residents within these districts, suburban legislators required the support of city political leaders and residents to win elections. But once apportioned their own seats in the legislature, newly elected suburban representatives found themselves in agreement with rural and small-town legislators just as often, if not more often, than with their urban neighbors. These representatives, like their mostly white constituents, had fled the increasingly nonwhite core cities for a reason and felt no inclination to appropriate taxpayer funds for sewer construction, busing for urban schoolchildren, and other items on the municipal agenda.[50]

Despite the lingering ills of urban America, reapportionment did bring about important transformations in American society and politics, not the least of which was an affirmation of the principle of majority rule. In fact, for Earl Warren, and no doubt other members of the Court, the reapportionment decisions articulated first and foremost a profound belief in the absolute necessity of majority rule in a democratic society. Over time, however, political operatives of both major parties have become increasingly successful at subverting the will of majorities without running afoul of the Court's mandate in *Reynolds*. In 1964, an analyst with the Library of Congress's Legislative Reference Service recognized the limits of the Court's reapportionment rulings and predicted quite prophetically that "we may be passing from the age of the grossly malapportioned district to that of the strangely gerrymandered one." Thus far the Supreme Court has refused to enter the thicket of political gerrymandering; to do so would require a decision as revolutionary and controversial as the reapportionment rulings of the 1960s.[51]

NOTES

1. Earl Warren, *The Memoirs of Chief Justice Earl Warren* (Lanham, Md.: Madison Books, 2001), 306–12; Anthony Lewis, "A Talk With Warren on Crime, the Court, the Country," *New York Times Magazine*, October 19, 1969, 34; Jim Newton, *Justice for All: Earl Warren and the Nation He Made* (New York: Riverhead Books, 2006), 425.

2. "The Governor's Vetoes," *New York Times*, May 29, 1965, 26.

3. *Baker v. Carr*, 369 U.S. 186 (1962); *Gray v. Sanders*, 372 U.S. 368 (1963); *Wesberry v. Sanders*, 376 U.S. 1 (1964); *Reynolds v. Sims*, 377 U.S. 533 (1964).

4. National Municipal League, "Compendium on Legislative Apportionment" (New York, 1962), iii–iv.

5. Benjamin Muse, *Virginia's Massive Resistance* (Bloomington: Indiana University Press, 1961), 30–31.

6. Jimmy Carter, *Turning Point: A Candidate, a State, and a Nation Come of Age* (New York: Times Books, 1992), 25–42 (quotations 26, 28); *Gray v. Sanders*, 376 U.S. 1 (1964); *Toombs v. Fortson*, 205 F. Supp. 248 (1962); Morris Abram, *The Day Is Short* (New York: Harcourt, Brace, Jovanovich, 1982): 48–50, 101–9.

7. Bernard Schwartz, *Super Chief: Earl Warren and His Supreme Court—A Judicial Biography* (New York: New York University Press, 1983), 504–5.

8. Ed Cray, *Chief Justice: A Biography of Earl Warren* (New York: Simon & Schuster, 1997), 433–34.

9. "Warren Stresses Legislative Role of Rural Counties," *Sacramento Bee*, November 21, 1947, 13; "Warren Opposes Reapportionment," *Los Angeles Times*, October 30, 1948, 1; "Redistricting: A Warren View in '48," *U. S. News & World Report*, 57 (July 6, 1964): 34.

10. Proposition 28 (California), "Legislative Reapportionment" (1926); Robert B. McKay, *Reapportionment: The Law and Politics of Equal Representation* (New York: The Twentieth Century Fund, 1965), 285–89; National Municipal League, "Compendium on Legislative Apportionment," iii–iv; Robert G. Dixon, Jr., *Democratic Representation: Reapportionment in Law and Politics* (New York: Oxford University Press, 1968), 370–71.

11. Proposition 13 (California), "Senate Reapportionment" (1948); Proposition 15 (California), "Senate Reapportionment" (1960); Proposition 23 (California), "Senate Reapportionment" (1962); Charles R. Adrian, "Policy Implications of Reapportionment: Conference on Apportionment and State Government," March 20, 1963, Box 259, Folder "Illinois-Indiana," Part IV, League of Women Voters Papers, Library of Congress, Washington, D.C. [hereinafter LWV Papers].

12. Dixon, *Democratic Representation*, 370–74; McKay, *Reapportionment*, 285–89; Charles A. Wellman, Chair, "Report of the State of California Study Commission on Senate Apportionment" (February 1962); Bill Boyarsky, "Why They Fight Against Apportionment," *Frontier*, 16 (March 1965): 11–13 (first quotation 12); "Proposition No. 13, Vote 'No,'" *California: Magazine of the Pacific*, 38 (October 1948): 3 (second quotation), Senator Randolph Collier Papers, LP 229: 340, California State Archives, Sacramento [hereinafter CSA].

13. Al Toffler to Mrs. Alexander Guyol, July 24, 1960, Box 886, Folder "Government—Reapportionment," Part III, LWV Papers.

14. Unites States Commission on Intergovernmental Relations, *A Report to the President for Transmittal to the Congress* (Washington: GPO, June 1955), 227–28, cited in Margaret Greenfield, Pamela Ford, and Donald R. Emery, "Legislative

Reapportionment: California in National Perspective," 1959 Legislative Problems, No. 7, Bureau of Public Administration, University of California at Berkeley, October 1959.

15. "Inventory of Work on Reapportionment By State Leagues of Women Voters," (Washington: LWV of the United States, February 1959); "Inventory of Work on Reapportionment By State Leagues of Women Voters" (Washington: LWV of the United States, revised January 1963).

16. "Housewife Agrees, It Has Lots To Do With The Price of Eggs," *The Oak Ridger* (Oak Ridge, Tennessee), December 1961, in Box 1040, Folder "Government Apportionment," LWV Papers.

17. "Inventory of Work on Reapportionment By State Leagues of Women Voters," (revised January 1963), 15–16, 28–29, 36–39; "Brief of J. Howard Edmondson, Governor of the State of Oklahoma, as *Amicus Curiae*," in *Baker v. Carr*, 369 U.S. 186 (1962). On the Minnesota case, see *Magraw v. Donovan*, 163 F. Supp. 184 (1958); Gene Graham, *One Man, One Vote: Baker v. Carr and the American Levellers* (Boston: Atlantic Monthly Books, 1972), 95–114.

18. John F. Kennedy, "The Shame of the States," *New York Times Magazine*, May 18, 1958, 12, 37–38, 40.

19. Kennedy, "Shame of the States," 40; "Brief of J. Howard Edmondson"; Gordon E. Baker, *State Constitutions: Reapportionment* (New York: National Municipal League, 1960); *Colegrove v. Green*, 328 U.S. 549 (1946); National Municipal League, "Compendium on Legislative Apportionment," sections on "Alabama," "Oregon," and "Tennessee."

20. Graham, *One Man, One Vote*, 117–78.

21. *Baker v. Carr*, 179 F. Supp. 824 (M.D. Tenn. 1959); "Brief *Amici Curiae* of the National Institute of Municipal Law Officers," filed in *Baker v. Carr*, 369 U.S. 186 (1962).

22. *Baker v. Carr*, 369 U.S. 186 (1962); "Opinions of William J. Brennan, Jr., October Term, 1961," Box 6, Folder 4, Part II, William J. Brennan, Jr., Papers, Library of Congress [hereinafter Brennan Papers].

23. Handwritten note of Earl Warren to William Brennan, Box 64, Folder 4, Part I, Brennan Papers.

24. Transcript of oral arguments in *Baker v. Carr*, October 9, 1961, 36–37 (first quotation), reprinted in Philip B. Kurland and Gerhard Casper, eds., *Landmark Briefs and Arguments of the Supreme Court of the United States: Constitutional Law*, Volume 56 (Arlington, Va.: University Publications of America, 1975), 651–52; Richard C. Cortner, *The Apportionment Cases* (Knoxville: University of Tennessee Press, 1970), 117, 131–32 (second quotation).

25. John F. Kennedy, "News Conference of March 29, 1962," *Public Papers of the Presidents of the United States* (Washington: GPO, 1963), 274; Cortner, *Apportionment Cases*, 144–45; "High Court Rules for Fully Representative Democracy," *Dayton* (Ohio) *Daily News*, March 28, 1962, 26, in Box 1266, Folder 5, William O. Douglas Papers, Library of Congress; *Engel v. Vitale*, 370 U.S. 421 (1962).

26. Cortner, *Apportionment Cases*, Appendix B, 273–76.

27. Author interview with Clarke Stallworth, November 8, 2005, Birmingham, Alabama; Author interview with George Peach Taylor, November 9, 2005, Tuscaloosa, Alabama; Author interview with John McConnell, May 9, 2006, Memphis, Tennessee; Jerome A. Cooper, " 'Segregating Together': Memories of a Birmingham Labor Lawyer," 69–71, Jerome A. Cooper Papers, Birmingham Public Library; Anthony Underwood, *A Progressive History of the Young Men's Business Club of Birmingham, Alabama, 1946–1970*, M.A. thesis, Samford University, 1980; Cortner, *Apportionment Cases*, 160–91.

28. *Sims v. Frink*, 208 F. Supp. 431 (1962).

29. Jack Bass, *Taming the Storm: The Life and Times of Judge Frank M. Johnson, Jr.* (New York: Anchor Books, 1994), 107–72.

30. Taylor Interview; Cortner, *Apportionment Cases*, 160–91.

31. Transcript of oral arguments in *Reynolds v. Sims*, November 13, 1963, 19–25, 34–46 (quotation 19), reprinted in Kurland and Casper, *Landmark Briefs and Arguments*, Volume 58, 997–1003, 1012–24; Cortner, *Apportionment Cases*, 192–221.

32. Transcript of oral arguments in *Reynolds v. Sims*, 46–56, reprinted in Kurland and Casper, *Landmark Briefs and Arguments*, 1024–34; Ken Gormley, *Archibald Cox: Conscience of a Nation* (Reading, Mass.: Addison-Wesley, 1997), 161–81; Cortner, *Apportionment Cases*, 195–98; "Brief for the United States as Amicus Curiae," filed in *Reynolds v. Sims*, 377 U.S. 533 (1962); Author interview with Bruce J. Terris, Washington, D.C., March 29, 2006.

33. *Reynolds v. Sims*, 377 U.S. 533 (first quotation at 555; second quotation at 562–63).

34. Cortner, *Apportionment Cases*, 227–36.

35. *Lucas v. Colorado General Assembly*, 377 U.S. 713 (quotation at 736–37); Cortner, *Apportionment Cases*, 214–19, 232–36.

36. Gormley, *Archibald Cox*, 176–77; Cortner, *Apportionment Cases*, 235–36. The Court rejected the viability of a federal system by reasoning that the original thirteen states were sovereign entities that had agreed to a Senate based on geography, but that counties and other political subdivisions had never been sovereign.

37. Elizabeth Yadlowsky, "Action With Respect To Apportionment of State Legislatures and Congressional Redistricting, 88th Congress," July 16, 1964, revised December 14, 1964, Legislative Reference Service, Library of Congress [hereinafter LRS]; Yadlowsky, "Action With Respect To Apportionment of State Legislatures and Congressional Redistricting in the 89th Congress: Through the Week Ending June 11, 1965," June 14, 1965, LRS; Edward Keynes, *The Dirksen Amendment: A Study of Legislative Strategy, Tactics and Public Policy*, Ph.D. dissertation, University of Wisconsin, 1967; David E. Kyvig, "Everett Dirksen's Constitutional Crusades," *Journal of the Illinois State Historical Society*, 95 (Spring 2002): 68–85; Kyvig, *Explicit and Authentic Acts* (Lawrence: University of Kansas Press, 1996), 370–79.

38. Keynes, "Dirksen Amendment," 143–44; Kyvig, "Everett Dirksen's Constitutional Crusades," 76–83; Kyvig, *Explicit and Authentic Acts*, 370–79; Carey McWilliams, "Government by Whitaker & Baxter," *The Nation,* 172 (April 14, 1951): 346–48; McWilliams, "Government by Whitaker & Baxter, II," *The Nation,* 172 (April 21, 1951): 366–69; McWilliams, "Government by Whitaker & Baxter, III," *The Nation,* 172 (May 5, 1951): 418–21; Irwin Ross, "The Supersalesmen of California Politics: Whitaker & Baxter," *Harper's Magazine,* 219 (July 1959): 55–61; Gabrielle Morris interview with Clement Sherman Whitaker, Jr., 101–15, State Government Oral History Program, CSA.

39. Materials on "Proposition 13: Senate Reapportionment (1948)," Box 8, Whitaker & Baxter Papers, California State Archives, Sacramento [hereinafter W&B Papers]; Newton Stearns to Secretary of State Frank M. Jordan, June 20, 1960, "Original Arguments For and Against Proposition No. 15, 1960 General Election," Secretary of State Election Records, 1960 General Election, Box 2, W&B Papers; Whitaker & Baxter, "Report Presented on Behalf of Californians Against Proposition No. 23: General Election, November 6, 1962," Senator Randolph Collier Papers, LP 229:334, CSA; Bill Boyarsky, "Why They Fight Against Apportionment," *Frontier,* 16 (March 1965): 11–13; C. William Queale to James Dorais, July 30, 1964, Clem Whitaker, Jr., to Sigvald Nielson, September 3, 1964, Sigvald Nielson to C. William Queale, Box 97, Folder "C. William Queale," W&B Papers; Press Release, March 8, 1965, Box 96, Folder "News Releases," W&B Papers; Lists of financial contributions, Box 99, "Solicitation (Correspondence, 1965–66)," W&B Papers.

40. James Musatti to Committee Members, November 29, 1965, Clem Whitaker, Jr., to Committee Members, November 30, 1965, Box 101 (unlabeled folder), W&B Papers; Press Release, January 19, 1966, Everett Dirksen Working Papers, Folder 2275, Everett McKinley Dirksen Papers, Dirksen Congressional Center, Pekin, Illinois; Interview with Clem Whitaker, 101–15, CSA.

41. Lists of financial contributions located in Box 99, "Contributions (Solicitation Lists)," W&B Papers; Complete set of press releases and all other activities undertaken by Whitaker & Baxter, in "Report to the Advisory Committee, Committee for Government of the People," May 6, 1966, Dirksen Working Papers, Folders 2284–88.

42. "Congress: Three-Time Loser," *Newsweek,* May 2, 1966, 19–20; Yadlowsky, "State Petitions and Memorials to Congress on the Subject of Apportionment of State Legislatures: 87th Congress—90th Congress," June 11, 1965, revised and updated by Johnny H. Killian, February 1, 1968, LRS; Various memos, Box 100, "State Check 1967," W&B Papers; Clem Whitaker, Jr., to Everett Dirksen, June 11, 1968, and other correspondence, Box 102, "Hold File: Reapportionment Current," W&B Papers; Everett Dirksen to Ted Stevens and John Butrovic, n.d., Ted Stevens to Clem Whitaker, Jr., April 14, 1967, Whitaker to Carl D. McMurray, February 16, 1967, Box 101, "Alaska," W&B Papers; Interview with Clem Whitaker, 104, CSA.

43. Kyvig, "Everett Dirksen's Constitutional Crusades," 76–83; Kyvig, *Explicit and Authentic Acts*, 370–79; E. W. Kenworthy, "A Political Phenomenon," *New York Times*, September 8, 1969, 1, 26; "Wisconsin Refuses to Become 34th State to Adopt Dirksen Plan," *New York Times*, November 5, 1969, 37.

44. George B. Merry, "Putting the Houses in Order," *Christian Science Monitor*, October 29, 1968, second section, 1; Cortner, *Apportionment Cases*, 253 (quotation); Johnny H. Killian, "Legislative Apportionment: The Background and Current Status of Developments in Each of the Fifty States," January 1966, 227–29, LRS.

45. Karl E. Meyer, "Shame of the States," *New Statesman,* 63 (April 6, 1962): 478.

46. William J. D. Boyd, "Suburbia Takes Over," *National Civic Review,* June 1965, 294–98; "One Person, One Vote—Who Wins, Who Loses," *U. S. News & World Report,* August 23, 1965, 42–44; Congressional Quarterly Service, "Representation and Apportionment" (Washington: Congressional Quarterly, 1966), 38–41.

47. Boyd, "Suburbia Takes Over," 294–98.

48. "Sweeping Decision," *Newsweek,* 63 (June 29, 1964): 22, 25; "After Redistricting Decision," *U. S. News & World Report,* 57 (July 6, 1964), 34–36; Congressional Quarterly Service, "Representation and Apportionment," 43–44; Bruce F. Norton, "Recent Supreme Court Decisions on Apportionment: Their Political Impact," LRS, August 12, 1964, 8–16; 88th Congress, Second Session, Senate; "The 1964 Platform of Republican National Convention," *Congressional Record* 110 (July 22, 1964); Keynes, "Dirksen Amendment," 88–92; Graham, *One Man, One Vote*, 272–73.

49. Graham, *One Man, One Vote*, 21–22, 274–75 (quotation 22).

50. Bill Kovach, "Some Lessons on Reapportionment," *The Reporter,* 37 (September 21, 1967): 26–32; Kenneth T. Jackson, *Crabgrass Frontier: The Suburbanization of the United States* (New York: Oxford University Press, 1985), 241–45.

51. Norton, "Recent Supreme Court Decisions on Apportionment," 28; *Vieth v. Jubelirer*, 541 U.S. 267 (2004); *Cox v. Larios*, 542 U.S. 947 (2004); *League of United Latin American Citizens v. Perry*, 126 S. Ct. 2594 (2006).

12

BEYOND THE SOUTHERN CROSS

The National Origins of the Religious Right

Kevin M. Kruse

In the popular imagination, the modern Religious Right is a creation of fundamentalist and evangelical Christians from the South. In recent decades, with leaders like the Reverends Jerry Falwell and Pat Robertson of Virginia serving as its most visible spokesmen and institutions such as the Southern Baptist Convention providing an activist core, assumptions about the southern roots of the Religious Right are certainly understandable. In truth, however, the initial political mobilization of religious conservatives stemmed from a much broader landscape, in terms of both region and religion. Geographically, the Religious Right represented a constituency stretching across the country. Supporters came from every state in the nation, with prominent religious and lay leaders hailing from the Midwest and Southwest almost as frequently as from the South. In its denominational scope, meanwhile, the movement extended well beyond the evangelical and fundamentalist faith of its most celebrated spokesmen, bringing together orthodox religious figures from a wide variety of Protestant denominations with like-minded Catholics, Jews, and Mormons.

Traditional narratives of the Religious Right have depicted these alliances across regions and religions as something of an afterthought to a political mobilization that began with evangelical and fundamentalist Christians in the South and only later extended to other parts of the country. Most famously, at a 1979 meeting in Lynchburg, Virginia—a meeting that would lead to the creation (and christening) of the Moral Majority— the New Right activist Paul Weyrich made the case for a coalition that extended beyond the independent Baptist preachers from the South who were gathered around him. "Out there is what one might call a moral majority—people who would agree on principles based on the Decalogue [the Ten Commandments], for example—but they have been separated by geographical and denominational differences and that has caused them to vote differently," he noted. "The key to any kind of political impact is to get these people united in some way, so they can see that they are battling the same thing and need to be unified."[1]

Closer inspection shows that the national alliances forged by this nascent Religious Right were taking shape long before the late 1970s. While leaders of the movement only belatedly recognized the commonalities between evangelical and fundamentalist southerners and other religious conservatives across the country, those at the grassroots had, in truth, been moving in common directions for decades. In their eyes, their movement never advocated a narrow ideology representative of a single sect or section but, rather, defended an ecumenical religious nationalism that embraced all traditional believers, regardless of their location or denomination. Only by adopting a national perspective, then, can scholars contextualize the fundamental convictions of the Religious Right—the firm belief that the nation was bound together by its shared religious faith and the fear that disaster would strike America if its faith should falter.

The roots of religious nationalism can be found not in a peculiar *place*— the antiquated "Christ-haunted South" of Flannery O'Connor's imagination—but, rather, in a particular *time*. During the international crisis and the domestic anticommunist panic of the early Cold War, the vast majority of Americans, regardless of their region or religion, came to understand their loyalties to God and to country as one and the same. They readily embraced a new religious nationalism, an ideology in which piety and patriotism were inextricably intertwined. While southern fundamentalist and evangelical Christians ultimately came to advance this worldview in stronger terms and adhered to it in greater numbers than other Americans, they were not solely, or even chiefly, responsible for its creation. Instead, a broadly ecumenical movement of Protestants, Catholics, and Jews led the way. Moreover, when the tenets of Cold War Christianity came under attack in later decades, southerners were not the first to rush to its defense in the political realm; religious leaders from the North, Midwest, and West took charge. In the final reckoning, the cause of religious nationalism was, not surprisingly, a national one.

Although its roots stretched back for centuries, American religious nationalism underwent a strong resurgence during the mid-twentieth century. As the Second World War drew near, political leaders feared that the foreign loyalties of more recent immigrants and even some old-stock citizens would lead to a paralyzing divisiveness on the home front, as various Americans allied themselves with their mother countries. To unite the people, civic leaders and government officials downplayed ethnic loyalties and instead stressed a religious heritage that they insisted all Americans held in common. Thus, a relatively new concept—the idea of a "Judeo-Christian tradition" running through American history and life—ascended to a place of prominence. Meanwhile, new "interfaith" organizations such as the National Conference for Christians and Jews (NCCJ) likewise stressed that Protestantism, Catholicism, and Judaism represented "the religions of democracy." Because these "three great faiths" shared the same spiritual heritage and moral codes that made the nation strong, doctrinal differences were largely irrelevant. "In all things religious," the NCCJ argued, "we Catholics, Jews and Protestants can be as separate as the fingers on a man's outstretched hand; in all things civic and American, we can be as united as a man's clenched fist."[2]

The connections between the three "religions of democracy" and American nationalism grew even stronger in the postwar era. "There is a religious boom on," noted Paul Hutchinson, editor of *Christian Century*. "Almost any clergyman or rabbi can swamp you with statistics to prove it." Indeed, while church attendance had slipped dramatically in previous decades, the 1950 census revealed that 59 percent of Americans now claimed a specific denominational affiliation. According to Gallup polls, church membership continued to grow at astounding rates during the early years of the Cold War, reaching 79 percent at mid-decade. By then, the amount spent on construction of new churches and synagogues topped $500 million annually and continued to climb. Sales of the Holy Bible, meanwhile, doubled between 1947 and 1952. Within a year of its publication in 1952, the Revised Standard Version sold more than 2 million copies; even then, printers kept presses rolling for years to meet the demand. Opinion polls asking which occupations were "doing the most good for the country" ranked religious leaders at the top. Unlike past religious booms, which had been marked by religious rivalry as much as religious revival, Americans did not see this latest resurgence as a competition among the main faiths. Instead, they viewed increasing religiosity as a unifying process that strengthened the nation as a whole. "In the last analysis," observed sociologist Will Herberg, "Protestant and Catholic and Jew stand united through their common anchorage in, and common allegiance to, the American Way of Life."[3]

Connections between this newfound "Judeo-Christian tradition" and American national identity were forged in the crucible of the Cold War. Regardless of their differences in terms of politics, religion, or region, most Americans agreed that the danger of communism lay not just in the military might of the Soviet Union but also in the spiritual threat of an ideology that rejected God. Republican Senator Joseph McCarthy of Wisconsin, a staunchly conservative Catholic, argued in 1950 that communism sought to destroy "all the honesty and decency that every

Protestant, Jew and Catholic [had] been taught at his mother's knee." Illinois Governor Adlai Stevenson, a liberal Unitarian who twice stood as the Democratic presidential nominee, wholly shared this interpretation of the "communist menace." "The anti-Christ stalks our world," he warned in 1952. "Organized communism seeks even to dethrone God from his central place in the universe. It attempts to uproot everywhere it goes the gentle and restraining influences of the religion of love and peace. One by one, the lamps of civilization go out." In pointed contrast to "godless communists," almost all Americans stressed their nation's religious heritage. "Our form of government," president-elect Dwight Eisenhower noted in 1952, "has no sense unless it is founded in a deeply-felt religious faith, and I don't care what it is. With us, of course, it is the Judeo-Christian concept, but it must be a religion that all men are created equal."[4]

During the two-term Eisenhower presidency, the federal government readily embraced the trappings of an ecumenical religious nationalism. The new president had never before belonged to a church, but he quickly converted to Presbyterianism, becoming the first chief executive to be baptized in the White House. Eisenhower also instituted the practice of an opening prayer at his very first cabinet meeting and likewise inaugurated the now-annual tradition of the presidential prayer breakfast. Congress, meanwhile, confirmed its understanding of the nation's religious identity in more concrete ways. In 1955, for instance, legislators added a prayer room to the Capitol building. To underscore its nonsectarian nature, the room's design reflected input from the two Protestant congressional chaplains, the assistant chancellor of the Roman Catholic Archdiocese of Washington, and the rabbi of the Washington Hebrew Congregation. In 1956, Congress passed a measure requiring that all first- and second-class mail be stamped with a reminder to "Pray for Peace." According to the bill's Catholic sponsor, the new postmark would serve as testament to "our dependence upon God and of our faith in his support" in the face of "ever-increasing attacks upon us by the forces of godlessness and atheism." That same year, Congress underscored its reliance on heavenly guidance by changing the nation's official motto to "In God We Trust." The phrase, which had appeared on American coins since the Civil War, would now grace postage stamps and paper currency as well. "As long as this country trusts in God," noted one of its many sponsors, "it will prevail."[5]

Of all the symbolic representations of the new religious nationalism, perhaps none was as significant as the addition of the phrase "under God" to the Pledge of Allegiance in 1954. Once again, the new religious symbolism had ecumenical origins. A Catholic fraternal organization, the Knights of Columbus, first proposed the change in 1952, but it would take a sermon from a Presbyterian minister, Reverend George Docherty, to make it manifest. Speaking to a Washington congregation that included the president and his wife, Docherty complained that something was missing from the pledge: "the characteristic and definitive factor in the American way of life." He observed that "apart from the mention of the phrase 'the United States of America,' it could be the pledge of any republic." Since only America was truly "one nation under God," Docherty urged the addition of that specific phrase to the pledge. Seventeen bills to require the change soon appeared in Congress, where support once again transcended divisions of party, region, and religion. "Let us join together, Protestant, Jew and Catholic, in taking this action," urged Congressman Peter Rodino, a Catholic Democrat from New Jersey. Not surprisingly, President Eisenhower readily endorsed the proposal. "We are reaffirming the transcendence of religious faith in America's heritage and future," he noted at the bill's signing. "In this way, we shall constantly strengthen those spiritual weapons which forever will be our country's most powerful resource, in peace or war."[6]

In such an environment, the concurrent rise of religious nationalism in evangelical and fundamentalist circles seemed wholly within the mainstream. Like their counterparts in other denominations, leading evangelicals encouraged the view that communism threatened religion. "Communism," Reverend Billy Graham thundered during a 1949 revival, "has decided against God, against Christ, against the Bible, and against all religion. Communism is not only an economic interpretation of life— communism is a religion that is inspired, directed, and motivated by the Devil himself who has declared war against Almighty God." As the Cold War intensified, so too did this evangelical attitude about the threat of communism. In 1960, for example, the National Association of Evangelicals (NAE)—an organization representing nearly forty denominations, some 28,000 churches, and 2 million evangelicals nationwide—issued an unequivocal defense of American anticommunism. "There is no such thing as a compromise with atheistic Communism," the NAE declared. "We cannot pursue a policy of 'live and let live' with Hell."[7]

Like many other Americans, evangelical and fundamentalist Christians argued that a religious revival represented the nation's only hope for salvation. Throughout the 1950s and 1960s, organizations such as Reverend Billy James Hargis's Christian Crusade, Reverend Carl McIntire's American Council of Christian Churches (ACCC), and Dr. Fred Schwarz's Christian Anti-Communism Crusade (CACC) campaigned aggressively for an America in which God and country were intricately intertwined. While all three stood further to the political right than the NAE, they shared with that organization a common message that Christian values were the true source of America's past strength and a widespread revival its only hope for survival. "I believe Christian people have to be political as well as religious," Hargis argued. "I don't think we are full Americans if we're not concerned about our nation and our politics as well as our faith." Notably, despite later assumptions about the distinctly southern roots of the

Religious Right, all three organizations were located outside the South. Hargis's Christian Crusade was headquartered in Tulsa, Oklahoma; McIntire's American Council of Christian Churches in Collingswood, New Jersey; and Schwarz's Christian Anti-Communist Crusade in Long Beach, California.[8]

While rooted in different regions, all three sought to have an impact on the national stage. Hargis and McIntire engaged in significant outreach programs through the media, spreading the gospel of religious nationalism simultaneously over the airwaves and in print. Between 1960 and 1964, Hargis's *Christian Crusade* newsletter nearly doubled its circulation from 58,000 to 98,600, while McIntire's *Christian Beacon* more than tripled its subscribers, from 20,000 to 66,500. Their radio presence was even more significant. In 1958, McIntire had been preaching the gospel of God and country over a single radio station; by 1964, 540 stations carried his program. Hargis took a different approach, using incredibly powerful Mexican superstations to blanket the South, Midwest, and Southwest with his nightly "Bad News" broadcasts. Meanwhile, Schwarz relied on a more personal appeal, traveling roughly 100,000 miles a year to hold rallies and weeklong "Anti-Communist Schools" across the country. These CACC programs commanded major venues and trumpeted appearances by local congressmen, national politicians, and conservative celebrities such as Ronald Reagan, John Wayne, and Pat Boone. A 1962 CACC tour of New York City, for example, featured an 8,000-person rally at Madison Square Garden, followed by a five-day-long anticommunism school at Carnegie Hall. That same year, the CACC held similar events in Los Angeles at the Shrine Auditorium and the Ambassador Hotel. In a sign of its growing popularity, CACC contributions doubled every year between 1957 and 1960 and then quadrupled in 1961, when the group received more than $1,250,000 in donations. Hargis's Christian Crusade, meanwhile, raised around $800,000 a year during the same era, while McIntire's organization saw contributions increase from less than $600,000 in 1958 to more than $3,200,000 in 1964.[9]

These organizations of conservative evangelicals and fundamentalists thrived in the late 1950s and early 1960s not because they stood outside the mainstream of American thought but because they reflected it so well. During the early years of the Cold War, the new conceptualization of America as a religious nation—firmly rooted in a "Judeo-Christian tradition," long sustained by religious faith, and now threatened by "godless communism"—became firmly entrenched in the popular imagination. Enshrined in mainstream discourse, the ideas and ideals of religious nationalism quickly seemed the norm. And when challenges to this reinvigorated union of God and country arose in the coming decades, many of these same religious conservatives would rise up to defend that union and, by extension, the country as a whole. Southern evangelicals and fundamentalists would, of course, eventually stand at the forefront of this movement. But in the earliest years of the political mobilization of religious conservatives, figures from other regions and religions led the way.

For conservative Christians, the first real attack on the religious nationalism of the Cold War era—and, as a result, the first real spark for their own political mobilization—came in a pair of U.S. Supreme Court rulings against prayer in public schools. Previously, religious conservatives had directed their energies against enemies looming outside the country, but the Court's decisions represented, in their eyes, a new threat rising from within. The first case, *Engel v. Vitale* (1962), involved the daily recitation of a nondenominational prayer composed by the New York Board of Regents: "Almighty God, we acknowledge our dependence on Thee, and we beg Thy blessings upon us, our parents, our teachers and our Country." The second, *Abington v. Schempp* (1963), arose from a requirement in Pennsylvania's public schools for daily readings from the Bible. In both cases, education officials had assumed such broadly drawn religious practices were perfectly acceptable. "We didn't have the slightest idea that the prayer we wrote would prove so controversial," a former chancellor of the New York Regents reflected. "At the time, one rabbi said he didn't see how anybody could take offense." The Supreme Court saw the matter differently, however, and declared both practices unconstitutional violations of the First Amendment's establishment clause.[10]

Although the Justices went to great lengths to reassure the nation that the rulings did not affect the "many manifestations in our public life of belief in God," countless Americans feared that the Cold War symbols of religious nationalism, only recently enshrined, would now be discarded. Indeed, of the thousands of complaints sent to the Court, the vast majority made direct invocations of such symbols. "All Americans are aware that our country was founded on faith in God," wrote a woman from Houston. "It is this faith that has made us a great nation, with our motto, 'In God We Trust,' and will continue to keep us so." "Is th[e] next step to be to declare unconstitutional the Congressional act of a few years ago inserting the phrase 'under God' in the Allegiance to the flag?" worried an Alabama Baptist. "And will the words 'In God We Trust' be stricken from our money? And will the Bible be taken from the courts of the land and from the Inaugural ceremonies of the president of the United States?" "How about next time around lets abolish all references to God in official documents," added a Fort Lauderdale woman. "Then the third time around lets imprison anyone mentioning God or attending a religious service, & fourth time around—set up the firing squad, & fifth—get your silver platter out & hand us over to you know who."[11]

The widespread outrage of religious conservatives testified to the power of religious nationalism in Cold War America. To their surprise, however, the major faiths that had so recently stood united now seemed in disarray, with only a few denominations offering strong opposition. The Catholic hierarchy took the lead and condemned *Engel* immediately. "The decision strikes at the very heart of the Godly tradition in which America's children have for so long been raised," said Francis Cardinal Spellman of New York. James Francis Cardinal McIntyre of Los Angeles likewise called the decision "shocking and scandalizing." Leaders in the Mormon Church were just as swift to denounce the Court. Mormon President David O. McKay lambasted *Engel* for severing "the connecting cord between the public schools of the United States and the source of divine intelligence, the Creator himself." *Schempp*, meanwhile, showed that the Court was "leading a Christian nation down the road to atheism." In contrast, other denominations reacted slowly, if at all. Indeed, in most of the mainline Protestant churches, clergy and lay leaders either supported the rulings or found themselves deeply divided on the matter. The Methodist General Conference, for instance, had to table a resolution in favor of the prayer rulings after a vote of 341 to 339.[12]

For their part, evangelicals and fundamentalists offered a mixed reaction. Initially *Engel* caused little alarm within either camp. Except for Billy Graham, few evangelical leaders denounced the decision, while fundamentalists seemed even less concerned. Carl McIntire explained that prayer "without the name of Jesus Christ was not a non-denominational prayer—it was simply a pagan prayer" and thus not worth the worry. *Schempp*'s prohibition of Bible reading, however, prompted many evangelicals and fundamentalists to action. McIntire denounced the second Supreme Court ruling in no uncertain terms. "A greater issue is at stake than simply Bible reading in the schools," he noted. "At stake is whether or not America may continue to honor and recognize God in the life of the nation." Likewise, the National Association of Evangelicals, which had grudgingly supported *Engel*, quickly denounced *Schempp* and called for a constitutional amendment to protect prayer and Bible reading in public schools. Other networks of evangelicals and fundamentalists, however, remained unmoved by either decision. In keeping with their traditional opposition to state control of religion, both the American Baptist Convention and the Southern Baptist Convention actually praised the rulings as guarantees of individual religious freedom.[13]

The uneven reaction of the major religious organizations to the school prayer rulings masked a widespread popular resentment. A 1962 Gallup poll showed that 79 percent of Americans supported school prayer, with the sentiment spread fairly evenly across the nation. In retrospect, visceral reactions from Lynchburg, Virginia, the small southern town that would later give rise to the ministry of Reverend Jerry Falwell, would not seem surprising. But similar outrage emerged across the continent in metropolitan Los Angeles. Indeed, opponents of the decision in these two communities expressed their anger in nearly identical terms. After the rulings, the mayor of Lynchburg wrote Chief Justice Earl Warren to explain "the real feeling of the people on a 'grass-roots' level....I am constantly being approached by people in all walks of life," the mayor noted. "It is almost unbelievable the amount of anxiety, mistrust, and disgust that is present among them. I have had businessmen whom I have known for years to almost shed tears" [talking about the decision]. Such shock and anger echoed in the suburbs of Los Angeles. "Here in Long Beach," a woman noted, "everyone from the checker in the market, the cashier in the coffee shop, to the beachcomber... is shaking his head in disbelief and wonder and, sometimes, rage." Despite their different surroundings, these religious conservatives had common reactions and sought common solutions. "I am concerned that the Supreme Court has carried the matter of individual freedom so far as to permit the atheistic minority to deprive the religious majority of a way of life which they hold dear, and one upon which our nation was founded," noted a minister from Lynchburg. "I think it is time for solid thinking Americans to rise up and do something about it." "From the buzzing around here," wrote a Long Beach resident in similar, if sharper terms, "angry hornets are about to descend on the stupid boys who poked the hornets' nest!"[14]

With resentment over the rulings widespread, religious conservatives swiftly rallied around a proposal to amend the U.S. Constitution to allow prayer and Bible reading in public schools. Just eight days after the *Engel* decision, all of the nation's governors—with the lone exception of New York's Nelson Rockefeller—issued a resolution urging such an amendment. Members of Congress reported that half of their constituent correspondence during the 1963–1964 term focused on the school prayer amendment, with letters in favor outweighing those against by a stunning margin of 20 to 1. In the two years following *Engel*, more than one hundred congressmen submitted versions of such an amendment, with support eventually coalescing around proposals from Republican Congressman Frank Becker in the House and Republican Minority Leader Everett Dirksen in the Senate. Meanwhile, a "Citizens Congressional Committee" formed to lobby aggressively on the bills' behalf. "Our Committee represents zealous, enthusiastic, and uncompromising individuals in every state and in every Congressional district in the nation," its leaders warned legislators. "We are now in a campaign to challenge every member of Congress to take a fighting stand in defense of the right of Christian devotions in our public institutions." As proof of their support, the committee noted that its petition was nearing three miles in length.[15]

Despite popular support in the South for the school-prayer amendment, the organizational energy came largely from other regions (figure 12.1). In political terms, none of the amendment's major sponsors or supporters was a southerner. Senator Dirksen and Congressman Becker represented

Illinois and New York, respectively, while the Citizens Congressional Committee had its headquarters in Los Angeles. In religious terms, the main thrust again came from the North and Midwest. The only religious bodies to testify on behalf of the 1966 Dirksen Amendment were the Greek Orthodox Diocese of North and South America, the National Association of Evangelicals, and the American Council of Christian Churches. Greek Orthodox headquarters were in New York City; the NAE had been founded in St. Louis and was based in Wheaton, Illinois; and the ACCC, the fundamentalist network led by Carl McIntire, operated from New Jersey. Efforts to enshrine religious nationalism into the Constitution and to legalize Bible reading and prayer in schools certainly had the support of southerners, but it was largely passive in nature.[16]

Although southern evangelicals and fundamentalists would become incredibly active in the politics of religious nationalism in later decades, they remained reluctant to get involved in the 1960s. Reverend Jerry Falwell, the future co-founder of the Moral Majority, originally refused to enter the political sphere. During the 1965 civil rights campaign in Selma,

FIGURE 12.1. The opposition of religious conservatives to the Supreme Court's decisions in the early 1960s banning officially sanctioned prayer and Bible reading in public schools has always been a national phenomenon. On March 7, 1984, more than two decades after these rulings, students representing all fifty states gathered in front of the U.S. Capitol for a school prayer rally sponsored by the Moral Majority. © Bettmann/CORBIS.

Alabama, he delivered a now-famous sermon, "Ministers and Marches," denouncing the involvement of religious figures in worldly affairs. "Preachers are not called to be politicians," Falwell cautioned. "Nowhere are we commissioned to reform the externals. We are not told to wage wars against bootleggers, liquor stores, gamblers, murderers, prostitutes, racketeers, prejudiced persons or institutions, or any other existing evil as such." True to his word, Falwell refused to take part in any political activity, even resigning a post in Lynchburg's antipoverty program in 1966 on grounds that it was "political" and therefore "not consistent with my calling as a minister of the Gospel." Reverend Pat Robertson, meanwhile, refused even to assist the 1966 reelection campaign of his father, U.S. Senator A. Willis Robertson. "I yearned to get into the fray," he later wrote, "but the Lord refused to give me the liberty. 'I have called you to my ministry,' he spoke to my heart. 'You cannot tie my eternal purposes to the success of any political candidate,... not even your own father.'" In a similar fashion, the Southern Baptist Convention remained purposefully aloof from political issues during the decade. Even efforts of moderate Baptists to pass a resolution at the 1968 convention that simply noted their concern over poverty and racism prompted a backlash among conservatives who worried about any involvement in worldly matters.[17]

Rather than enter the political battle over prayer in the public schools, many southern religious conservatives instead turned inward, working to develop private religious academies. Much of the literature on private Christian schools has focused exclusively on southern institutions, encouraging the impression that they were, in the parlance of the day, nothing more than "segregation academies" established to evade the court-ordered desegregation then sweeping through the region.[18] For many southern white conservatives, rulings against school prayer dovetailed with federal mandates for racial desegregation to convince them that the public schools had been lost to them forever. In its most famous formulation, this attitude was best represented in a complaint from Congressman George Andrews of Alabama: "They put the Negroes in the schools, and now they've driven God out." While racial motivations played a significant role in the creation of many private academies in the South, and in the decisions of countless parents to send their children to them, the regional reaction against the civil rights movement does not entirely explain the rise of private Christian schools across the country, especially in those regions where the political culture of Jim Crow had little history.[19]

For many involved in the Christian schools movement, both inside and outside the South, religious issues were the main concern. In late 1966, Reverend Falwell announced plans to open his own private religious school, Lynchburg Christian Academy, the following year. Although the *Lynchburg News* originally described the school as a "private academy for white students," Lynchburg Christian soon enrolled a few black students and helped refute charges that it had been inspired simply by racism. Instead, Falwell insisted, his primary motivation remained the rulings against public school prayer and other developments that indicated "the Christian world view was not only going to be pushed back but eliminated, and that another might replace it." Looking outside the South reveals that Falwell's complaints were echoed in countless other communities where court orders against segregated schooling were not as prominent. Conservative religious parents in Los Angeles continued to express concerns about secular public schools in language very similar to that found in Lynchburg. A suburban mother in Southern California found it "frightening to consider how atheistic thinking has and is infiltrating our schools." "In a true educational system," a Los Angeles parent complained, "patriotism, literature, art and science would be brought together with a faith in God in such a way in the daily lives of boys and girls as to affect their character and conduct throughout life. But in our 'progressive' system of education these things, broadly speaking, do not exist."[20]

Not surprisingly, private school growth in California closely paralleled the growth of Christian schools in the South. Reverend Tim LaHaye, a Baptist minister from Southern California who would help co-found the Moral Majority, was even more involved in the private school movement than Falwell. LaHaye's Scott Memorial Church owned and operated four grammar schools, two high schools, a college, and an Institute for Creation Research. Scattered across three separate campuses in the San Diego suburbs, the academies were large enough to constitute their own independent school district, the San Diego Christian Unified School System. LaHaye was by no means the only conservative leader involved in Christian academies there. By the early 1980s, there were more than 150 private religious schools in San Diego County alone. That local pattern was repeated throughout the state and nation. By Falwell's count, only 1,400 Christian schools were scattered across the country in the early 1960s, but well over 16,000 existed by 1980. Notably, many of the evangelical and fundamentalist leaders who would later play prominent roles in the Religious Right first became active in the Christian school movement. Looking over the background of state chairmen for the Moral Majority, one study discovered that twenty-five out of twenty-eight had previously sponsored Christian schools of their own.[21]

For much of the 1970s, these fundamentalist and evangelical leaders, especially those in the South, remained busy creating their own private schools and stayed, for the most part, outside the public realm of politics. As a result, when even greater threats to the worldview of conservative Protestants and Catholics emerged in the early 1970s—most notably, in the 1972 congressional proposal for an Equal Rights Amendment to the U.S. Constitution and the 1973 *Roe v. Wade* Supreme Court ruling supporting abortion rights—the duty to defend that worldview fell to others.

By the end of the 1970s, evangelical leaders in the South and elsewhere regularly condemned the proposed Equal Rights Amendment (ERA) as a threat to the divinely prescribed order of relationships between men and women. At the beginning of the decade, however, they remained unengaged in what would become a signature struggle of the Religious Right. *Christianity Today*, the leading publication for evangelical Protestants, even gave the ERA its enthusiastic support in 1970. "Simple justice," the magazine admonished, "calls for action." While *Christianity Today* gradually qualified this endorsement, its original stance showed that evangelicals were far from united against the ERA. In a similar vein, the Southern Baptist Convention never took a formal position on the amendment during the initial seven-year ratification period, waiting until 1980 to express its opposition. As southern evangelical leaders sat on the sidelines, other religious conservatives stepped forward. None was more important than Phyllis Schlafly, an archconservative Catholic activist from Illinois whose political career originated in the Cold War crusade against communism. Her husband had lectured for the Christian Anti-Communism Crusade; in her own writings, Schlafly advanced a similar-sounding defense of religious nationalism. In February 1972, she published an antifeminist manifesto that set forth the essential arguments of the anti-ERA movement, "What's Wrong with 'Equal Rights' for Women?" She argued that the family, not the individual, was "the basic unit of society, which is ingrained in the laws and customs of our Judeo-Christian civilization [and] is the single greatest achievement in the history of women's rights." In September 1972, Schlafly founded STOP ERA (Stop Taking Our Privileges), an organization that became the pivotal force of the anti-ERA movement.[22]

Religious conservatives rallied around Schlafly. According to one study, an overwhelming 98 percent of anti-ERA activists belonged to a church. Despite her own devout Catholicism, Schlafly encouraged a broadly ecumenical approach. "Our movement brought together...Protestants of all denominations, Catholics, Mormons, and Orthodox Jews," she recalled in a 1996 interview. "At our meetings, I taught them that, although they might be sitting next to someone who might not be saved, we could nevertheless work together on behalf of a political/social goal we all shared." In truth, while the national organization did embrace religious diversity, those local meetings were often dominated by a single faith. In Midwestern states such as Illinois, the organization was overwhelmingly Roman Catholic. In Mountain West states such as Utah, Nevada, and Arizona, much of the membership was Mormon. In Oklahoma, most key activists came from the Church of Christ. In the South, STOP ERA organizations were staffed by the Church of Christ and Southern Baptists, as well as members of smaller fundamentalist and independent Baptist churches. Interestingly, in many southern states, the presence of Church of Christ members in anti-ERA organizations was much more pronounced than their numbers in the general population. North Carolina's population, for example, was 23 percent Baptist and 0.2 percent Church of Christ, and yet the latter actually outnumbered the former in anti-ERA organizations, 45 to 36 percent. In Texas, Baptists accounted for 20 percent of the general population but only 9 percent of the anti-ERA activists; Church of Christ members, meanwhile, formed merely 2 percent of the state population but 60 percent of the anti-ERA base.[23]

Much as Southern Baptists were overshadowed in the anti-ERA struggle at the state level, southern states were likewise eclipsed in the national struggle. Histories of the ERA effort typically stress the initial rush of states moving to approve the amendment; by the end of 1974, thirty-three states had ratified the amendment, just five short of the needed total. During the same period, however, seventeen states rushed just as quickly to *reject* the ERA. Notably, that number included ten of the eleven states of the former Confederacy. Louisiana led the way in June 1972, followed swiftly by Arkansas, Virginia, Mississippi, North Carolina, South Carolina, Florida, and Alabama over the next twelve months. Georgia also rejected the ERA in January 1974. Technically, the amendment could be revisited in each state legislature, but none would reverse course. Indeed, the only southern state to change its stance was Tennessee, which passed the ERA during the initial rush for ratification but voted to rescind its support and reject the amendment in April 1974. By that time, the lines in the ERA struggle had been drawn, with all ten southeastern states forming a solid bloc of opposition. As a result, when the political struggle over the amendment peaked in the late 1970s and early 1980s, both sides focused their energies elsewhere, on the remaining swing states. These were located largely in the Midwest and Mountain West, with Illinois emerging as what one historian has termed "the most hard-fought state" of the ratification fight. Because the state organizations of STOP ERA in these regions were dominated by Catholics or Mormons, figures from those faiths stood at the forefront of the anti-ERA struggle in its climactic years (figure 12.2). In the end, the defeat of the ERA depended on *their* resistance, and not that of southern evangelicals, who were marginalized throughout the struggle.[24]

In an even more pronounced fashion, Catholics emerged as the key figures in the early "pro-life" movement. As they mobilized opposition to both birth control and abortion law liberalization in the late 1960s and early 1970s, Catholic leaders found evangelical Christians taking moderate to liberal stances on the issue. "In general, I would disagree with [the Catholic stance]," Billy Graham announced in 1968. "I believe in planned parenthood." That same year, twenty-five evangelical scholars issued a "Protestant Affirmation on the Control of Human Reproduction," in which they asserted that "abortion must be considered under certain circumstances." Baptist leaders, in particular, took this view. In 1970, an internal survey of Baptist ministers and lay leaders revealed widespread

FIGURE 12.2. Senators Jesse Helms (R-North Carolina, a Southern Baptist) and Orrin Hatch (R-Utah, a Mormon) with conservative activist Phyllis Schlafly, the Catholic and Illinois-based founder of STOP ERA, at a banquet in Washington on March 22, 1979. Schlafly worked to mobilize the Religious Right as an ecumenical and transregional force, as did her ally Jerry Falwell through the Moral Majority. This event celebrated the coalition of states in the South, Midwest, and Mountain West that had refused to ratify the Equal Rights Amendment. © AP Images/Charles Tasnadi.

support for abortion law liberalization. In cases where the woman's health was threatened by a pregnancy, nearly 70 percent of Baptist pastors and nearly 80 percent of Sunday School teachers supported abortion rights; in cases of rape or incest, 70 and 77 percent, respectively; and in cases of deformity of the unborn, 64 and 76 percent. Even Dr. W. A. Criswell, a fundamentalist minister who would later lead the conservative take-over of the Southern Baptist Convention, initially expressed a fairly liberal viewpoint on abortion. "I have always felt that it was only after a child was born and had life separate from its mother... that it became an individual person," he told *Christianity Today* a month after *Roe*. "It has always, therefore, seemed to me that what is best for the mother and for the future should be allowed."[25]

Catholic leaders thus created the pro-life movement largely on their own. Following the directives of Vatican II, the National Conference of

Catholic Bishops (NCCB) established what would become the leading anti-abortion umbrella organization of the 1970s, the National Right to Life Committee (NRLC). In its early years, the NRLC was so thoroughly a Catholic organization that it operated directly out of the NCCB offices. Only after *Roe*, with the recognition that abortion was becoming a polarizing political issue, did the Catholic Church make the committee an independent lay organization. In a conscious effort to attract members of other faiths, the NRLC elevated three consecutive Protestants to its presidency from 1973 to 1980. Despite these attempts to give the organization a Protestant face, its rank-and-file remained overwhelmingly Catholic. In 1974, an NRLC official estimated that non-Catholic membership amounted to less than 15 percent of the total; six years later, a survey showed that it still remained below 30 percent.[26]

For evangelicals, their longstanding assumption that abortion was a specifically "Catholic issue" was difficult to shake. Harold O. J. Brown, a prominent evangelical theologian, later recalled that the "fact that Catholics were out in front caused many Protestants to keep a low profile." Many, he said, had the attitude that "'if the Catholics are for it, we should be against it.'" In the years after *Roe*, however, a few pro-life evangelical leaders sought to win over their co-religionists. Now under a more conservative editorial hand, *Christianity Today* tried to rally its readers to the cause. In a 1976 editorial, "Is Abortion a Catholic Issue?" the magazine dismissed the titular question as a "smokescreen" and urged evangelicals to stop worrying about Catholic political influence and to start worrying about "the most fundamental of human rights, the right to life." Dr. C. Everett Koop and theologian Francis Schaefer further advanced the evangelical case against abortion in *Whatever Happened to the Human Race?* a best-selling book later disseminated widely as a five-part film series. Robert Holbrook, a prominent Southern Baptist minister, won election to the National Right to Life Committee, while other evangelicals formed parallel pro-life organizations such as Baptists for Life and Harold Brown's creation, the Christian Action Council. As a result of their energies, local ministers began to become involved. Reverend Falwell finally delivered his first sermon on the subject of abortion in 1978 and then quickly embraced the once "Catholic" cause as a priority of his own.[27]

As the 1970s wore on, these southern evangelical and fundamentalist leaders took an ever-increasing role in the political mobilization of religious conservatives across the country. Although they followed the lead of Catholics and Mormons in campaigns against the Equal Rights Amendment and abortion, conservative southern Protestants later stood at the forefront of the fight against homosexual rights. The overwhelming defeat of a 1977 proposal for a Dade County, Florida, gay rights ordinance depended upon the work of Anita Bryant, a devout Southern Baptist who joined forces with leading ministers from her denomination in the Save

Our Children organization. Southern Baptists tried to build upon their successful campaign in Florida with a 1978 effort to ban homosexual teachers in California, where they worked with like-minded local leaders such as Reverend Tim LaHaye. At a huge rally at the San Diego Convention Center, Jerry Falwell exhorted the crowd to support the cause. "We need this measure," he shouted, "to reverse the tide of moral decay that threatens California and our beloved nation." The initiative failed at the polls, yet the mobilization of religious leaders on this matter, and the new ties they forged across the nation, would have lasting effects.[28]

While social issues such as the ERA, abortion, and gay rights succeeded in drawing southern religious leaders out of their local concerns and into national politics in the late 1970s, a challenge from the federal government to those same local concerns also increased their activism. In an effort to stem white flight from southern public schools to "segregation academies," the Internal Revenue Service (IRS) initiated a new policy in 1970 to deny the charitable, and thus tax-exempt, status for white-only private schools. When it became clear that some of these schools still managed to retain their tax-exempt status, the IRS strengthened the guidelines in 1978. Private religious schools throughout the nation would now be required to demonstrate commitments to minority enrollment or outreach, or else lose the tax-exempt status essential to their financial survival. Not surprisingly, the guidelines generated a swift response from religious conservatives. Congress received more than 400,000 complaints, and opponents sent the IRS another 120,000, which one stunned official noted was "more than we've ever received on any other proposal." While religious conservatives across the nation were outraged at the guidelines, those outside the South emerged as its most effective critics. Racial discrimination had seemingly little to do with the formation of their own schools—or at least much less so than with those located in the South—and as a result, they were better able to defend the institutions on their religious merits. At the same time, Christian schools in other parts of the country stood by their southern counterparts to project a united front. In a letter to IRS Commissioner Jerome Kurtz, for example, the administrator of Liberty Christian Schools outside Los Angeles demanded that the guidelines be removed: "If they are not—and this is not a threat but a known fact—not only our small group but some 50,000,000 evangelicals in the U.S. will rise up."[29]

As confrontations over Christian schools and social issues revealed the common grassroots resentments of religious conservatives across the nation, fundamentalist and evangelical leaders finally realized the potential for a broad-based political movement. Fledgling local organizations that formed to address specific issues were soon augmented and interconnected by three broader, formal coalitions established in 1979— Christian Voice, the Moral Majority, and the Religious Roundtable. In these organizations, previously localized struggles to defend traditional religious values became linked and amplified as a national pro-America movement. Importantly, the leadership of each group reflected the geographical reach of religious nationalism. Jerry Falwell founded the Moral Majority along with Reverends Tim LaHaye of San Diego, Greg Dixon of Indianapolis, Charles Stanley of Atlanta, and James Kennedy of Fort Lauderdale. Christian Voice linked Pentecostal religious broadcaster Pat Robertson of Virginia with Reverends Richard Zone and Robert Grant of Los Angeles, while the Religious Roundtable brought Robertson together with Reverend James Robison of Fort Worth and business executive Ed McAteer of Memphis. In forming national alliances, these leaders strengthened the political clout of conservative Christians and reinforced their self-image as the representation of majority will.[30]

These new organizations reflected the ecumenical nature as well as the cross-country appeal of religious nationalism. As Falwell noted, "religious organizations are marching together who never worked with each other. Evangelicals, fundamentalists, conservatives, Catholics, and Mormons are all working together now." The leadership structure of Christian Voice, for example, reflected a wide range of religions. Its founder, Richard Grant, was a former Pentecostal minister; its legislative director, Gary Jarmin, a Southern Baptist who had worked for Reverend Sun Myung Moon; and the head of its direct-mail fund-raising organization, Jerry Hunsinger, a former Methodist minister. Through their efforts, Christian Voice's membership included 1,200 Protestant ministers of various denominations, as well as several hundred Catholic priests. The group's allies in the political realm also reflected an ecumenical approach. Sixteen members of Congress served on the congressional advisory committee of Christian Voice, including four Republican senators: Orrin Hatch of Utah, a Mormon; Roger Jepsen of Iowa, a Lutheran; Gordon Humphrey of New Hampshire, a Baptist; and James McClure of Idaho, a Methodist. "This is no false unity based on papering over doctrinal differences," observed organizer Paul Weyrich. "These leaders have concluded it is better to argue about denominational differences at another time. Right now, it is the agenda of those opposed to the Scriptures and the church which has brought us together."[31]

Ultimately, these coalitions formed by the new Religious Right, spanning divisions of region and religion alike, succeeded in crafting a major conservative movement with national implications. After 1980, the impression that religious conservatives had been essential to Ronald Reagan's electoral success ensured that the Religious Right would have a central place in the Republican Party and, through it, national politics, for decades to come. Although the new movement secured few concrete accomplishments in legal or legislative terms in its early years, it had tremendous success in its most important goal: bringing the concerns of conservative Christians to the center of American political culture. In time, the original coalitions faded away and were replaced by others, such as Pat Robertson's Christian Coalition (based in the suburbs of Norfolk, Virginia) and James Dobson's Focus on the Family (founded in suburban Los Angeles and now based in Colorado Springs). But the active involvement of grassroots religious conservatives—once thought to be beyond the pale, even by its future leaders—remained at the core of national political life. For a movement dedicated to making the voices of conservative Christians heard, throughout the country, such an accomplishment stands as a tremendous success, one brought about not by religious conservatives from a single sect or section but from a broad coalition working for a common end.

NOTES

1. William Martin, *With God on Our Side: The Rise of the Religious Right in America* (New York: Broadway Books, 1996), 200.

2. Wendy Wall, *Inventing the "American Way": The Politics of Consensus from the New Deal to the Civil Rights Movement* (New York: Oxford University Press, 2008), 84–86.

3. Paul Hutchinson, "Have We a 'New' Religion?" *Life,* April 11, 1955, 138; Joel A. Carpenter, *Revive Us Again: The Reawakening of American Fundamentalism* (New York: Oxford University Press, 1997), 213; Stephen J. Whitfield, *The Culture of the Cold War,* 2nd ed. (Baltimore: Johns Hopkins University Press, 1996), 83; Will Herberg, *Protestant Catholic Jew: An Essay in American Religious Sociology* (Chicago: University of Chicago Press, 1955, 1983), 246.

4. Herberg, *Protestant Catholic Jew,* 246; Mark Silk, *Spiritual Politics: Religion and America Since World War II* (New York: Simon and Schuster, 1988), 90, 87; Patrick Henry, "'And I Don't Care What It Is': The Tradition-History of a Civil Religion Proof-Text," *Journal of the American Academy of Religion,* 49 (1981): 41.

5. Herberg, *Protestant Catholic Jew,* 84; Whitfield, *Culture of the Cold War,* 81–88; Silk, *Spiritual Politics,* 100; *Washington Post,* July 24, 1956; *Congressional Record, House of Representatives,* 84th Cong., 1st Sess., 7795–96.

6. Silk, *Spiritual Politics,* 96–110; Whitfield, *Culture of the Cold War,* 88–89; *New York Times,* May, 9, 15, 23, June 15, 1954.

7. Silk, *Spiritual Politics,* 88; Billy Graham, "We Need Revival," reprinted in Billy Graham, *Revival in Our Time* (Wheaton, Ill.: Van Kampen Press, 1950), 69–80; *United Evangelical Action,* June 1960, 10.

8. Leo Ribuffo, *The Old Christian Right: The Protestant Far Right from the Great Depression to the Cold War* (Philadelphia: Temple University Press, 1983), 259–60; Martin, *With God on Our Side,* 37.

9. Martin, *With God on Our Side,* 76; Pamphlet, "What is the Christian Anti-Communism Crusade?", n.d., Box 43, Fred Schwarz to "Dear Friend," November 24, 1962, Box 44, Pamphlet, "Project Alert!" Winter 1962, Box 43, "CACC News

Letter," August 1962, copy in Box 44, Collection of Underground, Alternative and Extremist Literature, Special Collections, Charles E. Young Library, University of California at Los Angeles; Steve Bruce, *The Rise and Fall of the New Christian Right: Conservative Protestant Politics in America, 1978–1988* (Oxford: Clarendon Press, 1988), 11–12.

10. *Engel v. Vitale*, 370 U.S. 421 (1962); *School District of Abington Township v. Schempp*, 374 U.S. 203 (1963); Lynda Beck Fenwick, *Should the Children Pray?: A Historical, Judicial and Political Examination of Public School Prayer* (Waco, Tex.: Markham Press Fund, 1989), 130, 137.

11. Fenwick, *Should the Children Pray?* 133; Mrs. M. Busly to Hugo Black, April 9, 1962, Box 355, Cornelia O. Edington to Hugo Black, [July 1962], Box 354, Mary Crum to Hugo Black, July 4, 1962, Box 359, Hugo L. Black Papers, Manuscript Division, Library of Congress [hereinafter Black Papers].

12. *New York Times*, June 26, July 1, 1962; Dallin Oaks, "Religion in Public Life," *Ensign*, July 1990, 10; "A Tide Reversed," *Time*, June 19, 1964.

13. Daniel Kenneth Williams, *From the Pews to the Polls: The Formation of a Southern Christian Right*, Ph.D. dissertation, Brown University, 2000, 177–81; C. Emanuel Carson, Executive Director, Baptist Joint Committee on Public Affairs, to Harry Byrd, Jr., June 2, 1966, Box 260, Harry Flood Byrd Jr. Papers, Albert and Shirley Small Special Collections Library, University of Virginia.

14. "On Second Thought," *Time*, August 24, 1962; W. C. Vaughn to Hugo L. Black, June 22, 1963, W. C. Vaughn to Earl Warren, June 22, 1963, Box 356, Black Papers; Dorothy G. Wise to Craig Hosmer, July 6, 1962, Mary D. O'Hare to Craig Hosmer, July 1, 1962, Box 54, Craig Hosmer Papers, Special Collections, Edward L. Doheny, Jr., Memorial Library, University of Southern California; N. W. Crumpacker to A. Willis Robertson, July 27, 1966, Drawer 81, A. Willis Robertson Papers, Special Collections, Earl Gregg Swem Library, College of William and Mary [hereinafter Robertson Papers].

15. Fenwick, *Should the Children Pray?* 134; "A Tide Reversed," *Time* (June 19, 1964); *U.S. News and World Report* (May 4, 1964); Charles W. Winegarner, Citizens Congressional Committee, to A. Willis Robertson, January 15, 1964, Winegarner to "Dear Congressman," September 25, 1963, Drawer 72, Robertson Papers.

16. Williams, "From the Pews to the Polls," 189; *Newsweek*, August 29, 1966.

17. Jerry Falwell, *Strength for the Journey: An Autobiography* (New York: Simon and Schuster, 1987), 290; Susan Friend Harding, *The Book of Jerry Falwell: Fundamentalist Language and Politics* (Princeton: Princeton University Press, 2000), 22; *Washington Post*, May 14, 1966; Pat Robertson and Jamie Buckingham, *Shout It from the Housetops* (Plainfield, N.J.: Logos International, 1972), 179, cited in Justin Watson, *The Christian Coalition: Dreams of Restoration, Demands of Recognition* (New York: St. Martin's Press, 1997), 209, n. 24; Neil J. Young, *We Gather Together: Catholics, Mormons, Southern Baptists and the Question of Interfaith Politics, 1972–1984*, Ph.D. dissertation, Columbia University, 2008, 81.

18. David Nevin and Robert E. Bills, *The Schools that Fear Built: Segregationist Academies in the South* (Washington: Acropolis Books, 1976).

19. *U.S. News and World Report*, July 9, 1962; A. James Reichley, *Faith in Politics* (Washington: Brookings Institution, 2002), 144.

20. Reichley, *Faith in Politics*, 144; *Lynchburg News*, April 14, 1967; Falwell, *Strength for the Journey*, 298; Martin, *With God on Our Side*, 71; Paige B. Hooper to John H. Rousselot, June 25, 1962, Box 360, Thomas M. Manion to John H. Rousselot, July 12, 1962, Box 359, Black Papers.

21. *Los Angeles Times*, February 22, May 17, July 16, 1981; Robert C. Liebman, "Mobilizing the Moral Majority," in *The New Christian Right: Mobilization and Legitimation*, ed. Liebman and Robert Wuthnow (New York: Aldine Publishing Co., 1983), 59, 67; Frances FitzGerald, *Cities on a Hill: A Journey Through Contemporary American Cultures* (New York: Simon and Schuster, 1987), 130.

22. *Christianity Today*, November 6, 1970; Robert Booth Fowler, *A New Engagement: Evangelical Political Thought, 1966–1976* (Grand Rapids, Mich.: Eerdmans Publishing, 1982), 205–6; Young, *We Gather Together*, 240–41; Carol Felsenthal, *The Sweetheart of the Silent Majority: The Biography of Phyllis Schlafly* (New York: Doubleday, 1981), 108; Donald T. Critchlow, *Phyllis Schlafly and Grassroots Conservatism: A Woman's Crusade* (Princeton: Princeton University Press, 2005), 217.

23. Critchlow, *Phyllis Schlafly*, 221–22; Ruth Murray Brown, *For a "Christian America": A History of the Religious Right* (New York: Prometheus Books, 2002), 69–78.

24. U.S. Library of Congress, Congressional Research Service, Issue Brief Number IB74122, *Equal Rights Amendment (Proposed)*, by Leslie Gladstone (Washington, D.C., July 8, 1982); Critchlow, *Phyllis Schlafly*, 235.

25. *Christianity Today*, August 16, November 8, 1968; Young, *We Gather Together*, 142–44.

26. James Risen and Judy L. Thomas, *Wrath of Angels: The American Abortion War* (New York: Basic Books, 1999), 19–20; Young, *We Gather Together*, 148–49.

27. Martin, *With God on Our Side*, 193; *Christianity Today*, February 16, 1973, January 16, 1976; Scott Flipse, "Below-the-Belt Politics: Protestant Evangelicals, Abortion, and the Foundation of the New Religious Right, 1960–75," in *The Conservative Sixties*, ed. David Farber and Jeff Roche (New York: Peter Lang, 2003), 138–39.

28. Kenneth D. Wald, *Religion and Politics in the United States* (New York: St. Martin's Press, 1987), 187; Lisa McGirr, *Suburban Warriors: The Origins of the New American Right* (Princeton: Princeton University Press, 2001), 258; *Los Angeles Times*, October 31, November 3, 1978.

29. Bruce J. Schulman, *The Seventies: The Great Shift in American Culture, Society, and Politics* (New York: Free Press, 2001), 202; Peter Skerry, "Christian Schools versus the I.R.S." *The Public Interest*, 61 (Fall 1980): 19; Martin P. Claussen and Evelyn Bills Claussen, eds., *The Voice of Christian and Jewish Dissenters in America: U.S. Internal Revenue Service Hearings on Proposed 'Discrimination' Tax Controls Over Christian, Jewish, and Secular Private Schools, December 5, 6, 7, 8, 1978* (Washington: Piedmont Press, 1982), 172, cited in Joseph Crespino, "Segregation Academies or Church Schools?: Race, Religion, and Taxes in

Mississippi, 1970–1982," paper in author's possession; William D. Mewhinney to "Commissioner of IRS," October 23, 1978, Box 13, Mark Hannaford Papers, University Library, Special Collections and Archives, California State University, Long Beach.

30. *Los Angeles Times*, August 5, 1979, March 6, May 19, 1980; *Washington Post*, August 25, 1979; Sidney Blumenthal, "The Righteous Empire," *The New Republic*, October 22, 1984, 20, 22.

31. *Washington Post*, August 25, 1979; *Christianity Today*, November 2, 1979.

13

NEO-CONFEDERACY VERSUS THE NEW DEAL

The Regional Utopia of the Modern American Right

Nancy MacLean

"The 1984 Republican platform, all the ideas we supported there—from tax policy, to foreign policy; from individual rights to neighborhood security—are things that Jefferson Davis and his people believed in."

Congressman Trent Lott (Mississippi),

Southern Partisan, 1984

"Just when they seem engaged in revolutionizing themselves and things, in creating something that has never yet existed, precisely in such periods of revolutionary crisis they anxiously conjure up the spirits of the past to their service and borrow from them names, battle cries and costumes in order to present the new scene of world history in this time-honored disguise and this borrowed language."

Karl Marx, *The Eighteenth Brumaire of*

Louis Bonaparte, 1852

An odd metamorphosis has taken place in American politics since the 1960s: the party of Lincoln has become the haven of neo-Confederacy. Having long prided itself on saving the Union, the Republican Party has become home to those who lionize the slaveholding South and romanticize the Jim Crow South. This is a development that has attracted little notice in the press except when it goes too far to be ignored, as in 2002 when Senate Majority Leader Trent Lott, Republican from Mississippi, said that America would have been better off if the Dixiecrat revolt of 1948 had succeeded. Yet outside the limelight, many GOP leaders honor the icons of the Confederacy. To take just a few examples: in 1981, sixteen prominent Republican U.S. senators recommended M. E. Bradford to President Ronald Reagan as an "impeccable" scholar to head the National Endowment for the Humanities. Bradford, who described himself as an "unrepentant Southerner," had compared Lincoln to Hitler and denounced emancipation as a blow to "liberty." President George W. Bush, for his part, earlier in his career had ties to the Museum of the Confederacy, the United Daughters of the Confederacy, and the Sons of Confederate Veterans. The Republican leaders Phil Gramm, Dick Armey, John Ashcroft, and Newt Gingrich, among others, have given friendly interviews to *Southern Partisan,* an arch-Confederate journal that gives a "scalawag award" to those whites who stray from its right-wing views.[1]

What makes all of this especially intriguing is that these particular spirits of the past have been conjured up by actors engaged in a project of radical transformation. The GOP, as the former Labor Secretary Robert Reich observed with reference to the impact of globalization, has been "the party of 'Let 'er rip.' "[2] That is to say, the Republican Party has shown little concern with the destructive impact of hyper-capitalism; quite the contrary, it has sought to remove restraints that might ease the job loss and family and regional devastation that result from economic restructuring. Its ideas and policies are not exactly the embodiment of Burkean conservatism, with that tradition's regard for family security, community cohesion, and settled tradition. Why, then, do so many of those leading the way to the brave new world of Wal-Mart–style neoliberalism, a world in which government's hands are tied so as to allow capital maximum freedom, hearken back to the Confederacy, despite the obvious political risks of doing so now that anti-racists have voting power they lacked in the heyday of the Lost Cause?

The puzzle suggests the need for a sequel to C. Vann Woodward's classic 1951 study of postbellum America, *Reunion and Reaction.* The sequel would need to explore alterations in the composition and politics of the conservative business interests that have long dominated the Republican Party. It would have to take into account how the economic and population growth of the Sunbelt has enabled southern and western elites to eclipse the GOP's former leaders from the Northeast and Midwest.[3] It might explore how the historical mythology of neo-Confederacy, understood as a retrospective romanticization of the Old South and the secessionist project, has offered many themes of use to the longstanding dream among conservative northern Republicans of rolling back the New Deal. Its story would begin in the South, with aspiring white politicians who found in neo-Confederacy a font of legitimacy for their quest not only to limit black civil rights but also to free private property from effective regulation, substitute market dynamics for democratic processes, and undercut political challenges to this extreme makeover of the nation. One prime arena to look for the interregional transfer of ideas would be Congress, where the representatives of southern white planter interests in the old Democratic Party and of northern business conservatives in the old Republican Party allied repeatedly from the 1930s forward to block reforms ranging from labor rights to national health insurance.[4] As early as 1938, conservative southern politicians were using the mythology of the Civil War and Reconstruction to fight the second, more radical phase of the New Deal, with a rallying cry summed up by one historian as "The carpet-baggers are coming."[5]

But the proximate answer to this puzzle of the GOP's metamorphosis is the modern conservative movement. The conservative movement proved to be the main transmission belt carrying the spirit of Dixie into the Grand Old Party, from the time of the Manhattan-based *National Review*'s founding in 1955 to the election of the Californian Ronald Reagan to the presidency in 1980, and beyond. From the moment the mainstream Right coalesced around *National Review* as a self-conscious effort to overthrow the New Deal consensus regnant at mid-century—a consensus the publication's founders derided as "the Liberal orthodoxy"—that project has contained a strong element of neo-Confederacy. The leading proponents of the Old South as utopia were those later dubbed "paleo-conservatives," largely descendants of the Nashville Agrarians and their admirers among later northern-based conservatives. Yet where the Agrarians had used this mythology to critique corporate capitalism in the 1930s, the *National Review* intellectuals used it to free business from any significant restraint in the 1950s and thereafter. Sunbelt corporate neoliberals and northern neoconservatives have since displaced the paleo-conservatives from the front ranks of conservatism and relegated them to the wings. Yet their ideas were imbibed, or at least tolerated with virtually no public criticism, by northern and western libertarian and traditionalist conservatives less enamored of the Old South.[6]

The Right conjured a mythical region that bore little relation to the actual South, with its dramatic history of conflict between and within its major population groups and of dissent from the dominant conservative ethos. In the Right's odes to the Old South, classes never clashed, whites took care of blacks, planters shared the interests of city dwellers, men presided over orderly households, and liberalism and modernism were foreign imports that attracted no local buyers. Their South was a land of propertied gentlemen devoted to defending liberty for the good of all. That conservative leaders propounded this mythical South in the very years scholars and civil rights activists alike were exposing its fundamental falsity reveals a willful blindness to inconvenient empirical evidence.[7]

Their tenacity suggests the power of conservatives' felt need for a proving ground for their utopia: a model of actually existing conservatism that combined untrammeled property rights, a small state restricted largely to punitive functions, a hierarchical social order, and public religiosity. If we want to understand the radical reconstitution of the party of Lincoln, then, we need to look at those who did the most to engineer it: the thinkers and organizers in the orbit of *National Review*. From the time they first took aim at "the well-fed Right," as they called the moderate GOP leaders who had "made their peace with the New Deal," conservative movement builders looked south for support in their project.[8]

Although studies of conservatism have proliferated, its southern dimension has received surprisingly little attention until recently. There are myriad books and articles on varied aspects of the conservative project. Scholars have studied its intellectual moorings, its evolving grassroots base, its business backing, its institutional infrastructure, its gender and sexual politics, its religious dimension, and its impact on the major parties. Yet the parts played by region and race in the conservative ascendency have not received anything like the attention they deserve, in part because northern solipsism continues to distort what passes as national history.[9] Too many scholars still imagine that they can focus on the Northeast and Midwest and draw sound conclusions about national matters. In doing so, they often miss the potent role of race; in particular, they miss the resistance of so many whites to black advance, a national phenomenon that tended to play out most fiercely in the South until the last few decades. The evolution of modern conservatism since the 1950s cannot be understood without that.[10]

But neither can this movement be understood without region. So this chapter asks: What work did the invocation of a peculiar reading of southern history do for conservatives' core goal of achieving a U-turn in American social policy? The beginnings of an answer can be gleaned from *National Review* founder William F. Buckley, Jr., who wrote in his notorious 1957 argument for "Why the South Must Prevail": "Let us speak frankly. The South does not want to deprive the Negro of a vote for the sake of depriving him of the vote." No, there were instrumental reasons to do so that went beyond racial chauvinism—above all, policy questions to be decided by democratic process, "on which there is corporate disagreement between Negro and White." The civil rights movement was advancing a vision of democratic government active in the service of economic and social justice that conservatives viewed as an extension of the New Deal, the dismantling of which was their raison d'être. As the conservative publishing magnate Henry Regnery put their case years later, "the much larger issue" in the defense of racial segregation was "the usurpation by Washington of the authority of the states."[11] Activists and scholars alike have long dismissed such claims as mere window dressing for racism, but in fact they deserve closer attention in explanatory efforts. Precisely because the black struggle ended the quiescence of the McCarthy years and focused national attention on poverty and social injustice (to say nothing of providing a compelling new understanding of "freedom"), it proved the most significant obstacle to the Right's success.

That may explain why conservative leaders were willing to inflict damage on African Americans even if not primarily motivated by racism. In order to achieve rollback of the regulatory authority of the federal government, so as to restore property rights to their once-hegemonic standing, they had to clash with the civil rights movement, willy-nilly, whether or not they welcomed the confrontation. By ennobling the South's white rulers, neo-Confederacy made that task more palatable. It offered a way to ally with the political forces that were suppressing blacks without seeming to embrace their uglier features. Neo-Confederacy changed the subject, and thereby enabled the New York-based movement builders to tap into the potent grassroots energy of white reaction without acknowledging the truth of what they were doing. At a time when African Americans were gaining white sympathy and the nation's racialized form of capitalism was losing legitimacy as never before, the architects of the conservative movement enlisted a mythical southern past to deflect reform. Neo-Confederacy served their purposes, then, in matters that went beyond race and region.

After sketching the conservative movement's enthusiasm in its first formative decade for a fantasy version of the antebellum and Jim Crow South, this essay jumps forward in time to the post-1980 period in order to explore the continuing utility of these commitments for the Right's project in the emerging global order. The contemporary conservative movement, like the Republican Party it dominates, is a complex coalition, and for some of its member groups the nostalgia of neo-Confederacy has scant to negative appeal. The invocation of southern mythology is a sideshow now—yet one that still does important warm-up work for the feature act in the part of the country that yields the most reliable—indeed, avid—Republican voters. The fact that such a seemingly anachronistic show has not shut down completely demands analysis.

The *National Review* made no clear reference in its inaugural issue in November of 1955 to the grassroots movement for racial justice then sweeping the country, but the *Brown v. Board of Education* decision helped galvanize the new cause's founders. "From the day of the Supreme Court's unanimous ruling against racial segregation in the public schools," as the conservative journalist and former educator Felix Morley put it a few years later, "a resurgence of [a] political movement in behalf of States' Rights became probable."[12] That movement later came to prefer the less charged label "federalism," but its cause was indeed states' rights. Buckley announced the mission of the new magazine thus: to "stand athwart history, yelling, Stop." He and his colleagues at *National Review* pitted their cause against the very developments that had enabled the mounting challenge to racial hierarchy. The New Deal state, mass industrial labor unions, anti-colonialism in Africa and elsewhere, the right to dissent freely and organize nonviolent protest, social gospel Christianity and prophetic Judaism, nontraditional scholarship in the life sciences and social sciences—there was hardly a development that invigorated African-American organizing that did not antagonize spokesmen for the conservative cause. The Right's architects focused on fighting communism abroad and the welfare state at home. Yet a defense of white rule in the South was part of their cause from the outset, by tacit agreement a unifying force among otherwise quarreling libertarians, cultural traditionalists, and militant anticommunists. The consensus was evident when the leader widely credited with bringing "fusion" between the rival factions, *National Review* senior editor Frank Meyer, himself a New Yorker, denounced *Brown v. Board of Education* as a "rape of the Constitution."[13]

The intellectual architects of the conservative cause united across the Mason-Dixon line in a common defense of the old hierarchical order. In the wake of the Court's decision, the national movement reached out to the man who supplied the constitutional rationale for "massive resistance" to school desegregation: James Jackson Kilpatrick, editor of the *Richmond News Leader*. Resurrecting the pro-slavery states' rights doctrine of "interposition" for use against federal court-ordered integration, Kilpatrick exulted in how it was "catching fire across the lower South." The head of the white Citizens' Councils of Mississippi, one of the most ardent segregationists in America, praised Kilpatrick as "one of the South's most talented leaders."[14] The *National Review* agreed and chose Kilpatrick to be its voice on civil rights. Kilpatrick, who described himself as "only a little to the south of John C. Calhoun," did more than anyone else to make neo-Confederacy part of the postwar conservative mainstream.[15] With his help, Buckley obtained the mailing list of the Citizens' Councils in 1958: some 65,000 southern white conservatives who might appreciate the *National Review*. "Our position on states' rights is the same as your own," Buckley said in thanking William J. Simmons, the Mississippi-based leader of the regionwide organization that, in the words of the civil rights movement scholar Charles Payne, "pursu[ed] the agenda of the Ku Klux Klan with the demeanor of the Rotary." Simmons, in turn, praised the *National Review's* "contribution to the cause of political and social sanity."[16]

The appreciation that Simmons expressed made sense, because Buckley's magazine portrayed the white South's cause as not merely a regional concern but a vital national struggle. Other conservative opinion makers therefore sought to spread Kilpatrick's philosophy. Henry Regnery, the conservative book publisher and lifelong midwesterner, offered Kilpatrick an advance contract to write the book that became *The Sovereign States*, a bellicose brief for interposition to limit federal power. Regnery described their shared convictions without regional modifiers as simply "the conservative point of view" on "constitutional problems as a result of the Supreme Court decision."[17]

Supporting the white supremacist case against federal interference from Washington, conservative movement builders vehemently opposed civil rights legislation. The *National Review* broadcast attacks developed by southern defenders of segregation against the Civil Rights Act of 1964. As Buckley later reminded the magazine's publisher: "I feel a considerable debt of gratitude to the [Virginia] Commission [on Constitutional Government] for permitting us to publish free of charge and without assigning them the credit, the[ir] extensive analysis of the civil rights bill." The proposed Civil Rights Act of 1964, Commission Vice-Chairman Kilpatrick had written, "would undermine the most precious rights of property," of private businesses in particular. If "the citizen's right to discriminate" should "be destroyed, the whole basis of individual liberty is destroyed."[18] "The right to own, and possess, and manage property is vital," Kilpatrick insisted, as he portrayed any restriction on owners' rights as a death threat to the liberty envisioned by the nation's founders.[19] Robert Bork, then a young law professor at Yale, argued that it was sophistry to separate property rights and human rights; property rights were human rights of the highest order. The issue, he said, "is not whether racial prejudice is a good thing but whether individual men ought to be free to deal and associate with whom they please for whatever reasons appeal to them." For anyone to tell these white citizens "that even as individuals they may not act on their racial preferences" was "unsurpassed ugliness."[20] Defending the right to discriminate as a time-honored gauge of liberty, conservatives tried to derail civil rights reform.

The timing of this invocation of tradition becomes the more intriguing when set against the rapid economic development of the South. World War II and the Cold War had transformed the region. Coming on the heels of the shake-up in sharecropping during the Great Depression and the mass out-migration of farm workers that new federal agricultural policies prompted, the sudden economic diversification of the South thoroughly altered southern society. Business growth outside the old agricultural sector, encouraged by federal government contracts, remodeled the region's communities.[21] From the outset, the conservative movement attracted support from some of the regional elites in oil and textile manufacturing who were pioneering these changes.[22] What could such daily watchers of the bottom line gain from seemingly nostalgic odes to the likes of John C. Calhoun and to defiance of the federal government that twice in a century had resulted in defeat? Most whites of that generation were raised on the so-called Redeemers' interpretation of the Civil

War and Reconstruction, to be sure, so the opportunity existed to appeal to their mis-education.[23] And even staid, centrist northerners discovered the advantages of flattering white southern revanchism, as when General Dwight Eisenhower stood for the playing of "Dixie" before a delighted crowd in Columbia, South Carolina, while campaigning in the 1952 election.[24] But there was more to it than a bid to attract votes.

Neo-Confederacy appealed to conservatives as a way to advance their core mission of freeing capital from any effective restraint, especially that which used the democratic process in the interests of less powerful citizens of any description. Perhaps that is why *Nation's Business*, the official journal of the U.S. Chamber of Commerce, made James Kilpatrick one of its regular writers after he became nationally known for his pro-states' rights, anti-civil rights commentary, and why he was chosen as the keynote speaker for the first annual Conservative Awards Dinner in 1969.[25] From early on, in fact, northern as well as southern conservative thinkers identified the Union cause in the Civil War, Reconstruction, and the New Deal as interrelated aspects of a "Liberal" threat that usurped the rights of property owners and states. Conservative intellectuals who discussed Emancipation thus portrayed it as one of the greatest violations of the rights of private property in world history. For them, its import was not the freeing of persons but the expropriation of property. Wilmoore Kendall, the mentor of Buckley and Russell Kirk, claimed that the contemporary "war" between liberals and conservatives "began as a war of aggression, launched...by the Liberals," who attacked "the victim's territory in the 1860s and 1870s" in the form of "emancipation of the slaves in the name of equality, [and] the post-Civil War 'equality' amendments to the Constitution."[26] Northerners and southerners alike promoted a mythology of the Civil War and Reconstruction that depicted Dixie whites as victims and supported their demand for states' rights. A few rejected the national cause in their very terminology, speaking of "the War Between the States."[27]

In the Right's view, the social legislation of the New Deal deepened the outrage to the nation's founding creed that had begun seventy years earlier. "The tradition of Western civilization and the American republic," the venerable conservative strategist and *National Review* senior editor Frank Meyer insisted, had "been subjected to a revolutionary attack in the years since 1932," when Franklin D. Roosevelt won the presidential election and proceeded to offer Americans a "New Deal."[28] In conservatives' reckoning of how America veered off course, the pro-labor welfare state and racial justice were linked causes from the outset. By the 1950s, according to *National Review's* founding salvo, "the most alarming single danger to the American political system" was how "clever intriguers are reshaping both parties in the image of Babbitt, gone Social Democrat."[29] Conservatives felt, as one writer explained, "a positive hatred of redistributionist schemes" and "anything in the way of mandated equality." Standing against what another called "the characteristic leveling egalitarianism of the time," they argued that hierarchy was natural, inevitable, and desirable for a good society.[30]

On both sides of the Mason-Dixon line, conservatives understood liberty—their cardinal virtue—in the manner of the nation's slave-owning founders and their Confederate heirs. They viewed it as precious and essential to the preservation of republican institutions, yet something that only certain men were fit to exercise. Willmoore Kendall explained that one of the things that made liberals so odious was their *"egalitarian* principle," their deplorable belief in "one-man one-equal-vote." Seeing it as "manifestly dangerous" for "the inferior group" to be "granted political equality," James Burnham thought it eminently reasonable to "continue to want my group to have more than its arithmetic share in running things."[31] Insisting that the United States was a republic, not a democracy, they scorned majority rule and often defended restricted suffrage and other limits on voting rights, such as poll taxes.[32] They saw no contradiction between claiming to stand for liberty and opposing a movement seeking "freedom now," because they upheld a tradition that subordinated African Americans as outsiders to the polity. "Integration," said a writer in *Modern Age*, a conservative scholarly journal, "is patently a radical departure from the explicit provisions of the contract between the states that established the federal union."[33] What made "the White community" in the South "entitled" to use any means necessary to keep blacks from voting, Buckley explained—sounding for all the world like one of the gentlemen planters who overthrew Reconstruction—was that "it is the advanced race," so its "claims of civilization supersede those of universal suffrage."[34]

Conservative leaders constructed an image of the Jim Crow South that served as a mobilizing device for their intended audience across the nation. Leading thinkers of the movement exalted what Richard Weaver, the historian and author of the early conservative treatise *Ideas Have Consequences*, was wont to call "the regime of the South." Weaver and his fellows portrayed the segregated South as a kind of Shangri-La: a utopia of ordered liberty and civilized values. He defended the South's devotion to the "principle of exclusion" and an "aristocratic" social order against the "heavy assault" on its white leaders' rule "by Liberalism." Anthony Harrigan, the first executive director of the Southern States Industrial Council and a *National Review* writer, praised this region of "essential conservatism" for its "built-in power brake." To Russell Kirk, the South was "the citadel of tradition," the front line of defense for "civilization." "The South," he instructed readers, "need feel no shame for its defense of beliefs that were not concocted yesterday."[35]

This idea of the South—this imaginary, symbolic South—served its exponents as a homegrown example of conservatism in practice. An analogue to the Stalinist Left's "actually existing socialism," it provided a beacon from which conservatives could take their bearings. The Jim Crow South exemplified their ideal of state governments that vigorously upheld the rights of property against all other claims, resisted federal intrusion on their prerogatives, and confined their exertions to encouraging corporate capitalism and punishing crime, straying as little as possible onto the socialist-tainted ground of providing for the popular welfare. Conservatives "strive to re-establish a federal system of strictly divided powers," as Meyer put it, "and to repulse the encroachment of government, federal or state, over the economy and the individual lives of citizens." Why? Because "our right of property," as Arizona Senator Barry Goldwater avowed in making his case against the Civil Rights Act of 1964, "is probably our most sacred right."[36] Their determination to safeguard property drew conservatives, like homing pigeons, to the side of the South's white rulers.

Those conservative intellectuals who wrote about the South especially revered the most ardent advocates of property rights in American history: the defenders of chattel slavery, who invented a powerful constitutional and philosophical defense of inequality for a nation that worshiped opportunity. Later thinkers of the Right lifted up that constitutional tradition in order to prove that "conservatism is something deeper than mere defense of shares and dividends," as Russell Kirk quipped in his paean to South Carolina's John C. Calhoun and Virginia's John Randolph in *The Conservative Mind*. "Men are not created equal," announced Kirk, and so "the overmastering tendency of the past century and a half" toward "social egalitarianism" was a grievous error. "Aye," he intoned, articulating a core premise of his movement, "men are created different; and government which ignores this law becomes an unjust government, for it sacrifices nobility to mediocrity; it pulls down aspiring natures to gratify the inferior natures."[37]

Calhoun claimed a special place in the pantheon of historically inclined conservative thinkers thanks to the extreme states' rights position he staked out to fortify the power of property owners—in his case, slave owners—in national affairs. Aptly dubbed by historian Richard Hofstadter "the Marx of the master class," Calhoun devoted his acute intellect to figuring out how to subvert the will of the majority and restrict democracy so as to safeguard private property rights and protect white privilege.[38] In a tribute to him, the Vanderbilt professor and *National Review* writer Donald Davidson thus insisted that slavery was but "a minor issue": "the difficulty was with egalitarianism itself." Only those "realistic" enough to renounce "romanticism" and accept the inevitability that some were made to rule and others to serve were fit to govern wisely, a truth proved "when the carpet-bag governments had finally been expelled."[39] Calhoun had understood early on that his region could best restrain the nation's majority because it acted as "the great conservative power." "In this tendency to conflict in the North, between labor and capital," Calhoun had written over a century before his rediscovery by the right, "the South has been and ever will be found on the conservative side." Calhoun perceived a logic that became common sense among his latter-day admirers when he observed that "the assaults which are now directed against the institutions of the Southern States may be very easily directed against those [of the North] which uphold their own property and security."[40]

Another resource the modern conservative project found in looking south was skillful defenders of what conservatives liked to depict as "the Constitution as originally conceived."[41] As Felix Morley noted of white southerners' contribution, "to justify their part in the 'War Between the States' Southerners have had to study our constitutional history, and they are generally more familiar with it than are many in other sections of the country."[42] Here, too, the Right constructed a past that never existed. As the historian Garry Wills has shown, the Right's true heroes were the anti-Federalists—not the Constitution's advocates, but its enemies.[43]

Still, that tradition of tendentious interpretation in the guise of divining "original intent" was a powerful political tool. The legal scholar Cass Sunstein, for example, points to the *Dred Scott* decision as an early instance of judicial "originalism," noting that the Taney Court claimed obeisance to the Constitution's "true intent when it was adopted."[44] It is often forgotten today that the pioneers of so-called original-intent interpretation were defenders of slavery in the antebellum era and its apologists thereafter, who used their readings of the Constitution to limit what democratic government could do for the less powerful. That helps explain why *National Review* chose the Calhoun fan James Kilpatrick to serve as one of its two experts on the Constitution. As Frank Meyer later approvingly quoted Richard Weaver, another devotee of secessionist thought: "It took the study of John Calhoun to wake me up to a realization that a constitution is and should be primarily a negative document"—a restraint rather than an enabling framework.[45] Setting to work in argument with the Warren Court—which, in the words of one legal historian, was the first to stand for "equality of treatment as a necessary precondition of democracy"—conservative leaders sought to turn the judiciary back to its habits in the Gilded Age and the *Lochner* era, when justices repelled democratic attempts to advance the rights of working people as constitutional violations of the private property rights of corporations.[46] The Right's thinkers viewed the trend after 1937, when the Supreme Court made its peace with the New Deal and began limiting the autonomy of business in the interests of the majority, as the scratch that led to gangrene.

Many conservatives were similarly contemptuous of democratic amendments to the Constitution, above all the Fourteenth, which became the scaffold for many kinds of reform. Explaining his support for whites who deprived blacks of the vote, Buckley announced: "the Fourteenth and Fifteenth Amendments to the Constitution are regarded by much of the South as inorganic accretions to the original document, grafted upon it by victors-at-war by force." Attacks on the Fourteenth Amendment became a veritable cottage industry on the Right, a staple in its leaders' push for "authentic federalism."[47] In recent years, most conservatives have become more discreet, but as late as 1978 the publisher Henry Regnery insisted that the Fourteenth Amendment had never "properly" become "part of the Constitution" and was therefore illegitimate.[48]

Granted, neo-Confederacy was not the main thoroughfare on which the conservative movement traveled to power. Far more central and consequential to its day-to-day work were the promotion of militant anticommunism abroad and, at home, individual liberty through "free enterprise" and religious orthodoxy. Nor did every writer in the conservative camp work these byways. Indeed, some experts on the Right may object that this chapter conflates paleo-conservatives with the entire movement and therefore overlooks the ultimately more influential libertarians and neoconservatives.[49] Yet however much the latter groups differed from the former on some matters, it is striking how little they protested the neo-Confederate mythology. It is not yet clear what explains this silence. Perhaps the antistatism of the libertarians and the growing infatuation of neoconservatives with unfettered capitalism and American military power have led them to similar distortions of historical memory by different routes—at minimum, to politically convenient silence.[50]

Yet, what ultimately accounts best for the lack of challenges to neo-Confederacy among conservatives may well be its continuing utility to their overall project. Nowhere was its instrumental value better demonstrated than in the presidential election of 1964. By all accounts, Barry Goldwater was not himself a racist, let alone a neo-Confederate; he was first and foremost an economically minded libertarian, who even took out membership in the NAACP in his home state of Arizona. But for all that he differed from arch-segregationists such as Kilpatrick, Goldwater believed that the Republican Right should "hunt where the ducks are"—among white southerners.[51] Although he lost in a landslide in 1964, recent studies reveal that in the course of his spirited grassroots campaign, the Right attracted a mass following as never before, particularly among corporate conservatives in the suburbs of the broad Sunbelt. But outside his home state of Arizona, Goldwater scored his only electoral success in states of the Deep South, where white supremacy and economic conservatism usually went hand-in-hand, and even those who hewed to one seldom questioned the other. The Goldwater-Johnson race, the later Mississippi U.S. senator and senate majority leader Trent Lott noted, was "the first time that we really started thinking, 'Gee, maybe we are Republicans.'" In his once solidly Democratic state, 87 percent of voters, still overwhelmingly white, reached the same conclusion. The compound was unstable, but the shift toward the GOP was strong.[52]

After Goldwater's defeat and the passage of the Civil Rights Act of 1964 and the Voting Rights Act of 1965, the conservative sales pitch underwent significant modification. The Right's strategists learned, often under the tutelage of northern Jewish neoconservatives whose goals began to converge with theirs, that they must stop using overtly racial appeals if they wished to succeed in national politics. Early in that education, the veteran cold warrior and New York editor Irving Kristol thus thanked Buckley in 1964 for sending a *National Review* attack on school desegregation but warned that to argue the case "in terms of racial differences" was "political folly." Veteran conservative leaders such as Buckley, and even Kilpatrick himself, came to realize that they could achieve nearly all of the same ends by advocating "color-blind" policies.[53] As they ceased defending state-sponsored segregation, the neo-Confederacy with which they had once glorified it, now understood as a potential liability, also slipped from its once central place into the shadows.

What is most important here, however, is that although there was increasing electoral risk in being identified as racist after the mid-1960s, very few of the Right's leaders ever criticized neo-Confederate holdouts despite that risk (figure 13.1). The silence speaks loudly from a conservative movement that in recent decades has condemned Holocaust denial and anti-Semitism and has ritually demanded that African-American leaders denounce anti-Semitism even on the part of black individuals to whom they had no organizational or personal ties.[54] National conservative leaders have instead played a two-faced game, singing hosannas to color blindness on one side while whistling Dixie on the other. With so many Republican conservatives bowing to the mythical South without challenge from their peers, it seems fair to conclude that the enablers hold their tongues because they find that mythology useful in their overall quest to advance extreme property rights and undermine what remains of a welfare state.

A case in point of the national movement's continued exploitation of Confederate mythology was the 2004 runaway bestseller on the Right, entitled *The Politically Incorrect Guide to American History*. Commissioned by the oldest and most respectable conservative publishing house in the nation, Regnery, and featured prominently on the Web site of the *National Review*, the book sported a belligerent-looking Johnny Reb on its cover. The text popularized interpretations of southern history and the Civil War and Reconstruction long since discredited among scholars. It had chapters on such topics as "Why nullification isn't as crazy as it sounds" and sidebars that shared important lessons such as "Southern states had the

FIGURE 13.1. Despite the clear political dangers, even into the twenty-first century mainstream conservative Republican politicians continued to associate themselves with issues, symbols, and organizations inspired by the neo-Confederate Right. In this image, from the *Charlotte Observer* on February 4, 2000, political cartoonist Kevin Siers speculates on the lengths that then Governor George W. Bush of Texas went to win the 2000 Republican presidential primary in South Carolina. © NAS, North America Syndicate.

right to secede" and "The Fourteenth Amendment was never constitutionally ratified." Yet the neoconservative Max Boot was nearly alone on the Right in protesting.[55]

The matter of why and how neo-Confederacy continues to animate the conservative cause needs more examination. Its greatest long-term value to the Right would appear to be its contribution to the development of a radically altered jurisprudence for the twenty-first century global order. A sanitized version of neo-Confederacy has proved very helpful in transforming U.S. political economy through a historic rewriting of its legal rules to favor corporations and other property owners. Thanks to the judiciary's role in sustaining progressive reforms, from the right of workers to organize labor unions to the right of lesbian and gay citizens to marry, the courts have been a prime target of conservatives since *Brown v. Board of Education*.

By the 1970s, corporate interests had joined forces with the conservative movement in seeking the U-turn in public policy that has since been misleadingly labeled neoliberalism, as both looked to the courts to rein in reforms from occupational health and safety requirements to environmental standards. "No thoughtful person can question that the American economic system is under broad attack," Lewis Powell, the Virginia attorney whom President Nixon soon after appointed to the U.S. Supreme Court, wrote in his now famous 1971 memo for the U.S. Chamber of Commerce, in reference to the grassroots challenges to corporate power that arose in the sixties. Powell urged business executives to organize as never before to reclaim hegemony in arenas from "the campus" to the Congress, but he noted that "in the final analysis, the payoff" to such mobilization "is what government does," especially the federal courts. Powell wrote: "American business and the enterprise system have been affected as much by the courts as by the executive and legislative branches of government. Under our constitutional system, especially with an activist-minded Supreme Court, the judiciary may be the most important instrument for social, economic, and political change." Pointing to the success progressives had achieved in the courts, he urged "business interests" to take "a more aggressive attitude."[56]

The "revolt of the haves" in the years since has included the promotion of conservative legal foundations and organizations.[57] The premier such initiative is the Federalist Society, which since its founding as a national body in 1982 has enjoyed generous backing from foundations spawned by the conservative movement, including Olin, Scaife, Bradley, and Milliken. Federalist Society leaders have strategically presented the organization as a debating forum without a particular political agenda, and its over 30,000 members no doubt have varied goals, not least to enhance their prospects of preferential hiring in GOP administrations. But the Federalist Society's opposition to decades of labor, consumer, environmental, civil rights, and other protections appears indistinguishable from the southern states' rights tradition revived by the modern Right. Its officials do not advertise the connection, but the kinship is undeniable. No wonder, then, that the Federalist Society chose as its first executive director Eugene B. Meyer, not himself an attorney but an astute strategist and the home-schooled son of the *National Review* power broker who called *Brown v. Board of Education* a "rape of the Constitution."[58] Supreme Court Justice Stephen Breyer reminds those unaware of the portent of "original intent" jurisprudence that "the Constitution originally and intentionally ignored" the majority of those whom most of us now think of as "We the People." As Breyer puts it, "literalism has a tendency to undermine the Constitution's efforts to create a framework for democratic government."[59] That was precisely the goal of the conservative movement builders who set out in the mid-1950s to transform the nation with a mythical South as their guiding star.

The neo-Confederate project helped build the modern conservative cause in ways that demand more recognition and analysis, not least because that movement managed to transform a major party and with it the nation's political economy. Irving Kristol, who had been skeptical of the conservative movement at its founding yet went on to became one of its premier spokespersons, characterized what its organizers wrought thus: "*National Review*, it turns out, was part of a larger movement that created institutions which shaped and trained several thousand young conservatives, not so much to go forth and proclaim the gospel, as to go into the Republican party and take control of it."[60] Their triumph came in 1980 with the election of Ronald Reagan, the conservative movement's standard-bearer in electoral politics after 1966. Given that movement's history as described here, the push by the Reagan administration to recast the nation's judiciary with a "jurisprudence of original intention," as Attorney General Edwin Meese called it, has deeper and more frightening roots than most Americans realize.[61]

The metamorphosis of the Republican Party under the tutelage of such conservatives has made the contest over interpretation of the South's past ever more consequential to the nation's future. Neo-Confederacy played an important role in enabling that metamorphosis. Odes to the South of yesteryear served as a time-honored disguise and borrowed language with which conservatives presented a new scene in world history in familiar terms, offering "traditional" packaging for the ill-named "neoliberal" project, whose radical goal was to shred a century of popularly supported reform.

NOTES

1. On the Republicans and Bradford, see Nancy MacLean, *Freedom Is Not Enough: The Opening of the American Workplace* (Cambridge: Harvard University Press, 2006), 257–58; Paul M. Murphy, *The Rebuke of History: The Southern Agrarians and American Conservative Thought* (Chapel Hill: University of North Carolina Press, 2001), 232–33, 245–46. On Bush, see "Bush Close Ties to Neo-Confederate Groups Questioned," February 18, 2000, http://www.commondreams.org/news2000/0218–04.htm. For current exposure of neo-Confederacy, see the Southern Poverty Law Center Web site, http://www.splcenter.org/, especially "The Neo-Confederates" (Summer 2000), http://www.splcenter.org/intel/intelreport/article.jsp?aid=253; and the Web site maintained by independent scholar Edward Sebesta, http://www.templeofdemocracy.com/ (including Gramm, Armey, and Ashcroft).

2. Robert Reich, "America's Real Jobs Crisis," IPR Distinguished Public Policy Lecture, Northwestern University, Fall 2005.

3. For a fascinating start, see Michael Lind, "Conservative Elites and the Counterrevolution against the New Deal," in *Ruling America: A History of Wealth*

and Power in a Democracy, ed. Steve Fraser and Gary Gerstle (Cambridge: Harvard University Press, 2005); on party politics, Nicol C. Rae, *The Decline and Fall of the Liberal Republicans* (New York: Oxford, 1989).

4. For the formative years, see James T. Patterson, *Congressional Conservatism and the New Deal: The Growth of the Conservative Coalition in Congress, 1933–1939* (Lexington, University of Kentucky Press, 1967).

5. Bryant Simon, *A Fabric of Defeat: The Politics of South Carolina Millhands, 1910–1948* (Chapel Hill: University of North Carolina Press, 1998), 188.

6. On the centrality of *National Review* to the larger conservative project that ultimately transformed the GOP, see George H. Nash, *The Conservative Intellectual Movement in America since 1945* (New York: Basic Books, 1976); Patrick Allitt, *Catholic Intellectuals and Conservative Politics in America, 1950–1985* (Ithaca: Cornell University Press, 1993); Godfrey Hodgson, *The World Turned Right Side Up: A History of the Conservative Ascendancy in America* (Boston: Houghton Mifflin, 1996). On the paleo-conservatives, see Murphy, *Rebuke of History*.

7. For a sampling of the major works available in these years that uncovered a very different South, see W. E. B. DuBois, *Black Reconstruction in America; An Essay Toward a History of the Part which Black Folk Played in the Attempt to Reconstruct Democracy in America, 1860–1880* (1935); C. Vann Woodward, *Tom Watson: Agrarian Rebel* (1938), *Origins of the New South, 1877–1913* (1951), and *The Strange Career of Jim Crow* (1955); John Hope Franklin, *From Slavery to Freedom: A History of American Negroes* (1947), and *Reconstruction: After the Civil War* (1961); Kenneth M. Stampp, *The Peculiar Institution: Slavery in the Old South* (1956).

8. "Publisher's Statement," *National Review,* November 19, 1955, 5 [inaugural issue]. This is not to suggest that the South was the Right's only regional utopia: a mythical West also served important purposes. See Richard White, *"It's Your Misfortune and None of My Own": A New History of the American West* (Norman: University of Oklahoma Press, 1991), esp. 601–4.

9. Among the few scholars of the national conservative movement to explore in any depth the role of race in the early years are Hodgson, *World Turned Right Side Up*; Allitt, *Catholic Intellectuals and Conservative Politics*. Since this article was first conceived, several new and important southern-based studies have added to understanding the role of region in the Right's rise, among them: Kevin M. Kruse, *White Flight: Atlanta and the Making of Modern Conservatism* (Princeton: Princeton University Press, 2005); Matthew D. Lassiter, *The Silent Majority: Suburban Politics in the Sunbelt South* (Princeton: Princeton University Press, 2006); Joseph Crespino, *In Search of Another Country: Mississippi and the Conservative Counterrevolution* (Princeton: Princeton University Press, 2007).

10. For elaboration, see MacLean, *Freedom Is Not Enough,* esp. chapters 2, 7, and 9.

11. Buckley, "Why the South Must Prevail," *National Review,* August 24, 1957, 149; Henry Regnery, "Emerging Conservatism: Kilpatrick, Morley, and Burnham," *Modern Age,* Summer 1978, 237, 245.

12. Felix Morley, *Freedom and Federalism* (Chicago: Regnery, 1959), 171. Similarly, Kendall portrayed "the Right" as scattered in the early 1950s, with "the Rightists' most experienced and far-seeing commanders (Senator Byrd, Senator McCarran, and Senator McCarthy, for example)...conducting you might say their own little local wars" against "the Liberals" without coordination. Until, that is, they began to understand that they were faced with "a full-scale revolution"—presumably, when *Brown* focused their attention. Willmoore Kendall, *The Conservative Affirmation* (Chicago: Regnery, 1963), 9–10.

13. Frank S. Meyer, "The Court Challenges the Congress," in *The Conservative Mainstream* (New Rochelle, N.Y.: Arlington House, 1969), 163.

14. W. J. Simmons to S. E. Brookings, May 21, 1956, Box 8, Acc. 6626-b, James J. Kilpatrick Papers, 1908, 1963–1997, University of Virginia, Special Collections, Charlottesville, Virginia [hereinafter JJK Papers]; quotations from James J. Kilpatrick to Harry F. Byrd, December 28, 1955, Box 7, JJK Papers. See also Joseph J. Thorndike, " 'The Sometimes Sordid Level of Race and Segregation': James J. Kilpatrick and the Virginia Campaign against *Brown*," in *The Moderates' Dilemma: Massive Resistance to School Desegregation in Virginia*, ed. Matthew D. Lassiter and Andrew B. Lewis (Charlottesville, University Press of Virginia, 1998), esp. 56, 61–62.

15. Quoted in Charles Moritz, ed., *Current Biography* (H.W. Wilson, 1980), s.v. "Kilpatrick, James J(ackson)," 184. For sample correspondence, see Kilpatrick to William F. Buckley, June 7, 1956, Kilpatrick to Buckley, September 19, 1956, Buckley to Kilpatrick, September 21, 1956, Box 8, Acc. 6626-b, JJK Papers.

16. William F. Buckley to W. J. Simmons, September 10, 1958, Simmons to Buckley, September 5, 1958, Box 6, William F. Buckley, Jr. Papers, 1951–2002, Manuscripts and Archives, Yale University, New Haven, Connecticut [hereinafter WFB Papers]; Charles M. Payne, *I've Got the Light of Freedom: The Organizing Tradition and the Mississippi Freedom Struggle* (Berkeley: University of California Press, 1995), 34–35.

17. Henry Regnery to James J. Kilpatrick, March 14, 1956, Acc. 6626-b, Box 66, JJK papers.

18. James Jackson Kilpatrick, "Civil Rights and Legal Wrongs," *National Review* (September 24, 1963), 231, 234; Virginia Commission on Constitutional Government, *Civil Rights and Legal Wrongs* (Richmond, 1963).

19. Kilpatrick, "Remarks in Debate with Roy Wilkins, University of Minnesota," 1964, Box 3, Acc. 6626-c, JJK Papers.

20. Kilpatrick, "The Case for Conservatism," Remarks before the St. Johns Dinner Club, Jacksonville, April 22, 1964, Box 4, JJK Papers; Robert Bork, "Civil Rights—A Challenge," *New Republic*, August 31, 1963, 22–24.

21. Kirkpatrick Sale, *Power Shift: The Rise of the Southern Rim and its Challenge to the Eastern Establishment* (New York: Random House, 1975); James C. Cobb, *Industrialization and Southern Society, 1877–1984* (Lexington: University Press of Kentucky, 1984); Bruce J. Schulman, *From Cotton Belt to Sunbelt: Federal Policy,*

Economic Development, and the Transformation of the South (New York: Oxford University Press, 1991).

22. John B. Judis, *William F. Buckley, Jr.: Patron Saint of the Conservatives* (New York, Simon & Schuster, 1988), 121; Lind, "Conservative Elites."

23. David W. Blight, *Race and Reunion: The Civil War in American Memory* (Cambridge: Harvard University Press, 2001); W. Fitzhugh Brundage, *The Southern Past: A Clash of Race and Memory* (Cambridge: Harvard University Press, 2005). On how neo-Confederacy was built into the public landscape, see James W. Loewen, *Lies Across America: What Our Historical Sites Get Wrong* (New York: Simon & Schuster, 1999), esp. 38–39, 102–7.

24. Kari Frederickson, *The Dixiecrat Revolt and the End of the Solid South, 1932–1968* (Chapel Hill: University of North Carolina Press, 2001), 230–31.

25. *Current Biography* (1980), s.v. "Kilpatrick, James J(ackson), 184–87; Program, First Annual Conservative Awards Dinner, Sponsored by American Conservative Union, *Human Events, National Review,* and Young Americans for Freedom, Washington, D.C., October 4, 1969, Box 131, William A. Rusher Papers, Manuscript Division, Library of Congress, Washington, D.C.

26. Willmoore Kendall, "What is Conservatism?" *Conservative Affirmation,* 1–20; Buckley, "A Clarification," *National Review,* September 7, 1957, 199.

27. Morley, *Freedom and Federalism,* x; Buckley, "The Issue at Selma," *National Review,* March 9, 1965, 183.

28. Frank S. Meyer, "Introduction," *What Is Conservatism?* ed. Meyer (New York: Holt, Rinehart, and Winston, 1964), 3; Russell Kirk, "Prescription, Authority, and Ordered Freedom," in ibid., 32–35; Richard M. Weaver, *Ideas Have Consequences* (Chicago: University of Chicago Press, 1948), 35–51; Frank S. Meyer, "Conservatism," in *Left, Right and Center: Essays on Liberalism and Conservatism in the United States,* ed. Robert A. Goldwin (Chicago: Rand McNally, 1966), 3, 1.

29. "The Magazine's Credenda," *National Review,* November 19, 1955, 6 [inaugural issue].

30. Robert A. Nisbet, "The Conservative Movement in Perspective," *Public Interest,* 81 (1985), 129; Meyer, "Introduction," 3.

31. Buckley, "Why the South Must Prevail," 149; Kendall, *Conservative Affirmation,* 16–17; James Burnham, *Suicide of the West: An Essay on the Meaning and Destiny of Liberalism* (New York: The John Day Co., 1964), 86.

32. Kendall, *Conservative Affirmation,* 8, 16; Richard M. Weaver, "The Regime of the South," *National Review,* March 14, 1959, 589; Buckley, "Issue at Selma," 183.

33. John Court, "Integration in Historical Perspective," *Modern Age,* 2 (Fall 1958), 365; also Edward Stone, "A Backward and Forward Look at Integration," ibid., 372; Meyer, "Conservatism," 7.

34. Buckley, "Why the South Must Prevail," 149–50; see also Richard M. Weaver, *The Southern Tradition at Bay: A History of Postbellum Thought* (New Rochelle, N.Y.: Arlington House, 1968), 167–68.

35. Richard M. Weaver, "The Regime of the South," *National Review,* March 14, 1959, 587–89; Anthony Harrigan, "The South *Is* Different," *National Review,*

March 8, 1958, 225–27; Russell Kirk, "Norms, Conventions and the South," *Modern Age,* 2 (Fall 1958), 338–43.

36. Meyer, "Conservatism," 8; "Text of Goldwater Explanation of Vote Against Civil Rights Bill," *Congressional Quarterly Weekly Report,* 26 (June 26, 1964), 1297.

37. Russell Kirk, *The Conservative Mind, from Burke to Santayana* (Chicago: Henry Regnery Company, 1953), 160; Russell Kirk, "Prescription, Authority, and Ordered Freedom," *What Is Conservatism?* 33–34.

38. Richard Hofstadter, *The American Political Tradition and the Men Who Made It* (New York: Knopf, 1948), 68. *The Essential Calhoun* (New Brunswick: Transaction Publishers, 1992), by the neo-Confederate Clyde N. Wilson, won publication in The Library of Conservative Thought series, with an encomium by Russell Kirk. See N. Alan Cornett, "Russell Kirk's Southern Sensibilities: A Celebration," *Southern Partisan,* 14 (2nd Quarter, 1994), 39, 42.

39. Donald Davidson, *The Attack on Leviathan: Regionalism and Nationalism in the United States* (Glouster, Mass.: Peter Smith, 1962, original 1932), 269–70, 117; Buckley, "Why the South Must Prevail," 149; Kendall, *Conservative Affirmation,* 16–17; Burnham, *Suicide of the West,* 86.

40. Quoted in Hofstadter, *American Political Tradition,* 83.

41. Meyer, "Conservatism," 7; also M. Stanton Evans, "A Conservative Case for Freedom," *What Is Conservatism?* 67, 231.

42. Morley, *Freedom and Federalism,* 194.

43. Garry Wills, *A Necessary Evil: A History of American Distrust of Government* (New York: Simon & Schuster, 1999). My thanks to Wills for his helpful reading of an early draft of this essay and his informative recollections of the early years of *National Review.*

44. Cass R. Sunstein, *Radicals in Robes: Why Extreme Right-Wing Courts Are Wrong for America* (New York: Basic Books, 2005), 85–86.

45. Frank S. Meyer, "Richard M. Weaver: An Appreciation," *Modern Age,* 14 (Summer-Fall 1970), 248. The other *National Review* authority was L. Brent Bozell. His attack on the Warren Court, *The Warren Revolution: Reflections on the Consensus Society* (New Rochelle, N.Y.: Arlington House, 1966), is praised as "neglected work" in a recent scholarly brief for originalism: Jonathan O'Neill, *Originalism in American Law and Politics: A Constitutional History* (Baltimore: Johns Hopkins University Press, 2005), 76.

46. Morton J. Horwitz, *The Warren Court and the Pursuit of Justice* (New York: Hill & Wang, 1998), 81; on the *Lochner* era, see 76–77. In a recent article, Barry Friedman notes that the *Lochner* revisionism of late has failed to recognize its "devastating consequences for labor laws nationally"; Barry Friedman, "The History of the Countermajoritarian Difficulty, Part III: The Lesson of *Lochner,*" *N.Y.U. Law Review* 76 (2001): 1450, 1452. My thanks to Laura Kalman for generously providing this and other helpful legal citations.

47. Buckley, "A Clarification," *National Review,* September 7, 1957, 199; Morley, *Freedom and Federalism,* 172, 69. Donald Davidson complained that the Fourteenth Amendment was "raised up by a virtual *coup d'état*" as he mourned

that "history [was] being repeated" in the 1960s. "Preface" to Weaver, *Southern Tradition at Bay*, 24.

48. Regnery, "Emerging Conservatism," 238.

49. For the best treatment of the paleo-conservatives, see Murphy, *Rebuke of History*, which addresses their clash with neoconservatives on 245–47.

50. For examples of how other conservatives reached the same conclusions by different routes, see the "law and economics" legal scholarship of Richard Posner and Richard Epstein. For insightful discussion of conservative legal scholarship, see Laura Kalman, *The Strange Career of Legal Liberalism* (New Haven: Yale University Press, 1996), esp. 132–39.

51. Quoted in Frederickson, *Dixiecrat Revolt*, 236.

52. Lott quoted in Hodgson, *World Turned*, 108; Paul Gottfried and Thomas Fleming, *The Conservative Movement* (Boston: Twayne Publishers, 1988), 32. On conservative white southerners and the 1964 election, see Rick Perlstein, *Before the Storm: Barry Goldwater and the Unmaking of the American Consensus* (New York: Hill and Wang, 2001); Crespino, *In Search of Another Country*.

53. Irving Kristol to William F. Buckley, Nov. 23, 1964, Box 31, WFB Papers; on the makeover of the right in the 1970s, see MacLean, *Freedom Is Not Enough*, chapters 6 and 7. On how non-elite whites at the grassroots drew similar lessons about class-conscious "color blindness" as the best defense for racial privilege, see Kruse, *White Flight*, Lassiter, *Silent Majority*.

54. See, for example, William F. Buckley, Jr., *In Search of Anti-Semitism* (New York: Continuum, 1992).

55. Thomas E. Woods, Jr., *The Politically Incorrect Guide to American History* (Washington: Regnery, 2004), 40, 61, 77, 92; Max Boot, "Incorrect History," *Weekly Standard,* February 5, 2005, http://www.weeklystandard.com/Content/Public/Articles/000/000/005/246eaokp.asp?pg=1.

56. Internal Memorandum from Lewis F. Powell, Jr., to Eugene B. Sydnor, Jr., of the U.S. Chamber of Commerce, August 23, 1971, reprinted http://reclaimdemocracy.org/corporate_accountability/powell_memo_lewis.html. On neoliberalism as misnomer, see Nancy MacLean, "Southern Dominance in Borrowed Language: The Regional Origins of American Neo-Liberalism," in *New Landscapes of Inequality: Neoliberalism and the Erosion of Democracy in America*, ed. Jane L. Collins, Micaela di Leonardo, and Brett Williams (Santa Fe: School of American Research Press, 2008), 21–37.

57. Robert Kuttner, quoted in Thomas Ferguson and Joel Rogers, *Right Turn: The Decline of the Democrats and the Future of American Politics* (New York: Hill & Wang, 1986), 102, which also documents the mobilization of business interests, as does Thomas Byrne Edsall in *The New Politics of Inequality* (New York: Norton, 1984). For the process of the legal mobilization from a political science perspective, see Steven M. Teles, *The Rise of the Conservative Legal Movement* (Princeton: Princeton University Press, 2008).

58. Felix Morley, in his foundational conservative tract on federalism, thus argued that the "revival of Interposition" by advocates of massive resistance

to *Brown* was "a striking illustration of the tenacity of the federal tradition in American thinking, and a powerful weapon in the armory of those who seek to maintain the Republic"; Morley, *Freedom and Federalism*, 187. The Federalist Society is more guarded, but its approach to the Constitution has the potential to take the nation further back than 1954, as some legal scholars have begun warning (Sunstein, *Radicals in Robes*, esp. 63–65). On the Federalist Society, see Alliance for Justice, *Justice for Sale: Shortchanging the Public Interest for Private Gain* (Washington, 1993); Owen F. Fiss, "What Is the Federalist Society?" *Harvard Journal of Law & Public Policy*, 15 (January 1, 1992); Terry Carter, "The In Crowd: Conservatives Who Sought Refuge in the Federalist Society Gain Clout," *ABA Journal* (September 2001), 46–51 (quotation from 46, Meyer on 51); on preferential hiring, Eric Lichtblau, "Report Assails Political Hiring in Justice Department," *New York Times*, June 25, 2008, A1, 20. Most informative is Institute for Democracy Studies, *The Federalist Society and the Challenge to a Democratic Jurisprudence*, Briefing Paper, January 2001, which notes the organization's desire for "significant restrictions on Congress's authority to legislate," 1, 2; see also Wills, *Necessary Evil*, esp. 75–76.

59. Stephen Breyer, *Active Liberty: Interpreting Our Democratic Constitution* (New York: Knopf, 2005), 20, 131.

60. Irving Kristol, "American Conservatism, 1945–1995," *The Public Interest* (Fall 1995), 83. For the defeat of moderates, see Mary C. Brennan, *Turning Right in the Sixties: The Conservative Capture of the GOP* (Chapel Hill: University of North Carolina Press, 1995); Rae, *Decline of the Liberal Republicans*.

61. Kalman, *Strange Career of Legal Liberalism*, Meese quotation on 132, discussion on 132–39. See also Horwitz, *Warren Court*, 112–13. Yet as Kalman, Horwitz, and others have pointed out, judicial originalism has a longer and more multivalent genealogy and an ongoing appeal that makes engagement— rather than simple rejection—of it essential for those who would challenge the contemporary conservative interpretation of the Constitution. Laura Kalman, "Border Patrol: Reflections on the Turn to History in Legal Scholarship," *Fordham Law Review*, 66 (1997–1998), esp. 122–24; Morton J. Horwitz, "Foreword: The Constitution of Change: Legal Fundamentality Without Fundamentalism," *Harvard Law Review*, 107 (1993–1994), esp. 116–17; also see Jack N. Rakove, *Original Meanings: Politics and Ideas in the Making of the Constitution* (New York: Knopf, 1996).

INDEX

Proposition 187 (California), 249
Puerto Ricans, 32, 34, 36, 87, 237, 242, 249

racial gerrymandering. *See*
    gerrymandering, racial, of school
    attendance zones
racial imbalance, 33, 34, 37, 57, 111–12
Racial Imbalance Act of 1965
    (Massachusetts), 37, 57
Raines, Charles, 105
Randolph, A. Phillip, 174, 182
Reagan, Ronald
    anticommunism and, 291
    election of, 310, 323
    racial politics of, 6, 11, 18n9, 309
    Reagan era, 159
    Religious Right and, 303
Reagon, Bernice Johnson. *See* Johnson,
    Bernice
Reagon, Cordell, 122, 126–28, 134
reapportionment, 263. *See also*
    malapportionment; "one person, one
    vote"
    in Alabama, 270, 272–73
    in Colorado, 265, 274–75
    in Georgia, 264–65, 273
    in Illinois, 270, 275
    League of Women Voters on need for,
        269–70
    as national issue, 16, 266, 267f, 273
    in New York, 266, 273–74
    opponents of, 263–64, 268, 275–78, 276f
    racial discrimination and, 265–66
    suburbs as beneficiaries of, 264, 278–80
    in Tennessee, 264, 271
    Warren on, 263, 266, 279–80
Reconstruction, 52, 75, 107, 177
    "America's Second," 6, 101, 117n7
    mythology of, 310, 314–15, 320
Regnery, Henry, 311, 313–14, 319
Reich, Robert, 309
religious nationalism, 287–95. *See also*
    Religious Right
Religious Right. *See also* religious
    nationalism; *specific leaders and
    organizations*
    abortion and, 299–301
    anticommunism and, 290–91
    in California, 297, 302
    Catholics and, 286, 297–303
    Equal Rights Amendment and, 298–99,
        300f

gay rights and, 301–2
    as national movement, 286–87,
        294–95, 295f, 303–4
    origins of, 16–17, 287
    political realignment and, 286–87,
        298–304
    school prayer and, 292–95, 292f
    starting private schools, 296–97, 302
    southern leaders of, 286, 291–92,
        295–97, 301–4
Religious Roundtable, 302–3
Repent America, 163n21
Republican Party, 6. *See also*
    conservatism; *specific politicians*
    anti-immigration politics and, 234, 253
    debate over southern strategy and, 6,
        107–8, 319–20
    hyper-capitalism and, 309
    neo-Confederacy and, 308–23
    Religious Right and, 303
    suburbanization and, 107, 279
residential segregation. *See* segregation,
    housing
Reunion and Reaction (Woodward), 309
Reynolds v. Sims, 263, 264, 265–66,
    272–74
    backlash against, 275–78
Ribicoff, Abraham, 40, 113–14
Richmond, Virginia, 40, 42, 227
Richmond News Leader, 108, 313
Right. *See* conservatism; Religious Right
Rilling, Paul M., 114
Robertson, A. Willis, 296
Robertson, Pat, 286, 296, 303, 304
Robison, James, 303
Rockefeller, Nelson, 40, 88–89, 294
Rockefeller, Winthrop, 82–83
Rodino, Peter, 290
Roe v. Wade, 297, 300–301
Rogers, Chip, 234, 253
Roosevelt, Franklin D., 168, 174, 180, 315
    Roosevelt administration, 13
Rose, Harold, 223
Roth, Stephen, 42
Rumford Fair Housing Act, 1963, 10f,
    49, 66
Russell, Richard, 111

Salinas de Gortari, Carlos, 239
San Diego Christian Unified School
    System, 297
Saunders, George, 154